The Art and Scie Oracle Performance Tuning

Christopher Lawson

Apress™

The Art and Science of Oracle Performance Tuning
Copyright © 2004 by Christopher Lawson

ISBN (pbk): 1-59059-199-2

Printed and bound in the United States of America 2345678910

Technical Reviewers: Alice Backer, Sheldon Barry, Rob Benson, Chaim Katz, Brian Peasland
Editorial Board: Dan Appleman, Craig Berry, Gary Cornell, Tony Davis, Steven Rycroft, Julian Skinner, Martin Streicher, Jim Sumser, Karen Watterson, Gavin Wray, John Zukowski
Assistant Publisher: Grace Wong
Proofreader: Pauline Briggs
Indexer: Adrian Axinte
Artist: Paul Grove
Cover Designer: Kurt Krames
Manufacturing Manager: Tom Debolski

Distributed to the book trade in the United States by Springer-Verlag New York, Inc., 175 Fifth Avenue, New York, NY, 10010 and outside the United States by Springer-Verlag GmbH & Co. KG, Tiergartenstr. 17, 69112 Heidelberg, Germany.

In the United States: phone 1-800-SPRINGER, email orders@springer-ny.com, or visit http://www.springer-ny.com. Outside the United States: fax +49 6221 345229, email orders@springer.de, or visit http://www.springer.de.

For information on translations, please contact Apress directly at 2560 Ninth Street, Suite 219, Berkeley, CA 94710. Phone 510-549-5930, fax 510-549-5939, email info@apress.com, or visit http://www.apress.com.

The source code for this book is available to readers at http://www.apress.com in the Downloads section.

This book is dedicated to my wife, Karen.
Thank you for your patience and encouragement.
You made it all possible.

About the Author

Chris Lawson is an independent consultant who specializes in performance tuning of data warehouse and financial applications. His articles on database management and performance tuning have appeared in numerous technical journals, and he is a frequent speaker at Oracle conferences.

When he is not tracking down elusive performance problems, Chris teaches courses in Enterprise Database Systems for the University of Phoenix.

He is also the editor of the online magazine, *The Oracle Magician*, available at http://www.OracleMagician.com. Chris earned his B.S.E.E. and M.B.A degrees from the University of California, Irvine.

Chris lives with his wife and two daughters in Northern California, where they cheer for their favorite sports teams, the Oakland Raiders (*his* team) and the San Francisco 49ers (*her* team).

> *"This book is dedicated to my wife, Karen.*
> *Thank you for your patience and encouragement.*
> *You made it all possible."*

Acknowledgements

Writing a book on Oracle performance tuning is a big undertaking. Many others contributed substantially to this endeavor. Firstly, thanks to the Curlingstone editors: Timothy Briggs, Sarah Larder, and David Mercer. Their suggestions and corrections contributed greatly toward improving this book.

The technical review team was also instrumental in spotting mistakes and suggesting areas for improvement. To Brian Peasland, Chaim Katz, Sheldon Barry, Alice Backer, and Rob Benson, thank you all for your diligence!

A variety of other DBAs and colleagues also made useful suggestions and helped confirm the facts of the cases presented. Several of these DBAs were also featured in the case studies as examples of professionals who "put the customer first." Thanks to Pedro Reyes, Ron Wagner, Hector Pujol, Brian Keating, Sten Rognes, and Sammy Ho.

Don Burleson, editor of *Oracle Internals*, was also very supportive in encouraging me to pursue this work. I am grateful for his advice and guidance.

Thanks to Auerbach Publications for permission to use material from several of my earlier writings on performance tuning techniques. Credit is also due to Dr. Daniel Tow, of http://www.singingsql.com, who originally suggested the graphical method of analyzing table joins. My career has benefited greatly from the "Tow Method" of optimizing table joins. Thank you Daniel!

Finally, special thanks to Roger Schrag of Database Specialists (http://www.databasespecialists.com/) for use of his superb examples and definitions of wait events and execution plans. Besides being an outstanding DBA, Roger has proven to be a great colleague and friend. His valuable assistance is gratefully acknowledged.

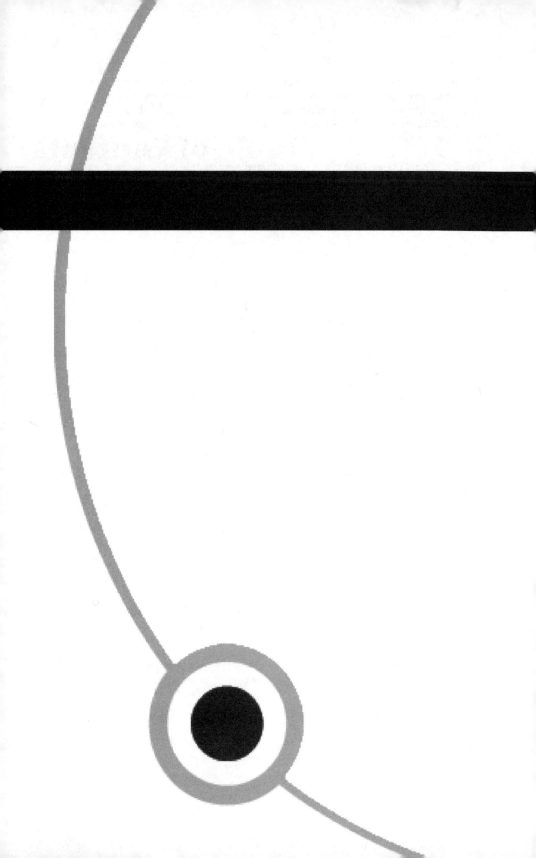

Table of Contents

Table of Contents

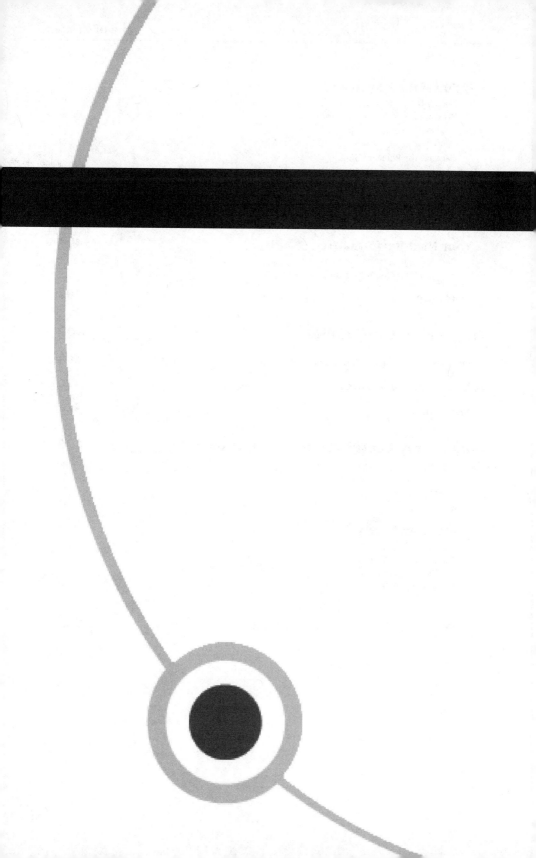

Introduction

Welcome to *The Art and Science of Oracle Performance Tuning*.

This book presents an approach to performance tuning, which is built on chapter by chapter. It is recommended that you follow the text through from beginning to end initially. Once set in the context of the Physician-to-Magician process, the technical information presented in later chapters will also be useful as a reference.

What You Need to Use this Book

You should understand the basic concepts behind relational databases and the various types of SQL statements. Although you don't need to be a SQL guru, you should know what a join is.

It is also assumed that you have a basic working knowledge of Oracle; for example, you know what init.ora parameters are, or what is meant by the Listener. You should already have experience in starting and stopping an Oracle database.

To follow the examples, you'll need:

❑ A working instance of Oracle: 8, 8i, or 9i

❑ SQL*Plus

❑ An account with DBA rights

The complete source code from the book is available for download at http://www.apress.com/.

Beyond these basics, you do not need to have any background in performance tuning.

Conventions

To help you understand what's going on, and in order to maintain consistency, we've used a number of conventions throughout the book:

> **These boxes hold tips for performance tuning.**

Reminders and background information are presented like this.

We present case studies like this:

Case Study: A Sample Case Study

Here's a case study to illustrate the point we're making.

The DBA tried to do things in a particular way– it didn't work. He tried another way, and it did. We learn from this.

Larger examples are introduced with headings like this:

Example: Tuning a Query

and example code is shown like this:

```
In our code examples, the code foreground style shows new,
important, and pertinent code.
Code background shows code that's less important in the present
context, or code that has been seen before.
```

Words that appear on the screen in menus like the File or Window menu are in a similar font to what you see on screen. URLs are also displayed in this font.

In the book text, we use a fixed-width font when we talk about databases, fields, values, elements, attributes, and other objects that may appear in code. Take, for example, the Customer table and the Customer_id field.

Customer Support

We always value hearing from our readers, and we want to know what you think about this book: what you liked, what you didn't like, and what you think we can do better next time. You can send us your comments by e-mail to support@apress.com. Please be sure to mention the book title in your message.

Errata

We've made every effort to make sure that there are no errors in the text or in the code in this book. However, no one is perfect and mistakes do occur. If you find an error in one of our books, like a spelling mistake or a faulty piece of code, we would be very grateful for feedback. By sending in errata you may save a future reader hours of frustration, and of course, you will be helping us provide even higher quality information. Simply visit the Apress web site, find this book's page, and submit your errata. Your information will be checked and, if correct, posted to the errata page for that title and used in subsequent editions of the book.

To see if there are any errata for this book on the web site, go to http://www.apress.com/, and locate the book's page.

E-mail Support

If you wish to get information about a problem in the book then e-mail support@apress.com. A typical e-mail should include the following things:

❑   The **title of the book**, **last four digits of the ISBN**, and **page number** of the problem in the Subject field.

❑   Your **name**, **contact information**, and the **problem** in the body of the message.

We *won't* send you junk mail. We need the details to save your time and ours. The Apress support process can only offer support for issues that are directly pertinent to the content of our published titles.

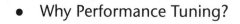

1

The Challenge of Performance Tuning

Database Administrators, or DBAs, perform a wide variety of tasks – some exciting, and others more routine. At most companies, the DBA doesn't have the option to pick and choose which tasks to perform. Typically, all the DBAs have to "pitch-in" and work on a wide variety of tasks, some pleasant, and others dull.

On the down side, not too many DBAs get really excited about setting up backups, monitoring disk space, or checking to see if the exports ran OK last night. For most DBAs, these tasks are not especially challenging, nor do they typically call for much creativity. Nevertheless, they are all critical to ensuring the integrity of important systems on which a firm depends.

There is another facet of DBA work, however, which many have found to be a definite plus. On the up side, performance tuning offers DBAs an entirely new arena in which to flex their muscles. Far from being routine or dull, performance tuning allows the analyst to exercise creativity and intelligence, and to solve baffling problems that are threatening a firm's success.

In this chapter, we take a step back and look at the big picture of performance tuning. We explore the proposition that performance tuning is not all science but, rather, a mixture of art and science. This means that the DBA must be *more* than a superb mathematician who cranks out answers to complex problems. Instead, the performance expert must have a flexible process that allows him to change tack as needed.

We will present an adaptable approach to performance tuning that I call **Physician-to-Magician**; with this method, the DBA "changes hats" in the various stages of the performance tuning process. Each stage has its own unique tasks, suited to what needs to be accomplished at that point.

Real-life scenarios will illustrate the challenge and excitement of Oracle performance tuning. In this chapter (and throughout the book), we will be using actual **case studies** whenever possible. This is useful for several reasons:

❑ Real-life examples are often more obscure than we could ever imagine.

❑ Historical examples can be used to illustrate a sound approach (or a blunder to avoid).

❑ It is easier to remember colorful cases compared to merely theoretical axioms; they are often much more interesting.

❑ Solutions to real cases may provide the reader with an answer to similar problems.

In addition to the various case studies in this chapter, we introduce our first performance tuning **hint**. These hints are observations and suggestions that I believe are critical points in understanding the performance tuning process. Some of the hints might seem obvious at first, but many of these common sense tips are not so commonly practiced.

Along with the Physician-to-Magician approach, we will also discuss some obstacles to performance tuning that the specialist may encounter. These include the "silver bullet" tendency, as well as the "guessing method" approach. These troublesome obstacles are covered in more depth in Chapter 2.

Finally, we conclude with a discussion of "preventative medicine." Ideally, DBAs, designers, and developers will strive to prevent many of the performance problems that are seen so frequently today. Let's begin...

Why Performance Tuning?

In contrast to more routine DBA tasks, performance tuning can be a fascinating part of database work. Most people do not realize, however, how rewarding it can be. This is unfortunate, because performance tuning is one of the DBA's greatest challenges, with both tangible and less obvious rewards. How many jobs provide the opportunity to be an instant "hero" who saves the day by fixing critical systems for a large corporation? Yet this is exactly what a skilled performance expert can accomplish.

Performance tuning skills are also in high demand. The following figure illustrates some skills that employers desire in newly hired Oracle DBAs. Notice that performance tuning is mentioned far more frequently than even basic skills, such as backup and recovery. Of all employers looking for Oracle DBAs, 42% mentioned performance tuning as a desired skill:

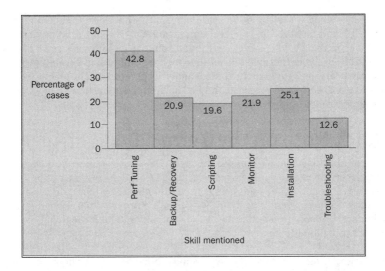

Source: DICE web site (http://www.dice.com/) on 3/7/2002. Sample size: 593 employers. DICE (Data Processing Independent Contractor Exchange) is a popular web site for software professionals.

These figures can be interpreted in several ways. Possibly, these skill sets are needed to address newly discovered performance problems that haven't yet been dealt with by a tuning specialist. It is also possible that they have been addressed – but not successfully! Whatever the explanation, it is clear that there is a big demand for Oracle DBAs who are also competent tuning professionals.

Note that the slightly lower demand for skill sets such as backup and recovery does NOT mean that these skills are less important to the company. Rather, it is a reflection of the *scarcity* of competent tuning professionals.

Why This Book?

Although many DBAs and designers are confronted with a challenge in Oracle performance tuning, many are not really sure where to start. They know that *something* must be done, but what? "Should I start changing the `init.ora` parameters? Or perhaps I should add more data files?"

Without a sound approach to performance tuning, one guess is as good as another, and will rarely lead anywhere. This guessing approach may be fun at first, but our bosses will seldom find the results satisfactory. We all want to employ a competent, logical approach to Oracle performance tuning – and get the corresponding results. This is a reasonable goal, whether the performance analyst is a permanent employee or a consultant.

This book is designed for those readers who want to learn and apply a systematic, step-by-step approach to resolving tough performance issues. The message of this book is a positive one: **There is no need to employ a guesswork, seat-of-the-pants approach to Oracle performance tuning**.

Of course, when we talk about a sound approach, that does not mean that technical content and expertise is unimportant. On the contrary, the best approach in the world is useless without a sound grounding in Oracle database operation. In the earlier portions of this book we emphasize a sound process; in later chapters, however, we introduce analytical methods. These methods include how to use the V$WAIT interface, how to solve table joins, how to use Consumer Resource Groups, and so on.

A Quick Note on the Term DBA

Throughout this book, we will use the term, **DBA**, or **Database Administrator**, when referring to a specialist who is tackling Oracle performance problems. In actuality, this person may not be a DBA at all – the performance analyst could be a lead developer, a senior designer, or perhaps a programmer. Depending on the individual organization and project, the company's "Oracle Magician" could be any of these individuals.

What's important is not whether a person is called a DBA, but how well they understand database fundamentals, and how well they apply a consistent, logical process to solving performance problems. After all, results are what the performance tuning game is all about. When a tough performance problem is resolved, management will be very appreciative – regardless of the person's title.

Who Should Read This Book?

This book is aimed at two groups of readers. The first group consists of those DBAs who have limited or moderate experience of Oracle performance tuning. Perhaps you have been a DBA for only a short time, or you have struggled with even how to *begin* solving performance issues. If this describes your situation, this book is for you. We will show you how to get started with Oracle performance tuning, and how to maximize your odds of success.

Besides new DBAs, this book will also help those readers who have already had some exposure to performance troubleshooting. Some of you have already analyzed a few simple performance issues. You might have successfully solved some problems by adding an index or two, or perhaps by rewriting some poorly defined SQL. Nevertheless, although you have achieved some success, you sense that you need to beef up your skills in Oracle tuning. You would like to handle much tougher performance issues that really challenge the analyst. If this describes your background and desires, this book is also for you.

If you are an experienced DBA, you will benefit from the discussion of some recent innovations in Oracle performance tuning. For instance, we will explore sophisticated techniques, such as using the **wait events** facility to isolate bottlenecks, and how to use the **star transformation** join to optimize data warehouse queries. Additionally, you will probably find the discussion of the Consumer Resource Manager and the section on a graphical method of analyzing table joins to be very helpful.

What You Need to Know

To gain the greatest benefit from reading this book, some basic knowledge of database operation is assumed. For instance, we assume you know what `init.ora` parameters are, or what we mean by the Listener. You should already have experience in starting and stopping an Oracle database.

You should also understand some of the very basic concepts in relational databases, such as the various types of SQL statements. Although you need not be a SQL guru, you should know what a join is.

Beyond these basics, you do not need to have any special background in performance tuning.

Good News for the Reader

Since you are reading this book, you are most likely interested in becoming an accomplished performance tuning analyst. You might already be employed in this capacity as a DBA tasked with improving performance, or you might be curious as to exactly how performance experts operate.

As with all professions, there will be new things to learn and obstacles to overcome. This book is written as a guide, or mentor, to help you get around those obstacles, by answering questions such as these:

❑   How do I get started?

❑   How can I master such a complex subject?

❑   How can I achieve remarkable performance tuning results?

The good news is that:

❑   Yes, you too can do these things!

❑   I'll show you a good way to start.

❑   It isn't really that hard!

The Physician-to-Magician Approach

The true way to become a performance tuning expert is not through technical sophistication, but rather by a good understanding of the overall approach. Many extremely bright DBAs do not do well at performance tuning because of a poor approach. Despite their intelligence and drive, they unwittingly hinder their own progress.

Performance problems take place in a certain *context*, typically a corporation with many other software professionals involved. This means that there are many aspects of human interaction that need to be considered. As we will see, this context means that DBAs sometimes have to play detective, separating the real information given to them by their colleagues from the illusory. At other times, they must try to figure out which problem should be solved.

Even with the root cause identified, the DBA must somehow fashion a solution that is acceptable to the other software engineers. The Oracle performance expert must deal with a variety of complications, many of which are not purely technical in nature. This wide scope of activity means that they must be **adaptable.**

The Need for Adaptability

To be effective, the performance expert must have a flexible approach that can address the different requirements within each performance assignment. In other words, the DBA must wear different "hats" as the performance tuning process unfolds. The effective performance analyst realizes that the methods used must *adapt* to the particular problem and to the people involved.

This multi-dimensional approach recognizes that much fact-gathering, analysis, and deduction must be applied – each according to its order in the performance assignment:

> **The performance expert must use a process that adapts to the various stages of the tuning assignment.**

Let's take a look at the different stages that we can identify in our successful performance tuning process:

The Steps From Physician to Magician

We begin with a summary:

1. **Define problem**: What is the chief complaint?

2. **Investigate**: Confirm/quantify the problem.

3. **Isolate root cause**: Home in on the essence of the problem.

4. **Devise a solution**: Fashion a solution to the environment.

5. **Implement a solution**: Make sure the solution fixes the problem.

We can liken each of these steps to the jobs carried out by other professionals. Let's take a look at each of these analogies in turn:

Step 1 – Physician

The performance analyst starts off as the physician, listening to his patient. When any of us visit a doctor, the doctor will soon ask, "What seems to be the trouble?" In medical clinics, this is called finding the **chief complaint**. The DBA must do the same thing; for instance, he may ask the questions, "How long is the query delay?" or "When does the problem occur?"

Step 2 – Detective

After defining the problem, the next step is investigation. Here, the DBA changes hats from physician to detective. The main objective in this step is to **recreate and quantify** the problem. For instance, the DBA-detective will strive to find important facts, such as the actual elapsed time of the query, or the number of disk and logical reads that are performed. In many cases, he will discover that the problem has nothing to do with the database at all. Sometimes, he or she will conclude that there isn't even a problem!

Step 3 – Pathologist

After the detective has gathered clues (and confirmed that a problem really exists), the Oracle Pathologist tries to find the **root cause** of the problem and isolate what it is that is causing our database so much distress. At this point, we have a great deal of good information, so there will be no need to make wild guesses. The Oracle Physician and Oracle Detective have given us their files, which contain a great amount of useful information. This information will help guide us to the source of the problem.

Step 4 – Artist

With the root cause of the problem identified, the task of the Oracle Artist is to **create an acceptable solution**. Whereas previous stages have required *analysis*, this stage requires *synthesis*. The Oracle Artist will have to consider the particular environment in fashioning a solution that is not just technically accurate, but also feasible. Both technical and organizational issues will need to be considered, so that the final solution is both technically accurate and acceptable to the customer.

Step 5 – Magician

Finally, the Oracle Magician will **implement and confirm the solution** devised by the previous steps. This is the most exciting part of the whole process; we now activate a solution that has been carefully prepared to clear the performance bottleneck. As a final step, we will also quantify the performance improvement for a subsequent report to management.

With the completion of Step 5, our database patient, formerly so sick and sluggish, now skips out of the infirmary with a clean bill of health. His "chart" has been updated to show his new vital signs, with a copy to grateful hospital management.

Underlying this approach, there are some fundamental principles that we will examine now.

Understanding, Not Trickery

Ironic as it sounds, the successful performance expert will strive to *avoid* tricks, such as special setups or unnecessarily complicated code.

In fact, using exotic solutions, understandable only by the select few in the "DBA-guru club," is a cruel disservice to your employer. The reason for this is simple. In future years, the firm will probably not understand what you did (or *why*). Documentation that you may have left will probably be lost. Other DBAs who were familiar with your work will be gone. The result of the tricky solution by the tricky DBA, is that the application is almost impossible to maintain.

In the very first case study of the book, we see how exciting performance tuning can be. We also get an illustration of the importance of a thorough understanding of basic principles of database operation:

Case Study: Police Department Arrests Otrace

Years ago, Rob went to an interview at a firm that creates public safety programs for police departments. The firm's IT manager wanted to see how the candidates approached their work; thus, the interview was actually an all-day mini-contract. In order to see how the candidate would tackle some difficult database issues, the IT manager demonstrated some performance problems the firm was experiencing with its Oracle 7.3 databases. He did not expect the DBA to solve the performance bottlenecks, but just to discuss what approach he would take.

After some small talk, the manager connected into an important production database and illustrated a particularly vexing problem. He demonstrated how the time to establish a connection in SQL*Plus seemed to be inordinately long (perhaps 30 seconds).

As Rob listened to the manager and observed the problem, he recalled that the symptoms being described perfectly matched a well-documented problem with an Oracle utility called **Otrace**.

The idea behind the Otrace utility was to record various types of database and SQL*Net activity; this information could then be used for later debugging.

With Otrace active, connections to SQL*Plus will take longer and longer over a period of months. This happens because Otrace builds and scans several special data files, which grow larger and larger with each new connection. As the file reaches several megabytes, delays become very noticeable. The following figure illustrates a typical degradation in time to establish a SQL*Plus connection:

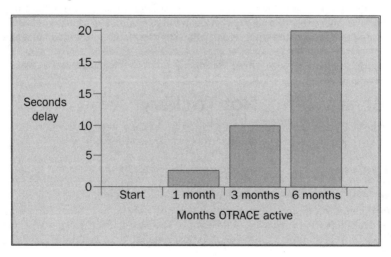

After Rob double-checked the documentation, he asked the manager to check the directory where the Otrace files were kept. Sure enough, there were several files that had grown large enough to be a problem. Rob suggested the manager remove the files and follow a simple procedure to reset Otrace. The manager did so, thereby removing the delay due to Otrace.

A quick test confirmed that SQL*Plus connections could now be established instantaneously. One of the firm's biggest performance problems was solved during the interview!

Needless to say, Rob felt pretty good about his showing in the interview. Unfortunately for him, it now appeared that one of the firm's biggest performance problems (and reasons for hiring a DBA) was now solved!

The Otrace performance problem was quickly solved, not because the DBA was incredibly smart, or knew some clever tricks, but because he was aware of some fundamental problems with the database, and recognized symptoms that matched a particular problem. In fact, that particular problem was well documented with an **Oracle Alert**.

An Oracle Alert is a document created by Oracle Corporation that warns the user community of some serious, or even catastrophic problem.

Anyone who had read the alert and had a good understanding of database operations would also have found the root cause rapidly.

This case demonstrates the dynamics of performance tuning and shows how a good grasp of database fundamentals can lead to remarkable results. On the other hand, without a sound grasp of the fundamentals, the DBA must resort to guessing. Of course, Oracle has long since solved the Otrace problem, but similar odd problems will undoubtedly pop-up in future database releases:

> **Nothing can substitute for a solid understanding of database principles.**

This hint might appear to be ridiculously obvious, but experience indicates that this maxim is not often followed in practice. I have witnessed many attempts, by both management and software engineers, to avoid the labor necessary to gain actual knowledge of Oracle fundamentals.

Avoiding Guesswork

We have stressed the importance of the tuning analyst following a sound *process*. The opposite of a sound approach is *guessing*. We will discuss the guessing approach in detail in Chapter 2.

As we have seen, though, it is very common for analysts, administrators, and managers to try to solve a thorny performance problem without attempting any real understanding of database principles. This scenario often manifests itself via some fantastic "tool" that will supposedly analyze the database and churn out the solution. This is sometimes called a **silver bullet**.

The Silver Bullet

Recall that our previous hint suggests that this approach is usually a waste of time. Trying to use some sort of tool without a good understanding of database operation will probably be fruitless.

The point is *not* that all these tools are designed badly. Some *are* poor, but others have been well designed by very competent teams or individuals. The point, rather, is that no tool can compensate for a lack of understanding on the part of the user. In the hands of a competent analyst, a tool can be very helpful.

In other words, *the wrong problem is being addressed*. Instead of focusing on achieving true understanding that will lead to the best solution, the focus is subtly shifted to a vain search for ways to avoid the labor that is required to achieve true understanding. The longing for these types of tricks is so great, that they will be discussed at length in Chapter 2.

In our Otrace case, the firm with the performance problem had experienced the degradation for *months*. The users suffered poor performance while nobody successfully resolved the problem. Were the firm's analysts simply very dull individuals? Of course not. The firm employed very intelligent people; but they simply did not have anyone who truly understood how an Oracle database worked.

Imagine if the firm with the Otrace problem had tried to avoid hiring a competent performance analyst, and persisted in trying to solve the performance problems via a silver bullet like some performance tool. Obviously, that course would have only led to frustration and embarrassment.

Solving the Wrong Problem

In solving the Otrace problem, note also that Rob did not waste time fooling around with the `init.ora` parameters – such as doubling the database buffers, increasing shared pool size, or perhaps some more sophisticated features, such as parallel processing. The novice DBA often applies solutions such as these incorrectly, and therefore fails to solve the real problem.

In the Otrace case study, the symptoms of the problem indicated that steps such as these would have been *completely irrelevant* to the problem in hand. Instead, the solution followed directly from careful listening to the exact problem – just like a doctor listening to the patient describe the symptoms.

Admittedly, it is a bit unusual to solve performance problems during the initial interview, but this scenario emphasizes the theme of this book: the importance of the *approach* that the DBA uses to solve performance problems. This leads us to another hint:

> **Successful performance tuning requires understanding of database principles, with a focus on uncovering the root cause of the bottleneck.**

In other words, the successful performance analyst is no smarter than other DBAs; he has simply learned an overall process that has proved successful. Trickery? No way.

The Big Secret Revealed

After years spent tuning Oracle systems, I have learned a surprising lesson. It is the subject of our next hint:

> **With a sound approach to performance tuning, many performance bottlenecks are actually very simple to correct.**

Considering the big demand for DBAs with performance tuning skills (see the earlier graph), this hint seems counter intuitive. Does this mean that performance tuning is trivial? Not quite. As we have seen with the Otrace situation, many performance tuning problems are incredibly easy to solve. With the wrong approach, these same problems are agonizingly difficult. The high demand for these skills indicates that many analysts do not have good understanding of Oracle principles, or do not bring a sound approach to performance analysis. Perhaps *both* are lacking in some cases.

The following figure illustrates the time required to solve the various performance tuning problems that I have encountered. In my opinion, this graph should be more or less similar for any competent performance analyst. Perhaps super-gurus could do better. In any case, note the large percentage of problems that were resolved within a few days or so; relatively few require many days of intense analysis:

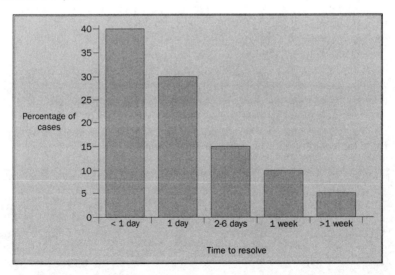

Solutions to the vast majority of performance problems do not require discussions with Oracle Corporation about tweaks or new patches. Instead, it is not unusual for a good performance tuning expert to make just a few changes that lead to markedly improved performance.

Of course, there will always be the odd problem that tests our intellectual prowess. Contrary to expectations raised by some, there will continue to be bugs in database software – whether Oracle, Sybase, Informix, DB2, or SQL Server. We will continue to see things like internal errors and bizarre database problems that test our skill. Nevertheless, the pattern is clear: many performance bottlenecks are resolved in just a few days.

Bizarre database problems seem to have a certain appeal though; thus, I have reserved for the final chapter of this book some of the craziest "database mysteries" I have seen.

Case Study: A Master Tuner Solves a Table Join

Years ago, I consulted for one of the world's aircraft manufacturers. The DBA group comprised about eight DBAs – some very experienced, but others just beginning their careers. I had the good fortune to work with a much more experienced DBA, who also happened to be an accomplished SQL tuning expert.

One morning, while sitting at my desk, I noticed that he was looking at something in a small package. He appeared to be quietly chuckling over some private joke. When I asked him about the small package, he showed me what it was – a nice pen and pencil set with the logo of the firm. He explained that the gift had just been presented to him, in appreciation for some SQL performance tuning work he had recently performed.

He (Ron), being a SQL performance expert, had been asked by another department to look at some long-running reports, and see if he could improve their runtime. Many of these troublesome reports involved table joins. This was an easy (actually trivial) assignment for Ron, because he fully understood the basics of table join techniques.

Ron explained that he had investigated the problem and isolated the bottleneck to one particularly bad piece of SQL code. Having found the root cause, Ron made a slight change in the table join, and *voila* – the problem was gone! The reports now ran in a very short time, the users were thrilled, and Ron immediately became the "hero" to this other department. A week later, to show their appreciation, they presented a gift to Ron.

We will take a closer look at the actual mechanics of table joins, and how we can code them for best performance, in Chapter 9.

As should be obvious from the scenarios presented, the path to tuning expertise is not based on clever equations, or silver bullets, but on an understanding of what steps must be performed to succeed in the performance tuning process.

Keeping Up With Oracle

Faced with a bewildering assortment of performance problems, many DBAs are understandably unsure of themselves when it comes to performance tuning. Without some time-proven approach, the whole process can be intimidating. After all, how can anyone keep up with all the new features?

The marketers of some SQL performance tuning tools exploit this apparent obstacle posed by the enormous breadth of Oracle options. In their marketing literature, some tool-sellers emphasize the impossibility of the DBA fully understanding how to deal with the many flavors of SQL. Continuing with this line of reasoning, the DBA must surely buy a tool (*their* tool) that can rapidly formulate and test a myriad of different SQL combinations.

The huge flaw in this line of reasoning is the assumption that effective performance tuning requires that the DBA understand all the features available in the most recent database version. In truth, the DBA who has a good grasp of database principles can easily account for many of the new bells and whistles in the latest database release. As the first two hints explained, sound understanding is the best long-term strategy to win in the game of performance tuning.

Consider the game of chess. In a chess match, there might be hundreds of possible moves, leading to thousands, then millions of combinations for all future moves. Does a good chess player actually consider *every* possible move? Of course not! It is only the poorest of players (or the crudest of computer programs) who uses that strategy. In reality, the master chess player knows the *principles* of the game, and only considers the options that show some promise, or appear to be relevant. The master's grasp of the game leads him to reject the vast majority of moves summarily.

Calculate Every Move?

The performance analyst can use the same reasoning. He doesn't need to try every option, because he knows that 99% of the choices are irrelevant. Consider the expert tuning analyst who sees a SQL statement that generates a huge amount of disk I/O. His good understanding leads him to reject 99% of the ideas that might theoretically be considered. The seasoned performance expert knows, for instance, that he must first focus on *why* the disk I/O's are occurring. Therefore, he will narrow down his investigation to answering questions that strike at the core of the problem. These include issues such as:

❑ Is there a full table scan occurring?

❑ What types of indexes are being used?

❑ Are the proper columns indexed?

We cover the detail of how the expert knows that these are the questions he needs answers to later in the book.

Performance Problems Yield to Sound Analysis

Experience shows that performance problems are good targets for the application of sound principles of database operation. In spite of the bewildering set of new database options that Oracle Corporation releases, there are some things that stay the same, even in a world of rapid database releases:

> **The principles of sound performance tuning do not change from version to version.**

To illustrate this hint, consider how the Oracle optimizer joins two tables. The concept of performing table joins has stayed much the same, even as database bells and whistles have been added. This means that, regardless of database version, the performance specialist must understand the difference between a nested loop and sort-merge join (for more on these, see Chapter 9). Armed with this understanding, a large number of SQL performance problems can be solved, regardless of the exact database version.

Of course, as technology advances there are some changes that must be noted, such as changes in the algorithm that the Oracle optimizer uses, or new efficiencies that are introduced In the case of table joins, for instance, the DBA should be aware of the hash joins method that is now often used. Nevertheless, this addition is an easy adjustment for the DBA who is already well acquainted with the other two methods that have been around longer. The DBA who already possesses a good understanding of performance tuning principles will have little trouble assimilating additional features such as these.

Art or Science?

Finally, we come to the question of "art or science?" Some specialists have argued that performance tuning is purely a science – simply the application of sound mathematics to a given problem. This notion is very appealing to technical practitioners, because it suggests a nice, clean, deterministic way to solve any problem. There will be no messiness.

Attractive as this idea is, it does not really appear to match reality. In the real world, life is messy and performance tuning is rarely 100% pure science. Rarely are performance problems handed to the DBA on a nice, clean index card, ready for calculations to begin.

In practice, performance problems take place in complex organizations, filled with the potential for misinformation and the effects of human egos. Instead of getting a well-defined problem report, the DBA often gets *half* an index card, with various smudges and contradictory annotations. Problems don't always start off as black and white issues.

Oops! There's Something Wrong with Your Application!

Even when the root cause of a performance problem can be determined through an heuristic, the solution often calls for creative thinking. For instance, creative thinking (and tact) is often needed when the root cause of a performance difficulty is traced to the application. The DBA may be *positive* that the application is to blame, but the developers may not be so anxious to hear that conclusion.

The designers may resist calls for changing their code, arguing that certain changes are too expensive, or simply not feasible. The professional performance expert cannot walk away at this point, but has an obligation to work with the designers to synthesize an acceptable solution. At this moment, the DBA is more of an artist than a scientist.

Thus, solving serious performance problems is not merely a mechanistic process, such as solving an equation in a school textbook. There are frequently other points to consider, such as determining what problem to solve, wading through misinformation, or dealing with the human factor. Of course, good analytical skills are necessary, but so are good *creative* skills. To ignore either aspect is to misunderstand how technical problems are solved *in practice*. Let's take a look at some case studies to illustrate these points:

Case Study: At some Firms, Performance Tuning is *all* Art!

Recently, while discussing the finer points of performance tuning with a friend, I brought up the notion of "art versus science". I should mention that this DBA works for a large financial firm, as a member of the DBA staff. At this company, there are certainly technical challenges, but much of my friend's time is spent using the softer skills, such as coordinating and discussing issues with developers, managers, and other DBAs. Also, since some of the analysts at the firm are just beginning their careers, he must spend much time educating, mentoring, and explaining issues to the more junior staff members.

Over lunch, I made the point that the DBA rarely walks into a situation with the performance problem nicely written out, as an equation to solve. This means, I continued, that the DBA must have a broader perspective than commonly believed. When I suggested that part of a DBA's work is really art, not science, he enthusiastically replied: "It's *all* art!"

For the DBA in this case, the *majority* of his time was spent on solving the "people" problems. Very little of his energies were spent on producing technical solutions.

Now I think, upon reflection, my friend would admit that his job is not *really* 100% art, but his point is instructive. Depending on the environment, simply being an analytical guru is not good enough. Technical problems do not exist in a vacuum.

In our next scenario, we review an interesting tuning problem that illustrates the importance of solving the right problem:

Case Study: Good Performance but Wrong SQL

At a San Francisco training firm, a DBA was tasked with improving the performance of six separate **Actuate** reports.

Actuate is a web-based application that allows reports to be sent over the Internet.

Most of the Actuate reports were completing in a minute or two, but six reports took up to 30 minutes to run. This run-time was considered unacceptable, especially since it represented *worse* performance than the system being replaced. Additionally, the slow reports were for some of the firm's most important customers, so it was important to identify and resolve this problem correctly.

Analysis showed that each of the problem reports had one thing in common: each report requested a huge amount of data, leading to a long delay as it was transferred over the network. In a manner of speaking, then, one could say that the *network* was the bottleneck, but that would be very misleading. Even though the network was in fact restricting the run-time, a more fruitful avenue of investigation would lead to the question: "*Why is the query being executed in the first place?*"

At this firm, the network bandwidth was fine; the delay time was simply due to the *size* of the data transfer. The real problem had nothing to do with how the network, or the database handled a particular SQL query, but why this query was being run.

With these facts in hand, the DBA met with the report designers, and explained why the report was requiring 30 minutes. The designers agreed that the large data transfer was usually unnecessary and they modified the reports to restrict unnecessarily large data transfers.

Consider how a tool would have handled the report problem. The tool could have offered suggestions on increasing the parallelism of the query, or perhaps trying a different join technique. Maybe spreading the disk I/O's across multiple spindles would have been advised. Of course, all "solutions" such as these would have completely missed the point.

The next scenario shows how just getting the right information to start with is often the biggest hurdle:

Case Study: The Cost of Misleading Information

At a division of a publishing and printing house, the IT manager reported a problem with a "slow database." He indicated, however, that he was sure the problem was related to network speed, and advised the DBA to concentrate on network problems. The DBA, being new to the firm, followed the manager's advice, but could not find anything wrong with the network. Suspecting a very serious, but subtle, network problem, he felt unqualified to take any further action.

A few months later, having some spare time, the DBA once again reviewed the slow connection times. This time, the DBA decided not to restrict the analysis to just the network, but to consider *all* possible causes. Investigation soon showed that initial connections to SQL*Plus required about 15 seconds. The same connection *locally* on the server also required 15 seconds. In other words, the network infrastructure was completely irrelevant. Further checking showed that the connections were slow due to some basic mistakes in database setup. The errors could have been easily corrected months earlier, had the DBA not been misled.

The previous case study shows how misleading information can completely sidetrack an investigation. The DBA was too quick to accept the advice, "concentrate on the network." This advice delayed by several months a solution to the performance bottleneck.

Proactive Tuning

Although many of the examples in this book are based on performance problems discovered after the system had already been released to production, it should be noted that it is preferable to correct problems *before* the system is rolled out. The cost to correct problems is orders of magnitude greater once the bug is lodged in a production system. Because of this, many IT shops employ extensive load testing in order to flush-out performance problems well before deployment.

In light of this, many of the case studies here reflect problems that were in fact corrected prior to production. The reality today, however, is that even with capable developers, many performance bottlenecks will be missed in development, and only addressed when the problem becomes so severe that immediate action is warranted.

This state of affairs is sometimes an indication that proper care has not been exercised during the development and testing phase. Ideally, applications should be thoroughly analyzed using load-testing techniques or similar means, in order to confirm the expected performance and scalability of the system.

Much has been written about the need to detect problems as early in the development process as possible. Learning from this, many large projects use strict quality assurance procedures in order to minimize undetected problems. For instance, the Software Engineering Institute (SEI) has developed rigorous procedures that are used by many Department of Defense projects in the United States (http://www.sei.cmu.edu/). Prospective contracting companies must be certified at a certain SEI level in order to be considered a qualified vendor. This process is used to minimize the huge costs that would be incurred to correct bugs that are found in production systems.

Database analysts, whether DBAs or designers, will naturally want to encourage thorough testing of applications for performance problems and scalability, and advise management about prospective performance problems *prior* to release into production.

Summary

In this chapter, we have introduced the proposition that Oracle performance tuning is neither fully art nor fully science. Although technical analysis is certainly a major element, many performance problems require the analyst to deal with a bewildering variety of personalities, and to sometimes separate fact from fiction.

Faced with the confusing set of environments in which performance problems occur, the DBA is forced to *adapt* the tuning process to the environment. This means that the DBA must use different tactics – or "change hats" during the process. We call this the Physician-to-Magician approach to performance tuning.

After looking at several real-life scenarios, we also discussed the importance of proactive tuning, in which the DBA or designer strives to *avoid* problems before they are allowed to impact production systems. Most of the principles discussed in this book will apply to both development and production systems.

In future chapters, we will go backstage to explore the steps followed by performance tuning experts. We will see that there *is* a good strategy for performance tuning – a strategy that adapts for each stage as the DBA exchanges one hat for another.

Before we put on our first hat and start the process, we need to pause and clear away some misconceptions about the Oracle tuning process. These pitfalls are the subject of the next chapter.

- Losing Strategies
- Faulty Approaches to Performance Tuning
    - The Silver Bullet Approach
    - Avoiding Work
    - The Quicky Training Class
    - Pet Ideas
    - Solving the Wrong Problem
    - The Guessing Method
    - Blame Should be Avoided
    - More Obstacles?

2

Why Many Tuning Strategies Fail

Before diving into an exposition of the Physician-to-Magician approach to database performance tuning, it is important to clear away some misconceptions about proper ways to perform the job first. To do this, we need to discuss some common ideas that sound good in theory, but work poorly in reality.

In this chapter we examine some of the most common mistaken practices, namely:

❑ Searching for the silver bullet
❑ Implementing a pet idea
❑ Solving the wrong problem
❑ Guessing

Within the silver bullet category, we will give special attention to three approaches that are extremely common:

❑ Buying a tool
❑ Buying more hardware
❑ Sending someone to a quick training class

To supplement the discussion, we present numerous case studies that illustrate the consequences of following one or more of these notions. We also consider why exotic solutions are often a distraction from solving the real problem. Following this, we conclude with an overview of some other obstacles that the performance specialist may encounter.

Losing Strategies

There really isn't any other way to say it – in this section we want to put the reader on the alert regarding some losing strategies. Many of these tuning strategies sound plausible to the novice but, in reality, they are strategies that fail most of the time.

It should be noted that some strategies that might have worked well in the past are now very dated. For instance, it used to be common practice to rely extensively on tuning ratios. Most modern-day experts, however, generally de-emphasize these ratios in favor of more sophisticated methods, such as the wait event facility (discussed extensively in Chapter 6).

Let me admit right away that the individuals suggesting (or following) poor performance tuning strategies are not dull, dimwitted, or challenged in any way. These people are often extremely intelligent staff who have a lot to offer. Unfortunately, they have simply not yet had the opportunity to develop a sound approach to Oracle performance tuning.

As we discuss these strategies, you may recognize an approach that you have used (or may still use!) This should not be an occasion for embarrassment, for we have *all* tried some of these approaches, or made similar mistakes in our careers. In fact, some of the case studies represent blunders that the author or some other (anonymous) DBA has made. The important thing is to recognize which approaches are not sound, and to abandon them for a strategy that is far more likely to produce the desired results.

Without a solid grounding in the performance tuning process, one is vulnerable to all kinds of seemingly useful suggestions, which in practice rarely bear fruit. Often, these ideas are put forward because, in the absence of a solid idea, any idea seems better than nothing. After all, if the DBA assigned to the job seems clueless, then we certainly shouldn't blame bystanders for offering pointers or attempting to fix the problem. Of course, the bystanders will occasionally be right! This might encourage the shoot from the hip approach, and lead to trying a solution again because it worked before.

Faulty Approaches to Performance Tuning

Although there are literally hundreds of mistaken ways to perform performance tuning, I have found that mistaken approaches to it generally fall into the four categories that we mentioned in the introduction to this chapter. Note that each approach discussed may indeed have some valid points. For instance, while it is a mistake to rush to buy new hardware quickly, the decision to buy new hardware may in fact turn out to be correct in some cases. Similarly, buying good software utilities or tools may indeed prove to be of great benefit in some cases.

In this section, we are going to run through each of those categories one by one, and discuss all the ramifications of choosing these flawed approaches.

The Silver Bullet Approach

Silver bullets are frequently the first option suggested, and they are a special favorite of management. By silver bullet, we mean something that very simply and cheaply solves a problem. On television, many advertisements promise fantastic results if the viewer would only buy their cleaning product – all problems simply melt away!

Of course, the term "silver bullet" is not usually mentioned by anyone, but that is what is meant (and what is hoped for). The silver bullet idea is very popular because it holds the promise of fantastic results at an amazingly low cost. Is it really any surprise that many engineers and managers respond to these offers?

The marketing bulletins from silver bullet firms promise astonishing results, without labor-intensive analysis. In other words; you, the discerning buyer, would be wise to purchase such a product. By simply buying this software or hardware, most problems disappear with almost no effort! Or so they would have you believe...

These types of solutions are often packaged as tidy, easy-to-install applications, in which the analyst simply turns the handle and out pops a solution! The marketing literature explains that the experts in the vendor's employ have already solved all the messy complications. All situations that could conceivably be encountered are covered (or they will be in the next release).

Maintain a Healthy Skepticism

Seasoned veterans, both analysts and managers, are properly skeptical of claims such as these. These silver bullets are reminiscent of perpetual motion machines that promise to run some sort of equipment without being supplied with any form of power. Although experienced DBAs do not usually fall for these magical claims, less experienced analysts often find the claims very credible. Of course, not all marketing claims are gross exaggerations, just as not all TV advertisements overstate their cases. The point is, listen to claims with a grain of salt.

In firms where little database expertise is available, these silver bullets – whether tools, hardware (or even consultants) – are especially appealing. After all, how can one evaluate the suitability of a certain solution if no one really knows how to solve Oracle performance problems? Without some in-house competence, the firm must rely upon the expertise of the vendor. Of course, the conflict of interest is obvious. The vendor will not be the one stuck with the problem if the silver bullet turns out only to be silver plated.

The search for silver bullets is not confined to the world of Oracle performance tuning. This same appetite for quick and easy solutions permeates the software development community. Just as database managers want a quick and cheap solution to performance problems, program managers also want quick and cheap solutions to project problems.

James A. Highsmith III has documented the phenomenon of searching for the silver bullet in his award-winning book entitled *Adaptive Software Development: A Collaborative Approach to Managing Complex Systems*, ISBN 0932633404. Highsmith notes that many capable project managers intuitively grasp for a quick solution that will always contain any messy problems, no matter how they transpire. Nevertheless, he says, *"There is no silver bullet"*.

In practice, management will not be able to surround and contain all problems of the future magically. They are simply fooling themselves with a vain hope. In spite of convincing empirical evidence against a silver bullet, Highsmith points out that management often continues to act as though this magic formula does exist.

There is No Silver Bullet

In spite of glowing marketing presentations, there isn't any one gadget that will contain all messy problems; it is unrealistic and contrary to the evidence to think that such a tool exists. Life simply is not that simple! The reality is that there will be situations that no one could have envisioned; this means that no one tool or operation will be adequate. Hence the performance analyst must adapt his process to the environment at hand.

At a minimum, the silver bullet approach is often a distraction to solving the real problem. Therefore, the performance analyst should caution management against embracing any suggestion that does not deal head-on with discovering the real source of the performance problem. Talking of which, let's look at our next hint:

> **There are no silver bullets that solve all performance problems. In the real world, analysis by a competent analyst is required.**

Avoiding Work

Of course, trying to save time and effort is fine. For instance, we shall see later that certain tools, in the hands of a competent DBA or other analyst, certainly have their place. The problem is not the tool per se, but rather the unrealistic expectation that there can be a substitute for actual competence.

One famous journalist, George Leonard, made a study of this quest to achieve success with only minimal effort. He points out in his classic work, *Mastery*, ISBN 0452267560, that *"The quick-fix, anti-mastery mentality touches almost everything in our lives"*. He uses the example of a tennis player who believes that he can became a good athlete in just a few months, with only a few hours practice a week. The eager novice even asks about some audiotapes that might be able to accelerate his learning process. Unfortunately, the new athlete becomes frustrated with the results, and usually gives up after a short while.

Leonard notes that, especially in America, this idea of a quick fix solution is rampant. Many want to get the satisfaction of complete mastery of some complicated subject without doing the hard work. We want to be a master via short cuts, special tricks, and the like. Hard work, and slow progress is too primitive and slow.

This whole idea of quick mastery without hard work is the impetus for the search for silver bullets. In the world of performance tuning, this means that we don't want to trouble ourselves with the hard work necessary to lay a good foundation. It is simply too hard to study the basics of Oracle database operation.

So what are some common ways to try to find a quick shortcut? Well, as mentioned in the introduction to this chapter, they are:

❑ Buying a tool

❑ Adding more hardware

❑ Sending someone to a quick training class

Let's briefly discuss some of the issues or concerns involved in these common shortcuts.

Buying A Tool

Buying a tool and buying more hardware tie for what appear to be the most common silver bullets that misfire, thus failing to solve performance problems, and leaving the customer with the initial problem.

Software tools are especially cheap, compared to the cost of competent DBAs; as a result, they hold a special attraction – for management in particular. For instance, a tool might be purchased for several thousand dollars for a single user license. Compare this to the claimed benefit, and it is easy to see why buying a tool has such a great appeal. With the claimed cost/benefit ratio, who can blame anyone for trying? What's surprising is not that some managers try a tool, but that some don't!

To give a rough idea of cost, one popular SQL tuning tool costs roughly $1,000 for a single user license. This tool performs SQL tuning by calculating the performance of a given SQL statement that is modified to include every possible SQL hint. This approach might seem a bit crude (like the chess computer program looking at all possible chess moves), but the price is right! Compare the cost of the tool to a senior DBA at roughly $100 per hour. The entire cost of the tool could be recouped in just over 1 day of wages to the DBA consultant! The appeal of this approach is self-evident.

Let us acknowledge right away that tools can be beneficial. It is certainly true that performance-tuning and design tools are often used by good DBAs. For instance, many fine DBAs use one of Quest Software's products, such as TOAD (Tool for Oracle Application Development). Others may opt for Oracle Enterprise Manager (OEM), or Embarcadero's DB Artisan. These are all fine GUI utilities that save the DBA the trouble of manually running many SQL scripts.

My own favorite, OEM Top Sessions, shows which sessions are consuming critical system resources, so that the analyst can concentrate his attention on them. This same OEM utility can also reveal exactly which SQL is being run, and the execution plan for that SQL. I find this tool very helpful, and have used it hundreds of times. It is simply more convenient than running SQL scripts manually.

Since many senior DBAs use tools such as TOAD or OEM, observers frequently draw the false conclusion that the tool is responsible for solving the problem. Of course, this is a completely erroneous conclusion, and leads us to our next hint:

> **Performance-tuning tools are valuable only to the extent that the user is competent and understands what the tool is doing.**

This hint simply states what is obvious to the person using the tool – a point that is missed by many observers. The tool may be very helpful for doing the manual labor, but the tool user must still direct the efforts to a certain purpose. We'll look at this in a little more detail in a moment.

A good performance DBA may or may not use a fancy GUI tool. Many excellent DBAs reject using tools in favor of using their own scripts run via the command line utility SQL*Plus. Their reasoning is that it is critical to understand exactly how the database is being queried, and not blindly trust a utility. In other words, for these DBAs, understanding and competence take precedence over convenience. Note, however, that one could exaggerate this notion to an extreme. For instance, is it really better always to use the command line? Of course not! If there is a tool that can ease your work, by all means consider using it!

Tools or No Tools

Experienced DBAs and managers recognize the problem with inappropriate reliance on tools. Excessive use of tools could suggest that the DBA might not really understand what is happening, but is simply selecting some menu options. In a shop that relies exclusively on tools, the question must then be asked, What if the tool can't handle the exact situation? What will happen in an emergency? Which DBA can I trust to solve a critical production problem? In other words, the fundamental competency of the DBA staff is in doubt.

Recognizing this issue, one senior manager at a large government agency even mandates that novice DBAs do not use tools. Instead, new DBAs are encouraged to develop and run scripts via SQL*Plus, so that they understand exactly what is happening behind the scenes. Only after the beginner shows clear understanding of database operation are they allowed to use tools such as Oracle's OEM.

While this might seem a little extreme, this particular manager wanted to be completely confident of the competency of her DBA staff. Of course, most DBAs will probably agree that this may be going too far. It isn't really necessary to abolish tools – just simply to use them wisely.

The DBA Drives the Tool

In many ways, the exact tool is irrelevant, because the DBA has a roadmap in his mind of where he is going. The tool smoothes the way a little (or a lot), and perhaps saves some grunt work of looking up scripts; but, in the end, the tool is not doing the performance tuning – the *DBA* is.

Consider an analogy in the medical world. If we visited the office of an experienced physician, we might see the doctor use a stethoscope in daily practice. Clearly, no one would suggest that simply having this tool makes anyone a competent doctor. We all know that a competent doctor uses his own judgment in picking whatever tools are most helpful in rendering good medical care. The act of removing the tool does not make the doctor incompetent; likewise, adding the tool cannot somehow make an incompetent doctor competent.

Let's turn to our next case study. It is an excellent example of what happens when someone tries to avoid the labor of analysis, and instead turns to a tool. This case exemplifies why no tool can substitute for true understanding (but some tools can provide the temporary illusion of competency!):

Case Study: The Joy of SQL Hints

On a new data warehouse project, the DBA who was supporting the design team was working with several report writers, making numerous suggestions on how to write better SQL code. Frequently, this meant asking the designer to include SQL hints.

SQL hints are simple syntax additions that guide the Oracle optimizer. We will discuss SQL hints in great detail later on in the book when we discuss the role of SQL in the tuning process.

Sometimes, however, the DBA needed to coach the designer in how to correct a poor report design.

After successfully correcting many reports, management became increasingly interested in using a tool to make life easier for the report writers (and presumably reducing the DBA expense). The DBA explained that someone on the project would need to have a good understanding of the database principles before a tool could ever be useful. The DBA noted that the analyst could be either a DBA or a lead designer, or perhaps someone else, but he explained that a tool would fail without some competent advisor.

The DBA continued his work with the report designers, and discovered one report with a particularly faulty design. This report ran poorly because it executed exactly the same SQL statement five times in a row. (The designers had prepared the report this way, because it saved them some formatting steps.)

Each of the five individual SQL statements ran well, with regard to what each statement needed to accomplish. A typical runtime for one SQL statement was about 30 seconds, which was an acceptable run-time for this report. Unfortunately, running the same code five times obviously slowed things down. Therefore, the DBA filed a bug report and asked the designers to correct the faulty design. (Note how taking a short-cut in the report design has already greatly increased the troubleshooting time.)

Weeks later, while performing some routine checks, the DBA happened to notice some unusual SQL code on the production system. A particular report, which turned out to be the earlier report with the five SQL statements, was using SQL code with hints that the DBA did not recognize. He was mystified as to how this report could ever have ended up in production without the correct fix. After investigating, he discovered that the designer had installed a tool, and asked the tool how to reduce the runtime. The tool, not knowing or caring about the five duplicate SQL queries, suggested a SQL hint as a way to optimize the individual SQL.

Of course, this solution had nothing to do with the root cause of the problem. The designer had decided to ignore the real problem (the five identical SQL statements); instead, he added the SQL hint that had been suggested by the tool. The hint had a marginal effect and, of course, the report time was unchanged. Falsely believing that the problem was now fixed, the designer released the code into production.

This case study illustrates how a tool can give a developer the illusion that he is well-equipped to solve performance problems. In reality, the poor choice made by the designer resulted in continuing performance problems in a critical production system. The unsatisfactory report simply had to be redesigned, as requested previously. The first short cut (running multiple SQL to save report formatting effort) was bad enough. The second short cut (using a tool to avoid a report redesign) cost the firm many hours in rework time, and extra effort by the QA team as well as the DBA.

Add More Hardware

Besides the buy a tool approach, another favorite silver bullet is buying larger servers, or bolting on more hardware. This approach is a time-honored (but rarely successful in the long run) method of trying to improve performance. Unfortunately, this option is often chosen with little thought of understanding or solving the real problem.

The line of thought here is very similar to the buy a tool approach, except that the stakes are generally higher. When management is considering purchase of new hardware, the performance problem is usually very urgent. Typically, the performance problem has been continuing for weeks or months, and a crisis has been reached. The desire is to solve the problem instantly. Often, management is in a panic and is willing to pay hundreds of thousands of dollars for a quick solution. In some cases, the buy the tool approach has already been tried and discarded.

Even though the new hardware solution is much more expensive than the buy the tool approach, it does have a certain genuine advantage – at least for the short term. New hardware, particularly if much more powerful than the existing system, can often buy time and delay facing the true problem. It is often true that faster CPUs will temporarily fix the problem, or at least mitigate some of the symptoms.

Of course, the problem with this approach is that it simply delays the real work that eventually must be done to resolve the root cause of the bottleneck. Faster CPUs will obviously not actually correct a poorly designed application – they will only mask the problem for a while.

Our next case study illustrates how the add more hardware approach works in practice. In this case, the company spent hundreds of thousands of dollars instead of solving the root cause of the performance problem. This is also an excellent example of what happens if no tuning process is in place:

Case Study: Bigger must be Better

At a wireless phone provider with many customers, there were performance problems involving a small Oracle financials application. Only a few modules in the Oracle apps program were actually used. The application was used to keep track of phone hardware that had been ordered by phone customers. As the number of phone subscribers grew, however, a performance bottleneck became noticeable; soon the program began to receive management's attention.

As weeks elapsed, the performance problems became more acute; however, it was not clear what to do because there was no application administrator. In other words, no one had ever been assigned responsibility for the application, and no one really knew how the application worked! None of the analysts on staff was really familiar with the application, and the DBAs were not seriously consulted. Amazingly, no competent performance analyst was even asked to evaluate the problem.

Not willing to spend time investigating, management decided to buy a much larger server, with many more CPUs. Then, the IT staff would migrate the application and database to the larger server. The DBAs were eventually invited to a meeting to explain the decision; however, it was apparent that the decision was final. None of the DBAs was asked to evaluate the performance problem.

The new hardware was purchased, and all applications were transferred. At first, the problems were successfully masked due to the increase in CPU power. Months later, however, performance problems once again arose. This time, help was requested, and one DBA was finally asked to investigate and locate the real root cause.

It turned out that many of the performance bottlenecks were easily corrected. Several of the changes were incredibly trivial; for example, one serious problem was resolved by very slight indexing changes. The application had provided certain standard indexes, assuming a certain data distribution. In the actual production environment, the data distribution was completely different, making a few more indexes necessary. Many of the problems were resolved in just a few hours.

As shown in this case study, the new hardware that was bolted on did have a temporary beneficial effect. That is the mixed blessing of using the buy-new-hardware approach; it sometimes provides temporary relief – but ultimately the root cause must be determined.

33

This case study of the bolt on more hardware approach illustrates an important principle, which is the subject of our next hint:

> **Adding hardware may temporarily mask a problem, but rarely solves the root cause of the problem.**

Let's move on now to look at another common silver bullet...

The Quick Training Class

Besides the silver bullet approaches of buying a tool and buying more hardware, there is also the idea of sending someone to a quick training course. The idea is to bolster up the in-house expertise for database tuning quickly. These classes are widely available from Oracle Corporation and Learning Tree International, as well as a growing list of online training providers. Typically, a student attends a one-week course, and then returns with a certificate acknowledging competence in the subject area.

At first glance, a training class seems a reasonable way to approach performance tuning, since it appears to head down the right path. After all, doesn't a training class address the fundamental problem of lack of understanding?

It is true that short training classes are often fun, or inspirational; they can certainly get the student off to a good start. Also, a good instructor can lay the foundation for future growth and guide the student to good resources.

Frequently, however, the expectations of a brief training class are completely unrealistic and unwarranted. Just as a fancy tool cannot substitute for actual understanding, so a quick training class cannot possibly provide much substance. The class is a good start (or refresher) but not the real thing.

This limitation will become obvious if we simply count up the total time that the student spends in actual hands-on performance tuning. In a typical one-week course, only about two hours of each day is spent on practicals – that is, actual performance tuning. This means that after completing a one-week performance-training course, the student has spent a total of about ten hours practicing this skill. Of course, many courses are shorter, and the online training courses rarely provide more hands-on experience.

The One-Week Doctor?

As a corollary to this argument, let's return to our medical example. Think how absurd it would be to send a medical student on a one- or two-week training class, and expect that the student would really be competent at the end of the course. Even after their extensive classroom training, medical students are required to spend several more years working under the eye of more experienced doctors. In other words, physicians are not considered competent until they have invested many years of study and practice.

Our next case study illustrates how reliance on a few training classes, or even an impressive certificate from a major corporation can lead to an embarrassing situation for a job applicant:

Case Study: Certified Professional?

During consulting assignments, I often have the opportunity to interview DBA candidates for my client. I use a list of about 30 questions that I have developed over several years. The questions are designed to show whether the candidate has just memorized some formulae, or whether he or she truly has an understanding of database operation.

The first five questions are very simple, and are designed to get the interview off to a good start. Many DBAs find these initial questions especially trivial. This is expected, because these questions are designed to be easy for experienced and competent DBAs, but too tough for imposters. In other words, the questions are based on practical matters, things that an experienced DBA would have done many times.

For example, one question simply asks the name of the SQL*Net files on the client and the server. The answers of course are: `tsnames.ora` and `listener.ora`. Clearly, these types of questions could not possibly be missed by any DBA with more than a few months experience.

I was asked to review the resume of one candidate, and then conduct a phone interview. I noted that the prospective DBA had his OCP (Oracle Certified Professional) certificate. In fact, this qualification was printed in bright red ink at the top of the resume. This was the first time I had met anyone with this certification, and I was curious how qualified this candidate would be.

I called the candidate and started the interview; however, I ran into a problem almost right away. In question 3, I ask the candidate how one chooses which database to connect to on a UNIX server. I was simply asking for information about setting `ORACLE_HOME` and `ORACLE_SID` – two extremely common environmental variables that are used on all UNIX databases. This question is so trivial that no candidate had ever missed it.

I asked the same question three different ways, without success. I tentatively concluded that I must be the problem; I was obviously not doing a good job at stating the question. I tried rephrasing the same question slightly differently. The candidate was still not able to answer the question.

The interview was very short and frustrating. I concluded that my inability to communicate was the source of the problem. Fortunately for me, however, a colleague, overhearing the interview, corrected my misconception. He had heard the question repeated several times, and assured me that it was clearly stated, and that no experienced DBA could possibly have not answered it correctly.

I finally came to the conclusion that the candidate had no experience whatsoever on UNIX systems. The OCP certification had been earned with little, if any, hands-on time. In other words, this certified professional did not even have the basics to begin supporting an Oracle database on UNIX.

Following the interview in this case study, I began to see a trend. I noticed that the certification process was sometimes being used as a credential in lieu of experience. This actually makes good sense. If a prospective DBA has very little experience, something must be offered to attest to the person's competence. After all, who would hire a DBA with no qualifications?

It seemed as though the experienced DBAs were not spending their time getting certified; they could already list years of experience on their resume, or provide testimonials from former employers. In addition, the job market at the time was so hot that no additional credentials were required.

For many months after this, I noticed a reverse correlation between actual DBA experience and OCP certification. That is, the candidates who claimed OCP certification fared much worse in answering even the simplest questions. (Of course, if I were to ask questions that happened to be covered in the training class, they would presumably do well on the interview.)

This case study is not meant to deride anyone who has gone through the trouble of obtaining Oracle certification, and wishes to become a DBA. Certainly, the goal of obtaining OCP certification is a worthy one. All things being equal, the DBA who has take the time and effort to achieve certification is ahead of the game. Now that the OCP exam has been around for several years, there are many fine DBAs who have achieved this certification. The point, rather, is that taking a few training classes, or getting a certificate does not in itself confer competence.

Qualified to Learn

At the college level, consider the years spent studying in order to earn a college diploma. Yet, after all that study, the recipient of a Bachelor's degree is really just a qualified beginner in the field of study. Mortimer Adler, the late Chairman of *Encyclopedia Britannica*, and editor of *Great Books of the Western World*, notes that the B.A. degree was never meant to be a sign of being learned, but rather that the graduates have become competent as learners. The graduates had obtained the skills of learning.

In other words, Adler points out, the graduate of a four-year college has learned the basics of how to learn, and is ready to begin a serious study of a profession. Thus, a fresh engineering graduate works under a senior engineer; a chemistry graduate likewise begins on simple lab assignments under the supervision of a senior chemist.

In no way would a new graduate in any field be considered a competent professional; years of experience are still required. For instance, some professions require that certification be preceded by at least several years of practical experience. This is true, for instance, for engineers desiring to get their PE (Professional Engineer) certification.

These examples suggest that a consensus exists as to what constitutes competence in a certain field. Clearly, years of study and practice are the norm in order to even attempt to demonstrate mastery of a complex subject. No one is considered to have obtained competency without meeting these requirements.

Compare these requirements for professional certification to the approximately ten hours of hands-on practice provided by a short training class in Oracle performance tuning. Even after accounting for possible differences in complexity between the various professions, the limitation of short-term training classes is obvious. Clearly, there is not the slightest chance that the graduate of one of these classes could possibly have be capable of solving Oracle performance problems consistently and competently:

> **Short-term training classes are a good starting point, but do not confer competence.**

A Good Start

In spite of their limitations, however, training classes certainly have their place. They are a legitimate option for helping someone get started on the path to true understanding of a complex subject. Many training firms provide Introduction to Oracle classes, or other introductory topics, such as Beginning Performance Tuning. These types of classes could be a good way to acquaint students with a new subject.

In addition, short training classes can be helpful in briefing more experienced practitioners on very specific technologies, or informing engineers about recent improvements in the field. For example, the New Features in Oracle 9i class could be very helpful in explaining to DBAs what new options are available in the latest database release. A class on Configuring Oracle Parallel Server could also be of great benefit to administrators starting out with this technology.

These types of classes are useful because their purpose is understood to be very limited. The introductory-type classes are expected simply to acquaint the students with a technology. Presumably, no one expects the student to be a master after an introductory class. The advantage of the application-specific classes is that they are very restricted in scope. Thus, the instruction can concentrate on one particular subject. Of course, it should be remembered that even specific classes such as Configuring Oracle Parallel Server don't really produce competency. They too, are simply a good starting point.

Our next case study shows the folly of overstating the benefit of training classes, and relying on them as a shortcut to instant mastery:

One of the world's largest electronic chip-making corporations prides itself on sending each employee to at least one week of training every year. Many employees take advantage of these training courses to brush-up on their skills, or explore some new areas to branch into. In certain cases, the corporation will provide more than the nominal one-week allotment.

One morning, the managers in the IT department were called to a meeting to discuss how to correct a deficiency in the department of certain critical IT skills. In particular, the department needed individuals with competence in VAX systems programming. After discussing possible employees who could meet this need, I remarked to the Director of IT that we simply did not have anyone in the department who had the expertise in the particular area.

No one disputed that observation, but the manager's response was surprising. He asked that I identify the training class that could correct this deficiency. That is, he wanted to simply send an employee to a one-week training course, which would supposedly transform the student into a fully qualified VAX systems programmer!

I was at a loss as to how to respond, since the manager's belief in a short training class seemed so unreasonable. It seemed obvious to me that actual competency in the particular skill could not possibly be achieved by attending a one-week training class.

In this case study, the manager's desire to produce competency by supplying a few hours of instruction illustrates the common notion that mastery in a complicated subject can be magically infused by a brief training class. Of course, the training class option mentioned in our case study was not successful in magically producing competent IT skills. Instead, the firm continued to suffer a deficiency in critical skills.

Over the succeeding months, increasing frustration led to management changes and continuing turmoil in the department. In later months, the firm decided to hire qualified workers with the necessary skills. The one week-per-year training was retained, but was used more as fill-in training.

By way of example, let's take a quick look at a sample tutorial that successfully helped developers.

Example: Sample Tutorial

The Powerpoint slide presented below demonstrates a one-hour lesson that was conducted for a publishing firm. The presentation was called *Five Points of Efficient SQL Queries*. This seminar was prepared when the DBA saw that many of the programmers were not aware of even the basics of index usage, and that fill-in training for those working on his project would be beneficial:

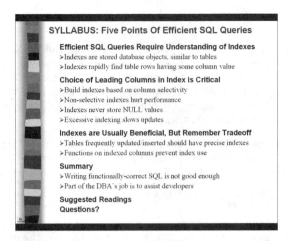

This mini-lesson was very much appreciated by the developers, and their designs immediately improved. They also saw that the DBA was treating them as equals, not just troublesome pests. This furthered the effort to build a trusting relationship with the designer team.

Of course, the benefit is two-fold. The benefit of preparing these lessons for the application team is that the DBA himself improves his grasp of the same database concepts.

For example, how many DBAs really know what a star transformation is? Or consider hash joins. Many DBAs have heard of them but few really understand how they work. By preparing a tutorial on subjects such as these, the DBA will vastly increase his knowledge and understanding. This gain in understanding will probably pay off later, as the DBA is confronted with a performance problem related to the subject of the tutorial.

In fact, by preparing a seminar on the subject of hash joins, the author came across an important journal article that laid the foundation for the join-processing algorithms used in the modern Oracle optimizer. The ideas in that article from the 1980's influenced not just Oracle, but the design of all major relational database systems. The point is, I was able to achieve this greater understanding as a result of preparing a mini-class for a customer:

> **Prepare mini-lessons on database performance topics, where appropriate.**

Of course, it is not really mandatory that the performance expert has these arcane journal articles memorized, or even knows the history behind the Oracle optimizer. The point, however, is that by spending the time and effort to build a presentation on this subject, the teacher will vastly improve his understanding of the topic. By conducting thorough research into a certain topic, the performance analyst will be much better qualified to handle related performance problems when they occur.

OK, that's all we are going to look into on the topic of silver bullets. Let's move on to the next mistaken approach in our list...

Pet Ideas

With this approach, the analyst has a solution in hand, and has been waiting for just the right moment to use it. These designs are often implemented without any real discussion, and the performance analyst may discover them already entrenched in the application. Very intelligent programmers or administrators, who just want to try something new, frequently advance these solutions. Who can blame them? It's fun to try tricky things.

These pre-packaged solutions are a lot of fun to implement, and sometimes they don't cause too many problems. At other times, however, the pet idea causes a lot of unnecessary work for DBAs. That's what happens in our next case study:

Case Study: A Raw Deal

The DBA team for a large aerospace company inherited a complicated database, used for storing engineering drawings for military aircraft. The uptime on this database was critical, since many engineers at the giant firm depended on it.

As the DBA team managed numerous databases already, adding another would normally not be an issue. This database had one feature, however, that set it apart: it had a pet idea entrenched in the design.

The complication in this database was that the disks were all configured for raw devices.

Raw devices are a way to set up disks so that they don't actually have a file system. This can provide some performance improvement because the steps involved in navigating the file system are eliminated. In contrast, disks that are set up the usual way are sometimes called cooked.

Now, raw devices are perfectly acceptable if warranted. If the raw devices had been configured to deal with extraordinary high disk I/O, this would be understandable; however, that was not the case for this database.

The original DBA, actually a very smart individual (and former systems administrator), simply implemented raw devices because he liked them. There had not been any serious analysis that indicated large disk I/O; it was simply assumed. No assessment of the extra load on the database group was ever performed. (Most likely, the previous administrator was simply not aware of the impact of his choice.)

This pet idea caused a great deal of consternation in the DBA group – with nothing to show for it. Many planning meetings were held to reconfigure the database to use a cooked file system. The main problem for the group was that this database was the only one in the company configured for raw devices. The backup/restore system that worked so well with all of the other databases had to be reconfigured just for this one database.

Of course, there were other complications also, such as the need to pre-plan raw disk partitions, the different procedures to use when adding more space in tablespaces, file-naming conventions, and so on. Hundreds of hours were spent on reconfiguring this simple database.

In this case study, all the extra housekeeping was due to one administrator's desire to implement a pet project. The database certainly worked, but at a large cost to the organization, with little to show for it otherwise.

Sometimes, the performance expert must re-educate the analysts or designers who have been subjected to someone's unique ideas. One of the strangest cases of pet ideas that I have seen is the subject of the next case study:

Case Study: Never Use Indexes!

A report-writer at a publishing company approached me one morning and asked for some advice on tuning his SQL code. This particular programmer was not too experienced, but he more than compensated for his inexperience by being very interested in improving his programs, and using good programming practice.

The programmer mentioned to me that he was new to SQL, and didn't understand what a former employee had coded. Could I review the program for him?

Scanning through the SQL, I noticed some strange syntax. In each WHERE clause, there were a few extra characters (single quotes) inserted so as to make index use impossible. It's important to remember when writing SQL that indexes have certain restrictions; in particular, indexes can only be used when a given column is referenced without any functions being applied to the field. This restriction occurs because an index is a look-up on the column values – not some function of the column values. (Recent innovations, in particular the function-index, have eased this restriction somewhat, but good designers still keep these indexing practices in mind.)

Each SQL statement was of this form:

```
SQL> SELECT Field1, Field2 ...
  2  FROM Table_X
  3  WHERE Field1 || '' = 'ABC'
  4  AND Field2 || '' = 'DEF';
```

For some crazy reason, the writer of this code had concatenated a null on each field, so that the optimizer would never use an index! Of course, this is occasionally done, but this same syntax was throughout the program.

I showed the report writer the odd syntax, and asked him why he didn't want to use indexes; he explained that the former employee always did it that way. After going over the basics of index usage, the programmer was able to correct his program with no further difficulties.

In this case study, for some odd reason, the former employee had a pet notion that SQL code should always include the syntax to avoid index usage. Fortunately, another programmer spotted the odd syntax and asked for assistance; otherwise, that same program could still be running, doing full table scans on each query!

Let's move onto our next approach, which is mistakenly solving the wrong problem...

Solving the Wrong Problem

With this approach, closely related to the pet idea, the analyst rejects (or never really considers) a careful, systematic means of finding the root cause of a performance bottleneck. Instead, the technical staff goes off at a tangent, solving problems that might be related, but which are not really the cause of the performance problem. Without a complete understanding of the bottleneck, it is not clear if certain technical issues are the problem itself, or whether they are merely symptoms of a more subtle cause.

One frequent manifestation of this approach is the tendency to assume an answer. Rather than expending the effort to identify the true root cause, some DBAs are tempted to skip the analysis and jump right to the solution.

Eliminating Possibilities

Solving the wrong problem can come about in several different ways. Some DBAs are often too quick to use their intuition to eliminate possibilities, or they simply fail to cast the net wide enough, thus focusing on only a few possible causes. This points out the need to establish the facts up front. At other times, the performance analyst can be led astray by suggestions that certain subsystems have already been ruled out. For instance, the application designers may point the DBA away from the application.

Being only human, application designers may resist divulging information that will reveal mistakes or poor design techniques. Later in the book we will discuss ways to isolate the root cause of performance problems; for now, however, remember that it is extremely common for a poor application design to hinder performance. In fact, this problem with the application design is probably the number one cause of performance bottlenecks. Nevertheless, many novice DBAs will ignore the application in favor of database-specific solutions.

This tendency to overlook some subsystems warrants another hint:

> **When performing a root cause analysis, consider all subsystems as potential suspects, until they are conclusively eliminated by first-hand analysis.**

An example of how one DBA (me) was fooled by misinformation is the subject of our next case study. Although this true case study relates to a Sybase database, the principles still apply to Oracle (or any other database for that matter):

Case Study: Trust but Verify!

I was asked to assist the design team in investigating and solving a certain problem in a web-based Java application. This program called various stored procedures, and some important users had complained that a certain function was very slow.

It was easily determined which function was being called. I asked the designer to isolate the Java code that was in question, so we could get an idea of how long the routine took. She quickly set up a test case and ran the program, reporting that the elapsed time was only a fraction of a second. She repeated the test several times, but each time the database appeared to respond very quickly.

At this point, we questioned whether the program actually had a performance problem; that is, we began to believe that the customer was in error. After several days of analyzing the stored procedure without any conclusive answers, I asked the production DBA to call this same procedure directly on the production system. This was almost an afterthought, because we both expected the procedure to finish instantaneously. The results were very surprising; the stored procedure did not run quickly, but actually ran for several minutes at least.

After reporting this contradictory finding to the designer, she investigated her test setup, and discovered that the sub-second response time she previously reported was simply the time to call the procedure, not the real time for the procedure to finish. It was simply a matter of a slight logical error in the script. Once we confirmed the true timing, the root cause of the problem was quickly located.

In this case study, the DBA was initially fooled by some misinformation. This led to the hasty elimination of one of the key subsystems, which later turned out to be the culprit. Note also that the DBA (the author) began to apply the blame-the-user approach to performance tuning prematurely. Once again, we see how critical it is to be sure of your facts. Don't be quick to assume facts not really proven, to accuse systems (or people), or to eliminate systems from consideration. We will discuss this approach a little later in the chapter.

Exotic Tuning Ideas

Another way of solving the wrong problem is by immediately branching off to try the more exotic tuning suggestions. These include changing some rare `init.ora` parameters, or activating the more unusual features in the database without good cause.

Some exotic solutions that may be unnecessary include:

❑   Assuming that raw disk partitions are required.

❑   Changing the value of more unusual `init.ora` parameters, for example, `spin_count` or `hash_multiblock_io_count`.

❑   Changing the degree of parallelism.

Note that none of these options is wrong in all circumstances. In some cases, one of these options may be appropriate, or even the best solution. The point, rather, is to try to use a systematic process that will lead to the simplest adequate solution to the problem. Try to find the solution with the fewest moving parts.

An example of using an exotic solution is the subject of our next case study:

43

Case Study: A Multi-Threaded Solution for a Single-Threaded Problem

A DBA for a large financial services company approached me one morning and explained his problem. Several of his databases had been configured for MTS (Multi-Threaded Server). Certain port numbers, listener names, and so on, had already been set up, based on a prior DBA's recommendation. Also, the client tnsnames.ora file had been established assuming this configuration for MTS. This file had been widely distributed to many database users.

The current DBA had come to realize that there was absolutely no reason whatsoever for MTS. His job was being complicated unnecessarily by a problem that didn't need to exist.

Of course, the MTS option has its place (on servers with insufficient memory or a huge number of connections). This option appears to work well in later versions of Oracle. Nevertheless, there are numerous cases in the Oracle bug database that are related only to MTS. Thus, unless this feature is really required, the DBA is simply introducing unnecessary complications, and possibly incurring a greater incidence of bugs.

The previous DBA, knowing that MTS makes efficient use of scarce memory resources, had implemented MTS without any real justification. In fact, there really was no memory problem. Of course, to be fair, it was probably not evident how many bugs would be related to MTS later on.

The DBA in this case study was faced with a dilemma, because many of the clients' network files had already been configured for MTS, and they did not want to reconfigure their workstations. Many months would transpire before Oracle could be cleanly reconfigured without the MTS option.

Achieving 100% Cache Hit Ratio

Another favorite of novice DBAs is to concentrate on some magic parameter to fix the problem at hand. It is tempting to believe that a simple change to an init.ora parameter could solve the performance problems; after all, what could be easier and faster than a quick change to the init.ora file, then to restart the database?

Often, it is easy to become obsessed with improving the database cache hit ratio so as to minimize disk I/O. All other factors are forgotten; the entire focus of the tuning effort becomes centered on this number; the novice believes that simply by making this number higher, the database must run faster.

The point often forgotten here is related to a concept called the *law of diminishing returns*. It means that increasing the database cache will initially provide a large bang for your buck. With each subsequent addition, however, the improvement will be slightly less. A database that has a reasonably sized cache will thus see virtually no improvement – even when large additions are made to the cache.

Of course, a good hit ratio is not necessarily a bad idea; but there are several more pertinent questions to ask first, for example:

❑ Why is there so much I/O in the first place?

❑ Is this I/O the actual root cause of the problem?

Keep in mind also that a very high hit ratio may itself indicate a problem. For instance, it is possible to write SQL that will result in a massive number of logical reads. The most common cause of this is called a **correlated subquery**. In this SQL, a read from one table is repeated for each row in another table. This can easily result in millions of logical reads, thus driving the hit ratio very high. The hit ratio indeed looks excellent, but it really is an indication of a terrible problem!

In other words, an obsession with the cache hit ratio is usually an attempt to solve the wrong problem. This ill-advised approach might work in a few rare cases where the database setup was drastically wrong, but this tactic is usually a distraction from solving the real problem.

Blaming the User

Another variation on the solve-the-wrong-problem approach is to insist that there is no problem. This is accomplished by simply blaming the user, and can be performed on any platform. This approach is an especially attractive option because the users are typically not present to defend themselves.

Of course, if the user is really not using the application correctly, this probably means that there is a problem with the application design or training, not the user. Obviously, applications should be designed so that it is virtually impossible to run a function that will degrade the system unnecessarily.

Now that we have finished with our tour of how DBAs might end up solving the wrong problem, let's look at the final incorrect approach to database tuning...

The Guessing Method

We have already briefly mentioned this sad, but very common method. For some reason, the guessing approach is mysteriously attractive. Many otherwise capable analysts feel compelled to start making wild guesses at a problem before the investigation has even started.

Perhaps the guessing tendency is due to the entrenched push by management for short-term results. Or maybe it is the desire to be the first to discover the solution. Of course, no one would ever admit that they are guessing, but that is exactly what often occurs.

Whatever the cause, the professional performance tuning expert must resist this tendency to engage in speculation. If nothing else, one's reputation is harmed by continually submitting erroneous answers not based on sound research. Most of the time a guess will be way off the mark and, eventually, the client will lose confidence in your ability to diagnose a problem.

The most extreme case of guessing that I have witnessed is illustrated in what I call the *Mad Guesser* case study. This real-life, jumbo-sized case study has an extra bonus; it also demonstrates several other erroneous approaches, including the solving-the-wrong-problem and buy-more-hardware tactics:

Case Study: The Mad Guesser

While consulting at a large medical instrumentation company, I was asked to review the performance of a certain database that had been experiencing severe performance problems. The project management team was considering buying a much larger server. (I found out years later that management had also been considering the option of simply canceling the project due to the continuing, unresolved performance problems).

Shortly after my involvement, the DBA for that project appeared, and while several of us watched, he frantically began to try different tactics to make the database work better. Unfortunately, he was not really willing to accept any help from his colleagues. The other DBAs would have been happy to assist him, but their assistance was not wanted. In the words of one DBA, he was wildly thrashing about for some resolution.

He suggested some big time-wasting efforts, such as increasing the size of redo logs, and spreading the disk I/O across more spindles.

Note: Adding more disks to a system is not at all a bad idea; spreading disk activity over a larger number of disks does tend to increase total throughput. In this particular case, however, there wasn't really anything that called for such a solution.

Adopting a more consistent and logical approach, several of the DBAs decided to perform a simple root cause analysis in order to define what the problems really were.

The analysis showed that all the performance problems were due to just a few SQL statements. These SQL statements required several million disk reads on each execution. Each hour, the database was forced to perform 12 million I/Os.

Once the problem was defined and the root cause was isolated, the solution was very simple. Just two corrections were required:

❑ Schedule a periodic rebuild of one index.

❑ Create a histogram for one index. We will discuss histograms in more detail in Chapter 12. The general idea of using a histogram, however, is to provide extra statistical information that tells the Oracle optimizer very precisely how data is distributed.

This situation exemplifies the guessing method at its finest. Without any investigation or analysis to try to find the root cause of the problem, the novice DBA desperately grasped at anything that could conceivably impact performance. His best course simply would have been to ask for help (in this case, he didn't really want any help!) Calm reflection and analysis would have revealed that there was no real reason to enlarge the redo logs.

The other inappropriate action of spreading I/O's across more disks, might be a good solution to some problems, but why was it done in this case? In fact, no one had ever taken the time to state exactly what the problem was clearly. Spreading the I/O across more disks need only have been considered when the I/O was first reduced to near-minimum. (In future chapters, we will discuss the important of first defining the problem.)

The program manager agreed to implement the very simple corrections, and the database was soon running smoothly. After these minor changes, disk I/O dropped to about 50 I/Os per hour. At this low rate, all of the database files could even have been on a single disk, showing just how inaccurate guessing can be.

At any rate, the project was not canceled, and the firm saved the time and effort of buying, setting-up, and migrating application and database to a larger server.

Once again, the solution here was not due to extraordinary aptitude by some special guru DBAs. Instead, it was simply an application of a sound process, with an insistence on avoiding the guessing method. As soon as the problem was clearly defined, the solution took almost no effort to identify.

Let's now move on to a topic that has less to do with the technical side of performance tuning, but is still an integral part of the overall tuning process. The following section deals with blame, and human interaction – or, more specifically, what we should avoid in these areas.

Blame Should be Avoided

With the Physician-to-Magician approach to performance tuning, it is important that you gain the trust of your database customers, whether they are the end users, designers, or programmers. This step is critical, because by gaining the users' confidence, the job of the performance expert actually becomes easier. Serious problems can be avoided, performance on the production system will probably be wonderful, and everyone on the team (including the DBA, of course) ends up looking like a genius.

In order to gain this trust, the DBA must avoid blaming the designer when performance is lacking, or a really poor design has been implemented. Instead of blame, the DBA can choose to assist the designer by focusing on the problem, not the person. This allows the designer to be part of the solution, rather than part of the problem; almost anyone would cooperate on these terms.

Not only should a performance expert refuse to point the finger of blame, they must also share the praise with the team when a performance bottleneck has been corrected. After all, the DBA is not a lone ranger, but depends on good teamwork; thus, the team should receive the credit:

> **Share the credit for solving performance problems.**

In contrast to this, if the designer is always getting blamed, or senses a hostile or accusatory tone in the DBA, he will simply choose to go around the DBA whenever possible. After all, no one wants to get blamed for a problem; no one wants to be yelled at. Everyone wants to be recognized for making a good contribution.

The Cost of a Poor Working Relationship

Unfortunately, the practice of bypassing the DBA is very common. As a result, poor designs are frequently implemented in production, where the cost to correct the error may be huge. A design flaw that is not detected until production can force decisions that would normally be considered foolish. For instance, a performance bottleneck on a major production server can be so damaging to the firm, that it has no choice but to buy new servers costing hundreds of thousands of dollars.

Usually, these production performance problems could have been easily prevented by a brief discussion with a competent DBA. This preventative medicine is usually cheap; the cure usually is not.

To guard against a tendency to blame, remember that our database users are really our customers; they depend on us for timely assistance, not blame. If nothing else, keep in mind that they could very well be the source of your new work!

Our next case study illustrates how a DBA's job was made simpler, and performance problems disappeared, all because of a trusting relationship with the designers:

Case Study: Please Check my Code

I had the pleasure of working with a diverse team of designers on an accounts-receivable system for a large insurance company. The team members were employees of a very large consulting services corporation; I was the only consultant not actually employed by that firm.

The "chemistry" on this team was especially good, and all the members appeared to work very well together. We had many occasions to review design ideas, and decide upon ways to produce a good application.

After some weeks of working together, one designer asked me to review his PL/SQL stored procedures, just to make sure he wasn't adding any serious design flaws. He provided a listing for me, and asked me to look over the code. I pointed out to him that often the people who most need code checking are the ones who would never ask for it.

It seemed to me that the attitude of this programmer had already prevented 90% of any possible problems. The fact that someone is open to a peer review already suggests the maturity and competence of the individual. That person *knows* that he might be missing something and wisely seeks the advice of others. (That same principle applies to DBAs.)

This case study illustrates the quality gain that results from a trusting relationship. The designers were willing to seek help because they knew that the DBA would not ridicule them. This project was a huge "win-win-win" situation. The DBA, the designers, and the company all benefited from a cooperative working relationship.

Have Pity on the Poor Users!

A good working relationship between the DBA and the users cannot be established if the DBA insists on criticizing the user for improper computer skills, or forgetting their password, or accidentally launching multiple sessions, and so forth.

The users depend on you to help them, so have pity on them if they are finding it hard to use their applications! In many companies, the users do not have significant computer backgrounds; most are not aware of how to run Oracle databases. Just as the patient is at the mercy of the physician, so our users are at the mercy of the Oracle DBA:

> **Don't blame the users.**

Our next case study illustrates the futility of the classic blame-the-user approach to performance tuning.

Case Study: You Have the Right to Remain Silent

While consulting for a shipping firm, I had an opportunity to do some performance analysis of the primary application. It generally performed adequately, but I noticed that occasionally there was a flurry of some (apparently) poorly designed SQL statements. At these times, many full table scans (on large tables) were performed, and some odd UNIX processes appeared to activate.

After talking to various users and designers, I finally saw what was happening. One feature of the application allowed the users to prepare a large shipment for processing. When this step was needed, the user simply selected a certain function key. Then, the program launched another program in the background. By design, the users would never see this second program; in fact, the application immediately returned control back to the user, while the other program continued to run. Of course, this design feature is not necessarily wrong in itself; it was simply part of the puzzle that needed to be unraveled.

This second program, run in the background, was the culprit. Its function was to create a Bill of Materials, so that certain products could be assembled and shipped. The program was not designed well, and what should have taken a few minutes actually consumed resources for nearly one hour.

After isolating the problem, I tried to create a solution that would be acceptable to the designers. It turned out that one of the senior designers was already aware of this problem. In fact, he had known about it for months. His solution was simple; he told the users to not perform that function so often. He was upset that the users failed to obey him. From his perspective, the users were the ones at fault!

Before we finish off this chapter, let's have a brief look at some of the other obstacles the DBA may encounter and have to overcome.

More Obstacles?

Just like Sherlock Holmes having to deal with the threats from his nemesis, Professor Moriarty, the DBA will likewise encounter various obstacles during the database treatment process. That's not to say that anyone will deliberately try to block your efforts; rather, it's just that performance tuning is not always an intuitive effort. This means that some of your brightest colleagues, without proper understanding of database fundamentals, may not be too helpful. Many well-meaning people will sometimes put forth ideas that will tend to sidetrack your work, if you are not careful.

Tired Users

One interesting obstacle sometimes occurs in shops where the DBA has overlooked ongoing performance problems. In spite of reports of performance problems, this DBA has chosen to ignore the bottleneck (or maybe he or she is simply too overworked to care).

In these cases, the users simply *tire* of complaining. Rather than informing the DBA of performance issues, they decide to live with problems rather than waste their time reporting them to someone who does nothing. In these cases, the DBA may simply remain ignorant of any new performance problems. This points out the importance of the DBA searching-out, proactively, significant performance issues. Don't wait for the users to complain!

Of course, this scenario leaves everyone in a bad state. The users continue to suffer slow performance, and the reputation of the DBA is wrecked. In Chapter 4, *Dealing with Humans*, we discuss suggestions of ways to improve the working relationship with the users. This will require that we accept the proposition that we work for the users, not the other way around. This perspective tends to change our attitude toward helping the users solve *their* problems.

Summary

In this chapter, we have examined some common errors encountered by the Oracle performance analyst. Many of these approaches appear attractive, because they promise large gain with virtually no work. These poor tactics provide the illusion of competence without having an actual sound grounding in Oracle database operation. Like a foundation built on sand, these tactics will support nothing, and usually lead to greater dissatisfaction.

We have seen that tools can never substitute for actual competence; the DBA drives the tool, not the other way around. Competent performance analysts may or may not use a tool. What is critical is the expertise of the individual, not the brand of the tool.

We also saw that many will try short-cutting the tuning process, instead of working to obtain genuine knowledge. These short cuts will eventually leave the analyst with very few options. The analyst without understanding of database fundamentals can generally only resort to tactics such as guesswork, or do whatever sounds good at that moment.

Finally, we also discussed a few other obstacles encountered by the performance specialist, including users who tire of complaining and no longer bring their concerns to the DBA. This situation implies a misunderstanding of the role of the DBA in a corporation. As we will see in Chapter 4, the DBA is employed in order to serve the users, not the other way around.

Having seen the consequences of these faulty ideas, the futility of following these well-meaning approaches should be obvious. The performance expert needs a consistent, sound approach that is not based on finding a silver bullet, or using pet ideas, tricks, or the guessing method. That is what the rest of the book is going to deliver and, in the next few chapters, we will look at what we should be doing when we are confronted by a serious performance problem. This means that it is now time to put on our first hat – the hat of the **Oracle Physician**.

- Define the Problem

    - Requirements

    - The Art of Requirements Definition

    - The Oracle Doctor's "Hippocratic Oath"

    - Not too Much Science (Yet)

- Find the Chief Complaint

    - Listen Carefully

    - Ask Questions Where Appropriate

    - See the Problem Demonstrated

    - Ask for Help if Necessary

3

The Oracle Physician

Now that we have discussed what strategies not to use when conducting performance tuning, it is time to present a tried and tested approach that really works. In this chapter, we discuss in detail step 1 in the Physician-to-Magician approach to Oracle performance tuning in detail.

We will discuss ways to get at the core of the user's difficulty; this chief complaint then becomes our problem statement. But, in order to do this, the Oracle Physician, like a true doctor, needs to listen to his patient carefully, without jumping to conclusions. These and other suggestions are discussed later in the chapter in the section entitled *The Oracle Doctor's Hippocratic Oath,* which is a list of suggested qualities that the performance tuning analyst should vow to maintain and uphold.

Other issues we will discuss in this chapter include:

❑   The difference between problems and solutions.
❑   The difficulties with vague descriptions of problems.
❑   Why it is a good idea to watch the user duplicate the problem.
❑   How to interview database users to find the real complaint.
❑   Why the DBA should not proceed until the problem can be clearly stated.

Before we dive into the Oracle Physician, let's review what the steps are in the Physician-to-Magician approach:

Physician	Detective	Pathologist	Artist	Magician
Define problem	Investigate	Isolate cause	Create solution	Implement

Let's don our physician's hat then, grab our stethoscope, and begin...

Define the Problem

This step seems very obvious, doesn't it? After all, how can we begin to solve a problem without knowing what needs to be solved? Unfortunately, this step is often skipped – leading to a great deal of wasted time, frustration, and embarrassment. Failure to define the actual difficulty is one of the biggest mistakes in performance tuning. However, by spending a little time up-front, the remainder of the process will run far more smoothly. So, we present ourselves as an Oracle Physician.

As a reminder, the Physician-to-Magician method is not a trick, but an adaptive process in which the performance analyst dons a different "hat" in each stage. In this stage, we are not trying to be analytical so much as empathetic. Above all, we want to hear what our customer is saying. A failure to define the performance problem precisely will undermine the rest of the tuning process:

> **Above all, listen to what your users are telling you.**

Requirements

For some reason, technical analysts seem to consider defining the problem as almost a waste of time, and not worthy of real analysis. In my experience, it is common for extremely intelligent software engineers to struggle with seeing the "big picture" that defines the actual problem to be solved. However, ignoring this step is a great error, and sets the process off to a shaky start.

In software development, the first phase of a project is always devoted to gathering information and defining requirements. In large government projects, for example, a Statement of Work and a System Requirements document are produced. Sometime,s a Memorandum of Understanding is developed to define how business is to be conducted between the two parties.

The field of requirements analysis is a busy one. For example:

❑ Entire books have been written on the subject of requirements analysis.

❑ Mini-courses have been conducted.

❑ Detailed US government specifications have been developed to guide the writing of requirements specifications.

❑ New computer programs have been designed to track the flow of requirements through the various phases of development.

❏ Applications based on Oracle databases have been used to track and distribute program requirements for large government projects.

The reason for all this attention should be clear; it is simply not rational to build a system with no clear idea of what it should do. As obvious as this statement seems, this axiom is often ignored. Many software engineers have worked on projects in which the direction was not clear; the requirements have simply "evolved" as programmers have sat down and started coding whatever appealed to them.

Admittedly, however, the tendency to skip the requirements phase has a certain appeal. After all, designing and coding is a lot more fun than interviewing the customer and writing a dull requirements specification. Nonetheless, experience proves that poor requirements definition often leads to wasted effort, or even "solving the wrong problem" when it comes to performance tuning.

The Art of Requirements Definition

Developing and documenting good requirements is itself something of an art. One must "stand back" and look at the big picture, without getting tangled up in all the details and proposed design.

Recall the many ill-advised approaches to performance tuning that were discussed in Chapter 2. Note that each of the poor strategies tended to skip one or more of the steps in the Physician-to-Magician process. Remember that this first phase in the performance tuning process is directed at defining the problem. We want to define the what, not the why or how. This means that we should avoid attempting to design a solution. As tempting as it is, try to resist the temptation to design a fix until you have a good problem definition:

> **Avoid jumping to solutions early in the tuning process.**

Let's have a look at a brief case study that illustrates the danger of jumping ahead:

Case Study: Putting the Cart Before the Horse

A report for a large publishing company was running badly. Each report required about 5 minutes to complete, which was unsatisfactory to the users. The users complained to the Systems Administrator, who decided to take immediate action. Eager to solve the problem, the administrator immediately added two more CPUs to the server. After all, if 4 CPUs were good, then 6 must be better!

Unfortunately, the new CPUs had only a marginal impact – the report was still too slow! A more careful analysis showed that the true cause of the slow report was not really related to processor speed. The difficulty was actually due to a missing index. Specifically, the query looked for rows based on an `Account_Id` field, which was not indexed.

In this case, simply by carefully defining then analyzing the problem, the solution was very simple. Instead, a lot of time, energy, and money were wasted for no reason.

No "Lone Rangers"

To do a good job of defining the problem, it is important to engage the customer. For one thing, what is important to the customer may not be the same as what *we* think is important. For example, the DBA might want to spend time resolving a report delay that is not really of concern to the customer. The customer might actually want the performance analyst to improve the online transaction response time. Of course, both issues would ideally be resolved, but the point is, listen to what the customer thinks is important.

This all means that it is not advisable to work in a vacuum, away from your customers. There might be a place in many corporations for the independent analyst, or "Lone Ranger"; but for the Oracle performance analyst, the Lone Ranger is not a valid alternative. Of course, there are some technical issues that can be worked on a purely technical basis (such as checking the V$Wait events), but the customer's input should never be taken for granted.

Working in a vacuum can lead to ignoring the customer. This approach will hardly lead to permanent solutions to difficult technical problems. How can the customer's problems be addressed properly if his input is ignored? Will the solution be adequate and truly get to the core of the problem? Probably not! The adequacy of the solution will correspond to how well the analyst has understood the problem in the first place. If the customer is ignored, then the solution is likely to be inadequate.

These suggestions are really no more than an admonition to remember who the customer is. Contrary to what some software engineers might think, the company does not exist to serve the database; rather the database exists to meet the needs of the corporation. This leads to our next hint:

> **The performance analyst is there to serve the users, not the other way around.**

In the next section, we suggest a code of conduct for the performance analyst, called the Hippocratic Oath. The doctor analogy seems fitting, because a good DBA is ever vigilant in taking care of his database, just as a physician takes care of people. The question to be addressed here is, "How can the Oracle performance analyst best serve the needs of the end-users?"

The Oracle Doctor's "Hippocratic Oath"

In a manner of speaking, databases do get "sick" and need help from the "DBA physician". The experienced doctor will use an efficient method to get to the issue quickly. How will he proceed?

Let's take a look at our ideal Oracle doctor. Here are some attributes that we might observe; the DBA will:

- seek to find the chief complaint.
- be a good listener.
- ask questions where appropriate.
- not blame the user.
- not try to prematurely solve the problem.
- ask the patient to demonstrate the problem.
- refer to a specialist when necessary.

All these attributes can be summed up in one idea: think of how you like to be treated, and do the same for your customers. This maxim leads to our next hint:

> **Start the task of performance tuning by treating your customers' problems seriously.**

Note also how little science is in play at this stage in the tuning process. So far, we have hardly mentioned SQL scripts, and have certainly not resorted to changing any `init.ora` parameters!

Not too Much Science (Yet)

Surprisingly, technical prowess is only a part of solving the performance problem. Of course, there are many exceptions. Sometimes the problem is extremely well defined and 100% technical in nature. For instance, a programmer may ask for assistance in performing a table join, or need advice on how to index certain tables. These issues are admittedly mostly science, and not too artistic.

Often, however, the problem will not be so clear; there may be many shades of gray involved. It may not even be known if there is a problem. Even if everyone recognizes that a problem exists, a clear problem definition is probably lacking.

To add extra confusion, personality or organization issues may be impeding progress. Certain groups or individuals may not talk to each other. In some situations, there may even be a dispute about who should try to fix the problem. Some groups may feel defensive, and resent anyone from the outside even looking at the problem.

All these complications suggest that human interaction can be very messy and unpredictable. Of course, this makes the entire tuning process much more interesting and colorful – but not really science. In the real world, problems are simply not handed to us like homework problems from a textbook.

Let's turn, then, to what the good "DBA-Doctor" should be doing.

Find the Chief Complaint

The overall goal of the Oracle Doctor is to find out what is wrong. By asking what the problem is, we are really trying to formulate a clear problem definition, just like a doctor asking their patient for a description of their ailments.

The Oracle doctor should strive to be as precise as possible; vagueness here will only impede later steps in the process. To prepare a good problem statement, interview the users. Ask them, "What seems to be the problem?"

Most users, delighted to find someone who cares, will be happy to spill the beans at this time. Many will be astonished that you are actually taking the time to help solve their problems.

Besides the simple question of "What seems to be the problem?" it is also important to follow up with more detailed questions, such as:

❑ Has this feature always run badly, or did it just start?

❑ When did you first notice the problem?

❑ What server or database are you connecting to?

❑ What username do you use?

❑ Does the function return the desired result, or does it abort?

❑ Have there been any changes to the program?

Of course, the users may not really know exactly what is wrong; in some cases, they may only be able to say, "Things seem sluggish. Please speed up the database". In cases like these, it is helpful to ask for examples of queries or reports that run poorly, and try to get as much detail as possible.

Here are some examples of good problem definitions:

Problem: The Accounting Quarterly Profit Report takes 5 hours to complete.

Details after User Interview:

❑ The report that is run is called QPR-001.

❑ Report was changed 3 weeks ago to add more detail.

❑ Database name: act1

❑ Server: fin01

❑ The report is run at midnight, and finishes at 5 a.m.

❑ There are no errors in the report; it just takes too long.

❑ The username is Bill Jones.

❑ The last quarter, it only took 2 hours to finish.

Note the very useful information about some changes that were recently made to this report. These details will be of great value in the next stage of the tuning process. Let's look at another example:

Problem: Typical user login takes one minute.

Details after User Interview:

❑ Tested with users: Bob Smith, Bill Jones, and Herman Johnson.

❑ Database name: qa_1

❑ Server: qa01

❑ This is the first time that this server and database have been used.

❑ Once users connect, everything is OK.

In the above example, the listed information is once again very helpful, even though the nature of the problem is completely different. Notice the very pertinent note that *this is the first time that this server and database have been used*. In other words, database connections have never worked properly. Let's look at one more slightly different example:

Problem: Program Customer Care has some slow running functions.

Details after User Interview:

❑ In particular, when searching for customer by phone number, the response time is about 1 minute.

❑ For example, search for the customer having a phone number of 909-101-5563.

❑ This feature has always performed badly, but it seems to be getting worse.

❑ Database: ccare01

❑ Server: cc_prod

Notice how helpful it is to know if the run-time has changed. If a certain report now takes three times as long as previously, that will probably be a valuable clue later on. For instance, that might suggest that the database size has drastically increased, and the application is not scaling well.

In our third example, it is relevant to know that the search by phone number has *never* worked well. Given this initial problem, it is not surprising that the performance would slowly get even worse (as would be the case if there were no index on the phone number).

"Your Database is Bad"

Frequently, the users will tell us a solution, or make a request, rather than provide a problem statement. (Sometimes even management will provide us with a solution.) As we saw in the last chapter, these well-meaning individuals may think they know what the solution is, but these statements should typically be put aside, until a more precise problem definition is formulated.

For example, the following problem definitions are either too vague, or presuppose a solution. They are all lacking pertinent details, such as server and database, username, and detailed timing information:

- ❑ **Problem:** The network is slow, causing my queries to take too long.
- ❑ **Problem:** Your database is slow; build another index.
- ❑ **Problem:** The database needs more memory because the application is failing.
- ❑ **Problem:** I need Parallel Query option to make my queries faster.
- ❑ **Problem:** I need version 8.1.6 because it is faster.
- ❑ **Problem:** I need raw devices. That will make the program run much faster because of fewer disk reads.

Note that many of these problems are in fact solutions. Once again, we see the tendency to jump ahead to devise a solution, even before we really understand the problem.

An example of what happens without a clear problem definition is illustrated in our next case study. This real-life example is like a chapter right out of a Kafka novel. All the players wander around aimlessly; no one knows what is going on (and we never did find out):

Case Study: Problem? What Problem?

I was asked to assist a designer who was troubleshooting a performance problem with a web-based application. The customer had apparently complained that certain features were running very slowly. Our task was to solve the problem.

Unfortunately, when we tried to get more detailed information about the problem, no one seemed to know anything. In fact, it wasn't clear exactly who had lodged the complaint, or which function was not working well. We just knew that this was "a very important customer!"

The problem definition could have read:

Problem: Production application runs poorly for company "A-one Devices.

Details:

- ❑ Server: `prod1`
- ❑ Not known how long this has been happening.
- ❑ Not known what function is involved.
- ❑ Username: unknown.
- ❑ Actual run-time: unknown.

Nevertheless, we were obliged to do *something* for this important customer. We spent nearly a week trying to solve this problem that had no definition. We ran various trials on our application, trying to pinpoint any performance bottlenecks, but could find nothing conclusive.

We never did find out what the problem was (or even if there ever *was* a problem). This entire episode occurred because there was no problem definition.

This last case study was one of the more bizarre performance tuning experiences, and provides a good illustration of how much time can be wasted when the requirements are not clearly defined.

Listen Carefully

The Oracle Doctor who is trying to resolve performance problems must start as an excellent listener. The analyst should put himself in the shoes of the database user, and try to see things their way. This is the best possible way to get started on a performance problem:

> **Simply listening to the user is a great way to begin performance analysis.**

As simple as it sounds, this step is incredibly challenging – probably much more difficult than solving most technical issues. Very few individuals have really mastered the art of good listening. As in other occupations, listening is a key step:

Case Study: "Who are You Again?"

While working as a DBA for a cellular phone company years ago, I was assigned to be the performance DBA. I wasn't exactly sure what this involved, but I suspected it had something to do with responding to the dozens of phone calls that were made to the primary DBA every day. (I sat across from the main production DBA, and the nature of the calls soon became obvious.) These calls were from irate users, complaining about slow performance.

The application was a customer care program, which allowed the company to keep track of all the customers. Each customer's name, address, phone number, and so on, were kept in a fairly large Oracle 7.3 database. Of course, the database was critical to the efforts of hundreds of customer service agents. These agents responded to phone calls from users, who had a multitude of questions and problems.

After watching the database for some time, I began discovering certain SQL queries that had some problems. These queries appeared to generate tens of thousands of disk reads per execution. To make matters worse, these queries were run very frequently. At any one time, there might be five of these queries running simultaneously.

I had detected these queries with this very simple SQL script:

```
SELECT Executions, Disk_Reads, Buffer_Gets, Sql_Text
FROM V$SQL
WHERE Disk_Reads/Executions > 1000;
```

I have found the above script to be probably the most valuable script to have; I have run it literally many hundreds of times. Its function is very simple: it returns the queries that have a very large disk reads-to-executions ratio. In other words, it identifies what I call the "heavy hitters," or SQL statements that consume resources beyond some reasonable threshold. In the script above, I am simply looking for SQL queries that consume more than 1000 disk reads each execution.

After running the above heavy hitters query many times on the phone company database, I began to see a pattern. The few queries that ran poorly appeared to be responsible for the majority of disk reads on the entire system!

The problem was not solved yet. At this point, I had successfully isolated the offending SQL statements, but I still didn't know what had caused the application to generate this poor SQL. Obviously, I needed to find out why the application was running these "funny" SQL statements. This would require some special investigation; there was no easy way to determine what the application was doing just by looking at the database server.

I decided to contact the customer service agents directly to try to glean whatever extra information I could. So, whenever I saw the bad SQL being run, I would track down the username, lookup the person's name in a cross-reference sheet, then call and interview the customer service agent. Once I introduced myself, I would simply ask them what steps they had performed just prior to the problem.

I was astonished to discover that few DBAs had ever talked to the end users. When I called, many of the users at first thought they had done something wrong, and that they were in trouble. Often, they became defensive, or invented remarkable stories about strange things the application was doing. Eventually, however, they came to understand that I was trying to help them, and were very helpful and cooperative. I would leave my phone number, and ask them to call me if they had any other problems. Many of the agents or their supervisors called me several times.

These phone calls opened up a channel between the end users and the DBA group. This new path of communication allowed us to identify certain critical problems in the application. Without directly communicating with the users, it would have been nearly impossible to discover what was really happening.

It turned out that the application had a poorly designed user interface. It was so unforgiving, that it led to many accidental mistakes by many service agents. The bad SQL statements would be executed whenever the user made a simple mistake, such as selecting the *Execute* function key, instead of the *Enter Customer Name* key. These mistakes were especially frequent because the two function keys were adjacent to one another.

This case illustrates the importance of actually listening to the user. The users were so surprised to have the DBA call them that they knew there must be trouble. Instead of being in trouble, however, they helped in correcting a huge flaw in the application. The correction saved many hours apiece for hundreds of customer service agents. The savings over some months amounted to hundreds of thousands of dollars in increased productivity.

This next case study, in a change of pace, illustrates the frustration that occurs when the courtesy of listening is absent:

Case Study: "Shut-up Already. I Know What You Want!"

On my very first consulting assignment, I worked for one of the world's largest corporations. There were many hundreds of people involved in IT, with hundreds of servers and PCs. The DBA team consisted of about eight DBAs – some were senior, but most were just starting DBA work.

The corporation had decided to use only one type of server. All these servers were maintained by a very capable outside service provider. The Systems Administrators in the outside firm were very competent, and especially cooperative. All of this contributed toward making my job much easier.

The only hitch in the whole system was that we weren't supposed to contact a Systems Administrator directly. Each DBA was required to call in a trouble ticket whenever he needed some help. The caller would be given a ticket by a help desk, and the Systems Administrator would call us back – usually very quickly. Although the ticket system was a little cumbersome, I understood the need to track problem reports, and so we gradually adjusted to this process. In fact, most calls to get a ticket went very smoothly, and without incident.

One day I needed a new directory to store some Oracle .dbf files. This oradata directory was to be placed under a certain file system. The permissions on the file system did not allow me to do this, so I had to call in a ticket.

I mentioned to the service representative who took the call that I wanted a subdirectory created in the file system /u01/usr. The person at the other end immediately responded, "OK, file system user". I corrected his misstatement and repeated my request – this time listing the exact letters. Once again, he replied, "OK, file system user".

Incredibly, we went through this same charade several more times. As my patience faded, I began to imagine various backdoor methods I could use to avoid dealing with this guy. Was there a way I could somehow "sneak-in" as root? Nevertheless, like a good DBA, I didn't succumb to the backdoor approach, although I was rapidly reaching the end of my tether.

Eventually, once the ticket-taker finally listened, I was able to communicate the very few words that defined where I needed the subdirectory created.

The encounter in the above case study lasted much longer than it should have. It required me to endure several minutes of frustration while the service person refused to listen. When he finally listened, he was able to see exactly what I needed; he accomplished the task in about 10 seconds.

The problem was due to one simple fact: the help-desk analyst simply didn't listen. He was so positive that he knew what I wanted, he actually could not hear what I was saying. In other words, he kept trying to skip the step of defining the problem.

Analytical Listening

Les Donaldson, in his best-selling book, *Conversational Magic* (Prentice Hall, ISBN: 0131721550), notes this common tendency simply not to listen to what others have to say. This often causes people to jump an erroneous conclusion:

> *"A basic problem with people who don't listen analytically is that they jump to conclusions. They hear only a phrase or sentence out of context, and jump to a conclusion. This often results in an argument which leaves a poor impression".*

Donaldson explains what he means by "analytical listening". This is the process of really trying to understand the other person's point of view. This also means avoiding the tendency to become "mentally argumentative" as the other person is speaking.

Let's consider another case, which more positively illustrates the listening principle. In this case study, the DBA actually listens to the user's problem:

Case Study: The Slow Medical Report

A Software QA engineer in a large medical group called the DBA one morning with a frantic request: "There is something wrong with your database. The screen takes over a minute to display. When can you have it fixed?"

This user was clearly very anxious to get the problem resolved. The DBA asked the user to explain exactly what application was being used, exactly what function was being performed, what parameters were set, and how long the process was taking.

The user immediately provided this information:

Application: Clinical Record System, Release 1.0
User: Ivan Z.
Database: QE1
Function: Display Patient Chart
Run-time: Between 1-2 minutes
Date range: Last 6 months
Patient: John Smith
Medical Record: 123456

Note that with this information in hand, the DBA had successfully completed the first phase of the Physician-to-Magician process. That is, the problem had been clearly defined. Note the specificity in the problem definition. The exact application name and function are provided, as well as the parameters used when calling this particular function. With this information well documented, any other DBA could easily duplicate the problem.

So far, only a small amount of time and effort had been required to produce this succinct problem definition. Thus far, the total elapsed time spent investigating was only about 20 minutes.

Note one interesting piece of information provided by the user: the date range was *6 months*. Without a careful discussion with the user, this critical piece of information would have been overlooked. The simple act of listening had gleaned the key to the entire puzzle. Let's see what happened next.

As part of the fact-gathering process, the DBA asked the user to run the exact function again. This time, however, the DBA monitored the session with the OEM (Oracle Enterprise Manager) Top Sessions utility. This tool has the capability to show the exact SQL that any user is running, as well as the execution plan (discussed in detail in Chapter 8) for that SQL.

When the DBA indicated he was ready to proceed, the user re-ran the problem area. Surprisingly, the OEM tool indicated that the SQL that was being run was really very trivial; the database activity was actually completed in just a few seconds.

Of course, this discovery eliminated any notion that the database itself was at fault. Nevertheless, the user who had just run the application emphatically claimed that there *was* a large delay – certainly far longer than just a few seconds. Well, he listened, and continued to search for the problem.

After extracting the SQL in question, the query was re-run in a SQL*Plus session, entirely separate from the application. (By running the query outside the application, attention could be focused entirely on the SQL of interest.) This test revealed the root cause of the problem: the query was extracting several megabytes of data. After retrieval from Oracle, the data then needed to be transferred over a medium-speed network to the client. Estimates showed that the elapsed time to accomplish this transfer would be about a minute. The time taken to extract the data from Oracle originally was irrelevant.

Note that other methods, besides running the query in SQL*Plus, could have also unearthed the large dataset issue. That is, this wasn't the only way to discover that piece of information. For instance, the Wait Facility would have shown that the Oracle was waiting for transfer of data over SQL*Net. In this example, however, the very simple act of trying the query in SQL*Plus was adequate to uncover the problem.

The DBA discussed these findings with the QA analyst, who confirmed that a very large set of data (six months of medical records) was being retrieved by the application for each patient. The analyst agreed that this seemed unnecessary; he volunteered to investigate why the program needed to retrieve such a large amount of information. (Later, the developers agreed to make a program modification to avoid the large dataset retrieval.)

This case shows that a DBA or other analyst who simply listens to a user's performance problem will create a very favorable impression. This is an important step to follow even if the evidence appears not to suggest anything wrong in the database. It is no secret that the database will not be at fault in many cases; for instance, the design of the application will be identified as the cause of many performance problems. Nonetheless, we owe the user the courtesy of listening even if we think he or she is wrong!

Ask Questions Where Appropriate

Since the objective of the Oracle Physician is to define the problem concisely and accurately, the DBA must do more than listen. He must also ask relevant questions that help put a good boundary around the problem, and better describe exactly the scenario in which the problem occurs. So, after the Oracle Physician has uncovered the chief complaint, he must follow up to get the details.

The questions should be aimed at further refining the problem that has been established. For instance, when a user reports that an application seems to be running too slowly, the tuning expert could ask the questions, "How long is the query delay?" and "When does the problem occur?"

Other pertinent questions to ask include:

❏ Did the program *ever* work right?

❏ Which users are complaining?

❏ What user login is being used?

❏ What is the application trying to do during the delay?

❏ What database version is being used?

❏ Is the connection remote or local?

❏ Is there more than one database involved?

❏ Is only one group of users experiencing the problem?

Often, the DBA will need to return later with more questions, following a preliminary investigation. For instance, if the DBA determines that the application is transferring large amounts of data over the network, an obvious follow-up question would be "Why is the application transferring all this data?"

Our next case study illustrates the importance of focused questioning to get to the heart of a performance problem:

Case Study: "Yes it's Slow, but that's Normal"

I was investigating a performance problem on an over-the-web training system that supported many thousands of users. In particular, I was trying to isolate which part of the program was responsible for a massive amount of disk reads that had been detected. This application was the core program for the firm. The entire existence of the firm depended on this application working perfectly.

Since I wasn't familiar with the particulars of the application, I asked one of the application administrators to demonstrate the use of the application. Specifically, I wanted to see how new users were added.

We sat down and accessed a web page that was the starting point for the program. We invented a new user name, and provided details such, as address, e-mail address, phone number, and so on. After providing this information, the administrator hit Enter, and we waited. She explained that there would be a short delay while the program processed the new user.

I confirmed that there was indeed a delay, and I immediately became suspicious. I knew that the program did not communicate at this point with any other systems. Thus, a delay of 30 seconds seemed completely unjustified. It seemed to me that adding a user should be a trivial event; perhaps a few index lookups, and a few table inserts. Why should there be a 30-second delay at this point?

I asked the administrator if she knew what the program was doing at this point. She did not know, but explained that this was the normal way the program worked. Aha!

No one had investigated because this long delay was *normal*. No one considered this anything to worry about.

A delay of only 30 seconds might seem minor, but in this very large system, literally *thousands* of new users could be added in a typical day. Apart from the inconvenience to each one of these new customers, there would be substantial resource usage that would degrade performance for all the other users.

Now that a problem had been clearly defined, it was easy to list the exact stored procedure that was responsible for the new user function. The procedure called only one major routine; this routine determined if any other existing users already had the same email address. In other words, the e-mail address was being used as a unique identifier for each user. Behind the scenes, the user's e-mail address, not his login id, was the way the application tracked each user.

Using the e-mail address was a perfectly fine design, since email addresses really are unique; the problem, rather, was the database check for a duplicate email address. I discovered that the e-mail address field was not indexed! So each time a new user was added, a full table scan of the large Users table had to be performed.

The new index was quickly added, and the production DBA noticed an immediate and large reduction in average resource consumption. Now, whenever a new user was added, there was no noticeable delay whatsoever. The system was truly working normally.

In the case study above, a simple question made it clear that there was a major performance difficulty in the application. Once the right question was asked, further analysis led to a simple technical solution. Note that the root cause, simply missing a one-column index, is a very common correction. The difficulty had nothing to do with technical sophistry, but simply *knowing what question to ask*:

> **Never accept slow response as "normal".**

See the Problem Demonstrated

This maxim is much easier to follow than the previous recommendation. Seeing the problem demonstrated firsthand is always a good idea. If the problem is not clear, it is very helpful to see the user run the program so that you can see exactly what is happening:

Whenever possible, get a first-hand look at the actual problem.

In some cases, you will quickly find that the real problem is non-existent. Being human, all of us are simply mistaken at one time or another. An independent observer ("another eye") looking at a supposed problem will often see something that immediately resolves the issue.

Ask for Help if Necessary

Just like the doctor, the tuning specialist should not hesitate to refer the user to another professional when appropriate. This decision should not be considered an admission of weakness, or a hint of incompetence. Instead, asking for help is often the wisest course of action; it is an excellent indication of a true professional. Referral is actually the professionally correct option in many cases.

Turning back to our medical analog, General Practice MDs do not try to treat skin cancer or heart disease. Similarly, an emergency room physician immediately calls for a psychiatric referral if a patient is having severe emotional problems. Clearly, no competent physician would attempt to resolve serious problems that are outside their own area of competency. In fact, they would probably be disciplined if they attempted to do so. In other words, we should call for help rather than drown in problems.

In the database world, the principle is similar; there is no reason to pretend to be competent in all areas. For instance, if it becomes clear that the problem is related to a network outage, don't waste their time or your own time pretending to be an expert on networks. If there is a certain problem related to the Unix kernel, ask the Systems Administrator for assistance:

Recognize when a problem is outside your area of competency. Don't pretend to be an expert in everything.

Remember the "Mad Guesser" from the Chapter 2 case study? (He was the DBA who wildly guessed at fixes to a serious performance problem.) His position at the firm could have been salvaged if he had simply asked for help. Unfortunately, he was not willing to take that step:

Case Study: Ask the Disk Doctor!

At a small dot-com firm in San Francisco, one of the Systems Administrators asked for advice on **stripe size** for the disks. (This term refers to the size of data that should be used when distributing data across a set of disks. Choosing this value is almost an art in itself.) The Systems Administrator was setting up a new server, and he wanted to take advantage of the information previously learned, so that the transfer of data to and from the disks would be as fast as possible.

One of the other DBAs, Igor, had spent an enormous time analyzing this very subject. He had been part of a team analyzing how to setup EMC disk systems for best performance. Clearly, Igor was *far* more qualified than I was to answer questions on disk striping. Therefore, I suggested that Igor was far more qualified on this subject than I was.

The Administrator consulted with my colleague, who was easily able to offer some valuable advice – probably far more accurate than I could have done.

This case simply illustrates the wisdom of not pretending to be an expert at everything. There's no shame in admitting that someone else is more qualified to address a certain problem. Your end customers will also appreciate your honesty in not exaggerating your own qualifications and of course, at the end of the day, the higher quality of the advice.

Summary

In this first step of the Physician-to-Magician process, we have explored the idea of how an effective performance analyst can imitate a caring doctor, serving his or her "patients". Just like a medical doctor, the tuning doctor needs to find out exactly what the main problem is. In medical terminology, this is called the patient's chief complaint.

This phase is critical to a good resolution of the client's performance bottleneck. Without a clear problem definition, the analyst will not know *which* problem to solve, and the odds of success will be greatly reduced. A clear problem statement lays a crucial foundation, upon which the later stages will be built. This method rejects all the guesswork, jumping to conclusions, and associated embarrassing results that arise from not following a sound process. Note also that the DBA can sometimes spot a subtle performance difficulty – even when the customer is not aware of the problem!

The performance specialist must be focused on solving the problem of the customers. This means that he cannot play the role of the Lone Ranger who works alone, and talks to the users only when absolutely necessary. Instead, the Oracle doctor, just like a medical doctor, should establish a good working relationship focused on resolving the user's performance problems.

The cases presented in this chapter give support to the proposition that performance tuning is rarely 100% science. A great many performance problems will not only test the technical competence of the analyst, but his people skills as well.

In many of the case studies we have examined, the tuning process seems to be closer to 100% *art*. This is typical of the tuning specialist's job. Real life is filled with misinformation as well as helpful characters who mean well, but may actually impede the performance analyst.

Step 1 of the Physician-to-Magician process has laid a good foundation for the Oracle performance expert. With a solid problem definition in hand, we are almost ready to switch hats, and transform ourselves into the Oracle Detective. First, however, we must examine a little more closely the perplexing issue of **how to deal with humans**. This is the subject of our next chapter.

- The People Factor in the Tuning Equation
- The Role of the DBA
    - Focus on Solving the Customer's Problem
    - Have a Positive Approach
    - Build a Trusting Relationship
    - Report Problems Accurately
    - Accept Responsibility
    - Avoid Accusations
    - Ask Questions
    - Accept Criticism

4

Dealing with Humans

In the previous chapter, we introduced the first stage of the Physician-to-Magician process, in which we suggested that the performance specialist actually begin the tuning process as the Oracle Doctor. We explained that in stage one, the DBA listens carefully to the user to define the trouble precisely.

After reading the various case studies, it should be clear by now why performance tuning is not really 100% science. The performance expert does not have the luxury of addressing only the technical side of the issue; he must also cope with people-problems.

In this chapter, we concentrate entirely on the soft skill of dealing with people. Of course, hundreds, if not thousands, of books have been written on the subject of human behavior and interpersonal relationships. Clearly, this book cannot be a definitive guide on all aspects of interpersonal behavior. Nonetheless, we can discuss those issues that the Oracle performance specialist is likely to encounter.

The theme of this chapter, and the key to achieving happy database customers, is that the performance specialist must focus his efforts on solving the customer's problem. Of course, this is not a novel idea – just one that needs a bit of emphasis.

The topics discussed in this chapter include:

❑ The "people factor" in the tuning equation.
❑ The role of the DBA.
❑ The importance of a positive approach.
❑ Building a trusting relationship.
❑ Accepting responsibility.
❑ Avoiding accusations.
❑ Admitting you could be wrong.

As always, we present several fun stories of true cases involving Oracle tuning problems. Many of these examples illustrate how Oracle analysts solved technical issues while facing some tough interpersonal battles. Some of the examples in this chapter illustrate what happens when the customer is given priority as the center of the tuning effort. In contrast, we will also look at a few counter examples.

The People Factor in the Tuning Equation

Rarely are Oracle performance issues nice, clean problems that are handed to you as a well-bounded technical equation to solve. On the contrary, problems occur in a messy environment with lots of vague or unclear facts. Sometimes, the analyst may be given misleading or even false information. At other times, he is pressured to emphasize certain areas, or even told to ignore some subsystems.

There are, typically, many people involved in a performance problem – designers, programmers, project managers and, of course, DBAs. Many of these people will not be pleased when you pin the bottleneck on their code or their design.

Some of these coworkers may be difficult personalities to contend with. Some people are arrogant and are simply not willing to cooperate. Others will seem cooperative – until your back is turned. Of course, some are a delight to work with, regardless of the situation.

These points simply reflect the reality that the *people factor* is a major consideration in Oracle performance tuning. Some of the most difficult issues for the performance specialist will not even involve technology; they will involve people. This means that one of the most important skills is *people management*.

Roadblocks

The DBA may encounter roadblocks constructed by individuals in the business. A **roadblock** is something that impedes progress, just like a barrier on the highway. Along the performance tuning highway, there are bound to be occasional obstructions. Some roadblocks are unintentional; others more deliberate. Usually meaning well, people will suggest ideas that they honestly think you should follow.

Here are some typical suggestions:

- ❏ "Our consultant, Bob, has already looked into that, so don't worry about that program."
- ❏ "We know the network is very fast, so disregard any network problems."
- ❏ "The tool we bought disagrees with your idea."
- ❏ "It wasn't my idea to bring you in here."
- ❏ "We want you to upgrade the database."
- ❏ "We don't use bind variables here."

The tuning specialist must deal with all of these comments – plus many other not-so-helpful suggestions.

If the performance tuning analyst tries to avoid these messy complications by secluding himself, and working like a hermit, he is misunderstanding the role of the DBA. The purpose of the DBA is to serve the users. Like the Oracle Doctor, this means helping our patients.

No matter how competent the DBA, a failure to work well with people can undermine the entire tuning effort. This is the subject of our next hint:

> **Failure to address the human side of performance tuning may doom your efforts.**

Thus, it is not good enough simply to be a technical wizard. A truly great performance-tuning expert must be able to cope with the human side as well.

The Role of the DBA

Some DBAs think that the company exists to nourish Oracle databases, and that the users are an unfortunate inconvenience. Of course, this is all wrong. DBAs and databases exist to serve the company, not the other way around. We may take pride in the fact that our databases are running very smoothly, with superb performance, but if the company doesn't make a profit, it doesn't matter.

Performance tuning assists our customers in reaching their goals. This means that performance tuning is not an end in itself. No one cares about the cache hit ratio if the database is not helping the corporation achieve its goals. Likewise, impressive architecture or some fancy database features are only meaningful if they advance the cause of our clients:

> **The purpose of performance tuning is to help our customers meet their goals.**

Focus on Solving the Customer's Problem

In order to maximize value for our employers, we must strive to fix their problems. This directed focus is important whether we are analyzing a tough performance problem, or simply setting up backups. The entire process must have, as its end goal, service to the customer.

The Physician-to-Magician approach recognizes this focus on meeting the needs of the customer. For instance, in Stage 1, the Oracle Physician builds up a definition of the problem based on how the customer sees it. Thus, the problem statement is always from the perspective of the customer, not the DBA. That is why we put such a great emphasis on listening in Stage 1.

Without patient listening, the performance analyst may not solve what is truly important to the customer. That would mean falling once more into the old trap of solving the wrong problem.

Of course, the customer may be completely in error in suggesting that the database is at fault. The user may simply be mistaken. That is why the next stage of the Physician-to-Magician process is dedicated to gathering facts to confirm and quantify the problem. These additional facts will help the tuning specialist see how the customer's perspective relates to what is happening in the database. What the customer sees on the "outside" is often surprisingly different from what the DBA sees on the "inside".

This customer focus continues throughout the tuning process. For instance, the Oracle Artist must fashion a solution that is acceptable to the designers and others in the firm. Some problems may have many solutions – but not all will be acceptable or appropriate. Even in the final stage, where the Oracle Magician is the main player, the DBA *closes the loop* by documenting how his solution solves the client's original problem. This confirms that the implemented solution has actually met the needs of the customer.

Have a Positive Approach

Put yourself at the desk of a mythical client. Now imagine that you have a really tough problem related to a database application. You have been worrying about this problem for days. Your boss calls you first thing every morning to demand a status report. Customers call your home at night. Your job might even be in jeopardy. Things are not looking good.

Is this an exaggeration? Not at all. The scenario above is played out every day at companies that rely on Oracle database applications to serve their customers. More and more, databases are expected to operate continuously around the clock, with no performance degradation. Senior managers in the firm do not really care what "excuses" you have for poor performance. Customers do not care why the application was down. They just want results.

Now, imagine how happy you would be, in this situation, if a database expert arrived. This expert clearly has a can-do attitude, with great confidence that he can speedily solve your problem. Naturally, you would greet this new arrival loudly and enthusiastically. At last! Someone who can help!

Of course, your customers demand competence as well; but the ideal approach is a mixture of both. This blend of technical know-how, mixed with a positive approach, illustrates the basic thrust of the Physician-to-Magician approach – a balanced mixture of art and science. The performance tuner will be less effective for ignoring one or the other.

The example of the busy manager just mentioned reminds us of exactly what performance specialists should do – willingly relieve the customer of a great burden. Let the worrying manager go back to his business, and forget about the database problem. Let the expert worry about the database problem. In other words, the performance expert takes the burden from the client.

Of course, this sharing of the burden and competent problem solving cannot possibly happen unless the Oracle performance specialist has an excellent grounding in the fundamentals of database operation. A novice who has exaggerated his skills should be quite nervous about taking on critical performance challenges for which he or she is unqualified. That's the time to ask for help.

Challenging, not Scary

A perplexing tuning scenario might sound scary for the Oracle tuning expert. However, many tuning experts look forward to taking on problems that appear to be far more difficult than your run-of-the-mill performance problems.

The reason that performance experts are not afraid of tough problems is very simple. To understand this, recall one of our very first hints: *many performance bottlenecks are actually very simple to correct.* Using the same logic, we find that this same point applies to production problems:

> **Performance problems on critical production systems are often not technically challenging.**

At first, this hint sounds crazy! How could a production problem be trivial? If it were simple to fix, wouldn't it have been solved a long time ago?

These are all reasonable objections that at first sound plausible. After all, most companies have bright analysts. Surely these bright engineers would have taken care of these trivial problems by now!

The key to understanding this apparent paradox is the observation that critical performance problems often exist due to non-technical reasons:

> **Performance problems on production systems often exist because of process problems, not technology.**

Consider, for instance, the logistics of changing code on a production system; this is usually not at all trivial. There will probably be several stages of testing and change approval cycles, in addition to the steps to make the change actually go live.

Of course, this does not mean that Oracle technology is not involved. The tuning process will certainly require technical analysis and troubleshooting, and the solution will probably require some technical modification. Nevertheless, the reason the problem exists in the first place is often due to a poor process, not due to the great complexity of the performance problem. For instance, perhaps the load testing was done at a feverish pace at the last minute. Maybe the designer forgot to tell the DBA about a last-minute alteration. Heaven forbid, maybe the DBA forgot to tell the designer about some eleventh hour switch.

Performance problems on production systems are often equally simple to resolve as problems on development systems. The main difference is that management is quite a bit more excited and motivated to do something about it in this case. Also, there is greater complexity in testing the solution, since significant changes cannot just be thrown into an important production database.

When a Positive Approach is Lacking

Our next case study illustrates how one person's attitude can be contagious – their positive (or negative) outlook can spread to others, and either buoy-up, or poison the atmosphere in a company:

Case Study: "Work Here; Never!"

It was my first day on the job as a consultant to a large medical company. I was told to talk to George, who would brief me on my duties, and tell me about the group to which I was assigned. George was one of the staff DBAs who had worked for the firm for about a year. He seemed to be competent, and supported several development databases.

George was an extremely bright individual; he graduated from a highly regarded university, and his intelligence was obvious to all. Unfortunately, his sour attitude more than compensated for any skills he brought to the job. In George's view, there was nothing right with the firm. He believed that no one was competent – basically, he thought all the managers and most of the technical staff were inept.

After several minutes of talking with George, I was ready to leave the company. His negative attitude was so depressing that I couldn't believe that anyone would want to work there! Unfortunately for me, my first day on the job was wrecked.

Of course, I found out later that George's view of the firm was very much mistaken. There were in fact numerous hard-working, very capable individuals in both management and the IT department. Over the course of several weeks, I met many competent analysts and managers who seemed to enjoy their work, and put in many hours.

Years later, I still stay in touch with friends I made at that company. In spite of a rough first day on the job, I stayed at the company for many months. Looking back, I see that the problem was not so much the company, as it was George's sour attitude.

In this case study, the real problem had little to do with the firm in question. The larger problem was really the lowered morale inflicted by the whims of just one individual. Not surprisingly, his sour attitude became well known throughout the company, and other analysts simply avoided him. (Perhaps that's what he intended in the first place.)

A DBA, designer, or programmer with a sour attitude has absolutely no hope of advancing in their career. Let's take a look at the flip side of the coin.

Build a Trusting Relationship

A positive attitude goes hand-in-hand with a trusting relationship. A performance analyst who has successfully established a position of trust will go very far. He or she won't have to look for clients – they will seek the DBA out.

One TV commercial shown recently asked, "Wouldn't it be great if you could trust your broker?" Well, this is the same sort of question that IT managers ask: "Wouldn't it be great if we could trust our DBA?"

The reality is, that there are not too many Oracle performance analysts who have earned the trust of their clients. Some Oracle analysts are technically savvy, but alienate their co-workers with their abrasive personalities. Others are very nice, but are not really technically competent. Either state leaves the client in an unsatisfactory position. That is why the Oracle analyst who can combine both traits, the art and the science, has a huge career advantage.

"Your Problem is Important to Me"

A genuine act of listening gives the customer the tacit message, "I think your problem is important". On the other hand, the database analyst who fails to seriously listen to his clients also gives them a message, "Your problems are not very important to me". Naturally, we want to send the former message to our customers.

For those interested in advancing their career, these are very relevant observations, with huge implications. In the medical world, the doctor who truly sympathizes with the problems of his patients will have a booming practice. Similarly, the performance expert who is competent as well as empathetic will have many firms vying for his or her skills.

Our next case study illustrates how valuable a trusting relationship can be. It's a simple lesson with a meaningful conclusion:

Case Study: "Have you checked with Hector?"

For the past ten years, McDonnell Douglas Corporation in Long Beach, California, has been designing and building the C-17 aircraft for the U.S. military. As might be expected, the size of this government project is massive, and the IT department employs hundreds of people.

During the late 1990s, the central DBA staff amounted to eight DBAs – a mix of both junior and senior staff. These DBAs supported nearly a hundred Oracle databases. In fact, at one point, one server alone was running 19 databases. This led one of the DBAs to post the sign: "Now serving: 56 databases." It seemed like the number on the chart had to be updated daily.

Clearly, with such a large number of databases, it was important to keep in touch with Oracle Corporation, in regard to new patches, important bulletins, and so on. To assist the team of DBAs, Oracle provided a full-time field-support consultant called Hector.

Hector was soon recognized as not only technically competent, but a person whom you could really trust to give you the "straight scoop", regardless of whether it led directly to more business for Oracle Corporation or not. It wasn't long before both DBAs and developers came to rely on Hector's counsel. If he didn't know the answer, he would try to find someone who did. Simply put, you could trust him to give you a straight answer. There was no conflict of interest. He just wanted to give the best advice possible. Of course, his work ethic obviously helped his employer as well.

Over the course of many months Hector's attitude of service and trustworthiness became well known. During those months whenever a major issue was discussed it was very common to hear someone say "Yes but have you checked with Hector?"

This case study leads us on to our next hint:

> **Giving your customers top priority should be considered comparable in importance to technical competence.**

Our next, and perhaps more important, case study is a good example of what can happen when an entire team is able to work together in an atmosphere of trust and respect. The team in this case study rapidly developed a prototype data warehouse in just a few months. Considering the track record of data warehouse projects, this effort was all the more astonishing. How was it done? Let's take a look, and see how they avoided the **death march**, or doomed project:

Case Study: We avoided the Death March!

One of the most pleasant and satisfying consulting engagements I have experienced was for a firm developing a new data warehouse application. The client needed to have information from a variety of different data sources merged into one Oracle 8i database. Some of the data would come from Sybase; other information would be transferred over database links from other Oracle instances.

The project team was fairly small; beginning with fewer than ten people, including just a few designers, a few administrators (system and database), quality assurance engineers, GUI interface experts, and a few managers to keep us on track. An outside consultant was used part-time for the overall data warehouse design. Most of the team members had never worked together before, and only the main architect had extensive experience of data warehouse design.

As the project began, a particular chemistry began to develop in the team that allowed the group to make far greater progress than I initially thought possible. For instance, the designers seemed to enjoy choosing seemingly impossible deadlines for themselves to meet. I kept quiet, believing that the deadlines were not realistic. Nevertheless, they kept on meeting these deadlines and, at the time, it wasn't clear exactly how they were achieving this.

Looking back on the project months later, I now realize what happened. Each person on the team simply began to trust and rely upon the others. Thus, the designers trusted the DBA to advise them on performance, and the DBA trusted the designers to prepare a sound design that would scale.

In addition, there were absolutely no turf wars. In other words, each person simply acknowledged the competency of the others, and trusted them to their job fully and correctly. No one claimed to know it all, and no one was afraid to ask for help or to acknowledge that they needed some guidance.

The atmosphere of trust on the project allowed the team to complete a prototype data warehouse in a very short time. In fact, a working design was operational in just a few months!

Following the completion of the above project, I was careful to document for the firm how well it went. To my consternation, management did not seem very surprised that the project went well. If only they knew how many data warehouses ended up as a death march project!

We should always try and engender a culture of trust within the working environment in order to achieve great results. One useful tool in establishing this trust is called the **Universal Law of Reciprocity**. It is extremely simple to state, but perhaps not so easy to do.

The Universal Law of Reciprocity

I had the good fortune to study with a superb instructor in the graduate program at the University of California, Irvine. The title of one particularly excellent class was Organizational Behavior. The professor had worked as a manager for many years, and was well acquainted with the latest research on interpersonal behavior within corporations.

The professor told the students about a philosophy that I have never forgotten. He called this maxim the Universal Law of Reciprocity, which means simply that people tend to treat you as you treat them. Thus, the DBA who scoffs at the problems of designers will probably receive similar treatment (and similar lack of cooperation). On the other hand, the analyst who clearly shows that he trusts the designers in their efforts to build a sound design will probably receive a similar courtesy in return.

I have found it to work very well in practice, as illustrated in our next case study:

Case Study: Poor Chemistry?

While working for a large financial services company, I was approached by the department manager. "Drop everything and get started on the HR project!" The manager explained that I was being assigned as the primary DBA on this project. I did not know why I was being assigned to this project (or anything else about the project, for that matter).

A team from a large, well-known consulting group was assigned to develop the application. I eventually discovered that they had had some sort of disagreement with the previous DBA, and the project had suffered. I heard stories about how poor the team chemistry was, and other tales of numerous disputes with the previous DBA.

In spite of all these reports, I was determined to start off on a good footing, so I completely disregarded all negative comments about the team. I would give them all the benefit of the doubt, and start off fresh. I would practice the Universal Law of Reciprocity, and hope for the best. If there were some conflicts, I was confident that we could negotiate some compromise.

I soon met all the members of the team. To my surprise, they all seemed normal and cooperative. (Perhaps I had expected an immediate attack.) Well, I thought, perhaps they will strike when I am not ready for them. I best keep my guard up.

In time, however, I realized that every person on the team was competent and very cooperative. They treated me very courteously, and I responded in kind. What started off as an apparently negative situation actually turned out to be one of the most positive experiences of my career.

The case study above illustrates an important point about why some projects succeed, and others fail miserably:

> **Trusting relationships on a project give the team a huge advantage.**

This hint suggests that a good working relationship not only helps the Oracle analyst, but the entire team. The project in the case study was very successful.

Report Problems Accurately

Most of us are eager to give a good report to our superiors; we may even be tempted to "sugar-coat" the extent of some performance problem, or perhaps gloss-over some significant barriers to success. This is only human, because we desire to give our superior the best news possible. No one wants to be the purveyor of bad news.

The best report, however, is not the one that underestimates the cost of a fix, or the one that trivializes the details of implementation. Just because you solved one database difficulty in 45 minutes does not mean that 45 minutes is a good estimate for all future issues.

Management has a right to expect a reasonable estimate of the effort required to solve a serious problem. To provide a good estimate, some detective work will have to be performed. After a little digging, maybe you will confirm that the problem really *is* a simple 1-hour job. You won't know, however, until you dig into the details a little bit.

One should also remember that changes to production systems are big events. For instance, changes in production applications or databases are usually accompanied by a significant amount of testing and configuration control. This is entirely proper, since the firm has a huge amount to lose if faulty changes are made. This means that a *simple code change* will probably be anything except simple, when all the mandatory steps are counted.

These observations suggest another hint, regarding how to report problems:

> **Do not give overly optimistic estimates of the time required to solve critical production problems.**

A number of times, I have seen DBAs or other administrators provide overly optimistic estimates of how long it would take to solve a crisis. These estimates were provided before they even knew what they were trying to solve. Remember though, that there is a difference between setting yourself a difficult target based on a good understanding of the problem, and setting an optimistic target based on a lack of understanding.

Avoid a Pompous Attitude

To foster a trusting relationship, it is important that all parties avoid a pompous attitude. Many of us have been on project teams that have certain difficult members who must always get their way. From sheer force of personality, these individuals often force the team to follow their recommendations.

Some engineers may be introverts by nature, who will opt to avoid a confrontation, and simply go along with the recommendation rather than make it an issue.

Even just one or two "swollen heads" on a team can completely destroy a team's good dynamic. Instead of working in a spirit of cooperation, meetings tend to be exercises in defending one's position, or justifying past work. Outside the meeting, programmers will do their job grudgingly. Instead of feeling that they are making a contribution, team players are reduced to the position of taking orders.

This type of situation is the opposite of trust. A pompous attitude really says to everyone else on the team, "You are not important. There is no reason to listen to your ideas". Obviously, a team with this chemistry will be at a huge disadvantage. Instead of benefiting from the minds of many people, from various backgrounds, the project degrades into just one person's design.

DBAs are some of the smartest people I know – really! In a few cases, however, it seems that a few heads get swollen a little out of proportion. Our next case study illustrates how one pompous individual was able to impede a project seriously, and create discord in an entire department.

Case Study: "I Am in Control!"

The DBAs in a large medical research corporation were having difficulty working with the lead Systems Administrator. As experienced DBAs know, the DBA-Systems Administrator relationship is critical to success, so this dysfunctional relationship was especially costly. None of the DBAs had been successful in working with this individual. The main issue was not so much the technical work done by the administrator; rather, his attitude.

I was invited to the next team meeting, and quickly saw what my colleagues were facing. Within this firm, the DBAs were really internal customers of the Systems Administrator (just as developers often are the internal customers of the DBA). Nevertheless, the Systems Administrator made it quite clear how things would work while he was on duty: "I am in control", he reminded us all. His attitude told us more than his words, however. Instead of treating us as valued customers (which we were), he treated us as pests that need to be controlled (if not altogether exterminated).

I attempted to reason with the administrator on some details that were causing friction with the DBAs. He was absolutely unwilling to see anything our way. Eventually, the DBAs were able to complete their project work, but with far less efficiency than might have been possible. The Systems Administrator succeeded only in establishing a reputation for pomposity.

This case study illustrates the serious damage that is caused by even one person with a pompous attitude. Of course, in the short run, there is not always an easy solution to these situations. In the long run, however, there is a useful and effective tactic, simply remember the following hint:

> **Treat your database customers with the same courtesy that you desire from others.**

Accept Responsibility

In some ways, the performance DBA has the best of all possible worlds. Firstly, performance problems can sometimes be a fascinating challenge to correct; secondly, the solution usually makes our customers extremely happy.

Typically, performance problems are usually so simple that no great brainpower is required. Occasionally, however, a really challenging bottleneck will emerge. Most senior performance analysts really enjoy solving these puzzles. So our next hint is as follows:

> **The majority of database-related performance problems CAN be completely corrected.**

It Could be the Database

A performance analyst who doesn't try to dodge the problem will impress many users. Immediately, a favorable impression of honesty and trustworthiness will be generated. Therefore, instead of ducking and weaving, be quick to admit that the database could indeed be the problem if that is what you believe it may be. This attitude will be like a refreshing breeze for your clients.

In spite of the clear advantage to the DBA who accepts responsibility, there are many who are too insecure, and as a result cannot bring themselves to accept any accountability. Instead, they choose to duck and weave whenever a problem appears. This misguided tactic of denying responsibility will not fool anyone for long, as this next case demonstrates:

Case study: "Fire, What Fire?"

While employed as a Systems Engineer for a large aerospace corporation, I had many occasions to troubleshoot problems with equipment designed for the US military. One large project involved a tank with radar-controlled anti-aircraft guns. This project was extremely complicated, with numerous independent computers talking with one another over a 1553-Bus. The entire project employed thousands of workers just at one company alone.

I was assigned to the Systems Integration team. This group comprised a small team of staff who were trained as specialists in troubleshooting problems with this system. We would travel around the country, working with the test engineers as the system was checked out. It was a lot of fun watching the system fire at remote control aircraft in isolated desert locations – but the results were not always good. The system was just incredibly complicated, and working out the bugs was taking a very long time.

While in the field, we would often consult with experts at the home office. For instance, when there was a problem with certain modules, we would often call the lead designer, in order to try to find the cause of the failure.

One of the more experienced designers, Rick, had the reputation for dodging any responsibility related to his particular module – the power distribution module. This particular module was very troublesome, and had a bad history. Nevertheless, no matter what happened, the problem was never in his module. Rick had developed an excellent track record of successfully repelling all suggestions that his module needed improvement. He had rejected almost all changes in his design, in spite of mounting evidence of problems.

One afternoon, I was called to investigate a problem with Rick's power module. The failure of the module had caused a complete stop in testing at the final checkout facility. By the time I arrived on-site, the technicians had already removed the cover to the power module. The cause of the failure was immediately apparent. A large power relay was completely burnt-up, with the smell of smoke still noticeable. We all laughed at this and realized that there was no way Rick could dodge this one – we finally had him!

I called Rick on the phone and (I'll admit, a little gleefully) gave him the bad news. Finally, I thought, he would have to admit to a design problem, and fix his design. However, when confronted with the undeniable evidence (charred relay, smell of smoke, and obvious fire) Rick calmly replied that there must be a problem with "a ventilation fan". Once again, I had underestimated Rick's ingenuity.

Rick continued in his job for a few months until he retired. His replacement, although not initially as technically savvy as Rick, had one huge advantage – he made no attempt to dodge problems. His realistic attitude finally led to several design changes, which resolved most of the problems. There were no more fires.

In this case study, one individual was able to block progress toward resolving a problem temporarily. His continuing failure to accept responsibility impeded the work of others, and simply delayed the inevitable. Everyone on the team lost.

Three Cheers for Database Problems!

The Oracle performance tuner benefits from an interesting paradox: surprisingly, the best problem is often one that really is in the database. This advantage is due to the simple fact that database problems are often relatively easy to correct, compared to the other options.

For example, suppose that an application user has complained of some sort of slow performance. Before we have actually gathered any facts, we must assume that anything could be to blame – network, application design, server setup, and so on. We simply can't eliminate anything.

If the problem is indeed traced to the database, the correction is often relatively painless. For instance, consider the following database changes that can usually be implemented relatively painlessly:

- New or modified indexes
- New table statistics
- Larger buffer cache
- Larger shared pool
- Pinning tables in memory
- Pinning packages in memory
- Larger redo logs
- More redo logs
- Different archive log destination
- Rollback segment sizing

The list goes on and on.

In other words, *many* database changes are extremely easy to implement. Of course, there are some that aren't quite as simple. One that comes to mind is a change in block size. Traditionally, this change would indeed be a big ordeal, requiring a complete rebuild of the database, but it is extremely unlikely that a block size mistake would really be the root cause of a critical performance problem.

In contrast to the relative ease of database changes, consider the plight of the developer, and the possible changes that he or she faces. A blunder in the application could require a complicated design change! A large design modification would have huge consequences – starting with a plethora of meetings, then continuing with detailed design analysis, several design reviews, and a variety of testing.

Of course, the Oracle DBA may also have to convince a change board to allow a database change; but for the database, this is usually only a slight hurdle. Changes such as new indexes, parameter changes, and so forth, are typically approved without much delay. This is reasonable, because these types of changes are normally easily reversed.

Of course, configuration control practices are important on the database side as well as for the application. For production systems, DBAs should indeed track changes to parameters and indexing. More than one DBA has had to "back-out" mistaken changes.

The large contrast between application design changes and database changes leads us to our next hint:

> **Performance problems due to database setup are often the easiest to correct.**

So, in the event of a problem, instead of becoming defensive about possible database glitches, we should be rooting for them. Three cheers for database problems!

Avoid Accusations

Our next suggestion for dealing with humans is to avoid accusations. The practice of trying to shift responsibility, or blaming others, is so common that we have already briefly touched on this point in the previous chapter. If for no other reason, this topic is worthy of further discussion simply because the practice of pointing fingers is so prevalent.

Whenever there is some problem, we all like to put the blame on someone else – and quickly. It seems to be so natural to make accusatory statements quickly. Yet how foolish we look when our rash actions have been exposed!

Trying to put blame on others is simply neither appropriate nor necessary for a competent Oracle analyst. In following the Physician-to-Magician approach, the performance analyst develops a logical case, based on sound analysis, for finding and correcting the root cause of a performance bottleneck.

When the Oracle Artist proposes a solution, it is clear that the solution has emanated from the findings of all his predecessors; namely, the Oracle Physician, Oracle Detective, and Oracle Pathologist. In other words, there is no stage in the process called the Accusing Stage, or the Oracle Accuser. Indeed, there is no need to accuse anyone; the process is based on a focus on the problem to be solved, not the people.

The Result of Accusations

In fact, by employing an accusatory manner, the Oracle specialist will only hinder his own case. No one likes to be unfairly accused (or even fairly accused, for that matter!)

What happens when we make accusations? Does this method serve our purposes? Of course not. The unlucky object of our accusations will only become defensive, and possibly starting pointing the finger of blame right back.

Accusations add little to the performance-tuning process. Even if the accusatory practice successfully resolves the performance problem, and wins the battle, you will have lost the war (and probably lost future work at that firm).

Our next case study illustrates the futility of blaming the users for performance problems:

Case Study: The Terminator, "I'll be Back!"

A large utility company had a customer-service application that severely stressed the server resources. In this application, approximately 600 customer service agents could simultaneously access the database, opening up about 1200 connections. (The program was designed to open up two connections for each user.)

This particular program had many holes that led to severe performance problems. For instance, when the agent searched for the records for a particular customer, the application allowed the agent to run the query with no name specified. In other words, the application allowed the users to run a null query. The null query executed a SQL statement without good selection criteria in the WHERE clause, thus causing full table scans of very large tables. The ill-formed query would try to return all entries – clearly something that the application was not supposed to do.

To make things worse, the function key for **Enter Name** was adjacent to the function key for **Execute Query.** Whenever the user made the simple mistake of depressing the wrong function key, the null query ran for about 15 minutes, consuming resources and spinning the disks.

After discovering the problem, management tried to solve it procedurally – that is, they told the agents to "stop doing that". The DBA gingerly tried questioning this approach, but his comments were ignored. It seemed to the DBA that management's approach was doomed to failure because it didn't really solve the problem. Instead, it just blamed the users.

Until the application could be changed, it was clear that more effective action was needed. Thus, one of the DBAs created a script called Terminator. This short program had a very simple function; it simply looked at all active sessions, compared the active SQL code to the null query, then terminated any corresponding user session.

> Note that the ideal fix would be to modify the application to disallow such queries, not to catch the problem after the fact. Unfortunately, however, the vendor was simply very slow to make any design changes; the application would not be corrected for several months.

The Terminator program was a big hit. At first, the DBAs ran it manually, perhaps once an hour, or whenever a large group of null queries were discovered. As confidence in the Terminator grew, it became clear that the script worked perfectly. Thus, the script was actually entered as a cron job, executed several times per hour.

> cron refers to the UNIX utility that activates periodic jobs. It is often used to run nightly reports, start back-up jobs, and so on.

For months, the Terminator script relieved the production system of a huge load of unnecessary table scans and disk spinning. Of course, no terminator script is necessary in cases where the application can be corrected quickly. In this case, however, a quick application fix was simply not going to happen.

Weeks later, a similar problem query was found in the same application. It likewise was responsible for consuming a huge amount of resources, with nothing to show for it. Following in the tradition of the `Terminator` program, the new program was called `Terminator2`, and likewise entered as a cron job.

In this case study, blaming the application users for an oversight in the application was akin to a teacher telling half the students in a class to "Stop failing your exams!" However, if many students in the class are failing, the problem is not with the students, but with the teacher.

The blame-the-users approach used in this case study also failed to recognize the simple fact of human nature: If some process makes it easy to err, many people will err. Large numbers of users doing the wrong thing is not an indication that many people are stupid, but rather that there is something radically wrong with the process – or in this case, the application.

Applications should be designed to prevent accidental mistakes, such as the ones noted in the case study. There should be restrictions or some type of error checking that preclude simple mistakes that lead to run-away queries. One solution is simply to reject queries that have unrealistic, or overly broad search criteria.

We see then that accusations are not only wrong in practice, they are also often wrong in principle. Let's explore a better way to dig into problems without casting blame.

Ask Questions

If accusations are not appropriate, then what approach should be used? A much better alternative to making accusations is the practice of asking questions. By asking a clearly phrased, neutral question, no finger of blame is being pointed.

When looking for a root cause, the Oracle specialist can make it clear that anything could be the problem – especially the database itself. In fact, the DBA should readily admit that perhaps the database is at fault. Asking questions is a non-threatening way to gather information.

By asking questions rather than accusing, the Oracle specialist makes it clear that no one person is being singled out. This creates a much more cooperative atmosphere, in which everyone is trying to solve the problem without worrying about who is to blame. With this approach, it is clear that there will be no consequences for anyone who has made a mistake. Most people are forgiving of an honest mistake or two, as long as your overall performance is good. (Of course, there *will* be consequences for someone who has misstated their qualifications and cannot competently perform their job!):

> **When investigating, ask questions – don't point the finger of blame.**

When an atmosphere of trust is established, the entire issue of who made the mistake becomes entirely irrelevant. The team looks for a *root cause*, not a *mistake* made by someone. Fortunately, this idea of looking for a solution, not a culprit, is a concept that management usually embraces quickly. Many good managers take the reasonable stance: "I just want the problem solved. I'm not concerned about who created it."

The next case study illustrates how asking questions, rather than blaming people can open up a few doors:

Case Study: The DBAs did it!

While assisting another DBA on a performance problem, I happened to discover certain SQL statements that for some reason consumed a massive amount of system resources. After monitoring the V$SQL area for a few days, I concluded that the offending SQL was coming from a batch job that was launched overnight, precisely at 1:00 A.M.

Due to the consistent (and exact) start time, I realized that the job was certainly a scheduled job, in cron (the UNIX job scheduling facility). There was nothing in the DBAs' cron jobs, so I concluded that one of the designers must own this process.

The exact SQL, along with the associated statistics, was easily retrieved from the V$SQL area. I sent an email to the application group, showing them the SQL, and, explaining that I was trying to correct a performance problem, asked if they knew what this SQL was doing.

The lead developer responded that this query was not theirs, but must be something that one of the DBAs had activated. I was very surprised by this response. None of the DBAs had any reason to develop or modify applications; that was not the job of the DBAs at the firm.

In the meantime, the lead Systems Administrator (in response to my query), tracked down the exact cron job. The entry did belong to the developers after all, as I had suspected. They admitted their error, and immediately applied the given corrections. The problem was completed resolved, to the satisfaction of everyone involved.

As a result of *asking questions*, rather than *blaming*, I was able to establish an excellent working relationship with the design team. We worked on several problems together over the next few months.

In this case, had I immediately blamed the developers, I might never have got their cooperation. They were sensitive enough that the mere act of asking a question was almost seen as a threat. Think of what would have happened if my email had stated, "I have isolated the problem and have found the cause to be you".

Accept Criticism

Closely aligned with admitting the possibility of being wrong, is the willingness to accept criticism. In most jobs, criticism is really no more than just the normal interaction with our boss. At our workplace, our superior critiques our report, suggests a better process, asks us to stop coming in at noon, and so forth. This is all fine, and part of our everyday lives.

For some, however, accepting technical criticism can be a particularly tough hurdle. Most DBAs, for instance, are justifiably proud of their ability to troubleshoot and solve many tough Oracle problems. Many senior analysts have spent years in the trenches, having to cope with numerous perplexing problems. Why should anyone with such experience be on the receiving end of pointed criticism?

Naturally, no one likes to be criticized, even if the criticism is well intended – a treatment commonly called **positive criticism**. On those occasions when remarks are made in a critical tone, it takes even more self-control to calmly accept the rebuke.

Why then, should the database guru be willing to accept critical comments? There are two excellent reasons:

❑　Accepting criticism leads to smoother cooperation with the customers.

❑　Accepting criticism leads to greater expertise on the part of the Oracle practitioner.

Thus, for purely self-serving reasons, the Oracle tuning specialist should be pliable. An attitude of humility not only smoothes relations with the customer, but also it helps the tuning analyst as well. This advantage accrues because all individuals grow and learn more by listening to criticism. All other things being equal, the one who is willing to be taught will learn far more than the one who is too proud to listen:

Accept criticism and learn from it.

Sometimes, criticism is really a back-handed compliment. That is, the person's ability is so highly regarded, that a rare mistake may be blown out of all proportion in jest, since it is understood by everyone that the culprit is exceedingly capable at what they do.

Summary

In this chapter we have explored many of the people problems that will definitely affect the success of the Oracle performance analyst. This *people* side of performance tuning is often overlooked, but these skills are very important in resolving serious Oracle problems. If the Oracle analyst chooses to deal with the people issues positively, many small problems will be forgotten, and the conflicts associated with larger problems will be eased.

Now that we have a good grounding in people management for these tricky people problems, it is time to change our hat. Let's pin-on our badge and grab our crime scene investigation kit; it's time for the Oracle Detective to make his entrance.

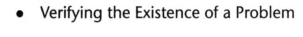

- Verifying the Existence of a Problem

- Quantify the Problem

- Note any Unusual Complications

The Oracle Detective

Once the Oracle Physician has clearly defined the problem, the next step requires an investigation. Here, the DBA switches hats from physician to detective. It is now time to "dig deeper" into the facts surrounding the performance problem.

Let's briefly review where we are in the Physician-to-Magician approach:

Physician	Detective	Pathologist	Artist	Magician
Define problem	Investigate	Isolate cause	Create solution	Implement

In this step, the Oracle Detective will strive to recreate and quantify the problem. At this point, thanks to the steadfast work of the Oracle Physician, we should have a very clear understanding of what the customer believes the problem to be.

Keep in mind, however, that the customer's description of the problem can sometimes *simply be mistaken*. This is the unavoidable reality of dealing with people. Despite their very best intentions, even experienced professionals will sometimes err. They will recall events imprecisely, mix-up the facts, or simply not fully understand the situation they are describing.

At crime scenes, for instance, eyewitnesses frequently give varying (or even totally contradictory) versions of events. For example, after a recent bank robbery in my hometown of Dublin, California, one customer in the bank described the bandits wearing masks. In contradiction to this, the bank's video cameras proved that this "eye witness" was completely mistaken. None of the robbers wore masks!

The bank customer honestly believed what he told the police; however, he was *simply mistaken*. In the same way, our customers can sometimes err. Thus, the Oracle Detective needs to be just a little cautious before accepting everything at "face value."

At this detection stage, we can begin our research into the details of the problem, to confirm or refute what has been reported. Note that we are not trying to solve the problem in this stage; rather, we are gathering details to use in the next step of our approach – the Oracle Pathologist. It will be our job to find the root cause of the problem in that phase of the process.

Practically speaking, however, it is possible that during this step, the Oracle Detective will unearth significant hints that point directly at the root cause. In fact, some simple problems may be completely resolved before the Oracle Pathologist even starts. Great! The sooner the problem is solved, the happier the customer. Normally, however, most problems will require a little more work.

In this chapter, we discuss how the Oracle Detective fits into the tuning process. What is the "Detective" supposed to do? Can't he just use a tool to do his job?

We discover that the Oracle Detective will actually be very busy. Specifically, he has three objectives:

- ❑ To confirm the problem.
- ❑ To quantify the problem.
- ❑ To note any unusual complications.

Although the Oracle Detective will not try to speed ahead to solve the problem, the facts uncovered will prove invaluable in succeeding steps. These facts will be critical in finding the root cause of the performance problem.

The Oracle Detective has many tools in his "crime scene investigation" kit. Some of these tools will be discussed here, such as using the V$ dynamic views (specifically VSQL, VSESSION, and V$PROCESS) to obtain statistics on recent SQL executions. We will also provide an overview of how to generate SQL trace files, and how to use the TKPROF utility to allow us to interpret them more easily. Several examples are provided to illustrate the use of this powerful tool.

The discussion of one important tool, however, is reserved for the following chapter, in which we continue our discussion of the Oracle Detective. In Chapter 6, we will examine in depth one of the most sophisticated investigative methods available to the Oracle Detective. This is the very powerful **wait event** facility that can be used to gather detailed information on most performance problems.

Clearly, then, the Oracle Detective will be very busy indeed. Our predecessor, the Oracle Physician, has provided valuable assistance to us in this regard – especially if he has already witnessed the performance bottleneck at first hand. We should dig a little deeper now, but not assume too much though. Besides, by simply confirming that the problem really exists, we will also be gathering pertinent facts about the bottleneck. Without further delay, let's grab our magnifying glass and get ready to gather clues.

Verifying the Existence of a Problem

What we really need to find out first is whether or not the problem actually exists. Also, if it does, is it database-related, or should a different specialist be recruited to resolve it?

The first step, then, is a simple one. The Oracle Detective should confirm first hand that something is awry with the database, the application, or some other subsystem that interacts with the database.

Surprisingly, the facts that are reported to the DBA are sometimes completely in error. That is, the purported performance bottleneck simply does not exist on occasion. This can happen, for instance, if the user is misled by some oddity in the application that may dupe him into believing it to be a performance problem. At other times, there might be a problem, but one that is completely different from what the user believes:

> **Do not assume that every performance problem is reported accurately.**

Therefore, so that no one wastes any more time, it is necessary to first confirm that a problem even exists. Fortunately, there are many ways to accomplish this confirmation, as we will see in the rest of this section of the chapter.

Does the Problem Really Exist?

It is critical that the Oracle Detective verify (and duplicate) a reported performance problem to confirm its existence. To achieve this, we can usually use any of these methods, either singly or in combination:

- Run through some basic troubleshooting steps and collect error messages from users.
- Re-run the application in a controlled environment.
- Check the application run logs.
- Query the V$SQL view to find the SQL statements.
- Monitor the application using a tool.

Let's take a look at each of these in turn.

> As the Oracle Detective gathers information about the performance bottleneck, clues about the eventual solution will often be obtained. These clues will be of great value when we are wearing our next hat, that of the Oracle Pathologist. Although, occasionally, the Oracle Detective finds such conclusive evidence about the cause of the problem, that an immediate solution is forthcoming.

Check the Basics

Prior to launching a detailed investigation, it is a good idea to perform some basic troubleshooting steps first. This will eliminate some obvious culprits, and possibly save us some embarrassment later:

> **Check the simple, basic things first.**

These basic steps, which only require a few minutes to perform, include:

- ❑ Check the alert log for the database being queried. Note any unusual error messages, such as space or rollback problems.
- ❑ Check for any other indications of space problems.
- ❑ Confirm that a file's AUTOEXTEND limit has not been met.
- ❑ Verify that the archive log file system is not full.
- ❑ Verify that the file system holding the Oracle executables is not full.
- ❑ Verify that the maximum number of users has not been hit.
- ❑ Verify that the file system holding the listener.log is not full.
- ❑ Verify that statistics have been generated.

Over time, as you gain experience with a certain system, you will be able to more quickly rule-out (or rule-in!) certain of these possibilities. For instance, if there are only a few users of a particular development database, it is not too likely that you have reached the maximum number of users.

For any particular site experiencing trouble, there will probably be other pertinent logs to check. For instance, web-based applications will certainly have logs related to the web server; checking these logs first can save the analyst a lot of trouble later.

Error Messages

It is also important to ask the users if they have experienced any error messages, such as ORA-nnn errors. These official error messages from the Oracle server can be very useful in diagnosing a problem.

There are usually other error messages, provided by the designers of whatever application is being used. These come in a many shapes and forms; the application might simply pass on the "official" Oracle error message, or it might provide its own error message. The usefulness of these will depend on how well they have been designed; but you should find out about them anyway, in case they yield useful clues.

Note that users often forget about an error message, or believe that it is unimportant. Do not assume that the users have given you all the information available; it may be necessary to probe gently to gather other useful clues.

> **Ask the user about specific error messages.**

Admittedly, checking logs, looking for file systems that are full, and asking the user about error messages is trivial in nature. It hardly seems fitting for an experienced detective. Like the police investigator, however, the Oracle Detective should not overlook any clue. It is better to take a few moments to fix the easy things first.

Remember that a great many performance problems are trivial to correct. Frequently, it is not necessary to perform sophisticated analyses, as problems are often extremely simple to correct. Imagine how foolish an Oracle performance expert would feel if he spent days analyzing a "tough" performance problem, only to discover that the solution was something trivial, like a full file system.

Assuming that the simple space and log checks have been done, and any error messages have been collected, it is appropriate for the Oracle Detective to confirm then that the performance problem exists.

Re-Run the Application in a Controlled Environment

One very simple way to verify a problem is to re-run the application, using the same parameters as noted in the original problem statement. Sometimes, this can be done on the production system without interfering with other users. At other times, this option is not possible, because the application might change some critical data, or otherwise interfere with other production users.

In some cases, it is best to watch the end-user as he executes the program. This is valuable, as it is always helpful for the DBA to understand more about the application. A side benefit of watching the user demonstrate the problem is that your customer will understand that you are serious about solving their problem; they will appreciate your interest.

Another advantage of watching the user re-stage the problem is that hints about the problem are frequently revealed. For instance, upon seeing an odd error message, the user might say something like, "Oh, we always get that problem. You can ignore that." Of course, the user could be wrong – perhaps the funny error message is critical to solving the problem.

By watching the user run the application, the Oracle analyst might also observe other performance problems that the user doesn't even realize are problems. The users might simply have become accustomed to certain poorly running functions, and not bothered to complain. This is where the performance analyst can really assist the customer:

> **Sometimes the users will not realize that they should complain about something.**

Typically, a good DBA will know roughly how long queries should take on their particular systems. For instance, most OLTP applications retrieve a few fields of user information upon connecting. This information is almost always related to a unique key, and thus often runs very rapidly. If the DBA notices that the user has to wait ten seconds for a successful login, then this delay should probably be investigated. Of course, there may be good reasons for this delay, but why not check it out?

Often, this demonstration of the application issue will need to be repeated, especially if the DBA activates SQL_TRACE (discussed later in this chapter). Tracing the application while a user is demonstrating the problem is an especially powerful tool for the Oracle Detective.

99

Check the Run Logs

There is another source of clues for the Oracle Detective. Many applications, especially those involving large batch jobs, keep track of long-running processes. For instance, sometimes the application designer has been clever enough to record the start and stop times for key steps in an application. When the designers have thoughtfully included this type of information, it is written to files called **run logs**. This extra information makes the job of the Oracle Detective much easier.

When run logs have been provided, we will need to determine what kind of logs the application writes, and then review each of them for significant delays. Once again, this is a simple step easily (and often) overlooked.

Remember that, surprisingly, even the designers are sometimes unaware of application logs. For instance, this could happen in a firm where there has been a large staff turnover and the current programmers are not aware of all the steps taken by their predecessors:

> **Don't assume that the application has no run logs, even if no one knows of any!**

Our next case study illustrates the great "evidentiary" value found in good run logs. In this case, the designer had the foresight to record the exact start and stop time for each major step in a large data-load operation:

Case Study: Data Warehouse Loading

A small design team for a dot com firm was troubleshooting their data warehouse ETL (Extract-Transform-Load) process. The entire process was running much slower than expected, which was impacting the reports needed for the firm's customers. If the ETL process was delayed, then the data would not be current the next day. Therefore, the designer asked the DBA for assistance.

Fortunately for the DBA, the lead data warehouse architect had designed the ETL process in a modular fashion, with excellent logging of each step. For example, the start and finish times for each part of the process were recorded in the ETL log for that day. In addition, the table names and row counts were also listed. It was as though the architect had foreseen some performance problems, and had wisely built in the best possible tool.

The DBA was astonished at how cleverly designed the entire ETL process was; without too much difficulty, he was able to isolate a few SQL statements that needed to be tuned. There were different logs for each day, so an increase in processing time for any step was easily identified by comparing them. Furthermore, these same logs were used throughout the project – not just in correcting major bottlenecks, but also in optimizing the time for the entire process. It was possible to check the performance of each step in the complex data-loading process easily.

In this case study, solving the performance problem became a trivial task, thanks to the foresight of the lead architect on the project. The start and finish timestamps feature certainly took some effort to design and test, but the effort paid back almost immediately. Without the run logs, just trying to figure out the culprit could have taken many hours or days.

The term **metric the application** is sometimes used to describe recording the performance of an application. Some applications even let the analyst set different granularity of runtime logging, depending on what they are trying to accomplish. These features are all very useful in diagnosing difficult problems:

> **Well-designed run logs can save the performance tuner a tremendous amount of time**

This case also reinforces the wisdom of "preventative medicine." While not all performance problems will successfully be prevented, some simple design features can make resolution of these problems far easier. A little time spent beforehand can save many days later in the project.

Our next case study again illustrates the value of run logs in assisting the Oracle analyst. In this case, a little digging was required to find the right log to use:

Case Study: Runaway Logs

At a small firm, I was working with the Systems Administrator to troubleshoot a "runaway" application. (It was a runaway application because it seemed to be using more and more disk space for no apparent reason.) The application was designed to keep track of how many web site hits the company received. It did this by processing web logs for the several web servers employed. The firm's business was conducted exclusively over the Internet, so the intensity of web site traffic was crucial to the firm's success.

I noticed, with alarm, that this particular application was causing the database size to grow rapidly as the web site activity for the firm increased. Unfortunately for me, the server had been set up originally to handle only a small database. In fact, the System Administrator reported that the server had already reached the physical limit on disks, and he would have to order extra racks to hold additional ones. In the meantime, disk space was very scarce.

Certain parts of the application were beginning to fail as the disk capacity was reached. No one at the company knew the exact details of how the application worked, but the problem appeared to be related to the file systems becoming full. In order to fix the application, it would be necessary to gather more details on the problem, but none of the DBAs or Systems Administrators had seen this problem before; in other words, we didn't have much to go on.

There were indeed some run logs for the application, but it was not clear how they could be used. We had many questions, but not many answers. For instance, would any of the logs reveal database-related problems, or were the logs for some other purpose? How many logs were there? Did the Oracle user have access to them all, or were the logs intended for use only by the root user?

Investigation showed that there were several logs that could be of help. For example, one log showed the details of each stage in the application as the program processed the numerous web logs. If anything, this particular log had too much detail; also, it was very difficult to relate the entries in this log to database problems. One other log, however, appeared more promising; it showed various errors encountered in the application, and provided clues as to what the problem was.

Several days of further investigation revealed what was happening; the application was designed to create then drop indexes dynamically, toward the end of its processing. The purpose of these temporary indexes was to speed up the purging of old web log listings in the database. So, when the application could not create these indexes, it could no longer purge the extraneous data. (This also explained why the database seemed to grow faster than expected – the purging of data was not working properly.)

The Systems Administrator temporarily provided some file space so that these "extra" indexes could be created; this in turn allowed the application to purge the old data. Finally, the DBA performed several exports and imports to shrink the space required by some of the largest tables and indexes. All these steps combined to reduce the disk requirements of the database significantly, and give everyone some breathing room.

Now that we knew the value of the application logs (and that they even existed), we were able to monitor the success of each night's run easily, and watch for the recurrence of any similar problems.

The database problem discussed in the case above was easily rectified once we knew how to use the application logs. Without these logs, it would have been very tough to discover that the application was creating then dropping indexes every night. Of course, once we knew that the application did this, it was simple to ensure proper operation.

Query the V$SQL View to Find the SQL Statements

Besides checking the application logs, there are other, very simple ways to see what is going on. In many cases, it is extremely helpful to capture the actual SQL statements that have been issued by the application. One way to do this is to activate SQL_TRACE for the session of interest. This will build a trace file that will include all database queries.

For now, however, consider an even more basic approach – simply query the V$SQL view to list all SQL statements in the shared pool. This is one of my favorite ways to see what is going on. I have used this method many hundreds of times to find troublesome SQL statements:

> Observing SQL statements in the V$SQL area is one of the most indispensable tools available to the Oracle performance analyst.

Every competent Oracle tuning analyst must know how to use the V$SQL view. The reason for this is simple; a large number of performance problems are due to poorly designed or incorrectly optimized SQL code. In fact, entire books have been written on the subject of SQL optimization. Some of these books have proved so useful that they have turned out to be essential resources for the Oracle tuning expert; for example, *Oracle SQL High Performance Tuning, 2nd Edition* by Guy Harrison (Prentice Hall, ISBN: 0130123811).

As the subject is so central to the subject of Oracle performance tuning, several chapters of this book (8 and 9) have been reserved just for SQL optimization techniques.

Using the V$SQL View

The V$SQL view contains extremely useful information on recently executed SQL statements.

> *A definition of the columns in the V$SQL view can be found in Appendix A.*

By querying the V$SQL view, the Oracle Detective can discover very pertinent clues, such as:

❑ Actual SQL statement processed.

❑ Number of times executed.

❑ Number of disk reads.

❑ Number of logical reads.

❑ First load time.

Several of our previous case studies have already hinted at ways to use the V$SQL view. Typical queries against this view will fetch the fields SQL_TEXT, as well as critical statistics such as DISK_READS, and BUFFER_GETS.

When interrogating the V$SQL view, some restriction should be placed in the query; otherwise, a huge list of SQL statements will be retrieved. For instance, one good idea would be to retrieve only those SQL statements that have a large number of disk reads. At other times, the analyst might be looking for SQL statements that have a specific number of executions.

Our first example shows the most common use of the V$SQL view – listing SQL statements that consume a large number of disk reads per execution.

Example: Finding SQL Statements with Excessive Disk Reads

This query restricts the result set to SQL statements that consume at least 10,000 blocks read from disk for each execution:

```
SQL> SELECT Executions EXEC, Disk_Reads DISK,
  2    Sql_Text TEXT
  3  FROM V$SQL
  4  WHERE Disk_Reads/(.01 + executions) > 10000;
```

```
EXEC     DISK TEXT
----  -------- --------------------------
   5    79204  SELECT Ename FROM Emp;
```

In this example, it looks as though the SQL statement in question is retrieving every single employee name from a very full Emp table. The problem, of course, is that each of the executions required about 16000 disk reads! (79,204/5).

Note the small decimal .01 in the query, inserted in the denominator so as to preclude a divide by zero error. Of course, any small number would be fine.

Besides looking only for excessive disk reads, it is wise to look for exorbitant numbers of logical reads as well. Although not as expensive as disk reads, there is nevertheless a cost associated with each logical read. The logical reads are associated with the column called BUFFER_GETS in the V$SQL view.

Example: Find SQL with Excessive Logical Reads

This query is a slight modification of the above. It looks for excessive BUFFER_GETS in the search criteria instead of DISK_READS:

```
SQL> SELECT Executions EXEC, Buffer_Gets LOG, Sql_text TEXT
  2  FROM V$SQL
  3  WHERE (Buffer_Gets/(.01 + executions) > 20000);

EXEC     LOG TEXT
----  -------- --------------------------
   5   121305  SELECT Ename FROM Emp;
```

This script, which also finds the same questionable SQL statement, recognizes the importance of checking for logical reads as well as disk I/O. Excessive logical reads frequently indicate problem SQL statements. However, this script sets a higher threshold for logical reads – 20,000 per execution versus the 10,000 for disk reads that we used in our previous query. This recognizes the higher cost of disk reads. For each particular database, these values can be adjusted up or down, depending on the exact circumstances.

During the search for troublesome SQL statements, be cautious when using a criterion based on disk reads. Once data is cached, the number of disk reads will probably fall sharply on subsequent executions, especially if the query is run several times in quick succession. Logical reads, on the other hand, will be nearly identical on subsequent executions.

Not all problems are due to high I/O per execution; sometimes the cumulative effect is the problem. These SQL statements are unearthed in our next example.

This query restricts the results to SQL statements that have consumed at least 1,000,000 blocks read from disk – total for all executions:

```
SQL> SELECT Executions EXEC, Disk_Reads DISK, Sql_text TEXT
  2  FROM V$SQL
  3  WHERE Disk_Reads > 1000000;

   EXEC       DISK TEXT
 -------  --------- ------------------------------------------
 1231421    3518234 UPDATE lock_table SET CODE = :b0;
```

In this example, each execution of the listed SQL statement runs fine, consuming only about 3 disk reads per execution (3,518,234/1,231,421). The problem here is not due to a poorly tuned SQL statement; rather, it is due to the huge number of executions. The Oracle Detective would certainly want to know why this statement has been executed over one million times, or why it was not cached.

Complications from not Using Bind Variables

Sometimes there are many "forms" of the same basic SQL statement. An example would be a SQL statement that retrieves certain columns based on Employee_id; each version of this statement differs only by the exact Employee_id specified in the WHERE clause. In these situations, the application forms a slightly different SQL statement over and over. The Oracle engine must then deal with these myriad forms of slightly different SQL statements separately.

The better option, is a design in which the application re-uses the *identical* SQL statement. This can be accomplished by using **bind variables**, which make it possible to not specify the changing value literally, but with a variable instead. Rather than thousands of slight different SQL statements being sent to Oracle, the *same* SQL statement is re-used, where the queries do not vary syntactically.

When a bind variable is used, the actual SQL presented to the Oracle engine will show the bind variable in the form :nx, where n is a letter, and x is a number (typically 0). Thus, a query that retrieves rows based on employee id would look something like this:

```
SELECT Emp_Name, Emp_Phone
FROM Emp
WHERE Emp_id = :b0   [that is, bind variable];
```

When searching for "bad" SQL, the lack of bind variables presents a slight difficulty; the query of V$SQL might return hundreds or even thousands of different SQL statements. Each SQL statement differs only slightly; nevertheless, the shared SQL area (shared pool) in memory will consider the statements unique.

In these scenarios, the question for the Oracle Detective is, how to group all the similar statements together? That is, how can we get the basic form of the SQL in question, but not be overwhelmed with thousands of individual statements?

There are several ways to accomplish this, and each analyst will choose the option most convenient for them. One very simple way is to group the SQL statements by the amount of memory they consume. This tactic works because SQL statements that are identical except for one parameter typically consume exactly the same amount of memory. In the V$SQL view, this field is called PERSISTENT_MEM. Thus, by grouping the results based on the PERSISTENT_MEM values, we can spot patterns much more easily. Our next example shows how to accomplish this.

Example: Finding Bad SQL Forms

This query finds SQL forms that consume at least 1,000,000 blocks read from the disk, the total for all executions of the same form:

```
SQL> SELECT Persistent_Mem MEM, SUM (Disk_Reads) DISK
  2  FROM V$SQL
  3  GROUP BY Persistent_Mem
  4  HAVING SUM (Disk_Reads) > 1000000
  5  ORDER BY SUM (Disk_Reads);

MEM    DISK
----   --------
 422   1014157
 516   1084906
 163   2004713
 682   5719359
```

We see from this query that SQL statements having a memory usage of exactly 682 bytes are responsible for over 5 million disk reads. Having identified this row, the next step for the Oracle Detective would probably be to list some of the individual SQL statements having the shown value for Persistent_Mem.

When using this method, note that there will occasionally be other, "innocent" SQL statements that happen to have exactly the same value for PERSISTENT_MEM. This is usually only a minor inconvenience, and is easily rectified. When unwanted SQL statements are retrieved, it is easy enough to eliminate the innocent SQL; simply modify the script that queries V$SQL to include a restriction that filters out the unwanted SQL statements. One way would be to filter the result set based on a certain number of disk reads, logical reads, or perhaps the letters that begin the SQL_TEXT. For instance, the Substr function could be used to select only the first 80 characters. Then, a grouping could be formed based on this subset of the SQL text. Of course, this method will only work in some cases, depending on the exact form of the SQL text.

Example: Group Almost Identical Queries

Here is an example of how to find SQL statements that are almost identical (and thus may not be using bind variables). The following query uses the Substr function to consider only the first 50 characters of the SQL statement. We use the HAVING clause to consider only those statements that have been issued at least 50 times. We provide the heading Similar_SQL, and order the results by the number of occurrences:

```
SQL> SELECT Substr (Sql_Text, 1,50) Similar_SQL, COUNT (*)
  2  FROM V$SQL
  3  GROUP BY Substr (Sql_Text, 1, 50)
  4  HAVING COUNT (*) > 1000
  5  ORDER BY COUNT (*);
```

This code would list and count the occurrence of SQL statements that are identical for at least the first 50 characters. The following such SQL statements would qualify, since they are identical for over 50 characters:

```
SELECT Emp_Name, Emp_Dept, Emp_Supervisor, Emp_Phone
FROM Emp
WHERE Emp_Name = 'Joe Smith';
```

```
SELECT Emp_Name, Emp_Dept, Emp_Supervisor, Emp_Phone
FROM Emp
WHERE Emp_Name = 'Bobby Jones';
```

Our next case study illustrates one big problem that was solved – just by looking at the V$SQL view:

Case Study: When Does One Million not Equal One Million?

A team of consultants was working on a data warehouse for a large financial services firm. This particular project had never been successful; it had been attempted several times, and ended in failure each time. The firm had once again restarted the project, but the prototype application was experiencing severe performance problems.

Although the application appeared to work functionally, the data load time was much longer than expected, and was completely unacceptable. The DBA supporting the project asked me to investigate. She suggested that I examine the SQL to see if anything could be done.

Since the problem had already been well defined (that is, "Data loading for load program takes 20 hours"), I began to gather clues. As I had been requested to look for poorly running SQL, my first step was to check the V$SQL area.

Surprisingly, examination of the V$SQL area showed that there were no SQL statements that consumed excessive resources per execution. By querying the V$SQL view, it was easy to discover that a variety of SQL statements had been run – but all ran very well! Each SQL statement consumed perhaps a few disk reads and about 20 logical reads – certainly no cause for concern. Clearly, the optimizer executed each SQL statement with great efficiency.

Further investigation revealed an astonishing fact, and explained why the load required an entire day of processing: Although each SQL statement was indeed very efficient, the program ran each SQL statement millions of times! Here is the result of my query on the V$SQL view (restricted to just the time frame of interest):

107

```
SQL> SELECT Executions, Sql_Text, Disk_Reads
  2  FROM V$SQL
  3  WHERE First_Load_Time LIKE '%14-JAN-1999%';

SQL_TEXT                                    EXECUTIONS  DISK_READS
-------------------------------------       ----------  ----------
SELECT Account_id, Last_Name,                 3132564      104185
First_Name
FROM ACCOUNT
WHERE Account_id = :b0    [that is, bind variable]
AND Account_status = :b1  [that is, bind variable];
```

In this case, the number of disk reads or logical reads was not especially relevant. It was the execution count that was the key to the bottleneck. There will always be a certain minimum time for executing any SQL statement – no matter how well tuned. Millions of executions will almost certainly cause a huge delay.

The designers of the data warehouse used stored procedures as the basis for data loading. There is nothing specifically wrong with using PL/SQL procedures, but here a trap had been sprung; they had designed the program to loop through each row to be loaded. Of course, this caused a huge delay. There is no way any form of SQL tuning can overcome such a huge design flaw. Instead of using database efficiencies to process a huge set of rows (perhaps 100,000) at a time, the application was designed to process each row individually.

At the next meeting of the data warehouse project, I gave the team the bad news, "The database is working extremely efficiently," I explained. "The problem is in the design of the data-loading module. Instead of treating the data as a large group, and then performing set processing; the program is using a PL/SQL procedure that loops through every single row. With this design, the database efficiency is academic, as no amount of optimization can correct for a design flaw like this."

It turns out that I was not the only one to come to this conclusion. When I finished my summary, another consultant in the room chirped up, "That is what I already told them!"

Sadly, the data warehouse project was canceled again.

This leads us to our next hint:

> **Remember to look for excessive execution counts, as well as excessive logical or physical I/O.**

In the case study above, one million transactions of one row is definitely not equivalent to one execution of one million rows. By making this erroneous assumption, the designers doomed the project. The difference in processing time was enormous, and the design had to be completely discarded because the whole idea of row-by-row processing was embedded in various PL/SQL routines. These were now seen to be of very poor design, and management decided it was not worth the effort to start them again from scratch.

V$SQL Limitations

When querying the V$SQL view, remember that the statistics are not kept in memory forever; depending on the size of the shared pool, statistics may soon "age-out", thus making the statistics useless. In most cases, however, the statistics will exist, and will prove to be of immense value.

In some cases, it is also helpful to flush the shared pool prior to running the application in question. This will reset the statistics in this view, so that there will be no confusion about which statistics were from prior operations. In other words, this is almost like a "mini trace" process, in which SQL statements are identified. Of course, the flush operation should be considered carefully on production systems, since this act could degrade future SQL operations slightly. (After a flush, the Oracle engine will have to repeat parsing for every SQL statement received, because each one will be seen as new.)

For SQL that originated in a stored PL/SQL procedure, note that the SQL shown in the V$SQL view may be slightly different from the code that is actually in the PL/SQL object. For instance, there will probably be a difference in capitalization, with the V$SQL view showing the SQL all in upper case. In addition, there will typically be slight syntax differences. These variations complicate the DBA's job a little, because one cannot search for exactly the same code that is listed in the stored procedure. The differences are usually so slight, however, that this does not prove to be a major issue.

Monitor the Application Using a Tool

Another useful way for the Oracle Detective to confirm a performance problem is to use some type of session monitoring or tracing tool. Options such as **TOAD**, or **Oracle Enterprise Manager** (**OEM**), can be very helpful at this stage.

> For information on TOAD, see http://www.quest.com/toad/;
> OEM information is available at
> http://otn.oracle.com/software/products/oem/.

For instance, Oracle's OEM **Top Sessions** tool will indicate exactly which SQL is being run for any session. It can also be used to show resource consumption, for example disk reads, for any session.

There are many other utilities that provide similar capability – including tools such as those produced by Quest, Embarcadero, BMC, and many other firms. Remember that these tools are actually reading the same tables and views that can be read with a simple SQL*Plus script. Behind the scenes, these tools are in fact querying various V$ views, such as V$SQL and V$SESSION. The main benefit of these utilities is not that they query some "secret" tables not usually available, but rather that they provide convenient and easy formatting of results from the ones we can already access. They also save time looking up scripts, correcting syntax, and so on.

When considering a utility or tool to aid your investigations, keep in mind that the exact tool is not the important point; in fact, many very successful (and competent) DBAs use only their own scripts, and prefer to not use any other tool. This is not a bad choice at all; a set of good performance tuning scripts is a huge asset in the hands of a competent performance specialist. When tools are used, the features will vary as the product undergoes new releases. Certain new bells and whistles will be added, and others will be dropped. With well-written scripts, on the other hand, new database releases typically necessitate only minor changes.

The analyst who comes to depend on a tool will be in trouble if that particular tool is not available. On the other hand, the performance analyst who truly understands the concepts involved will often do just as well even when no tool is available. All things being equal, the analyst who truly understands Oracle database operations will vastly outperform other analysts who feel obligated to use some tool:

> **Do not become dependent on any one tool to analyze performance problems.**

Watch for Active Versus Inactive Sessions

Frequently, when observing a particular user session, the DBA will notice some SQL that seems to be running continuously. This can happen, for instance, if the session is blocked, or if the SQL statement is badly tuned, and is really running the entire time. A blocked session can occur if one session tries to update a particular row that a different session is in the process of changing. The session waiting will be **blocked**, and the other session will be the **blocker**. Of course, blocking in a production application can be catastrophic, and will certainly lead to many complaints about a slow system. The point is, the session being blocked will be shown as *active*.

Typically, on a large OLTP system, the vast majority of sessions are inactive – that is, they are not really "doing" anything. The user is still connected to the database, but no queries are being run at present.

A large number of inactive users is very reasonable for many types of applications, because the end users on these systems often spend most of their time talking to the customers, rather than waiting for database queries to finish. Queries on these systems almost always finish in just a second or so. Thus, on a well-designed OLTP system, it is not uncommon for 95% of all sessions to be "inactive".

Now we have finished verifying that a problem does in fact exist, let's move on to quantifying it.

Quantify the Problem

Assuming that the Oracle Detective has successfully confirmed that there is a performance problem, we are now ready to dig deeper, and assign some numbers to it. In other words, we enhance the problem statement to specify the actual performance impact – typically in terms of the time that the users are being delayed.

For example, a problem statement that starts as "Accounting report run too slow" might be enhanced to say, "Accounting report takes 97 minutes to complete." With this extra information, the analyst can clearly see the magnitude of the problem – in this case, it is really serious!

Quantifying the problem is critical, and helps us in these ways:

❏   Numbers, (such as time) indicate the actual severity of the problem.

❏   Numbers associated with the **was condition** (that is, the state in which we found the problem - or the **baseline**) will be used later to illustrate any improvement in performance. Without knowing the was condition, how do you know how much improvement you have made, and whether *enough* improvement has been accomplished?

❏   Numbers give us a feel for how much effort should be expended.

Sometimes, after the problem has been quantified, there is a consensus that the whole issue is simply not worth the time. In other words, the problem may be deemed so trivial that no further action is warranted. For instance, if a problem SQL statement only requires a small fraction of a second to execute, it is not clear that anyone should spend time working to speed it up. (Of course, if that SQL statement is executed millions of times, then the effort should certainly be expended.)

Frequently, however, the quantification step reveals that the problem is even worse than expected. In either case, once the quantitative data is gathered, the performance expert will know the true magnitude of the problem, and can plan his effort accordingly.

Questions to Ask

When quantifying the problem, there are several key areas to investigate. Some questions that the Oracle Detective should consider include:

❏   What is the elapsed time of the query?

❏   What is the CPU time consumed?

❏   How many disk reads are performed?

❏   How many logical reads are performed?

❏   How many times was the SQL statement executed?

❏   Is there a large network transfer? (Note that with multi-tier applications, there can be *multiple* network transfers.)

❏   Does the application use database links? If so, what other database is involved?

❏   Is there any other server activity? If so, what and when?

❏   Are there other processes blocking the job?

There are several ways to obtain statistics, such as elapsed time, CPU time, disk I/O, logical I/O, and number of executions.

Methods

We have already discussed using the V$SQL view to provide this type information, but there are also some more sophisticated techniques for gathering clues and quantifying the performance degradation. These methods require a little more work, but are often well worth the effort. A few of the best methods include:

- ❑ Activating SQL_TRACE
- ❑ Using TKPROF to report the statistics traced
- ❑ Wait event analysis (using wait event dynamic views)

We discuss the first two methods in this chapter. The last method, wait event analysis, is so important that the next chapter is reserved entirely for discussing it.

Generating Trace Files

A very powerful tool for the Oracle Detective is the SQL_TRACE feature. With SQL_TRACE turned on, it is possible to capture the step-by-step database activity of either one session, or the entire database. It is very simple to start, and the clues it provides are extremely valuable. Remember, however, to turn off tracing when you are done, or you might find that it starts to slow down the performance of your database!

SQL_TRACE can be used to help debug many issues, including the following:

- ❑ An application performs a SQL query upon startup. This query is not working as expected. The DBA needs to know exactly what that query is.

- ❑ An application encounters some sort of error, but no one knows what the problem is. For example, an error that occurs because a database table cannot be found will appear in the trace file. By looking at the SQL statement just executed, you can easily isolate the problem.

- ❑ Certain triggers appear to fire, but no one knows what is causing the firing. (A trigger is a PL/SQL routine that is set to activate when activity, such as an INSERT, or UPDATE, occurs on a specified table.)

- ❑ A data load seems to "get stuck" at some step, but it is not clear exactly where.

This leads us onto our next hint, which is as follows:

> **SQL tracing is a very powerful tool for finding out exactly what an application is doing.**

How do I Start the Trace?

The DBA has two choices for starting a trace; either trace a particular session, or trace the entire database instance. Both have their uses, and it is important to understand clearly how to activate each method.

If tracing is desired for the entire database, simply change one `init.ora` parameter, then restart the database:

```
SQL_TRACE = True
```

Tracing all database activity, though performed occasionally, is actually not the typical use of SQL_TRACE. The main reason for this is that the amount of information generated is huge, and the DBA may spend a considerable amount of time wading through it to find what he wants. On UNIX systems, even the daemon processes, such as pmon and smon, will be traced! In other words, only a very small amount of the information will probably be useful; most will just get in the way. Thus, the trace feature for the entire database should be used infrequently; the performance degradation will be significant, and there will be the further nuisance of large trace files.

In some cases, however, tracing the entire database is appropriate. For example, suppose that a certain part of a program needs to be analyzed; ideally, only the active session would be traced, but the program design is such that each user is only briefly connected to the database. This makes it nearly impossible to trace just a single session. Without changing the application, how could just one session be traced?

Session Level Tracing

A much more common use of SQL_TRACE is to trace just a single session. The traced session can be your own, or that of a different user. For your own session, simply issue the following command in SQL*Plus:

```
ALTER SESSION SET Sql_Trace = True;
```

Similarly, to disable tracing for your own session, simply issue this command:

```
ALTER SESSION SET Sql_Trace = False;
```

However, you might ask how an application could issue the above statements. The answer is, it probably cannot, without actually changing the application code. Rarely do applications have convenient SQL*Plus sessions running in which anyone can add new SQL*Plus commands. There are exceptions, of course, but this tactic is frequently not possible.

This brings us to the most useful way to invoke SQL_TRACE; tracing a particular database session – one that is not your own.

In order to activate tracing for another session, it is first necessary to obtain the SID and Serial# for that session. This is easily retrieved from the V$SESSION dynamic view (see Appendix A for a definition of this view's columns). Once these two parameters are known, the following command is issued:

```
SQL> EXECUTE SYS.dbms_system.set_sql_trace_in_session (SID, -
  2  Serial#, True);
```

Tracing is turned off in a similar fashion:

```
SQL> EXECUTE SYS.dbms_system.set_sql_trace_in_session (SID, -
  2  Serial#, False);
```

Note that some versions of Oracle seem unable to re-activate SQL_TRACE for an on-going session, once Trace has been turned off. A simple workaround is to have the user disconnect, then re-initiate a new session.

Where is the Trace File?

When SQL_TRACE is activated for a session, Oracle will create a trace file in the udump admin area. Remember that the file will not really exist until the trace is actually activated. Note that this destination is specified by an init.ora parameter, USER_DUMP_DEST. Typically, this entry will look like this:

```
USER_DUMP_DEST = /u01/app/oracle/admin/testdb/udump
```

When trace is enabled, all database operations will be written to the trace file in the directory specified. The file is not overwritten by each operation; instead, entries for each new operation are appended to the trace file. For very long tracing operations, keep in mind that the file size will be limited by the init.ora parameter Max_Dump_File_Size.

Note that this directory is typically not the same directory as the one used for the Oracle background processes. Those processes use the bdump directory, as specified by the init.ora parameter, BACKGROUND_DUMP_DEST. Thus, there should be no mix-up or intermingling of these files, as long as different locations are specified for the respective parameters in the init.ora file.

It is sometimes convenient to perform a simple SQL query to make sure that tracing is really on; any valid SQL statement is fine. As soon as the SQL is run, the trace file will be visible in the udump directory. In the event that there are other files already in that directory, look for the file with the most recent time stamp. The file name will look a little odd; on UNIX systems, the name of the trace file will include the operating system PID of the server process writing the trace file.

It is sometimes useful to place certain statements, or **flags**, in the trace file. This is easily accomplished when the trace process is initially activated. For example, suppose that a data warehouse process is being debugged. The analyst wishes to mark the trace file by including a note about the module that is being analyzed. This is accomplished with the following command from SQL*Plus, where Data Warehouse module 1 should be replaced by the flag text you wish to use:

```
ALTER SESSION /* Data Warehouse module 1 */
SET Sql_Trace = TRUE;
```

If many different trace files are being generated, this will assist the analyst in identifying which trace is which:

> **Use a SQL hint to place flags in the SQL trace file**

Timing Information

To obtain the maximum benefit from the trace files (and subsequent interpretation by TKPROF), the timing flag should be turned on. By default, timing is turned off, which means that useful information will be unavailable. Thus, it is good practice to activate timing by including the following `init.ora` parameter:

```
Timed_Statistics = True
```

It is common practice to keep timed statistics on for the entire database; there is really no reason to turn the timing off, since the performance load is very slight. Most DBAs activate timing statistics for their production databases:

> **Keep TIMED_STATISTICS turned on for databases that may need performance analysis.**

Should timing not be active for the database as a whole, it is simple to activate dynamically. For an individual session, timing is easily enabled with the following:

```
ALTER SESSION SET Timed_Statistics = True;
```

For the database as a whole, statistics may be activated with the following command:

```
ALTER SYSTEM SET Timed_Statistics = True;
```

To turn off statistics, a similar command is issued simply by substituting `True` with `False`.

`TIMED_STATISTICS` only produces very slight performance degradation; the benefit far outweighs the cost.

Permissions and File Sizes

UNIX systems have a restriction on reading the trace file. On most systems, the operating system user must be in the `dba` group in order to be able to read the trace files. In most cases, this is not an issue, since the DBA is typically the only one examining trace files. If necessary, however, this restriction is easily loosened using the following entry in the `init.ora` file:

```
_trace_files_public = True
```

115

Another consideration is the size of the trace files. It is possible to restrain the total size of trace files in the udump directory by limiting the maximum size of any one trace file. This is accomplished by using another init.ora parameter, MAX_DUMP_FILE_SIZE. The units of this parameter are 512 bytes. If you are running an extensive trace session, it may be necessary to increase the value of this parameter.

For example, to limit each trace file to 5 MB, the following entry would be specified in the init.ora file:

```
max_dump_file_size = 10240
```

On UNIX systems, this file size limit can also be dynamically altered, by using the oradebug facility to remove the file size restriction.

> oradebug is a utility that is used infrequently to perform a few odd chores. For instance, it can perform tasks like setting tracing levels for debugging, or listing the shared memory segments in use on a UNIX server. Note that oradebug may become less important as Oracle more fully incorporates its features into commonly used tools.

To view all the oradebug commands, simply enter oradebug help from svrmgrl or SQL*Plus.

With Oradebug, it is first necessary to find the Oracle PID for the process responsible for the trace file. This is accomplished by querying the dynamic view, V$PROCESS (a definition of this view's columns can be found in Appendix A). For instance, assume that PID number 1000 is writing to a trace file that is nearing its maximum size. Knowing the PID value, we can remove the size restriction by using the following SQL*Plus syntax:

```
CONNECT / AS Sysdba
ORADEBUG SETORAPID 1000
ORADEBUG UNLIMIT
```

That about wraps it up for permissions and file sizes; let's move on to look at TKPROF.

TKPROF

Now that we have explored how to create SQL trace files, we need to discuss how to read them. This brings us onto TKPROF – one of the oldest (and most useful) utilities that the Oracle Corporation has designed. TKPROF stands for Transient Kernel Profiler (now you know why everyone just calls it TKPROF). It is a proven, mature tool that thousands of DBAs and designers have relied upon for many years. This utility has the added advantage of also being very simple to use.

The purpose of TKPROF is to read SQL trace files and format the contents for easier reading and analysis. A tool such as TKPROF is indispensable, because trace files are very cryptic and, therefore difficult to understand. Although theoretically possible, very few DBAs actually spend their time reading the raw SQL trace files.

Starting TKPROF

TKPROF is a command line utility that is very easy to activate. Here is how you start it:

```
TKPROF <trace file> <output file> [EXPLAIN=<username/password>]
[SYS=n] \ [INSERT=<filename>] [RECORD=<filename>]
[SORT=<keyword>]
```

Although this syntax looks very complicated, it does show all the possible options. Typically, however, only a few options and keywords are used, so the actual command typed will generally be much shorter. For example, with no options selected, the command syntax is simply:

```
TKPROF <trace file> <output file>
```

To interpret the trace file, file1.trc, and produce a report, OUTFILE, the following command would be issued at the command prompt or UNIX shell:

```
TKPROF file1.trc OUTFILE
```

This form of activation is very simple and will not provide any execution plans, but the report may still be useful to the analyst. If nothing else, the report will include the SQL statements that were executed.

A more useful way to use TKPROF is to ask the utility to provide the execution plan for the SQL statements that are in the trace file. This is accomplished by using the special word, EXPLAIN, followed by a database username and password. Thus, continuing with our sample raw trace file called file1.trc, we can generate a report showing the execution plan with the following syntax:

```
TKPROF file1.trc OUTFILE EXPLAIN=chris/gold
```

With this command, TKPROF will rapidly determine the execution plan for the SQL statements in file file1.trc, and include these plans and associated statistics in the output report file, OUTFILE. It is important to use the same username as the session that was traced. Thus, in our example, the username and password for the Chris account is provided so that the execution plans may be determined.

It is sometimes difficult to remember the exact syntax for all the various TKPROF options and keywords. To activate the help screen and list them, simply enter TKPROF by itself.

Overview of TKPROF Report

A typical TKPROF report is shown below. As you can see, the first part of each report will include some preliminary information, such as TKPROF version, the date and time the report was generated, the name of the trace file, the sort option used, and a brief definition of the column headings in the report:

```
TKPROF: Release 8.1.6.1.0 - Production on Wed Aug 9 19:06:36
2000

(c) Copyright 1999 Oracle Corporation.  All rights reserved.

Trace file: example.trc
Sort options: default
********************************************************************
count    = number of times OCI procedure was executed
cpu      = cpu time in seconds executing
elapsed  = elapsed time in seconds executing
disk     = number of physical reads of buffers from disk
query    = number of buffers gotten for consistent read
current  = number of buffers gotten in current mode (usually
                                                     for update)
rows     = number of rows processed by the fetch or execute
                                                           call
********************************************************************

ALTER SESSION /* TKPROF example */ SET sql_trace = True

call       count     cpu   elapsed   disk  query  current  rows
-------   -------  ------ --------- ------ ------ -------- -----
Parse          0    0.00      0.00      0      0        0     0
Execute        1    0.00      0.00      0      0        0     0
Fetch          0    0.00      0.00      0      0        0     0
-------   -------  ------ --------- ------ ------ -------- -----
total          1    0.00      0.00      0      0        0     0

Misses in library cache during parse: 0
Misses in library cache during execute: 1
Optimizer goal: CHOOSE
Parsing user id: 34  (RSCHRAG)
********************************************************************

ALTER SESSION SET timed_statistics = True

call       count     cpu   elapsed   disk  query  current  rows
-------   -------  ------ --------- ------ ------ -------- -----
Parse          1    0.00      0.00      0      0        0     0
Execute        1    0.00      0.00      0      0        0     0
Fetch          0    0.00      0.00      0      0        0     0
-------   -------  ------ --------- ------ ------ -------- -----
total          2    0.00      0.00      0      0        0     0

Misses in library cache during parse: 1
Optimizer goal: CHOOSE
Parsing user id: 34  (RSCHRAG)
********************************************************************

SELECT a.customer_name, a.customer_number,
       b.invoice_number, b.invoice_type, b.invoice_date,
       b.total_amount, c.line_number, c.part_number,
       c.quantity, c.unit_cost
FROM   customers a, invoices b, invoice_items c
```

```
WHERE   c.invoice_id = :b1
AND     c.line_number = :b2
AND     b.invoice_id = c.invoice_id
AND     a.customer_id = b.customer_id
```

call	count	cpu	elapsed	disk	query	current	rows
Parse	1	0.05	0.02	0	0	0	0
Execute	1	0.00	0.00	0	0	0	0
Fetch	2	0.00	0.00	8	8	0	1
total	4	0.05	0.02	8	8	0	1

```
Misses in library cache during parse: 1
Optimizer goal: CHOOSE
Parsing user id: 34  (RSCHRAG)
```

```
Rows    Row Source Operation
-------  --------------------------------------------------------
      1  NESTED LOOPS
      1   NESTED LOOPS
      1    TABLE ACCESS BY INDEX ROWID INVOICE_ITEMS
      1     INDEX UNIQUE SCAN (object id 21892)
      1    TABLE ACCESS BY INDEX ROWID INVOICES
      1     INDEX UNIQUE SCAN (object id 21889)
      1   TABLE ACCESS BY INDEX ROWID CUSTOMERS
      1    INDEX UNIQUE SCAN (object id 21887)
```

```
Rows    Execution Plan
-------  --------------------------------------------------------
      0  SELECT STATEMENT   GOAL: CHOOSE
      1   NESTED LOOPS
      1    NESTED LOOPS
      1     TABLE ACCESS   GOAL: ANALYZED (BY INDEX ROWID) OF
               'INVOICE_ITEMS'
      1       INDEX   GOAL: ANALYZED (UNIQUE SCAN) OF
                 'INVOICE_ITEMS_PK' (UNIQUE)
      1     TABLE ACCESS   GOAL: ANALYZED (BY INDEX ROWID) OF
               'INVOICES'
      1       INDEX   GOAL: ANALYZED (UNIQUE SCAN) OF
                 'INVOICES_PK' (UNIQUE)
      1     TABLE ACCESS   GOAL: ANALYZED (BY INDEX ROWID) OF
               'CUSTOMERS'
      1       INDEX   GOAL: ANALYZED (UNIQUE SCAN) OF
                 'CUSTOMERS_PK' (UNIQUE)
```

```
*************************************************************
```

```
ALTER SESSION SET sql_trace = False
```

call	count	cpu	elapsed	disk	query	current	rows
Parse	1	0.00	0.00	0	0	0	0
Execute	1	0.00	0.00	0	0	0	0
Fetch	0	0.00	0.00	0	0	0	0

```
   -------  -------  ------  ---------  ------  ------  --------  -----
   total        2   0.00       0.00        0       0         0      0

   Misses in library cache during parse: 1
   Optimizer goal: CHOOSE
   Parsing user id: 34   (RSCHRAG)

   ****************************************************************

   OVERALL TOTALS FOR ALL NON-RECURSIVE STATEMENTS

   call       count    cpu    elapsed   disk  query  current  rows
   -------  -------  ------  ---------  ------  ------  --------  -----
   Parse        3   0.05       0.02        0       0         0      0
   Execute      4   0.00       0.00        0       0         0      0
   Fetch        2   0.00       0.00        8       8         0      1
   -------  -------  ------  ---------  ------  ------  --------  -----
   total        9   0.05       0.02        8       8         0      1

   Misses in library cache during parse: 3
   Misses in library cache during execute: 1

   OVERALL TOTALS FOR ALL RECURSIVE STATEMENTS

   call       count    cpu    elapsed   disk  query  current  rows
   -------  -------  ------  ---------  ------  ------  --------  -----
   Parse       24   0.02       0.04        1       0         1      0
   Execute     62   0.01       0.05        0       0         0      0
   Fetch      126   0.02       0.02        6     198         0    100
   -------  -------  ------  ---------  ------  ------  --------  -----
   total      212   0.05       0.11        7     198         1    100

   Misses in library cache during parse: 11

        4   user  SQL statements in session.
       24   internal SQL statements in session.
       28   SQL statements in session.
        1   statement EXPLAINed in this session.
   ****************************************************************
   Trace file: example.trc
   Trace file compatibility: 8.00.04
   Sort options: default

        1   session in tracefile.
        4   user  SQL statements in trace file.
       24   internal SQL statements in trace file.
       28   SQL statements in trace file.
       15   unique SQL statements in trace file.
        1   SQL statements EXPLAINed using schema:
            RSCHRAG.prof$plan_table
              Default table was used.
              Table was created.
              Table was dropped.
      381   lines in trace file.
```

In addition the report shows an entry for each unique SQL statement that was executed while tracing was active. Besides the actual SQL statement executed, it also lists statistics showing values for parsing, execution, and fetching (that is, the actual retrieving of data blocks needed) for each SQL statement. In this sample report, notice that the very first SQL statement listed is the actual statement to activate tracing:

```
ALTER SESSION /* TKPROF example */ SET sql_trace = True
```

Note also that very similar SQL statements (if there are any) will show up as separate entries. When bind variables are used, however, only one entry will be shown (with multiple executions of the same SQL statement noted).

Asterisks separate the SQL statements in the TKPROF report; thus, we can see that the next SQL statement issued was:

```
ALTER SESSION SET timed_statistics = True
```

In addition to SQL statements that are generated by applications, there will also be entries for "recursive operations" run by the database engine for housekeeping tasks, such as management of the data dictionary. At the end of each report are summary statistics – both for non-recursive, and recursive statements.

TKPROF Report Examples

The great power of TKPROF, and an understanding of the statistics, can be seen best by looking at a short excerpt of a TKPROF report. Consider the excerpt shown below:

```
*******************************************************************

SELECT    table_name
FROM      user_tables
ORDER BY  table_name

call       count     cpu    elapsed    disk   query  current   rows
-------   -------   ------  ---------  ------  ------  --------  -----
Parse          1    0.01       0.02       0       0         0      0
Execute        1    0.00       0.00       0       0         0      0
Fetch         14    0.59       0.99       0   33633         0    194
-------   -------   ------  ---------  ------  ------  --------  -----
total         16    0.60       1.01       0   33633         0    194

Misses in library cache during parse: 1
Optimizer goal: CHOOSE
Parsing user id: RSCHRAG
```

As mentioned previously, a row of asterisks indicates a new SQL entry. In this case, the TKPROF entry was produced for the following SQL statement executed from SQL*Plus:

```
SELECT table_name
FROM user_tables
ORDER BY table_name;
```

Looking at the statistics below the SQL statement, we see the actual count for some key database operations; there was one parse operation, which required 0.01 CPU seconds and 0.02 elapsed seconds:

```
call       count    cpu    elapsed  disk  query  current  rows
-------    -------  ------  -------- ----- ------ -------- -----
Parse          1    0.01      0.02     0      0        0     0
```

The columns at the right indicate that there were 0 physical disk I/Os and 0 buffer gets required. In other words, all information required to parse this statement must have already been in the dictionary cache in the SGA.

The next line in the report shows that there was one Execute operation:

```
Execute        1    0.00      0.00     0      0        0     0
```

The time to accomplish this is less than the threshold of 0.01 seconds, thus the value of 0.00 is shown in both the cpu and elapsed columns. Of course, this SQL statement did not really run instantaneously; rather, the database engine is deferring the work until the first row is fetched.

The next line, Fetch, shows where most of the work took place:

```
Fetch         14    0.59      0.99     0  33633        0   194
```

This entry indicates that there were 14 fetch calls, retrieving a total of 194 rows, and consuming a total of 0.59 CPU seconds and 0.99 seconds of elapsed time. There were no physical disk I/Os performed during these operations, but 33,633 buffers were fetched in consistent mode (consistent gets). This implies that there were 33,633 hits in the buffer cache and no misses.

Since the SQL in this example was run from SQL*Plus, we can surmise that SQL*Plus must use some type of "array interface" to fetch multiple rows on one fetch call. That is, although 194 rows were fetched, there were not 194 fetches (just 14).

The last few lines in this report provide some other useful information:

```
Misses in library cache during parse: 1
Optimizer goal: CHOOSE
Parsing user id: RSCHRAG
```

There was one miss in the library cache, which means that the SQL statement was not already in the shared pool. The optimizer mode was set to CHOOSE, and the operations took place in the RSCHRAG schema.

The next example shows the remaining statistical information that can appear in a TKPROF report:

```
      Rows  Row Source Operation
   -------  ---------------------------------------------------------
       194  SORT ORDER BY
       194   NESTED LOOPS
       195    NESTED LOOPS OUTER
       195     NESTED LOOPS OUTER
       195      NESTED LOOPS
     11146       TABLE ACCESS BY INDEX ROWID OBJ$
     11146        INDEX RANGE SCAN (object id 34)
     11339       TABLE ACCESS CLUSTER TAB$
     12665        INDEX UNIQUE SCAN (object id 3)
        33       INDEX UNIQUE SCAN (object id 33)
       193      TABLE ACCESS CLUSTER SEG$
       387       INDEX UNIQUE SCAN (object id 9)
       194     TABLE ACCESS CLUSTER TS$
       388      INDEX UNIQUE SCAN (object id 7)


      Rows  Execution Plan
   -------  ---------------------------------------------------------
         0  SELECT STATEMENT    GOAL: CHOOSE
       194   SORT (ORDER BY)
       194    NESTED LOOPS
       195     NESTED LOOPS (OUTER)
       195      NESTED LOOPS (OUTER)
       195       NESTED LOOPS
     11146        TABLE ACCESS (BY INDEX ROWID) OF 'OBJ$'
     11146         INDEX (RANGE SCAN) OF 'I_OBJ2' (UNIQUE)
     11339        TABLE ACCESS (CLUSTER) OF 'TAB$'
     12665         INDEX (UNIQUE SCAN) OF 'I_OBJ#' (NON-UNIQUE)
        33        INDEX (UNIQUE SCAN) OF 'I_OBJ1' (UNIQUE)
       193       TABLE ACCESS (CLUSTER) OF 'SEG$'
       387        INDEX (UNIQUE SCAN) OF 'I_FILE#_BLOCK#'
                    (NON-UNIQUE)
       194      TABLE ACCESS (CLUSTER) OF 'TS$'
       388       INDEX (UNIQUE SCAN) OF 'I_TS#' (NON-UNIQUE)
```

When TKPROF is executed with the EXPLAIN keyword, execution plan information will also be listed in the report – as shown here. First, however, there is a set of data called a Row Source Operation listing; this is very similar to an execution plan, but not the real thing. The real execution plan follows.

The execution plan provided in the TKPROF report conveys the same information as is available via the EXPLAIN PLAN statement and the autotrace SQL*Plus feature. However, there is one major difference; the TKPROF version shows the actual count of rows processed. Of course, this makes sense because the TKPROF report is counting actual operations performed during the trace interval.

We can see in our example report the exact work the database engine had to perform. This information may also prove valuable, depending on the exact performance problem:

❑   11,146 range scans were performed against the i_obj2 index.

❑   11,146 accesses on the obj$ table.

❑   12,665 non-unique lookups on the i_obj# index.

❑   11,339 accesses on the tab$ table, and so on.

123

Recursion

Some TKPROF reports will have an additional entry for recursive depth. In the previous example there was no entry, meaning that the SQL statements were executed without recursion. When recursion is involved, the report will show the recursion depth next to the parsing user.

There are several ways in which recursion occurs: data dictionary operations, use of database triggers, and use of stored procedures. For instance, suppose a SQL statement needs an object that is not already in the dictionary cache; a recursive query will be performed to fetch the object definition into the dictionary cache. Another type of recursive action would also be required to perform space allocation for a dictionary-managed tablespace.

Database triggers and stored procedures can also cause recursion. When a trigger fires, the subsequent statements will run at a recursion depth of one. If the trigger in turn calls a stored procedure, the recursion depth could increase to 2. This could continue through any number of levels, as we can see in the figure below.

In the figure, there is a trigger (set to fire on INSERTs) on table Emp. When a user inserts rows into this table, the trigger fires. The trigger in turn calls a stored procedure, which calls a stored procedure, and so on. In this illustration, we see that the recursive depth advances all the way to 4:

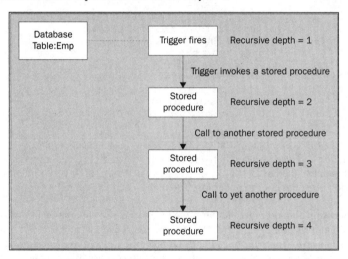

Further Useful Features

Let's take a quick look at some of the other useful TKPROF features that you might want to use.

sys

When invoking TKPROF, there is a special option that can be used to reduce the complexity of the output report. In particular, the activity generated by the sys user can be excluded from the output report if the following clause is used:

```
SYS=n
```

The n simply means "No, I don't want to see the activity from the sys user". In most cases, this option will speed up the analysis, because the report file will be much smaller, and restricted to application-specific activity only.

sort

Another useful keyword is SORT; this option causes the report to list SQL statements in order of resource consumption. sort options include sorting by CPU time fetching and CPU time parsing.

insert

With this keyword, TKPROF will create a script to populate a useful table called tkprof_table. One row will be inserted in this table for each SQL statement displayed in the report. Each row will contain the text of the SQL statement traced, plus all the statistics displayed in the report.

In other words, the insert keyword causes all TKPROF statistics to be transferred into the database! This could be useful for analysis of very complicated scenarios in which the DBA needs to analyze and manipulate the statistics.

record

With this keyword, TKPROF will generate another type of SQL list in addition to the regular report. This SQL script will contain a copy of each SQL statement that was run by the application while tracing was enabled. The same information is already available in the TKPROF report itself, but this feature might reduce the logistics of cutting and pasting.

TKPROF with MTS

Tracing a database session on an instance with Multi-Threaded Server (MTS) is a complicated affair, because each different server process may create a separate trace file for its particular set of operations. In order to perform analysis on the traced events it will, therefore, be necessary to read multiple trace files to get the full picture of how the application interacted with the database.

Furthermore, if multiple sessions are being traced at once, it will be hard to tell which operations in the trace file belong to which session. For these reasons, we should use dedicated server mode when tracing a database session with SQL_TRACE:

> **If possible, avoid MTS when activating SQL_TRACE.**

Now we have finished running through the features of the very useful TKPROF, let's return to our Oracle Detective steps and take a look at our last major topic in this chapter.

Note any Unusual Complications

Finally, the Oracle Detective should note any unusual features or setup that might be relevant to the performance bottleneck. The presence of these unusual features doesn't mean that they are necessarily *causing* the performance problem – only that you should be aware of their impact.

For instance, the analyst would certainly want to take note of any connections to a heterogeneous database, such as DB2 or Sybase. Other questions that might be asked include:

- ❏ Is the transparent gateway being used?
- ❏ Is MTS active?
- ❏ Is Oracle Names being used?
- ❏ Are there any peculiar `init.ora` parameters in use?
- ❏ Is the database using an extreme value for block size?
- ❏ Are bit-map indexes being used?
- ❏ For a data warehouse, is Star Transformation enabled? (Star transformation is a sophisticated type of join that Oracle may use when working with very large tables; this feature is discussed in detail in Chapter 9.)

Obviously there are hundreds, if not thousands, of special circumstances that can apply. There is no way to list all possibilities; therefore, the performance analyst needs to be thorough in "digging up" all the relevant facts. The Oracle Detective need not conclusively determine that factors such as those listed above are causing the performance degradation; rather, these facts should simply be noted at this time.

Summary

In this chapter, we have introduced the reader to the Oracle Detective, and explored some ways that the Detective conducts his investigation. Starting in this chapter, the Oracle specialist's job becomes more nearly science, as opposed to art. The Oracle Detective is interested in facts – not speculation.

In this stage, the detective is trying to:

- ❏ Confirm the problem.
- ❏ Quantify the problem.
- ❏ Note any unusual complications.

Before trying to quantify any performance problem, the performance analyst should confirm that the problem even exists. Many so-called performance problems are not problems at all, but rather misunderstandings based on incomplete information. The wise performance analyst will take a few minutes to confirm the problem before starting an investigation that could be time-consuming.

The Oracle Detective should be careful to check the "easy" things first. This includes investigating such things as the database logs, space on the file system, and maximum number of processes. By performing these basic checks first, many easily solved problems can be fixed rapidly. These simple steps also save much wasted time.

The analyst also needs to be aware of the usefulness of application run logs, if they exist. These logs frequently contain clues as to what ails the application or the database.

One of the most useful ways to confirm and quantify a problem is via the V$SQL view. This view contains all recently run SQL statements, along with statistics that show resource consumption; thus it allows the analyst to spot most poorly performing SQL statements. Queries can be based on finding SQL that exceed a threshold of many disk reads per execution, or even the cumulative amount of I/O for all executions. It is also possible to uncover poorly designed SQL statements that are not using bind variables.

We also presented an overview of other powerful resources available to the tuning specialist. SQL_TRACE is a useful way to find out what an application is doing. Since the SQL trace output file is difficult to interpret, tracing is usually used in conjunction with another powerful utility – TKPROF. This tool provides a wealth of information to the performance analyst, such as execution plans, list of SQL executed, CPU statistics, disk and logical I/O, and so on.

Finally, we concluded this chapter with a recommendation that the performance analyst be alert for any unusual complications that might be impacting database performance.

In the next few chapters, we will discuss many other ways that the Oracle Detective can gather clues. We will build upon our introduction to SQL_TRACE and TKPROF as we explore ways to detect and solve a wide variety of Oracle performance problems. More specifically, the next chapter will go on to explore using wait events as a method of collecting more information.

- What Are You Waiting For?

- Types of Wait Events

- An Overview of the Views

- Tracing Using System Event 10046

- Examples of Using the Wait Event Facility

- Important Caveats

6

Gathering More Clues

Now that we have introduced the Oracle Detective, and discussed his charter, we are ready to discuss some more of the most important tools in his detective's kit. As a reminder, let's recall where we are in the *Physician-to-Magician* approach: the problem has been clearly defined by the Oracle Physician, and we are in the *investigation* phase. The Oracle Detective is busily gathering clues at this point:

Physician	Detective	Pathologist	Artist	Magician
Define problem	Investigate	Isolate cause	Create solution	Implement

As part of the investigation, the Oracle Detective needs to use the best techniques available. Although there is a variety of performance tuning utilities and tools available, there is actually a simpler (and cheaper) solution that many senior DBAs have adopted. In recent times, more and more DBAs are beginning to use the **wait events** facility for investigating performance problems. These dynamic views contain information on what the database is waiting for.

This entire chapter is devoted to explaining how to use the wait events facility. It has the following structure, with the emphasis on practical application through examples and case studies:

❑ The concept of **waiting** and how it can be used to solve performance problems.

❑ Different types of wait events for an Oracle database.

❑ The four database views that show wait events, and how to use each view.

❑ How to use the special parameters that show more information for each wait event.

❑ How to use a special tracing mode, **event 10046**, to find out more information.

❑ Case studies that illustrate the use of these wait event techniques in the every-day work of DBAs.

❑ Some caveats and restrictions – what the wait facility *cannot* do.

Although there is other documentation on the wait event views (such as that provided by Oracle itself), practical instruction and examples are rare. In this chapter, we discuss in detail the *practical use* of these views. We present numerous examples, and real-life case studies of how this powerful facility can be used to solve perplexing performance problems.

What Are You Waiting For?

Consider for a moment what the performance analyst is trying to do; he or she is trying to find out *what is taking so long*. Well, let's consider what can make a task take a long time. First of all, we need to recognize that the total time for a task to complete consists of two components: the time spent **waiting**, plus the time actually spent **servicing** (that is, really doing) the task. Suppose for instance, that you have taken your car to be serviced. The mechanic works on your car for a while, and then decides that he needs to order a part. This will mean a delay, as he waits for the part to be delivered. Once he gets the part, he resumes his work, and (hopefully) completes the job. The total time for the task to complete consists of the mechanic's actual effort plus the time he spent waiting for the part.

In the database world, we can examine both aspects—*waiting* and *doing*. In this chapter, however, we will be looking especially at the *waiting* aspect. If the user is waiting for the database, why not find out what the database is waiting for? If we knew what was delaying the database, then perhaps we could do something about it.

Suppose, for instance, the performance analyst knew for a fact that the Oracle engine was spending an inordinate amount of time reading one block at a time from disk. That information would be extremely valuable in helping resolve a performance complaint. In this scenario, the DBA would certainly want to understand why the reads were only single-block, as opposed to multi-block.

The investigator might reason, for example, that an absence of multi-block reads could be an indication that the init.ora parameter controlling multi-block reads has been set improperly. Thus, he would immediately check the value of the parameter, DB_FILE_MULTIBLOCK_READ_COUNT. He might also want to verify that the server and disk systems can actually perform the assumed number of multi-block reads.

Similarly, suppose the DBA knew *for a fact* that the Oracle engine was waiting for completion of a transfer of a large amount of data over SQL*Net. The astute performance analyst would immediately question why this large transfer was occurring. He might wonder if the user had mistakenly requested a huge data set, or if there were some flaw in the application that encouraged such a transfer.

The wait event facility allows the DBA to ascertain precisely this sort of information. A systematic approach based on wait events is a far more effective process than simply looking at cache hit ratios, or other similar statistics.

The analyst who truly understands Oracle architecture will be in a far better position to realize the full benefit of the wait event facility. For instance, if you understand what a particular wait event is, and why it could be causing a delay, then you will be in an excellent position to do something about resolving it. In pursuit of that end, we cover some of the most important wait events in this chapter.

Types of Wait Events

In an Oracle database, each process is either actively doing something, or waiting for something to happen. The whole philosophy of the wait method of performance analysis is to determine what Oracle is waiting for, and decide if any of the detected wait events can be eliminated

Here are some ideas of what the database engine could be waiting for. Any one of these could potentially lead to a performance bottleneck:

- ❑ Writing to disk
- ❑ Reading from disk
- ❑ SQL*Net traffic to and from the client
- ❑ Writing to the control file (the .ctl file)
- ❑ Reading from the control file
- ❑ Writing to the redo log file
- ❑ Locks and latches
- ❑ Waiting for space in the log buffer

Unfortunately, the analyst cannot simply focus on the *worst* wait events, because many wait events are *normal*. Over the course of a day, it is usual for the database engine to wait many times, for a variety of reasons. Most of these waits are expected, and neither the DBA nor the end users will even be aware of these delays.

For example, it is very common for the database to wait for a user to supply input. This situation is especially true for OLTP (Online Transaction Processing) applications. While the database is waiting for the user, a certain wait event will accrue wait time. Oracle calls this particular event SQL*Net message from client. Naturally, large values for this wait event do *not* indicate a performance problem, but merely a normal state of operation.

Normal and Abnormal Wait Events

The trick, then, is to find out which of the wait events is *not* normal. This is a bit of a challenge, since many of the longest wait times that are detected will actually be irrelevant, or pertain to options that are not being used. There are some guidelines, however, that can help the performance analyst. There is a particular group of events (known as **idle events**) that can be ignored for most databases; this group is listed overleaf:

We will see one example later, however, in which a "normal" wait didn't turn out to be so normal! Be careful not to ignore these events blindly.

client message	PX Idle Wait
dispatcher timer	rdbms ipc message
lock manager wait for remote message	smon timer
Null event	SQL*Net message from client
parallel query dequeue	SQL*Net message to client
pipe get	SQL*Net more data from client
PL/SQL lock timer	virtual circuit status
pmon timer	wakeup time manager

Some experience with the wait views will be needed before the analyst begins to get a feel for which information is critical and which wait events on his particular system can safely be disregarded. Wait events will clearly depend on exactly which application that is being used; so for each database, the normal wait events might be a little different. The examples provided later in this chapter will help get you started:

> **Become familiar with the wait events that are normal and abnormal in your particular environment.**

On the other hand, certain events are very important and should generally not be disregarded. These events indicate preventable performance delays; thus, they will prove useful to the Oracle Detective as he investigates performance bottlenecks.

The following table includes these most pertinent wait events:

Wait Event	Description
enqueue	The process is waiting on an enqueue*. This commonly occurs when one user is trying to update a row in a table that is currently being updated by another user.
library cache pin	The process wants to pin an object in memory in the library cache for examination, ensuring no other processes can update the object at the same time. This happens when you are compiling or parsing a PL/SQL object or a view.
library cache load lock	The process is waiting for the opportunity to load an object or a piece of an object into the library cache. (Only one process can load an object or a piece of an object at a time.)

Wait Event	Description
latch free	The process is waiting for a latch** held by another process. (This wait event does not apply to processes that are spinning while waiting for a latch; when a process is spinning, it is not waiting.)
buffer busy waits	The process wants to access a data block that is currently not in memory, but another process has already issued an I/O request to read the block into memory. (The process is waiting for the other process to finish bringing the block into memory.)
control file sequential read	The process is waiting for blocks to be read from a control file.
control file parallel write	The process has issued multiple I/O requests in parallel to write blocks to all control files, and is waiting for all the writes to complete.
log buffer space	The process is waiting for space to become available in the log buffer. (Space becomes available only after LGWR has written the current contents of the log buffer to disk.) This typically happens when applications generate redo faster than LGWR can write it to disk.
log file sequential read	The process is waiting for blocks to be read from the online redo log into memory. This primarily occurs at instance startup and when the ARCH process archives have filled online redo logs.
log file parallel write	The process is waiting for blocks to be written to all online redo log members in one group. LGWR is typically the only process to see this wait event. It will wait until all blocks have been written to all members.
log file sync	The process is waiting for LGWR to finish flushing the log buffer to disk. This occurs when a user commits a transaction. (A transaction is not considered committed until all the redo to recover the transaction has been successfully written to disk.)

Table continued on following page

Wait Event	Description
db file scattered read	The process has issued an I/O request to read a series of contiguous blocks from a data file into the buffer cache, and is waiting for the operation to complete. This typically happens during a full table scan or full index scan.
db file sequential read	The process has issued an I/O request to read one block from a data file into the buffer cache, and is waiting for the operation to complete. This typically happens during an index lookup or a fetch from a table by row id when the required data block is not already in memory. Do not be misled by the confusing name of this wait event!
db file parallel read	The process has issued multiple I/O requests in parallel to read blocks from data files into memory, and is waiting for all requests to complete. The documentation says this wait event occurs only during recovery, but in fact it also occurs during regular activity when a process batches many single-block I/O requests together and issues them in parallel. (In spite of the name, you will not see this wait event during parallel query or parallel DML. In those cases wait events with PX in their names occur instead.)
db file parallel write	The process, typically DBWR, has issued multiple I/O requests in parallel to write dirty blocks from the buffer cache to disk, and is waiting for all requests to complete.
direct path read, direct path write	The process has issued asynchronous I/O requests that bypass the buffer cache, and is waiting for them to complete. These wait events typically involve sort segments.

An enqueue is a sophisticated type of locking feature that Oracle uses to protect internal objects (such as the V$ views). The processes needing access to a certain object are called waiters. They are given a place in line, or queue, hence the name enqueue. The enqueue locking structure makes use of the operating system lock manager; and allows sharing of resources, depending on the type of access that is requested.

** In contrast to enqueues, the `latch` locking mechanism grants access to only one process, and does not put waiters in an ordered queue; instead, the requesting process waits a brief time ("spins"), and then again requests access. If access is still denied, the process "sleeps" a short while, and then retries.

The wait views, which hold information about the wait events, indicate what activity is holding up the processing, but they don't show *why*. That is, the wait views are not really an end point, but a good starting point. Once some clues are identified, the analyst will usually need to look at other areas to help identify the underlying cause of the delay.

For instance, if the wait views indicate that the Oracle engine is waiting for disk I/O, the analyst will probably want to find out which SQL statement is responsible for that activity. Thus, he will probably decide to query the V$SQL view, which will show the exact SQL that has been run. In fact, querying the V$SQL view will be a subsequent step in many cases. Just as the wait event indicates the area of delay, the V$SQL view identifies the actual SQL statement that is responsible for the delay.

Timed Statistics

When preparing to use the wait facility, note that the `init.ora` parameter TIMED_STATISTICS should be set to True; otherwise, no timing information will be available in the wait views. If queries from any of the wait views always return 0 for the wait times, then it is likely that this parameter has inadvertently been set to False. Recall that, generally speaking, it is perfectly fine to leave TIMED_STATISTICS set to True; there is only a very slight performance impact.

This parameter can also be dynamically changed, as we saw in the previous chapter, using the command:

```
Alter System Set TIMED_STATISTICS = TRUE;
```

Turning statistics off is similar:

```
ALTER SYSTEM SET Timed_Statistics = False;
```

An Overview of the Views

Wait information is contained in a set of four views – three of which are dynamic, and one static. Dynamic views contain rows that can change from one moment to the next; static views are really more "lookup" views, their information does not change. These views record exactly what the database is waiting for, and how long it has been waiting. In fact, the only difficulty with using the wait views is that there is *too much* information!

Admittedly, some, if not all, of the information in the wait views is also available in other tables or views in the data dictionary. The performance analyst might wonder, then, why this facility is so valuable. The advantage of the wait views is that all information is nicely bundled together for easy access.

135

The four wait views are summarized in the following table. These views are accessible to DBAs, or other database users who have been granted the system privilege SELECT ANY TABLE or the role SELECT_CATALOG:

View	Description
V$EVENT_NAME	List of all wait events and definition of the associated parameters, P1-P3.
V$SYSTEM_EVENT	List of all wait event statistics for the entire instance.
V$SESSION_EVENT	List of all wait event statistics, grouped by SID.
V$SESSION_WAIT	Detailed information on the current wait event for a session. (If none, statistics are for the most recent wait event.)

Note that the column definitions for each of these views are given in Appendix A of this book.

Note also that the Oracle documentation provides a nice set of reference information on the wait views. See the Database Reference *Release 2 (9.2), Appendix A at* http://otn.oracle.com/. *Topics covered in that appendix include: Displaying Wait Events, Wait Events and Parameters, Parameter Descriptions, and Wait Event Descriptions.*

V$EVENT_NAME

The simplest view, V$EVENT_NAME, is really a static "look-up" table. It simply defines all the possible wait events for the particular version of Oracle being used. This is very important information, because each Oracle version has hundreds of wait events.

In this view, each event listed has an associated NAME and EVENT#. Additionally, for each event, there are fields that identify up to three parameters for each event (PARAMETER1, PARAMETER2, and PARAMETER3). These three parameters contain extra information about the event. Often, this additional information is very useful in determining what is causing the wait event in question.

For example, one wait event is called db file scattered read. This is "Oracle lingo" for a multi-block read – that is, a read that retrieves more than one block at a time. (This is a common operation for full table scans.) For this event, Oracle provides information further defining the multi-block read. The three parameters for this event are:

Field	Value	Definition
PARAMETER1	file#	What file number is being read
PARAMETER2	block#	Where the multi-block read starts
PARAMETER3	blocks	How many blocks have been read

V$SYSTEM_EVENT

The V$SYSTEM_EVENT view is the highest-level view; it contains cumulative wait statistics for all events for the entire instance. The numbers listed in this view are fairly simple in principle; for each wait event, it shows how many times a process had to wait, how many times the process gave up, plus the average and cumulative wait times. Note that wait times are shown in centiseconds – or hundredths of a second.

A few simple examples will be helpful in illustrating how the V$SYSTEM_EVENT view can be used.

Example: Waiting for Multi-block Reads

On a production database experiencing performance problems, suppose the DBA suspects there may be an issue with multi-block reads. Therefore, he wishes to obtain the cumulative wait time for all processes that have waited for multi-block reads.

The event in question is called a **scattered read** by the Oracle engine. Thus, the analyst could use the following SQL to find the total time waited for this event since the instance started:

```
SQL> SELECT Event, Time_Waited
  2  FROM V$SYSTEM_EVENT
  3  WHERE Event = 'db file scattered read';

EVENT                        TIME_WAITED
---------------------------  ------------
db file scattered read            357122
```

Remembering that the times listed are in *centiseconds*, this result tells us that the total time waited has been 3571.22 seconds, or slightly less than one hour.

Example: Waiting for the Redo Log Buffer?

Let's build on this example; we have already done some investigation, but we need to gather more information before we can go any further. Suppose there is some performance problem related to extremely high transaction rates. The users are complaining of an annoying 10 second delay for some apparently simple steps in the application.

The DBA for this system suspects that the high transaction rate is causing some problem with free redo log buffers; this could happen, for example, if the redo log buffers cannot be written to disk quickly enough. The DBA wants to confirm these suspicions. There is a wait event called log buffer space that will help him here. Relatively high values for this event would indicate that the Oracle engine is being impeded by a lack of fresh space in the log buffer.

The following SQL could be used to find the statistics related to this wait event. In this example, we will list the total time waited, and average time waited due to this event:

```
SQL> SELECT Event, Time_Waited, Average_Wait
  2  FROM V$SYSTEM_EVENT
  3  WHERE Event = 'log buffer space';

EVENT                   TIME_WAITED     AVERAGE_WAIT
------------------      -------------   ----------------
log buffer space            1477                   92
```

This result tells us that only about 15 seconds (14.77) of delay is due to problems with log buffer space. The average wait was .92 seconds, or less than 1 second. Recall that the users have already informed us that the problem is a *10* second delay. Apparently, then, we must be mistaken in our theory about redo log buffers. Clearly, an average delay of 1 second cannot possibly be responsible for the delay that the users see. This Oracle Detective must look elsewhere for his root cause.

> *Remember that the values read from the V$SYSTEM_EVENT view are for the entire span of time since the instance was started.*

V$SESSION_EVENT

The V$SESSION_EVENT is very similar to the V$SYSTEM_EVENT view. As its name implies, this view contains statistics for recent wait events, grouped by *sessions*. The statistics provided are identical to the V$SYSTEM_EVENT view – but correlated by session. As with the other view, statistics will be indicated in **centiseconds**, or hundredths of a second.

In typical use, the DBA will first determine the SID for the suspect session from the V$SESSION view (remember, there is a definition for the columns in this view in Appendix A, if you need to refer back). Then, this value is used to restrict the query from the V$SESSION_EVENT table, so that information from irrelevant sessions can be filtered out. Alternatively, the V$SESSION view can be joined directly to the V$SESSION_EVENT view.

> *Note that V$SESSION is not one of the four wait views; however, it is sometimes helpful to use this view in conjunction with the others.*

It is important to remember that this view only provides statistics for sessions that are currently active; in other words, once the session is gone, so are the statistics!

Example: Which User is Experiencing Long Waits?

Suppose that the performance DBA suspects that there is a problem with excessive SQL*Net traffic from the database to the client. This could happen, for instance, if a report user is constantly requesting a large dump from the database, thus producing a bottleneck on the network.

In this example, we will assume that we don't know which session is the culprit; therefore, we would like to list the statistics for all sessions having any significant network traffic. (Remember again that the statistics will only be available if the user is *still connected*.)

To retrieve this information, we will simply join the V$SESSION view to the V$SESSION_EVENT view, and list the wait statistics for all sessions (still connected) in which the total wait time exceeds 100 seconds (or 10000 centiseconds):

```
SQL> SELECT V.Sid, Username, Time_Waited, Average_Wait
  2  FROM V$SESSION_EVENT V, V$SESSION S
  3  WHERE Event = 'SQL*Net message to client'
  4  AND V.SID = S.SID
  5  AND Time_Waited > 10000
  6  ORDER BY Time_Waited DESC;

 SID Username      TIME_WAITED      AVERAGE_WAIT
 ---- -----------  -------------    ------------------
  19 Acctg              942120            104390
  21 Jim                 43964               599
  23 Chris               11034              9032
```

The result reveals that the user, Acctg has been experiencing very long waits. The total time waited for SQL*Net messages going from the database to the client is 9421.20 seconds, or about 157 minutes. On average, this user has had to wait 1043.90 seconds for each SQL*Net transfer to complete.

Of course, since we are just seeing waits for users still connected to the database, there could have been even longer waits for other users who have since disconnected. The V$SESSION_EVENT view will no longer have information about those users.

So far, we have seen that the V$SYSTEM_EVENT and V$SESSION_EVENT views can provide useful summary information on possible bottlenecks. V$SYSTEM_EVENT is probably most useful to query first to discover extraordinary wait events for the database as a whole. Then, the DBA can "drill-down" in V$SESSION_EVENT to try to find suspicious waits to a particular session.

Notwithstanding the great usefulness of both these views, none of the views discussed thus far provide any specifics on any one particular wait. That is, they provide overall, cumulative information, but aren't really helpful in examining a *specific occasion* in which a wait event is being triggered. That information is contained in the last wait view that we will discuss, V$SESSION_WAIT.

V$SESSION_WAIT

Fortunately for the Oracle Detective, instantaneous information is readily available in the V$SESSION_WAIT view. This view provides detailed information on exactly what a particular session is waiting for at that moment. It reveals specifics on the current event – or just-completed wait if there are no current waits. Clearly, this view is quite a bit different from the other views, and must be used in a slightly different way. Once again, this view is only useful for currently connected sessions.

V$SESSION_WAIT contains wait information grouped by SID, just like the V$SESSION_EVENT view; however, much more information is available here. For each SID, detailed information is provided for the exact event that is currently "holding up" the user.

The fields in this view are more cryptic than in the other wait views; for example, the field STATE is a bit tricky. This field shows whether the respective session is currently waiting, or not. Depending on the value of STATE, we can determine either how long the process has been waiting, or the total time waited for the most recent wait event just completed for that session:

STATE	Value	Definition
Waiting	Session is waiting	See time in SECONDS_IN_WAIT
Waited Known Time	Session not waiting	See time in WAIT_TIME
Waited Unknown Time	Session not waiting	Wait time not available
Waited Short Time	Session not waiting	Wait time not available

This means that in order to find the wait time, we must actually use *different columns*, depending on the definition of STATE. Thus, for a session currently waiting, the column SECONDS_IN_WAIT should be used. For a completed wait event, the field WAIT_TIME is used. If the value of STATE is either Waited Unknown Time, or Waited Short Time, then the value for WAIT_TIME has no meaning. Unfortunately, to add to this confusion, the field SECONDS_IN_WAIT uses *seconds*, not centiseconds, as the unit of measurement.

> *Note that the above definitions are also available in the official Oracle documentation. For Oracle 9i, see the Database Reference Release 2 (9.2), Appendix A.*

Timing information for completed wait events will only be available if TIMED_STATISTICS is set to True, and the actual wait time is above the minimum threshold of .01 seconds. If TIMED_STATISTICS is not activated, column STATE will indicate Waited Unknown Time. If the wait event is less than one centisecond, column STATE will show Waited Short Time.

Interpreting the Parameter Fields for V$SESSION_WAIT

If you review the fields in V$SESSION_WAIT, it might at first appear that many of them are for some arcane, internal use. This is actually not the case; some of these "cryptic" parameters are in fact the most valuable! Even though the cryptic *names* are not especially meaningful to most of us, the *content* certainly is.

The fields P1, P2, and P3 contain the values for three *parameters* that are associated with a specific wait event; the parameters provide more detailed information about the wait event. The parameter *names* are provided in the respective fields P1TEXT, P2TEXT, and P3TEXT.

Using these parameters is not as difficult as it might seem at first; their value is best illustrated through an example.

Example: Which File and Block are Being Read?

Assume that we are investigating performance problems with a production database. We have narrowed the investigation to one particular user (SID=19), and one type of wait event. The wait event of interest corresponds to a *multi-block read*. We are interested in finding out as much information about this multi-block read as possible. We would especially like to find out which file and blocks are being read.

Using our three parameters (P1-P3), a simple query can find out exactly which file and block number were involved. First, however, let's confirm that the completed wait event was indeed a wait due to multi-block reads.

Since we are interested in a completed wait event, we will be looking at column WAIT_TIME (not SECONDS_IN_WAIT, which is for ongoing waits). To confirm that the completed wait event was for multi-block reads, we query the V$SESSION_WAIT view and retrieve column EVENT, which describes the wait event:

```
SQL> SELECT Event, Wait_Time
  2  FROM V$SESSION_WAIT
  3  WHERE SID = 19;

EVENT                           WAIT_TIME
------------------------------  ---------

db file scattered read                 21
```

The results of this query tell us that the most recent wait event for session 19 was indeed for a multi-block read. The session waited .21 seconds for the multi-block read to complete.

Now, let's find out some more information on this event; specifically, let's find out exactly which file and block were involved. To do that, we will need to fetch the P1-P3 parameter columns. To help us relate the values to the definition, we will also retrieve the P1-P3 TEXT columns. Our query now looks like this:

```
SQL> SELECT P1Text, P1, P2Text, P2, P3Text, P3
  2  FROM V$SESSION_WAIT
  3  WHERE SID = 19;

P1TEXT    P1 P2TEXT       P2 P3TEXT       P3
-------  ---- ---------  ----- ---------  ----
file#      17 block#      2102 blocks       32
```

141

Note that this query assumes that the most recent event has not changed. When in doubt, also include the field EVENT in the query, just to be sure.

The results of this query tell us that the multi-block read was for file number 17 (see P1), starting at block number 2102 (see P2). A total of 32 blocks were read (see P3).

Upon seeing these results, a good performance specialist would recall that the number of blocks read at a time is limited by the value of the init.ora DB_FILE_MULTI_BLOCK_READ_COUNT parameter. In our example, this had been set to 32. This limitation is reflected in the P3 parameter, which indeed shows that a total of 32 blocks were read at one time.

The great value of the P1-P3 parameters is obvious; if the DBA needed to know the exact name of file #17, that data could easily be retrieved from the view DBA_DATA_FILES.

Let's take a look now at one of the most interesting uses of the wait event facility. We will see another good use of those mysterious P1 through P3 parameters we've been talking about.

Tracing Using System Event 10046

We come now to a very special way to use wait events. Recall that a particular session, or even the entire database, can be traced. A typical use of tracing involves setting the init.ora parameter SQL_TRACE = True, then restarting the database. All activity is then written to a trace dump file that is stored in the udump admin directory. Alternatively, a more selective (and helpful) use of the trace facility requires the DBA to execute a special Sys package, and activate tracing on one specific session, as follows:

```
EXECUTE Sys.Dbms_System.Set_Sql_Trace_In_Session (SID, -Serial#,
True);
```

Besides these "normal" ways to use tracing, there is also a "special" trace mechanism, which is even more helpful when working with wait events. This is called **event 10046**. Trace files written using this event have very special characteristics, in that they show much more detailed information. In particular, they can show the value of bind variables and the special P1-P3 parameters associated with wait events.

Event 10046 is a **system event**. These are most commonly used for debugging an unusual database problem. When a system trace event is set, a trace file is created, which can then by reviewed by the DBA, or submitted to Oracle support for analysis. For example, a trace event could be used to trace the database activity at the time of some database internal error.

Here are the various levels that are used with event 10046:

System Event Setting	Effect
10046 trace name context forever, level 1	Uses standard SQL_TRACE (default).
10046 trace name context forever, level 4	Enables SQL_TRACE with bind variable values included in trace file.
10046 trace name context forever, level 8	Enables SQL_TRACE with wait event information included in trace file.
10046 trace name context forever, level 12	Equivalent to level 4 and level 8 together. Enables SQL_TRACE with bind variable values and wait event information included in trace file.

As shown, display of the wait event parameters requires that level 8 be set. Thus, to set event 10046 for your *own* session the following syntax would be required:

```
SQL> ALTER SESSION SET events '10046 trace name context
  2  forever, level 8';
```

Just like setting a trace for another session, it is similarly possible to set Event 10046 for another session, using the Sys procedure Set_Ev. Interestingly, Oracle Corporation likes to hide this method of activating event 10046; they claim that it was really designed for "internal use." Nevertheless, the Oracle support analysts (for example, on Metalink) will provide clues on its use.

It is first necessary to obtain the SID and Serial# from V$SESSION. With this information, Event 10046 tracing can be activated using the syntax:

```
Exec Sys.Dbms_System.Set_Ev (SID, Serial#, 10046, level, '');
```

Note that the last argument is two single quotes.

For example, to activate trace event 10046 at level 8 for a database user having SID = 23 and Serial# = 44, we would run the following command from SQL*Plus:

```
SQL> EXEC Sys.Dbms_System.Set_Ev (23, 44, 10046, 8, '');
```

To deactivate tracing, simply repeat the call, and set level 0, like this:

```
SQL> EXEC Sys.Dbms_System.Set_Ev (23, 44, 10046, 0, '');
```

Here is a sample trace file that was created via event 10046 :

```
PARSING IN CURSOR #1 len=80 dep=0 uid=502 oct=3 lid=502
tim=2293771931 hv=2293373707 ad='511dca20'
SELECT /*+ FULL */ SUM (LENGTH(notes))
FROM   customer_calls
WHERE status = :x
PARSING IN CURSOR #1 len=80 dep=0 uid=502 oct=3 lid=502
tim=2293771931 hv=2293373707 ad='511dca20'
SELECT /*+ FULL */ SUM (LENGTH(notes))
FROM   customer_calls
WHERE   status = :x
END OF STMT
PARSE #1:c=0,e=0,p=0,cr=0,cu=0,mis=1,r=0,dep=0,og=0,tim=2293771931
BINDS #1:
   bind 0: dty=2 mxl=22(22) mal=00 scl=00 pre=00 oacflg=03 oacfl2=0
   size=24 offset=0
      bfp=09717724 bln=22 avl=02 flg=05
      value=43
EXEC #1:c=0,e=0,p=0,cr=0,cu=0,mis=0,r=0,dep=0,og=4,tim=2293771931
WAIT #1: nam='SQL*Net message to client' ela= 0 p1=675562835 p2=1 p3=0
WAIT #1: nam='db file scattered read' ela= 3 p1=17 p2=923 p3=8
WAIT #1: nam='db file scattered read' ela= 1 p1=17 p2=931 p3=8
WAIT #1: nam='db file scattered read' ela= 2 p1=17 p2=939 3=8
WAIT #1: nam='db file sequential read' ela= 0 p1=17 p2=947 p3=1
WAIT #1: nam='db file scattered read' ela= 3 p1=17 p2=1657 p3=8
WAIT #1: nam='db file scattered read' ela= 1 p1=17 p2=1665 p3=8
WAIT #1: nam='db file scattered read' ela= 2 p1=17 p2=1673 p3=8
WAIT #1: nam='db file scattered read' ela= 0 p1=17 p2=1681 p3=8
WAIT #1: nam='db file scattered read' ela= 3 p1=17 p2=1761 p3=8
WAIT #1: nam='db file scattered read' ela= 1 p1=17 p2=1769 p3=8
WAIT #1: nam='db file scattered read' ela= 1 p1=17 p2=1777 p3=8
```

As we can see, near the top of the trace file, tracing was activated while the SQL statement below was being run:

```
SELECT /*+ FULL */ SUM (LENGTH(notes))
FROM   customer_calls
WHERE status = :x
```

Note that we have successfully retrieved the various parameters for wait events. At the lines beginning with the phrase, WAIT #1, the values for the parameters P1, P2, and P3 are all shown. (The labels p1 – p3 will be shown in lowercase.):

```
WAIT #1: nam='SQL*Net message to client' ela= 0 p1=675562835 p2=1 p3=0
WAIT #1: nam='db file scattered read' ela= 3 p1=17 p2=923 p3=8
WAIT #1: nam='db file scattered read' ela= 1 p1=17 p2=931 p3=8
...
```

Notice also that many of the waits are for scattered reads. Recall that for scattered reads, the following parameters apply:

❑   P1: file number

❑   P2: block number

❑   P3: number of blocks read

Of course, if we had forgotten what the parameters meant, we could have simply queried the view V$EVENT_NAME to list the definitions of each parameter for this wait event.

In the sample trace file, we see that the reads were from file number 17 (because p1=17), and that the typical read was for eight blocks at a time (p3=8). The fact that the read was never larger than eight blocks at a time suggests that the database instance could have had DB_FILE_MULTIBLOCK_READ_COUNT set to 8, or possibly that eight blocks was the maximum read size possible for this particular server.

When setting this special level of trace using event 10046, remember there is definitely a price to pay for this extreme level of detail. Since one line of text is printed for each wait event, there is clearly some drag on the database. Therefore, be sure to use this event sparingly, and terminate the trace activity when all necessary information has been gathered:

> **Use Event 10046 sparingly, as performance will be degraded while this event is active.**

Examples of Using the Wait Event Facility

We now present four real-life case studies that illustrate the practical use of the wait event facility. In each case, the wait event facility played a pivotal role in tracking down the root cause of the performance problem. The "culprit" in each case is completely different, exemplifying the versatility of this approach:

Case Study: Caught in the Web

An application that relied on dynamic web pages was experiencing performance problems. Without too much trouble, the DBA was able to isolate the problem to a particular instance of SQL code. The code was really quite simple, and was of the form:

```
SELECT COUNT (*)
FROM    Customer_Inquiries
WHERE   Status_code = :b1
AND     Status_date > :b2;
```

The developer had suggested to the DBA that his database had "some sort of problem". He based this conclusion on the fact that an index was available, thus the query should be using the index to run quickly. He assumed that index usage implies fast response.

Upon investigation, the DBA confirmed that an index was in fact being used. Using the EXPLAIN PLAN command, the DBA was able to obtain a listing of the execution plan for the query:

```
Execution Plan
-----------------------------------------------------------
0    SELECT STATEMENT Optimizer=CHOOSE
1  0   SORT (AGGREGATE)
2  1     TABLE ACCESS (BY INDEX ROWID) OF 'CUSTOMER_INQUIRIES'
3  2       INDEX (RANGE SCAN) OF 'CUSTOMER_INQ' (NON-UNIQUE)
```

As shown above, the Oracle optimizer is indeed using an index. This index, CUSTOMER_INQ is actually a concatenated index (having more than one column). Here, however, this should not be a particular problem, because the leading column is the STATUS_CODE field. Since the leading column in the index matches the WHERE clause field, the index is available to this query. (The second column defined in the index is unrelated to the query.)

While technically a better index choice might be an index *without* the second, superfluous column, this slight detail should not have caused a significant performance lag. (The STATUS_DATE column was not indexed; this portion of the SQL code was not an issue in this example.)

The DBA decided to use the wait event facility to gather relevant details on the problem. He asked the user to repeat the problem function, but this time to stay connected to the database so that the wait information would not be deleted.

After running the problem query, the V$SESSION_EVENT view contained the following data for the session in question:

EVENT	TOTAL_WAITS	TIME_WAITED
db file scattered read	15	3
db file sequential read	6209	140
latch free	2	1
SQL*Net message to client	8	0
SQL*Net message from client	7	21285

The DBA thought that a few things looked odd about these numbers; in particular, why was there such a large number of sequential reads (6209 non multi-block reads)? Since he knew definitely, via the EXPLAIN PLAN output, that an index was being used, he reasoned that these reads must correspond to index lookups. If a full table scan had been performed, many of the reads should have been *multi*-block reads.

Although there was a huge number of sequential reads, there was other data that confused the issue and seemed contradictory. In particular, the query result above shows that the total time waited was only 1.4 seconds. This seems puzzling. How could the large number of reads be a problem if the total wait was only 1.4 seconds? Surely a wait of 1.4 seconds is not a significant issue.

Being suspicious of the large number of reads, the DBA decided to dig deeper; he wanted to know how many rows actually fulfilled the Status_Code condition (Status_code = :b1). Thus, he asked the developers what value was typically used for the bind variables in the WHERE clause.

If there was any confusion about the actual values, the bind variables could have been identified using event 10046, at level 4.

The DBA discovered that the SQL WHERE clause actually eliminated almost no rows! The optimizer, badly fooled (because of the very odd distribution of data), was using an index to find all table entries where the Status_Code was set to 12. Unfortunately, *almost all the rows* had a Status_Code of 12! The Oracle engine thus had to fetch repeatedly and process about 90% of the rows in the table – obviously a very poor optimization technique. In fact, the optimizer was using the worst execution plan possible!

The DBA in this example recommended a very minor change to the SQL code so that the index would *not* be used. The developers were given two options here; a SQL hint could be added to the SQL code to force a full table scan or, alternatively, the WHERE clause in the statement could be changed to "nullify the index". (Both of these ideas are discussed in a later chapter; the main point here is that the index usage needed to be stopped.)

After the application change, the problem statement was re-run, yielding a vastly changed set of wait statistics:

```
EVENT                          TOTAL_WAITS    TIME_WAITED
----------------------------   ------------   ------------
db file scattered read                 460             13
db file sequential read                  3              1
latch free                               1              0
SQL*Net message to client               10              0
SQL*Net message from client              9          18317
```

Note the very large reduction in sequential reads – from 6209 to 3! This change confirmed that the ineffective index lookup was successfully eliminated. Since a full table scan was now being used, there was also an increase in scattered reads from 15 to 460, which is exactly what we would expect for this new execution plan.

This case illustrates a real trap that analysts can fall into, and reminds us of an important point to remember about wait events; wait event statistics do not include CPU time consumed, or time spent *waiting* for the CPU to become free. Here, the fact that the total wait time was 1.4 seconds said nothing about how long the CPU actually worked! Remember our earlier illustration of the auto mechanic; the time to service the car included time waiting for the part plus time doing the *actual work* – you would be misled if you only considered the time waiting for the part.

Of course, the mere fact that the actual CPU run-time is unknown does not constitute proof that there is a major bottleneck with the CPU. Nevertheless, the DBA in this case thought that the large number of sequential reads was odd, and believed that it suggested a need for further investigation.

Our next case study illustrates a completely different performance problem. This case shows how using trace events can also help with locking problems:

A production support group became alarmed when nightly batch processing significantly degraded after a new data source was added to the job. The developer group, not being familiar with the Physician-to-Magician approach to performance tuning, decided to bolt on more hardware and, thus, they added more CPUs to the server. (Recall that this is one of the primary Silver Bullet approaches that rarely works.) Not surprisingly, this change did little to improve the run-time.

The DBA, on the other hand, understood the importance of gathering facts about a performance problem before proposing a solution. As a result, he decided to use the V$SYSTEM_EVENT view in order to take a quick glance at the overall system. He used a simple script to display the wait event activity for the instance over a 30 second time interval:

```
CREATE TABLE previous_events
AS
SELECT SYSDATE timestamp, V$SYSTEM_EVENT.*
FROM    V$SYSTEM_EVENT;
EXECUTE dbms_lock.sleep (30);
SELECT   A.event,
         A.total_waits - NVL (B.total_waits, 0) total_waits,
         A.time_waited - NVL (B.time_waited, 0) time_waited
FROM     V$SYSTEM_EVENT A, previous_events B
WHERE    B.event (+) = A.event
ORDER BY A.event;
```

In this script, we first capture all the waits for the entire database to use as a baseline; this is the B table in the join of the second query. Then, 30 seconds later, after the call to the sleep routine, we generate a summary of the waits that accrued *over just the previous 30-second span.*

Note that the this script uses the NVL function; this is necessary to make the arithmetic work properly. If the baseline table does not have any waits for an event, it will not contain a row for that event. To do the subtraction in the second query, however, we need to have *some* entry; hence when we do the subtraction, we use the NVL function to force a zero whenever there is not a row in the baseline (B) table.

In many cases, it is especially helpful to run a script such as this during the problem period. Simply take two separate readings, and then look to see what the Oracle engine was waiting for during the period in question.

This is the same method used by Oracle's utlbstat utility, and other similar tools. Another more sophisticated option is to use Oracle's statspack utility (this is such an excellent utility that we devote most of Chapter 10 to it).

Using his script, the DBA was able to obtain the wait statistics for a 30 second interval:

```
EVENT                              TOTAL_WAITS   TIME_WAITED
--------------------------------   -----------   -----------
LGWR wait for redo copy                    115            41
buffer busy waits                           53            26
control file parallel write                 45            44
control file sequential read                25             0
db file scattered read                     932           107
db file sequential read                  76089          6726
direct path read                           211            19
direct path write                          212            15
enqueue                                     37          5646
file identify                                2             0
file open                                   37             0
free buffer waits                           11           711
latch free                                  52            44
log buffer space                             2             8
log file parallel write                   4388          1047
log file sequential read                   153            91
log file single write                        2             6
log file switch completion                   2            24
write complete waits                         6           517
```

Note that the idle events are not listed, as they are not relevant.

The DBA in this case was familiar with the everyday wait events in his particular environment. (Recall that we mentioned earlier the benefit of being acquainted with your particular setup, so that you can more easily spot unusual wait conditions.) As a result, he was able to note an unusual reading for the enqueue wait event. For the 30-second period that was measured, all processes waiting for enqueues collectively spent a total of 56.46 seconds. More understandable perhaps, was the figure of 67.26 seconds spent waiting for single-block reads to complete (db file sequential read).

As with all wait events, there are the P1-P3 parameters that provide more information about the specific wait event. For the enqueue wait event, the DBA is provided with three pieces of information:

P1RAW: the first two bytes are the ASCII codes of the lock type, and the last two bytes are the requested lock mode

P2: same as ID1 column in the V$LOCK view
P3: same as ID2 column in the V$LOCK view

A definition of the columns in the V$LOCK view is included in Appendix A.

To gather more information, the DBA decided to activate system event 10046, and trace the session while it ran through the problem area. He was especially interested in confirming that some type of lock event was related to the delays.

Thus, the DBA activated event 10046 tracing at level 8. The trace file was automatically generated in the udump destination directory. Since level 8 was selected, this also caused a dump of the wait event information, including the P1, P2, and P3 wait parameters.

The trace file contained the following:

```
EXEC #5:c=0,e=0,p=3,cr=2,cu=1,mis=0,r=1,dep=1,og=4,tim=2313020980
XCTEND rlbk=0, rd_only=0
WAIT #1: nam='write complete waits' ela= 11 p1=3 p2=2 p3=0
WAIT #4: nam='db file sequential read' ela= 4 p1=10 p2=12815 p3=1
WAIT #4: nam='db file sequential read' ela= 1 p1=10 p2=12865 p3=1
WAIT #4: nam='db file sequential read' ela= 5 p1=3 p2=858 p3=1
====================
PARSING IN CURSOR #4 len=65 dep=1 uid=502 oct=6 lid=502
tim=2313021001 hv=417623354 ad='55855844'
UPDATE CUSTOMER_CALLS SET ATTR_3 = :b1 WHERE CUSTOMER_CALL_ID=:b2
END OF STMT
EXEC #4:c=1,e=10,p=3,cr=2,cu=3,mis=0,r=1,dep=1,og=4,tim=2313021001
WAIT #5: nam='db file sequential read' ela= 0 p1=10 p2=5789 p3=1
WAIT #5: nam='enqueue' ela= 307 p1=1415053318 p2=196705 p3=6744
WAIT #5: nam='enqueue' ela= 307 p1=1415053318 p2=196705 p3=6744
WAIT #5: nam='enqueue' ela= 53 p1=1415053318 p2=196705 p3=6744
WAIT #5: nam='db file sequential read' ela= 0 p1=10 p2=586 p3=1
WAIT #5: nam='db file sequential read' ela= 1 p1=3 p2=858 p3=1
EXEC #5:c=0,e=668,p=3,cr=5,cu=3,mis=0,r=1,dep=1,og=4,tim=2313021669
```

On reviewing this report, the DBA observed that there were several enqueue wait events; this seemed to confirm that there was some sort of lock contention occurring. Since the trace file also listed the SQL code run:

UPDATE CUSTOMER_CALLS SET ATTR_3 = :b1 WHERE CUSTOMER_CALL_ID=:b2
the DBA was then able to focus his attention on the exact code being run at the time of the waits.

Knowing the SQL statement involved in the locking turned out to be enough information to diagnose the contention problem and develop a fix. The DBA worked with the developers to redesign the batch programs so that locking time would be extremely brief. This was accomplished by using very brief transactions (called **autonomous transactions**). Using this approach, the locks on critical path rows were held for only extremely short periods of time. As a further preventative measure, the team adjusted the schedules of the programs in the nightly run schedule.

This case study, amongst other things, shows us an important technique that is the subject of our next hint:

> **Take two readings of wait events to isolate the ones that are contributing to performance delays.**

Note that the DBA in this case study could not simply have looked at the dynamic views for locks (such as V$LOCKED_OBJECT) to see which sessions were causing the blocking. This tactic would not have worked because the locking views only contain information during the time that the blocking *actually occurs*. The time of blocking in some cases (like this one) will simply be too brief to use the locking views.

Let's move on to our next case now, which will help us to understand further how the Oracle Detective can use wait events to help find the root cause of a performance problem, and gather clues along the way:

Case Study: Slow Query Without a Query

A client-server application was taking several seconds to bring up a certain form. The users complained constantly, but the developers were confounded. The paradox was that the delay was occurring before the user had even run any query! The only thing occurring during startup was a retrieval of standard reference data.

No one could understand why retrieving reference data should lead to a performance log-jam. The same data was used throughout the application, and it was confirmed that the data blocks were *already* in the buffer cache. This confirmation eliminated the possibility that excessive disk I/O was the cause of the bottleneck. Additionally, all the SQL code associated with this data retrieval had been examined, and was known to run very quickly.

The DBA set up an experiment that made use of wait events. He asked one user to log into the application, but not run any query whatsoever. After the user completed this step, the DBA examined the V$SESSION_EVENT view. She noticed one thing that looked very peculiar; there were almost 20,000 occurrences of the SQL*Net message from client event. The total wait time for this event was 300 seconds.

Normally, this SQL*Net wait event is not an issue – it is typically an idle event that can be safely ignored. A process waits on the SQL*Net message from client event when Oracle has completed a request from a user and is waiting for the next request; so, high wait times for this event are common in front-end applications that spend a lot of time waiting for the user to do something.

As a result, the 300 seconds of wait time in this case did not seem unusual; what did seem odd, however, was the high number of wait *times*. Therefore, the DBA decided to investigate further, focusing on this event.

She asked the developers for their assistance in conducting a very precise experiment. They were asked to modify the application temporarily by turning off timed statistics immediately after the initialization was complete. In this way, the statistics in the V$SESSION_EVENT view would reflect wait times during the form start up phase only.

Running the modified application yielded the following information in the V$SESSION_EVENT view:

```
EVENT                           TOTAL_WAITS   TIME_WAITED
---------------------------     -----------   -----------
SQL*Net message to client             18520             6
SQL*Net message from client           18519          1064
```

This information further confirmed that there was a huge number of waits associated with SQL*Net messages during the form start up. Furthermore, the wait time was over 10 seconds; this exactly corresponded to the delay that was annoying the users. Continuing the investigation, the DBA retrieved some key statistics from V$SESSTAT for the session in question:

```
NAME                            VALUE
---------------------------     ------
session logical reads            9295
CPU used by this session           82
physical reads                      0
```

Note: the V$SESSTAT view contains a wide variety of statistics, grouped by the particular session involved.

This data suggested that the database engine was using almost one second (0.82 seconds) of CPU time to perform 9,295 logical reads of data blocks. As the DBA had already suspected, there were no disk reads; that is, all the data blocks were already in the buffer cache.

It turned out that there were exactly 9,245 rows of reference data being retrieved each time a user logged in. Retrieving that many rows would not have been disastrous, except that the application code was fetching the data *one row at a time*! To make matters worse, for each row retrieved, there were two network roundtrips. This explained the 18,520 waits for SQL*Net messages.

With the root cause of the problem clearly identified, a correction was not difficult. The application developers modified the program to use Oracle's array processing interface, which allowed the form to fetch 100 rows at a time. This led to a hundred-fold reduction in waits associated with SQL*Net network roundtrips.

With the application modified to fetch 100 rows at a time, the waits and session statistics looked like this:

```
EVENT                           TOTAL_WAITS  TIME_WAITED
---------------------------     -----------  -----------
SQL*Net message to client              200            0
SQL*Net message from client            199           28

NAME                            VALUE
---------------------------     ----------
session logical reads            135
CPU used by this session           3
physical reads                     0
```

The new wait statistics confirmed the huge improvement. As the application was fetching 100 rows at a time, the team was able to improve response time dramatically by reducing network roundtrips – and reduce CPU usage on the database server at the same time.

This case study illustrates how useful the wait event facility can be as a way to focus on the actual bottleneck. In this case, note that the DBA started with the V$SESSION_EVENT view in order to get his first set of clues. From there, he gathered more details, and confirmed the solution using the V$SESSTAT view.

Our next case study begins with a "floundering" database server. In this example, nothing seems to work well—even the simplest of queries. This case study shows the broad range of problems that can be investigated using the wait event facility:

Case Study: The Case of the Floundering Database Server

A small group of DBAs were investigating a database server that seemed completely overwhelmed. For example, simply connecting to the database took a few seconds. A query selecting from SYS.DUAL, that should have run instantly, took more than a second. In short, everything on this system ran very slowly.

A look at V$SYSTEM_EVENT showed the following top wait events:

```
EVENT                            TIME_WAITED
-------------------------------  -----------
SQL*Net message to client            174398
log file parallel write              297297
log file sync                        326284
write complete waits                 402284
control file parallel write          501697
db file scattered read               612671
db file sequential read             2459961
pmon timer                         31839833
smon timer                         31974216
db file parallel write           1353916234
rdbms ipc message                6579264389
latch free                       8161581692
SQL*Net message from client     15517359160
```

At first, some of these entries might seem alarming, due to the very large numbers; note, however, that large numbers for idle events are normal. For instance, as discussed in the previous case, the event SQL*Net message from client usually means that Oracle is simply waiting for the user to do something.

The DBA noticed one event, however, that seemed wrong in the context of his system; the latch free statistic seemed excessive, particularly since the instance had only been running for seven days. He queried the columns PARENT_NAME and LONGHOLD_COUNT in the V$LATCH_MISSES view to gather additional information on a possible latch problem. Here is the query and result:

```
SQL> SELECT PARENT_NAME, SUM (LONGHOLD_COUNT)
  2    FROM V$LATCH_MISSES
  3    GROUP BY PARENT_NAME
  4    ORDER BY SUM (LONGHOLD_COUNT);
PARENT_NAME                      SUM(LONGHOLD_COUNT)
-------------------------------  -------------------
```

```
redo writing                             238
redo allocation                          373
Active checkpoint queue latch            377
mostly latch-free SCN                    458
redo copy                                482
enqueue hash chains                      614
enqueues                                 637
Checkpoint queue latch                   790
session allocation                      1131
messages                                1328
session idle bit                        2106
latch wait list                         5977
modify parameter values                 6242
cache buffers chains                    9876
row cache objects                      38899
cache buffers lru chain               125352
shared pool                          4041451
library cache                        4423229
```

The data suggested that the database was suffering from severe latch contention in the library cache. This prompted the DBA to check if there were an unusual number of unique SQL statements being issued without bind variables, which would explain the statistics.

The library cache houses the recently used SQL statements, so that they can be reused without parsing a SQL statement afresh. If bind variables are not used, these statements in the library cache will continually be turned over, and the benefit lost.

A look at the dynamic view V$SQL confirmed what the DBA had suspected; there were over 36,000 SQL statements in the shared pool, almost all of which had been executed exactly once. Obviously, the application was employing literal values in the SQL statements instead of using bind variables. This was, in turn, causing constant misses in the library cache and a steady churn of SQL statements through the shared SQL area. To make matters worse, the shared pool had been sized overly large at 400 MB.

Setting a massive size for the shared pool is a common, and usually incorrect, reaction to excessive misses in the library cache. If the application does not use bind variables, drastic increases in the shared pool will only make matters worse; it will not be possible to decrease misses, since almost every single SQL statement will be completely different.

Without bind variables, there will be a constant influx of distinct SQL statements that will almost always result in a library cache miss. By increasing the shared pool, there will be *even more* SQL statements for the database engine to search through, and an *even longer* LRU list for Oracle to maintain.

Faced with these issues, the DBA supporting this application could not fix the application quickly, but he was able to do something about the improper sizing of the shared pool. He immediately reduced the shared pool to a more reasonable value (100 MB), which dramatically reduced the effort the database spent managing the library cache. This in turn reduced latch contention, boosting performance in the process.

One might wonder if the reduced shared pool in the above case would cause a reduced library cache hit ratio. This did not happen, because the shared pool was still large enough to hold the few SQL statements that were executed many times.

Now we have seen how useful wait events can be, let's take a look at some of the limitations that the Oracle Detective should be aware of.

Important Caveats

A few caveats concerning wait events are in order; as valuable as the wait event facility is, it will not catch 100% of all performance problems. Just like any other "tool", the performance analyst needs to be aware of the limitations of the method.

Delays not Due to the Database

First of all, it is important to understand that the wait views will only provide clues for *database-specific* performance problems. Of course, this should be obvious, and it hardly seems necessary to mention it; nevertheless, remember that many performance problems will turn out to be completely unrelated to the database. This means that the performance analyst should never be too quick to rule out all possible subsystems that are used in the application.

For instance, consider a situation where users complain about poor performance for a web-based application. Since Oracle is used as the back-end, the database is a natural suspect. (And of course, it really *could* be the culprit, you don't know it isn't until you've found another root cause!) Upon investigation, however, the DBA discovers that the bottleneck is really due to delays spent transferring data from the web server to the client. Oracle fetches this data rapidly, so nothing will look amiss in any of the database views; the wait event views will probably reveal nothing, except for the typical idle events, such as SQL*Net message from client.

CPU Time not Detected

Secondly, and perhaps more importantly, the wait events do not include CPU activity consumed by Oracle – that is, the time that the Oracle engine actually spends working. This is not a bug, but rather a distinction: *working* is not the same thing as *waiting*.

Consider the analogy of a clerk at a supermarket, where there is only one line open. In the clerk's line are twenty customers, impatiently tapping their feet, wondering what is taking so long. The customers are certainly waiting, but what about the clerk? What are the things that he is waiting for? The answer is, the clerk is waiting for nothing! He is going at full speed. There are no "wait events" that could be cleared-away to make him work faster.

In the same way, if the Oracle engine is going full speed, performing complex calculations or other CPU-intensive processing, this activity will not be reflected in the wait views. This is a startling, but critical fact to keep in mind. By neglecting this limitation, many poorly performing SQL statements could easily be overlooked:

> **Remember that the wait views do not include CPU processing time.**

Logical Reads not Detected

Thirdly, note that logical reads will not be indicated as a wait event. This may not seem like a major limitation, but logical reads are frequently a factor in performance optimization. Naturally, the performance analyst will concentrate more on disk I/O; but in some cases, it will be logical, not physical, reads that are the culprit.

One example of a situation requiring many logical reads would be a poorly designed correlated sub-query, in which the inner-query is badly optimized. In this scenario, the same buffers would be used many thousands, or even millions, of times. Clearly, this type of SQL would run badly, but the performance analyst would *miss* the problem by relying exclusively on the wait events facility.

Time Resolution

Lastly, recall that the resolution of event wait times is .01 seconds. It is, therefore, possible that many "housekeeping" events may not ever show any wait time. For instance, the wait time for SQL*Net message to client may often be less than this minimum threshold; this means that the total count of wait events is not totally accurate. Of course, these events are the ones typically ignored anyway, so this limitation is not very serious

Summary

In this chapter, we have explored the powerful capabilities of the wait event facility. By observing unusual wait times, the Oracle performance analyst can discover what the database is "waiting for." Many, but not all, database-related performance problems can be detected using these wait events. When faced with a really tough problem, this facility can provide valuable clues that otherwise might be hard to come by.

We explored, using examples, various ways that the wait events can be used to gather more clues about typical performance problems. In each case, the performance analyst queried one or more views to narrow down his list of culprits to those related to unusually long or frequent wait events.

The great power and versatility of the wait event facility suggests that all serious performance analysts need to be acquainted with it. Without an understanding of how to use these views, the Oracle Detective will be "handcuffed" in his efforts to optimize the performance of Oracle databases.

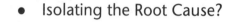

- Isolating the Root Cause?

- Identify Performance Degradation Sources

- Simplify

- Divide and Conquer

- The Timeline Method

- Common Causes of Performance Problems

- Other Practical Suggestions for Finding the Root Cause

7

The Oracle Pathologist

Now that we have identified what the problem is, and have quantified it, we are ready to find the root cause. In order to accomplish this, the tuning specialist takes off the hat of the detective, and dons the hat of the pathologist. As the Oracle pathologist, the tuning specialist will endeavor to find the disease that is the primary cause of the performance problem.

To recap, this is where we are in the Physician-to-Magician approach:

Physician	Detective	Pathologist	Artist	Magician
Define Problem	Investigate	Isolate cause	Create solution	Implement

We are at a critical stage in the performance tuning process, but much good work has already taken place. Results from the previous phases will help the tuning analyst concentrate his attention on the key problem areas.

This phase of the Physician-to-Magician process is somewhat different from the previous stage, in that it is very close to pure analysis – the people side of things has more-or-less been taken care of. In other words, this part of this process is much closer to 100% science. There will still be room for creativity and ingenuity, but this stage emphasizes analytical skills rather than artistry and people skills.

The Oracle Pathologist will strive to find the root cause of the performance problem. The subject of root cause analysis can be very broad; thus, we have devoted four entire chapters to this important topic:

- ❑ Chapter 7: *The Oracle Pathologist*
- ❑ Chapter 8: *Analyzing SQL Bottlenecks*
- ❑ Chapter 9: *Analyzing SQL Joins*
- ❑ Chapter 10: *The Pathologist's Tool Kit*

In this lead off chapter, we first provide an overview of the main tasks of the Oracle Pathologist. We also look at exactly what it means to **isolate a root cause**. In other words, what exactly is the performance analyst trying to accomplish? Understanding the nature of a root cause helps us to understand the true objective of the database pathologist. This in turn leads us to a logical procedure for isolating root causes.

There are several techniques that the analyst can use to pinpoint the root cause. In this chapter, we discuss how to use the following methods:

- ❑ The **simplify** technique
- ❑ The **divide and conquer** technique
- ❑ The **timeline** technique

At the end of the chapter, we also briefly give a few other suggestions for finding the root cause

To help the reader get a general feel for the topic, we also provide a survey of the most common root causes. This will acquaint us with the various possibilities that often turn out to be the culprit.

The Oracle Pathologist has a big job waiting! Let's grab the evidence bag, scrub-up, and get our microscope ready...

Isolating the Root Cause?

The phrase "isolate the root cause" is often used to describe troubleshooting – whether in an Oracle database, user application, or some completely unrelated field. These exact words, or very similar words, are used when describing the effort to resolve a wide variety of problems.

The notion of isolating the root cause appears to fit just about any type of technical problem. We follow the same sort of reasoning, and ask the same type of questions, whether the problem is small or gigantic. The same general approach is suitable for dealing with a car problem or with a national security problem!

The above observation is very convenient for performance troubleshooters, since we can follow the same principles, regardless of the details surrounding the problem. What, then, are these principles and how do we isolate the root cause?

Some Useful Steps to Follow

We are going to begin this section with a hint that will best summarize what we have to do to isolate the root cause of a problem:

> **Isolating the root cause requires the performance analyst to separate the interactions, identify the source, and confirm the effect.**

Let's take a more detailed look at each of the phrases of the above hint.

Separate the Subsystem Interactions

First, then, the analyst must clearly *distinguish* between many possible interactions. This means, for instance, that the tuning specialist should clearly identify and quantify the performance degradation that is due to network issues, as opposed to database-specific problems. It does no one any good to announce that the root cause of a serious performance problem is a slowdown due to network bottleneck combined with poorly optimized SQL statements. Further, statements such as this suggest that the performance analyst has not really completed the job.

The root cause that is ultimately identified will normally not be mixed with others. Of course, there are cases where several flaws contribute to a problem, but the Oracle analyst should be vigilant not to just "lump together" several causes. On rare occasions, a DBA will come across some system that is so badly designed that there are layer upon layer of problems. Fortunately, however, this is not the norm.

Identify the Source

Secondly, along with separating the various potential causes, the analyst needs to clearly identify the cause, or source, of the problem. The previous steps in our approach have provided us with many facts and possible suspects; now the Oracle Pathologist needs to point the finger at the guilty party. Of course, once the various ingredients in the performance puzzle can be distinguished, the job of identifying should be much easier.

As a practical matter, it is helpful for the Oracle expert to clearly announce what that root cause turned out to be. After all, the client usually is curious to know what caused the performance problem. Managers in the firm will naturally want learn how to prevent a reccurrence, and technicians will want to know if they had guessed correctly. You owe it to your client to give them a clear summary of the issue.

Confirm the Effect

Thirdly, the Oracle analyst must confirm that the cause that has already been separated and identified is really the prime cause that has led to the performance problem. What good is it to separate and identify something that turns out *not* to be the prime cause of the problem?

Just like the witness who identifies the wrong suspect, presenting the wrong root cause is disastrous. Management will probably remember that a significant amount of time and money has been expended for no reason! This error can be avoided by remembering to confirm your theory as to what is causing the performance bottleneck.

We can sum up the three components of a root cause in our next hint:

> **The root cause is the identifiable source that has led to observable performance degradation.**

If we grant the notion that the Oracle Pathologist is tasked with finding the root cause, then we have already found a logical way for him or her to proceed. These three ideas – separate the interactions, identify the source, and confirm the effect, suggest a reasonable approach to performing the job of Oracle Pathologist.

Now that we have established a theory for how the Oracle Pathologist should operate, let's look at how this works in practice.

Identify Performance Degradation Sources

The Oracle Pathologist must identify the performance degradation that is caused by each subsystem. Performance problems do not confine themselves to just one subsystem. For instance, there will generally be at least *some* sort of application that accesses the Oracle database over some sort of network. Clearly, Oracle databases cannot achieve anything by themselves; useful programs must be designed to retrieve and format the data in a manner helpful to the users.

Already, then, we have identified three subsystems that will possibly be involved in every performance problem: database, application, and network. In addition, there are often other subsystems involved, such as web servers, application servers, report servers, remote databases and data feeds, and so on. Theoretically, even the client setup can impact performance.

Amazingly, many analysts spend days troubleshooting a performance problem without even bothering to identify which subsystem could conceivably be responsible. Many hours are wasted chasing performance issues on systems that are completely uninvolved! (The old guessing approach strikes again!)

Identify the Real Contributors

Since there will always be multiple subsystems that could theoretically be the cause of a performance problem, it will be necessary to determine which subsystems are contributing in reality to the performance problem that is being analyzed:

> **Identify the approximate performance degradation due to each subsystem.**

Of course, each subsystem will probably add some delay, which is normal. Even a perfectly operating network with massive bandwidth will induce a fraction of a second delay. Usually, such small delays can be safely ignored, but if the performance problem really did result from a sub-second issue, even these miniscule delays would have to be considered.

Putting aside these trivial performance delays, the analyst should look for large, unexpected delays in each candidate subsystem that are roughly the same size as the performance problem. Thus, if the users are complaining of a 10-minute delay, don't waste your time trying to tune SQL code that contributes a total of 10 seconds delay. The 10-second delay might become important later on, but is probably not relevant now:

> **Look for subsystem delays that are of the same order of magnitude as the overall performance problem.**

When small performance problems, such as the above 10-second delay, are found, simply make note of them for future consideration. Although they do not warrant investigation right now, they probably will later. After the hot performance problem is resolved, the focus can shift to correcting even these smaller issues.

Performance Budgets

In aerospace companies that are constructing massive, complicated electronic systems, each subsystem within the machine is often assigned an error budget. This budget represents the subsystem's permissible contribution to the total error of the system as a whole. This is a common way of making sure that the total system error remains within the required specification.

For a radar tracking system, for example, suppose that the end customer has specified that the final tracking error must be no larger than 0.10 degrees. The chief designer might assign the following error budget:

Measurable Entity	Degrees Error, Maximum
Antenna	.004
Calculation error	.003
Optics	.015

The same principle applies to performance tuning; the total response time comprises various contributions from each of the components. Some of the contributions will be negligible, but each subsystem will contribute something to the total delay.

Normally, each subsystem causes slight degradation that is within our expectations. Performance bottlenecks occur when one or more of these subsystems begin to operate outside their error budget. So, when the total error (in our case, the elapsed *run-time*) is not acceptable, then a good first step is to identify the individual error contributors.

Let's look at an example:

Example: Slow Form

Consider a performance problem in an Oracle Forms application. A certain screen seems to delay about 45 seconds when a particular function or form is requested. The user reports that the screen eventually displays correctly, but the delay seems odd. Why should there be such a long delay for a relatively simple form?

163

The Oracle performance analyst, having read the chapter on using SQL_TRACE (Chapter 5), turns on SQL tracing and uncovers the SQL statement that was run for this function. (Alternatively, the application itself may have kept run logs of the SQL statements.)

We observe that the SQL code for this part of the application simply finds the total revenue for each contract that began in the past year:

```
SELECT Contract_Name, C.Contract_Number, SUM (Revenue)
FROM Contract C, Acts_Received A
WHERE C.Contract_Number = A.Contract_Number
AND C.Start_Date > (Sysdate - 365)
GROUP BY Contract_Name, Contract_Number;
```

The subsystems involved in this application include not only the database, but many others as well. There are at least seven subsystems involved, namely:

❑ database
❑ database to application server
❑ application server to web server
❑ web server to client
❑ web server
❑ application server
❑ client web browser

The complete database-network-application system is shown in the following diagram:

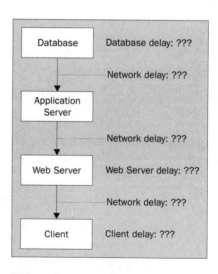

At this point, the analyst cannot (and should not) form any conclusions concerning which subsystem is the source of the problem; the performance bottleneck could originate at *any* of these subsystems. Perhaps the database is responsible for the 45-second delay; on the other hand, any of the network traffic could cause a large delay. Another possibility is that the client's workstation is the real bottleneck.

164

The Oracle analyst can easily assign a number to the delay directly attributable to the database. In our example, assume that the DBA tested the previous query in SQL*Plus. He has modified the original SQL so that the results are placed in another Oracle table, rather than displayed on the screen. This is important so that the elapsed time is not simply a measure of how fast the CRT can display the rows.

To check the database performance for this query, the DBA started SQL*Plus, set TIMING ON, and then ran the following transaction:

```
SQL> CREATE TABLE X UNRECOVERABLE AS
  2  SELECT Contract_Name, Contract_Number, SUM (Revenue)
  3  FROM Contract C, Acts_Received A
  4  WHERE C.Contract_Number = A.Contract_Number
  5  AND C.Start_Date > (Sysdate - 365)
  6  GROUP BY Contract_Name, Contract_Number;
```

Note the keyword UNRECOVERABLE. This was added so that there would be no logging for this transaction. That is, there will be no delay due to writes to the redo logs. Although this was not absolutely necessary for this test, logging might slow down the transaction slightly, and give a run-time a bit too high. In addition, remember that the SQL in the actual application is a query, not a transaction; thus, there is no logging in the real application.

The DBA completed his test; the elapsed run-time for this query was 1.80 seconds. (Second and subsequent queries were faster, since much of the data was cached.) This value can now be assigned to the database delay shown in the previous diagram. It is now apparent that the database alone cannot possibly be responsible for a delay of 45 seconds; one of the other subsystems must be the culprit.

While running the SQL test, the DBA discovered an interesting fact; the sample SQL caused about 10,000 contract values to be inserted into table X. As the firm only has a few dozen customers, this result is strange. How can the query return such a large result set? Since the test SQL uses the same data as the actual application, this means that this part of the application requires 10,000 rows to be transferred over several network hops: from the database to the application server, to the web server, then finally to the client.

Estimating that each row is about 50 bytes (roughly 10 bytes each for contract number and dollar value, plus 30 bytes for the contract name); this means that about 500 KB would be transferred several times, as the data hops between the various servers. Having discovered this fact, a delay of 45 seconds begins to look very fast!

Further investigation revealed that the Contracts table contained nearly 10,000 extra contracts. These bogus entries were actually just test data that had been inadvertently left in the Contract table. (Note that the books for this firm are arranged such that the number of contracts is always relatively small. Should there *really* be 10,000 contracts, the issue would have to be revisited.) After removal of the extra entries, the application was re-run. The run-time for the form in question was now less than three seconds.

Let's now look at the first of the promised methods for isolating a root cause. The first suggestion is to **simplify**.

Simplify

Besides identifying the delays due to the various subsystems, it is often helpful to simplify. This approach is especially useful when applied to SQL tuning, but the concept can be applied to many technical issues. When applied to SQL code, the idea is to remove irrelevant distractions from the query, such as formatting, irrelevant functions, simple lookup tables, and so on.

Often, what begins as a very formidable problem looks less intimidating once these distractions are removed. This simple step helps the analyst focus on the real core of the performance problem.

Simplifying SQL Queries

SQL queries will often contain a huge number of fields in the SELECT list. To further complicate the issue, a variety of different functions may also be used – such as TRIM, UPPER, TO_CHAR, and so forth.

The large number of fields and functions often makes the task look harder than it really is. If nothing else, a huge SELECT list makes it difficult to see the entire SQL statement on one page, forcing the analyst to shift his attention from page to page. It is amazing how much easier a problem seems when the essential problem can be cleanly listed on a single page:

> **Reduce a complicated SQL query to the essence of what the query is doing.**

The object of simplifying is to reduce the SQL code down to the essence of the query (or transaction). This is really half the battle! When the core code can be clearly identified, the analyst has already gone a long way towards finding the root cause. Of course, this simplification step must be done carefully, so as not to remove anything of substance inadvertently.

Once a satisfactory correction has been formulated, based on the simplified code, the analyst can confirm the solution by repeating the test with the original SQL.

Remove Irrelevant Information

A good first step in simplifying is to note which parts of a complicated SQL query have little to do with the performance of the entire SQL statement. For example, certain columns in the SELECT list may be duplicated in other parts of the SELECT list.

Consider the simple query below. In this case, it looks as though the application required that the column Last_Name be listed in two places:

```
SELECT Last_Name LASTNAME, Last_Name || First_Name FULLNAME
FROM Emp
WHERE Emp_No > 1000;
```

Let's look at the work that the Oracle engine has to perform to run this query. Does it retrieve each row twice, since the SQL query specifies the Last_Name column twice? No, it does not! The optimizer simply uses the value that was retrieved the first time. In other words, for purposes of analyzing the performance, the duplicate columns do not materially affect the optimizer.

This observation is good news for the performance analyst, since many SQL queries contain duplicate fields. The simplification step is clear; for purposes of performance tuning, the original query can be rewritten as:

```
SELECT Last_Name, First_Name
FROM Emp
WHERE Emp_No > 1000;
```

Note that the column titles, LASTNAME and FULLNAME have also been removed. The application needed these column titles, but we do not. This is another simple step to make things a bit easier (and shorter). The optimizer does not alter its operation just because the output is going to be given a special name. Why not get rid of these distractions?

Irrelevant Functions

Functions that are placed in the SELECT clause are also an unwelcome distraction. Consider the following SQL:

```
SQL> SELECT DECODE (Acctg_Number, 1, 3), Acctg_Dept || '-001'
  2  FROM Acctg
  3  WHERE User_id > 100;
```

In this example, the decode function and the concatenate operator are distractions that complicate our work. The decode function simply substitutes one value for another, and the concatenate operator | | just appends a few characters. Clearly, neither has any relevance to the execution plan for the SQL statement. The Oracle optimizer will normally not be affected by functions in the SELECT clause.

> A possible exception would be if the DBA has created one or more indexes on a function. Then, the presence of that exact function in the SELECT clause could modify the execution plan, since the optimizer could use the special index to retrieve the information more rapidly.

The revised SQL code is:

```
SQL> SELECT Acctg_Number, Acctg_Dept
  2  FROM Acctg
  3  WHERE User_id > 100;
```

An observer might wonder, "Don't these functions cause the CPU to perform more work?" Yes, they do. The database engine must calculate each function for each row retrieved. If many thousands or millions of rows were being retrieved, this fact would certainly have to be considered. Practically speaking, however, these minor delays will normally be far less than the real performance bottleneck. As always, the performance analyst is looking for contributed delays that are in the ballpark of the total system delay.

One caution, however; some applications may make use of user-created PL/SQL functions. These functions cannot simply be removed from the SELECT list. In fact, the function could be the root cause of the problem! For instance, an application might employ a function that actually performs many full table scans, with the associated logical and physical reads. By removing this custom function from the SELECT list, the entire performance issue is changed.

Apart from this, you may be saying to yourself that the presence of one or two functions in the SELECT clause does not complicate matters too much; why bother removing them? For one thing, the ability to find the essential SQL is a useful technique to encourage. Get in the habit of zooming in on the core issue while discarding the noise.

The habit of simplifying SQL will prove most valuable when very large SQL queries need to be analyzed. What seemed like a trivial change in a short SQL statement could become a substantial simplification when faced with a SQL statement that joins a dozen tables.

Simplify, but not too Far!

The trick in the simplification approach is to make the original SQL simpler – without changing the essence of the code. That is, the revised SQL should require the Oracle engine to accomplish the same work as the original SQL. Thus, if the original SQL requires the optimizer to join certain tables, then obviously, the simplified SQL must do the same. Otherwise, the subsequent analysis will not be helpful, and the proposed solution will fail when tried with the original SQL.

Redundant Columns

Sometimes SQL simplification requires that certain columns be temporarily removed from the SELECT list. These are cases where a large number of columns in the SELECT clause have no bearing on the execution plan – they just clutter up the analysis. These columns optionally may be removed from the SELECT clause as long as the table access method does not change.

For example, if the original execution plan required an index lookup followed by a table access, then the revised SQL should use the same method. Consider the following demonstration; the SQL code shown is based on an actual production problem. The original SQL was as follows:

```
SELECT Account_Name, Account_id, Address,
       Custom_1, Custom_2, Custom_3, Custom_4, Custom_5,
       Custom_6, Custom_7, Custom_8, Custom_9, Custom_10,
       Custom_11, Custom_12, Custom_13, Custom_14, Custom_15,
       Custom_16, Custom_17, Custom_18, Custom_19, Custom_20
FROM Account_Security
WHERE Account_id = 894123;
```

After simplification, it looked like this:

```
SELECT Account_Name, Account_id, Address
FROM Account_Security
WHERE Account_id = 894123;
```

This rewrite at first seems completely incorrect! How can all those columns be eliminated and have no effect on the query? Surely the new SQL will be much easier for the optimizer to execute.

In actuality, the two SQL statements will run in very much the same fashion. This is true because the Oracle access method (and therefore the execution plan) is identical in both cases. The presence of the extra columns has a negligible effect on the actual work that the Oracle engine has to perform.

Let's pause for a moment to discuss a commonly used term. When we discuss the way in which the optimizer executes SQL, we use the term execution plan. Just as it sounds, an execution plan describes how Oracle tackles a particular SQL statement. It addresses questions such as: which table is read? Which indexes are used? If there is a join, how are the tables joined? Are there any parallel operations?

In practice, many DBAs refer to this information as the explain plan; but technically, that really means the step we take to get the execution plan, not the plan itself. We provide extensive coverage of generating and interpreting execution plans in Chapter 8.

Getting back to our example; in the original version, none of the Custom columns are accessible via index, so that a table access to get those fields will always be required. In the second version, a table access is still required, because the Address column is likewise not available via an index. In both cases, a table access will be required.

The execution plan for both SQL statements is the same:

```
ID PARENT OPERATION                        OBJECT_NAME
--- ------ ------------------------------- ----------------
  0         SELECT STATEMENT
  1      0  TABLE ACCESS BY INDEX ROWID     ACCOUNT_SECURITY
  2      1    INDEX UNIQUE SCAN             ACCT_ID_IDX
```

We see that an index (based on Account_Id) is used first. This is indicated by the operation INDEX UNIQUE SCAN. The index tells the optimizer which row number in the ACCOUNT_SECURITY table has an entry for the specified Account_Id.

After this index lookup, the optimizer proceeds to perform the operation TABLE ACCESS of the ACCOUNT_SECURITY table. This access retrieves the columns that are needed; in other words, those listed in the SELECT clause.

The database will have to perform the same work, using the same execution plan for both SQL statements.

Large Transactions

When a multiple-transaction set is the problem under analysis, one easy way to simplify the performance problem is to break one large transaction into smaller mini-transactions. What remains will be just a few (frequently only *one*) SQL statements. In this way, the analyst can eliminate the portions that execute quickly, and not waste time on irrelevant code.

This principle is easily stated, but how is the performance analyst to accomplish it? How is one to separate the good SQL from the bad? One easy way to distinguish among the various SQL statements in a transaction is to trace the application while it is running. Recall that SQL_TRACE can be activated for the entire database if necessary, by setting the parameter, SQL_TRACE = True, or for one particular session by calling the stored procedure, Sys.dbms_system.set_sql_trace_in_session.

Then, by using TKPROF to format the trace file, it will be clear which SQL statements are really holding things up. This step should be pretty easy, because the elapsed times for each SQL statement are clearly listed in each TKPROF report.

Occasionally, the application itself might also have run logs that define the time spent on various transactions. This will also aid the analyst in his effort to home-in on the actual SQL code responsible for the bottleneck. With that said, let's now move on to look at the second method for isolating the root cause of a problem.

Divide and Conquer

Closely related to simplifying is breaking the problem into pieces, or the divide and conquer method. Actually, this approach is really just another form of simplifying. The principle is the same – we want to try to remove distractions and irrelevant information, so that what remains is the *essence* of the problem

> **Identify and remove irrelevant elements that don't contribute to the problem.**

The division approach works very well in SQL tuning because most SQL statement difficulties are due to a very few causes. This observation also explains why a true expert in SQL tuning is usually so successful; in many cases, all that needs to be done is to resolve a small number of problems – perhaps just one!

Of course, having just one core issue to solve cannot be guaranteed in every case, but this observation should be encouraging news to Oracle professionals – especially those interested in SQL tuning:

> **Many performance problems can be improved substantially by making just one or two corrections.**

Breaking up SQL Code

The divide and conquer approach is especially useful when tackling complicated SQL code. Often, what begins as a very complex SQL problem can be separated into several parts, each of which is much more manageable. In some cases, the separation of SQL code into parts is very obvious; in other cases, more work will be required.

To illustrate this approach, consider the following SQL statement. This code retrieves a list of employees from three separate tables, meeting three separate conditions:

```
SQL> SELECT Emp_name
  2  FROM Emp
  3  WHERE Zip_Code LIKE '92%'
  4  UNION
  5  SELECT Emp_name FROM Term_Employees
  6  WHERE Term_Date < Sysdate - 365
  7  UNION
  8  SELECT Emp_name FROM Managers
  9  WHERE dept_id = 1000;
```

If this SQL statement were to have a performance problem, the separation tactic would be very obvious – simply divide the SQL before each UNION statement. Then, attention could be individually directed at each of the three SQL statements; each statement could be checked for good run-time. Of course, most SQL statements will not be so trivial; nevertheless, the concept will be the same.

Consider this slightly more complicated example:

```
SQL> SELECT Emp_name
  2  FROM Emp
  3  WHERE Dept_id IN
  4   (SELECT Dept_id FROM Dept
  5    WHERE Dept_Name LIKE 'ENGINEER%');
```

This SQL statement can easily be divided into an outer query and an inner query. The inner query runs first, and then it feeds the rows into the outer query. Naturally, both pieces must run efficiently if the entire statement is to run well.

Firstly, then, we must determine which of the two parts is the problem. Is it the outer query, or the inner query? Let's separate them, and find out.

First, list the inner query:

```
SELECT Dept_id
FROM Dept
WHERE Dept_Name LIKE 'ENGINEER%';
```

Then, the outer query could be modeled as:

```
SELECT Emp_name
FROM Emp
WHERE  Dept_id IN 'N';
```

Now that the SQL is broken into its parts, simple timing tests will easily show which piece is the culprit. To check the timing of the outer query, one approach would be simply to substitute a typical value for N and check the performance for this one small SQL statement in SQL*Plus.

171

Simplification of Table Joins

A more sophisticated use of the divide and conquer approach can be applied to table joins. Simplification of table joins is important, because of the frequency of this form of SQL. It is very common to have SQL statements with a variety of table joins, in which only one or two of the tables joined are causing the performance problem.

We cover table joins very extensively in Chapter 9, but let's briefly define our terms. A join is a SQL query that uses information from two or more tables. The tables can be joined because they have corresponding columns. For example, one table might contain the fields Name, Address, and Phone_Number; a second table might have the fields Name and Occupation. These two tables could be part of a SQL join based on the column that they have in common, namely the Name field. We call the table that we use first the **driving** table; the second table is called the **driven** table. We will see in Chapter 9 the various ways that the Oracle optimizer can handle these forms of queries.

In complicated SQL queries involving table joins, one useful tactic is to remove a few of the tables in the join in order to simplify it, and thereby distinguish which tables really are performance drivers for the SQL in question. In other words, we try to find out which tables are on the critical path – which ones are really the performance drivers.

Let's look at an example:

Example: One Join at a Time

The following figure illustrates a simple query with five tables involved in joins. In this example, we are not concerned with the exact method of joining:

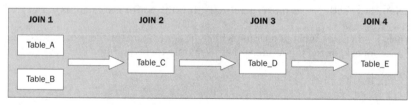

The five tables used in the join are: Table_A, Table_B, Table_C, Table_D, and Table_E. Let's assume they are listed in the join order, left to right, in the figure. Table_A is the driving table in the first join, and Table_B is the driven table. The result from the first join then becomes the driver for the second join, and so on.

The SQL used for this query is:

```
SQL> SELECT A. Emp_id
  2   FROM Table_A A, Table_B B, Table_C C, Table_D D,
  3   Table_E E
  4   WHERE A. Deptno = B.Deptno
  5   AND B.Site = C.Site
  6   AND C.Division = D.Division
  7   AND D.Office = E.Office;
```

In this example, note that none of the columns from tables B through E are even listed in the SELECT clause. This means that we don't really want to *see* the values from these tables; we only want to use their information in the join conditions.

Assuming that there is a performance problem with this query, we are faced with the question, "which join or which table is causing the bottleneck?"

One good way to answer that question is to systematically divide the SQL statement, thus greatly simplifying the root cause analysis. By splitting the SQL into pieces, the core of the performance problem can be quickly determined.

There are several good ways to start. One idea that immediately comes to mind is to eliminate Table_D and Table_E from the SQL entirely. This would then leave us with the very simple join shown here:

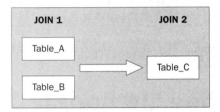

Notice that we have roughly divided the SQL statement in half. The next step would be to run the simplified SQL that persists in only Table_A through Table_C, and check performance. The objective would be to see if the problem stays with Table_A through Table_C, or whether the problem has disappeared.

Note that this simplification process requires that the SELECT clause be modified each time a table is removed from consideration. Thus, when Table_D and Table_E are removed, fields that originate from these tables will need to be eliminated from the SELECT clause. This leaves us with this SQL:

```
SQL> SELECT A. Emp_id
  2  FROM Table_A A, Table_B B, Table_C C
  3  WHERE A. Deptno = B.Deptno
  4  AND B.Site = C.Site;
```

When simplifying table join code as a method of understanding a more complex expression, it is important that the simplified SQL retains the same join order and join method as the original. Otherwise, we are not comparing apples to apples, and our analysis will be misleading. Thus, in our example, we should verify that the simplified SQL has an execution plan that joins the tables in order Table_A, Table_B, Table_C. Later, once the root cause has been identified and we are ready to change the SQL, we can use whatever join order we deem best.

Suppose that our simplified query with just a few joins still runs poorly. Since there are only three tables (and two joins) involved, the troubleshooting process has been greatly simplified. There are not too many choices left to investigate.

On the other hand, if the simplified query runs well, the next logical step would be to add back `Table_D`, then `Table_E`, and determine at which point the performance problem returns.

The overall goal of the simplification approach is to choose a method that reduces the complexity of the performance tuning process. This may involve the DBA chosing to break a given problem into two, employing a temporary table in the process.

Temporary tables are often used to make a problem more manageable – not because they have to be used. Admittedly, creating a temporary table might incur a slight performance decrease; the tradeoff is the increased maintainability of the program.

> **Be wary of SQL performance improvements that make it difficult to understand what is happening.**

Now let's move onto the final method of determining the root cause of a performance problem.

The Timeline Method

Another useful way to isolate a root cause is to find out what changed. Some performance difficulties occur on systems that had previously been performing fine. All functions had been performing normally, and suddenly the users report that the system is nearly unusable.

In some cases, it will be helpful to create a timeline of events leading up to the performance problem. For example, suppose that the performance of a customer service application suddenly went bad. The timeline might look like this:

Monday	Tuesday	Wednesday	Thursday	Friday
All OK	CPU #1 replacement	Code update	Rebuild indexes	New stats

The performance expert will naturally want to investigate the changes shown on Tuesday through Thursday. On Tuesday, for instance, we note that CPU #1 was replaced. This seems to indicate that there was a major hardware problem. What happened? Was the CPU satisfactorily changed? If so, how did the load on the system change?

The analyst will also want to look into the application and database modifications on Wednesday, Thursday, and Friday. Why were the indexes rebuilt – were there any database problems leading up to that decision? Why were new statistics gathered – and was the same sample size used?

If anything, people are sometimes too suspicious of changes made just prior to the discovery of a performance problem. It is very convenient having an immediate scapegoat to blame. Remember, however, that the exact start time of a performance problem is frequently not precisely known. In fact, many issues reported as new performance problems are actually old problems that were never reported. Believing that the performance problem has just begun, the Oracle analyst could easily jump to wrong conclusions, blaming some harmless change made a day earlier:

> **Performance problems are frequently reported inaccurately. Gather facts, not conjecture.**

Even when a performance problem is accurately reported, it should be remembered that performance problems that occur after a program or database change are not necessarily caused by the change:

> **Changes made prior to performance problems are not necessarily the cause of the bottleneck.**

Sometimes, it really *is* just a coincidence. It is very easy to become so fixated on finding what changed that the analyst mistakenly finds a correlation where none exists.

Common Causes of Performance Problems

For the analyst who is just beginning his or her career in Oracle performance tuning, it will be helpful to list some of the most common root causes of performance issues. Admittedly, this sample is not truly scientific in the statistical sense, but it should nonetheless prove useful in getting a feel for what kinds of things often are the culprits.

In my experience, root causes frequently fall into the following categories:

- ❑ Application design and interaction with database
- ❑ Database design
- ❑ Indexing
- ❑ init.ora parameters
- ❑ Problems from competing batch jobs
- ❑ Hardware (including networks)

Application and database design issues are almost always involved in correcting performance problems. At the other end, rarely have I seen problems that are truly caused by inadequate hardware sizing – it happens, but not too often.

175

Different DBAs will certainly have their own way of grouping root causes, but most DBAs and performance analysts recognize that application design is often at the heart of a performance problem. By application design, we must specifically consider *how the application talks to the* database. This usually leads the analyst to examine the exact construction of the SQL statement that originates at the application:

> **The number 1 performance issue is how the application interacts with the database.**

More than any other cause, the method in which the application retrieves data from the database is the key to resolving many performance issues. In fact, this principle applies even if the database is not Oracle!

In general, relational databases, whether Oracle, SQL Sever, DB2, Sybase, or Informix, follow similar steps in executing queries. When a query is received for processing, the database engine accesses many of the same type of database objects.

For instance, each database flavor uses indexes to speed access to information in tables. Each database must also deal efficiently with table joins (albeit with slightly different versions of join algorithms). Each database must protect the integrity of data through some sort of locking mechanisms. This similarity means that the skills learned in tuning Oracle performance problems will probably transfer to other database brands.

Application Design

The application design is very often a critical piece of the performance puzzle. Good application design permits (but does not guarantee) excellent response time. An especially poor application design may make good performance nearly impossible to achieve.

For instance, an application that encourages users to retrieve a gigantic result set (say, 50 Mb) will certainly run poorly, no matter how well the Oracle database operates. This large data transfer will cause a long delay – no matter what the performance analyst does:

> **Good database design cannot counteract poor application design.**

This principle explains why *every* subsystem must be considered. It only takes one weak link to wreck the overall performance. Since there are hundreds of potential problems with application design, let's have a quick look at some very frequent design flaws that occur time and again.

First, the application logic may be designed to handle results from very small tables only. This is another way of saying that the application will not scale. Usually, this also means that there had been no load/scalability testing.

Unfortunately, it is extremely common for a vendor-supplied application only to have been tested with tables of trivial size. Incredible as it seems, many applications are only tested with tables filled with fewer than 100 rows! The minute that these tables are populated with a realistic set of data, the application grinds to a halt:

> **Even the poorest of applications may run well with only a few rows in the database tables.**

Second, the application uses an algorithm that processes rows one by one, as opposed to an entire set. As in the previous problem, this only becomes an issue when a realistic set of data is used in testing. This problem mainly applies to data warehouse loading algorithms in which it is critical to process many thousands of rows as a group.

Third, the SQL defined by the application might preclude index usage. Developers will often mistakenly put functions in the WHERE clause, which often prevents index usage. The following SQL code will block index usage for the column Cust_Name:

```
SQL> SELECT Cust_Name
  2    FROM Customers C, Accounts A
  3   WHERE C.Account_id = A.Account_id
  4     AND UPPER(Cust_Name) = 'SMITH';
```

The Oracle engine cannot use an index on Cust_Name to address this query, because the query doesn't care about Cust_Name; it cares about UPPER (Cust_Name). Recent versions of Oracle, however, allow the DBA to create function-based indexes. Just as it sounds, we create an index on the result of a function, not the raw value itself. In this case, we would create an index on UPPER (Cust_Name).

The real question, however, is why the database is not storing the customer names in a consistent format; that is, why does the SQL query have to reformat the data? These questions are the issue in our next case study:

Case Study: Trouble with Trouble Tickets

One of the most popular help desk applications relies on an Oracle database to store all the trouble ticket information. In one particular company, the group that supported this application complained to the DBA that the nightly update was beginning to run very slowly. Each night, the application had to refresh various database tables with updated customer information.

The root cause of the performance bottleneck was easy to discover; the nightly batch job was being degraded by a single SQL statement. This SQL statement had the UPPER function hard coded into the program:

```
SQL> INSERT INTO Cust
  2  SELECT Cust_Name, Cust_Id
  3  FROM Old_Cust
  4  WHERE UPPER (Cust_Name) LIKE 'A%';
```

As shown above, the program first looked for, then inserted all new trouble tickets for the A customers. Next, it would proceed to the B customers, and so on. Since these customer names were not stored in a consistent format, the nightly batch job had to correct all the names dynamically; hence the use of the UPPER function, which turns the letters into upper case. This same correction was applied every night.

The DBA documented the design flaw and recommended two steps:
Note to production: this list starts with 1.

Perform a one-time update of the customer names to use a consistent format (in this case, all upper case);

Request that the vendor modify their program so that all subsequent customer entries be saved in upper case.

The vendor in this case agreed to the modification suggested, and provided a patch release of the program. Next, the DBA performed a one-time update to all customer names to convert them to the consistent case.

The nightly batch job was then able to complete in a fraction of the previous time. The modified application stored all names in a consistent format, making any sort of function unnecessary.

Note that the application in the above case study was a major application used throughout the nation. There were probably dozens, if not hundreds of companies experiencing the same problem! Thus, problems with scalability are not limited to just "mom and pop" (small, home-grown) applications. Many well-known applications make similar mistakes, leading to performance degradation as the database grows.

Fourth, the SQL might cause tables to be joined in an inefficient order. Deciding the order of table joins is almost an art in itself. Although including a large number of tables in one SQL statement does make the job a little trickier, performance should not necessarily be bad as more tables are added to the join. We reserve an entire chapter for this important subject: Chapter 9, *Analyzing Table Joins*.

Next, the application may encourage large transfers of data across the network from the server to the client. Transferring many megabytes of data from the database to the user is a sure way to degrade performance. Besides the "hop" over the network to the end user, there are frequently additional delays due to transfers to the application server, report server, web server, and so on. In cases like this, no matter how perfectly the database runs, the best it can do is not make the problem any worse.

Frequently, the end user will not be aware of the large data transfer. For example, the application may not actually display to the user the entire result set at one time. Some reporting applications, for instance, accept the entire result set from the database, then feed it to the client a few pages at a time. The end user may only see one page of data, but behind the scenes, the total amount of work and network transfers can be huge.

Finally, the application could allow empty searches, in which the WHERE clause is empty. Many applications do a poor job of restricting user queries to what is reasonable. Very often, the user can mistakenly forget to enter some restrictive criteria, and the application will execute the query anyway. The lack of search criteria means that all data will be retrieved.

Consider the following SQL; it fetches the name and grade for an Oracle "OCP" (Oracle Certified Professional) course for all students who live in Glasgow, who graduated in the past month:

```
SQL> SELECT Student_Name, Grade
  2  FROM Student_Tab S, Grade_Tab G
  3  WHERE S.Student_id = G.Student_id
  4  AND S.Home_Town = 'Glasgow'
  5  AND S.Grad_Date > (Sysdate - 30)
  6  AND G.Course = 'ORACLE OCP';

Student_Name          Grade
-----------------     -----
Herman Smith          A-
Bob Hernandez         B+
Susan Johnson         C+
```

This query is well written, and the performance should be fine. What would happen if a user ran the same query, but with no restrictions? The following query would return the grade of every student in the college, for every course:

```
SQL> SELECT Student_Name, Grade
  2  FROM Student_Tab S, Grade_Tab G
  3  WHERE S.Student_id = G.Student_id;

Student_Name          Grade
-------------------+--------
Robert Aagor          D
Robert Aagor          A
Robert Aagor          B+

...                   **

Herbert Abbot         C-
Herbert Abbot         A-
Herbert Abbot         A

...                   **
```

The results of this query would be completely unusable; the database would have performed unnecessary work, and the network delay would have been substantial. Additionally, other users would possibly have suffered performance degradation due to the unavailability of resources.

Database Design

Besides problems that may occur with the application design, the database design may itself be faulty. The DBA may have forgotten to perform some critical task (such as gathering statistics), or there might have been miscommunication between the design team and the DBAs, leading to wrong or missing indexes.

Here are some common errors on the database side:

❑ Unnecessary database feature wrongly activated

❑ Old statistics fool the optimizer

❑ Skewed data but no histograms built

❑ Index with excessive columns

❑ Stagnant indexes (need rebuilding)

❑ Missing/wrong indexes

In this list, some of the items are arguably really application issues. Index problems could probably be classified as either a database problem or an application problem. The DBA might assist with indexing suggestions, but indexes are really closely related to the application. Indexes exist in order to assist access to application objects, so one could argue that they are really part of application design.

The DBA might have implemented an overly complex design, such as using Oracle Advanced Replication, where a much simpler design could have worked equally well. Or, perhaps the MTS (Multi-Threaded Server) option is being used for no real reason.

init.ora Parameters

Oracle databases are tremendously resilient when it comes to operating well in spite of incorrect initialization parameters. Occasionally, however, the database has been set up so poorly that the database engine struggles to accomplish even simple queries.

Some typical errors with these parameters include:

❑ Greatly undersized SGA, for example, Db_block_buffers set too low (or so high that the memory on the server is exhausted).

❑ Greatly oversized shared pool.

❑ Unusual or exotic features used unnecessarily, for example MTS.

❑ Wrong setting for Db_File_Multiblock_Read_Count.

Nowadays, many new DBAs are unreasonably biased in favor of bigger is better for database caches; thus, undersized database caches are becoming rarer. In their place are oversized shared pools. A huge shared pool is often created when the application uses many unique SQL statements (for example, bind variables are not used). The large pool often makes things worse, because for each SQL statement issued, the Oracle engine has to search through the pool looking for matches. (The solution, of course, is to reduce the massive number of distinct SQL statements, not to create a huge shared pool.)

Setting the parameter `Db_File_Multiblock_Read_Count` is a bit trickier. It is normally set to the maximum number of Oracle blocks that can be read from disk at one time (traditionally, a total of 64 KB – but new servers often have a far greater capacity, sometimes even 1 MB). A low value means that multi-block reads will be unnecessarily restricted; a high value (beyond the actual capability of the server) means that the optimizer incorrectly believes that multi-block reads are more efficient than they really are. This in turn leads the optimizer to incorrectly favor full table scans instead of index lookups.

Interference from Batch Jobs

Sometimes, neither the database nor the application is at fault. Instead, some other process on the server is interfering with efficient database operation by consuming resources. For instance, in one of our previous case studies involving a data warehouse, one batch job interfered with another by locking access to some rows. In other situations, there might be regular maintenance that is mistakenly scheduled at the wrong time.

Our next case study illustrates how other batch jobs can lead to performance problems:

Case Study: Backed-up Backups

A DBA supporting a data warehouse application was trying to determine why the run-time for the nightly data extract was inconsistent. The nightly data extraction began just after midnight, and normally ran until 2:30 A.M. Sometimes, however, the time stretched out about 20 minutes longer.

The logs for the data extraction showed that one step in the data extraction (pull of data from a Sybase system) usually took about one minute. Occasionally, however, the time would grow. The logs showed that the number of rows retrieved from this one table in the Sybase database was nearly identical every night; even when the time was much greater, the number of rows varied by only a few percent.

The DBA started keeping a logbook to try to understand what was happening. All the other steps in the nightly data load ran very consistently – perhaps just a few percent or so variance each night. The steps both prior to and following the odd one ran fine.

The DBA mentioned this phenomenon to one of the Systems Administrators. The Sys Admin explained that the network bandwidth between the various production servers was so great, that the network could not possibly be responsible for the delay of a relatively small data transfer.

Another Systems Administrator, the one responsible for data backups, explained to the DBA that all backups had been shifted outside the midnight to 3 A.M. time window, thus avoiding any conflicts.

The DBA continued to log the runtime of the various data loads. All the facts indicated that there was some process that activated at exactly the same time every night. Finally, the DBA prepared to activate a special monitor to determine what processes were running on the server at that time. At this point, the backup Systems Administrator revealed that one of the backup jobs had been missed, and was indeed running at 1:30 every morning. Depending on the exact runtime of the backup job, there would sometimes be resource competition between the database server and the backup processes. When they both ran at the same time, database performance was severely degraded.

In this case study, it would have been understandable if the performance analyst had focused on either the Sybase data source or the application that pulled the data from Sybase. In this case, however, there was nothing wrong with either the application or the database; the root cause was interference from a batch job that had been incorrectly scheduled.

Hardware

On some occasions, there may actually be a resource problem with a hardware component; for instance, there could be so few disk drives installed, that disk I/O over the few spindles drags down performance. This scenario appears to occur less frequently, now that disk drives are so inexpensive. Also, most firms use striping to distribute files across multiple disks.

Rather than having too few disks, the more common difficulty is that the busy, or "hot", files are lumped together, instead of being more evenly distributed across the entire set of drives.

For applications requiring large transfers of data over a network, the network bandwidth may become an issue. Our next case study illustrates this problem.

Case Study: Local or Long-Distance?

A financial firm was re-evaluating its software development process. They wanted the various designers to be able to model the new application using a design tool, and be able to share the model within the group. The company decided to use the Erwin modeling tool, along with the ModelMart repository. With this setup, each designer checks out the up-to-date model, performs their work, and then checks-in the changes to the repository.

The DBA on the job was familiar with the Erwin product, and quickly had a sample repository for the designers to use. Testing showed that everything was working well; the DBA was able to create a small model, check it out, and so on. There seemed to be no problems. The DBA told the designers to give it a try.

When the designers tried to use the ModelMart repository, they experienced massive delays. In fact, even the act of logging in required about 30 seconds! The supervisor called the DBA and complained about the problem.

The DBA went to the office down the street where the designers worked. He first tried connecting over SQL*Plus to the database. The connection was established without a hitch, not immediately, but it seemed ok nonetheless.

Tests with the application, however, did not go so well. The DBA confirmed that using the application to connect to the database did elicit a long delay, about 15 to 30 seconds, just as the designers said.

The DBA put a trace on the application (activated SQL_TRACE) to see what was happening. The trace file showed that after login, the application transferred a moderate amount of data (about 500 rows) to the client. This did not seem a large amount of data, but it appeared to be the only difference between the SQL*Plus login, and the ModelMart login.

Armed with this new information, the DBA began to get suspicious of the network speed between the two buildings. (The designers were in one building; the database server was in another.) He ran a simple ping test to see how fast the network responded. To his astonishment, a simple ping sometimes took one second to accomplish.

While network response times can vary greatly, a reasonable estimate for a ping might be roughly 25 ms; thus, a one-second delay represents nearly 2 orders of magnitude degradation. A delay of 1 second on average is unbelievably bad.

He then tried transferring (via ftp) a few small files. The file transfer test confirmed that the network bandwidth between the two buildings was severely limited. Even the smallest data transfers would take a few seconds.

Discussions with the network group revealed that the network between the two buildings had been set up as a temporary measure. The network technicians were well aware of this bottleneck, but there was nothing they could do in the short run.

Unfortunately, the users who wanted to use the ModelMart application were all located in one building, and the server (and the DBA) in another. There was simply no way that a model could possibly be transferred over this severely limited network. Since a simple login required 15 seconds, a transfer of the entire application model would probably take an entire hour! Obviously, this would make the system completely unusable.

The DBA explained the problem to the project manager. She understood, and reluctantly agreed to postpone the ModelMart project. The entire project had to be delayed for months, until a more suitable network architecture could be implemented.

Of course, there were other potential options, for example, moving people, moving servers; but the real core of the problem was the network. All other solutions would be dodging the fundamental issue that needed to be addressed. Fortunately, the network administrators readily accepted responsibility for correcting these network issues.

Another potential hardware problem is related to CPUs. On some servers, the number of CPUs installed may be too few in number (or too slow). This situation is sometimes due not only to a desire to minimize hardware costs, but also as a way to reduce licensing fees. This phenomenon occurs because the price of some software packages is proportional to the number of CPUs installed. For some sophisticated software packages, this means that the licensing cost per CPU can be very high – even hundreds of thousands of dollars. Naturally, this pricing scheme encourages IT managers to try fewer CPUs, at least at first.

Note that the database server is supposed to be CPU-limited; that is, in a very well-tuned system, the other bottlenecks, such as disk I/O and network limitations, should have already been eliminated. In this ideal case, adding more (or faster) CPUs will naturally improve performance. Of course, the important question is, have the other bottlenecks really been addressed?

Recall our analogy of the clerk in the supermarket, servicing a long list of customers waiting in the checkout line. Once all the supplies and equipment have been provided to the clerk, there is only one thing left to do; employ more (or faster) workers. Prior to hiring more staff, however, the supermarket management will be very careful to make sure that all the clerks are performing at peak efficiency:

> **Well-tuned database systems are normally CPU-limited.**

Although there are undoubtedly some cases where all other bottlenecks have been addressed, and more CPUs are appropriate; this option is not usually the first alternative that the performance specialist should consider. Although some performance gain is normally achieved by adding more CPUs, it is better first to find out why the CPU load is very high. If an underlying problem is never investigated, the addition of more CPUs may buy a brief respite, but the real problem will still exist. For instance, an excessive number of logical reads will tend to drive the CPU load very high. It might be tempting to bolt-on more CPUs immediately, but the correct approach is to tune the SQL that is causing the excessive logical reads.

Other Practical Suggestions for Finding the Root Cause

There are some easy ways to make the job of the Oracle Pathologist a little easier. Consider what the Oracle Pathologist is trying to do; he is trying to reduce the overall elapsed time of SQL processing. Thus, it is important to have an easy way to determine exactly what the runtime is.

Another practical issue is how to handle large result sets. How can the analyst find the runtime of a SQL statement that returns 100,000 rows? How can the display time be separated from the actual run-time?

Simple Timing Tests

When testing SQL statements for elapsed time, it is convenient simply to be able to run the query in SQL*Plus, with timing set to ON. (The command in SQL*Plus is simply Set Timing ON). Although not as sophisticated as running SQL_TRACE (followed by TKPROF), this simple test is actually good enough for reviewing many problems.

Simple test runs using tools such as SQL*Plus are often more than adequate to confirm a problem and get a feel for the magnitude of the bottleneck. Of course, the analyst is still free to choose a more sophisticated approach if necessary; in practice, however, a quick check in SQL*Plus is often a good first step:

> **Use simple methods, such as SQL*Plus timing, to obtain approximate run-times.**

For instance, a customer with a one-minute performance bottleneck really doesn't care whether the performance problem is technically 59.3 seconds, 65.2 seconds, or any other similar number. All the performance analyst needs to know is that the delay is about one minute. Admittedly, using SQL*Plus is not exactly the same as running the same SQL from the application – but it is usually good enough to allow the Oracle expert to diagnose the problem.

Large Result Sets

In some cases, a query returns so many rows that the time to display the rows becomes the driving factor for the total execution time. This makes it difficult to distinguish between actual database-related time and the time to display the result set. When running the query in SQL*Plus, the long display time will probably mask the underlying problem, or exaggerate the actual run-time.

There are several ways around this difficulty. One simple way is to reword the SQL code to insert the results into a temporary table, rather than actually displaying the results. For example, consider a large query that returns 10000 rows. (Assume for this example that indexes are not being used). Note how the SQL could be rewritten to facilitate a simple timing test:

The original SQL:

```
SELECT Emp_Number
FROM Dept
WHERE Emp_Number > 100;
```

can be re-written as:

```
INSERT INTO Temp_Tab
 (SELECT Emp_Number
  FROM Dept
  WHERE Emp_Number > 100);
```

A possible disadvantage of this approach is that when SQL*Plus Autotrace is being used to display the execution plan, the INSERT method will prevent the execution plan from being shown. The Timing function in SQL*Plus will still function, however.

An alternative way to achieve the same result is to modify the SELECT clause to specify a function rather than the raw data. Instead of returning each row, we simply force the optimizer to fetch each row as though it is going to be displayed. The execution plan will normally remain the same, and SQL*Plus AUTOTRACE will work fine.

Continuing with our same example, this is how the SQL text could be reworded. The original SQL:

```
SELECT Emp_Number
FROM Dept
WHERE Emp_Number > 100;
```

can be rewritten as:

```
SELECT MAX (Emp_Number)
FROM Dept
WHERE Emp_Number > 100;
```

By using the function MAX, there is little change in the work that the Oracle engine will have to perform. The Oracle engine will still have to retrieve exactly the same rows as before; the only difference is that they will not be displayed. Admittedly, there will be a very slight impact due to the new function, but this effect is usually negligible – especially when compared to the magnitude of the performance problem being investigated.

When simplifying a SQL query to use the function approach, be careful not to disturb the execution plan. For instance, if certain fields are removed from the SELECT clause, the optimizer may modify the execution plan to take advantage of the lessened requirement. For instance, with fields removed from the SELECT clause, an index access might retrieve all the information needed, where a table access was required before. When in doubt, compare the execution plans for the two SQL statements.

Summary

In this chapter, we have presented a general overview of exactly what the Oracle Pathologist is trying to accomplish, as well as a procedure that he can follow. We learned that the very definition of root cause suggests a few courses of action that we might follow. They follow, namely:

- The simplify technique to remove unnecessary distractions and complications.
- The divide and conquer technique to break complicated problems into manageable pieces.
- The timeline technique to discover what changed.

We also saw that, amongst other things, performance problems frequently arise because the SQL code executed on the server is poorly optimized. This means that the Oracle Pathologist must become an expert in optimizing SQL code.

Chapters 8 through 10 continue our discussion about the Oracle Pathologist, and his critical job of finding a root cause. These follow-on chapters deal in detail with topics that a competent performance analyst will need to understand. The critical topic of SQL optimization is discussed in the next chapter.

8

Analyzing SQL Bottlenecks

SQL performance tuning is probably the number one most important technical skill for the Oracle tuning specialist to master. The importance of this skill is simply a consequence of the statistics of performance problems. In practice, a large number of performance tuning cases will boil down to resolving some issue with one or more SQL statements. Even in those cases where the ultimate root cause is not a poor SQL query, the performance of the SQL statement will probably have to be verified.

Thus, proficiency in SQL tuning is a must have for the performance specialist. By mastering it, an entire new dimension is opened to the Oracle expert. For instance, when faced with a perplexing SQL statement, the master of SQL tuning will be able to explain how the Oracle optimizer is handling the SQL, and what options there are for altering the performance.

SQL performance tuning is a big topic; a complete discussion of it would fill an entire book. In fact, some of the most widely read (and respected) Oracle technology books are those written specifically on this topic. Nevertheless, in spite of its overwhelming breadth, we can still introduce the main principles of this important subject. The purpose of this chapter, then is to cover the ideas and steps that are fundamental to the craft of SQL tuning.

We open the chapter with a discussion of the role of SQL tuning, answering question such as how does SQL tuning fit into the big picture of Oracle performance tuning? What kind of issues will the performance specialist face? How difficult are the problems to resolve? What are some benefits of performing SQL tuning?

Following this, the main points we discuss are as follows:

❑   Overview of SQL tuning

❑   Database and optimizer changes and upgrades

❑ Where should we begin with respect to SQL tuning?

❑ Execution plans

❑ Tips on SQL tuning

Throughout this chapter, we provide detailed examples and sample SQL code to illustrate the concepts discussed. We also include case studies that demonstrate how to use the recommended steps in the tuning process. As always, the goal is to give the reader the knowledge necessary to practice the ideas that are suggested here. Let's begin…

The Role of SQL Tuning

Many software professionals do not grasp the great importance of SQL tuning. This misunderstanding is ironic, because experience shows that SQL tuning is central to the entire performance tuning process:

> **Expertise in SQL tuning is a critical skill for the Oracle performance specialist.**

Less experienced DBAs and analysts are sometimes quick to dismiss SQL tuning in favor of (apparently) easier, more dramatic steps. For instance, some beginners might try moving around the database files (the .dbf files) in an effort to even-out the disk traffic, without really attempting to understand why there is so much disk I/O in the first place. This approach, as misguided as it is, is certainly appealing; after all, why not distribute the problem across as many disks as possible?

In reality, however, few performance problems are genuinely solved by addressing only the symptoms. While spreading high disk traffic over more disks is certainly not a bad concept (and can indeed lessen the severity of the problem), it doesn't really address the root cause. More often, problem resolution comes down to understanding what the SQL code is doing. Since SQL is the fundamental language, or one of the core structures of relational databases, it should not be too surprising that SQL difficulties are often the core of the performance problem as well. SQL is critical because it is the language by which we communicate with the database.

Good News for the SQL Analyst

Fortunately for the Oracle performance analyst, poorly performing SQL code is frequently very simple to correct – once the basic principles are understood. Once the analyst sees how the Oracle optimizer is handling the SQL statement, there is a wide variety of options that can be used to entice the Oracle engine to execute the SQL statement faster:

> **With an understanding of the basics, poorly performing SQL code is often easily corrected.**

The reason that poor SQL is often simple to correct is because many SQL-related problems have simple underlying causes. Once the performance analyst comprehends the cause of the SQL difficulty, the solution is not far away.

Of course, there will be exceptions – those thorny (and rare) problems that few Oracle analysts have seen before; certainly these puzzles will indeed test the skill of the Oracle expert. In general, however, many SQL difficulties are trivial to resolve.

For example, some common SQL issues include the following:

- ❏ Missing indexes
- ❏ Indexes with wrong columns
- ❏ Mixed up data types
- ❏ Functions interfering with index usage
- ❏ Wrong order of table joins
- ❏ Missing optimizer statistics (the DBA forgot to run the ANALYZE command on a table)
- ❏ Processing a single row versus a set

These are just a few of the many ways that poorly-designed SQL code can cause delays. We will provide various examples that illustrate real-life cases of SQL problems. As we will see, even though some common steps (such as spreading the disk traffic over more disks, or making a simple change to an init.ora parameter) resolve a performance difficulty, it is very common for a simple SQL-related change to fix a problem:

> **Many performance problems are completely resolved by a simple change to the SQL processing.**

Many Oracle analysts have been hailed as heroes by knowing how to deal with SQL problems. Often, difficult performance problems have been solved quickly and easily with simple fixes, such as correcting an index definition, or a minor change to join order.

Side Benefits of SQL Analysis

Even if the SQL in question runs fine as written, the process of SQL analysis will often reveal an application design problem, if one is present. The analyst could discover, for instance, that the SQL statement is only processing one row at a time, when an entire set of data should be processed. Or, the SQL might be retrieving many rows for statistical processing on the application server, when those same calculations could be made on the server – without transferring the rows themselves.

This case demonstrates an instance where the SQL statement executes well, but the SQL should never have been executed in the first place. If the performance analyst were to spend his or her time optimizing the SQL code, the real problem would be missed!

This wrong SQL error lies at the center of our next case study:

Case Study: The Wrong Intersection

A data warehouse program for a university required that new information be loaded every night. This was called incremental processing. Rather than reload the entire set of data, only the altered data was added. Thus, each night, the records for new students or courses were transferred from the operational OLTP system into the data warehouse.

The time to accomplish the nightly load was increasing bit by bit. Initially, the run time had been a little over one hour; this time had gradually increased to about 3 ½ hours for all nightly processing. Some possible improvements had been identified for the future, but it was desired that every possible one be identified, because the database was expected to greatly increase in size. What completed in 3 ½ hours now could easily translate into much longer in the future.

There were hundreds of steps performed each night; many of the simple steps ran in just a few seconds. The run logs for the data warehouse showed one step, however, that stood out as taking more time than the other processing. Each occurrence of this routine consumed a few minutes, and the routine was run in several different variations; thus, this routine was using more than its fair share of the nightly run time.

The purpose of this routine was to compare two tables (one very large, one small), and delete the rows that were in common between the two. (This was done as part of the method to insert only the *new* accounts.)

The SQL looked like this:

```
SQL> DELETE FROM Old_Data
  2  WHERE (Act_id, Dept_id)
  3  IN (SELECT Act_id, Dept_id FROM Old_Data
  4  INTERSECT
  5  SELECT Act_id, Dept_id FROM New_Data);
```

At first, this SQL code might appear reasonable; it simply identifies which rows are in common, and then submits them for deletion.

Actually, there is a subtle, but very serious, flaw in this SQL – but it has nothing to do with optimization! Let's look very carefully at what the SQL really does:

1. Retrieve all rows from Old_Data

2. Retrieve all rows from New_Data

3. Use the INTERSECT function to find the rows that are in common

4. Delete these rows from the Old_Data table.

This SQL code had already been examined by the DBA; it had been thoroughly optimized, and actually ran pretty well. (The concern was that future additions to the database would make this time grow significantly.)

The problem with the SQL code shown above is not that it is poorly optimized, but rather, that the entire approach is in error! If we look carefully, we can see that the code is performing a large amount of unnecessary processing. Specifically, Step 3 is completely unnecessary – we don't need to first find the rows that are in common.

Instead, a much more efficient approach is to just perform the delete based on the list of rows in the other table; if the Old_Data table does not have those rows, the delete does nothing.

In the new SQL that the DBA suggested, Step 3 is entirely eliminated, leaving the simpler (and faster SQL):

```
SQL> DELETE FROM Old_Data
  2  WHERE (Act_id, Dept_id)
  3  IN (SELECT Act_id, Dept_id FROM New_Data);
```

The new SQL simply deletes from the Old_Data table any rows that are in the New_Data table. This has exactly the same effect has the original SQL, but without the Intersect processing.

In this case study, concentrating on making the existing SQL more efficient would have missed the entire issue – it was the wrong SQL in the first place. In the rush to optimize the SQL, no one noticed that it was the wrong SQL!

> **Don't assume that the SQL code is actually doing what it is supposed to.**

That wraps up our brief discussion on the role of SQL tuning; but, the performance specialist will also need to cope with changes that are made with each new database release. So, before we move onto the section dealing with how we begin our SQL analysis, let's take a quick look at what to do with any new database features. Hopefully, these changes will help us, and make our job a little easier.

Handling New Database Features

Each new database release from Oracle includes a wide array of changes, including bug fixes, new features, and optimizer improvements. The optimizer design is tweaked by the Oracle designers in most new versions so that it performs optimally for the broadest possible range of SQL queries and transactions.

In most cases, new bells and whistles will be added, and obsolete features will be removed. Also, generally, problems reported in previous versions will also be fixed. In a few cases, however, new bugs will be introduced. (Later in the book, we discuss some helpful resources on the Oracle web site that will keep the DBA informed of major bugs, such as any security problems with new releases.)

Consider the large number of changes to the database that have been made in recent years. For instance, here are some of the features introduced in Oracle 9i:

Feature	Function
Online Table Redefinition	A new PL/SQL package, which provides a way to redefine tables online. With this option, the database can remain up and running at the same time that changes are being made to a production table.
Suspending a database	A new ALTER SYSTEM statement provides the capability to temporarily halt all input and output to database files. The current transactions complete, but new requests are queued.
Quiescing a database	This new feature allows the DBA to temporarily disallow all operations except for administrative functions.
Expanded archiving destinations	You can now archive the online redo logs to a total of 10 archive destinations.
Multiple block sizes	This feature provides for nonstandard block sizes, in which the system tablespace is set to one block size, and other tablespaces to a different block size. This option is especially useful when it is necessary to move a tablespace to a different database, which has a different block size.
Oracle Managed Files	With this feature, it is not necessary to explicitly name a new database file; Oracle automatically provides a unique name for the file (and deletes the file when not needed).
Automatic delete of data file	This feature permits the database itself to drop a .dbf file when a tablespace is dropped by the DBA. Traditionally, this has been a manual operation.
External Tables	This allows the database to read a table outside the database, just like the SQL*Loader utility. Access is provided via table access drivers.
Database Time Zone	When creating a database, the DBA can now specify a local time zone.
Transaction Naming	In Oracle 9i, the DBA can assign a name to a transaction. This is useful in distributed systems, in which certain transactions may need to be specifically identified and cancelled.
Monitoring index usage	A new option for the ALTER INDEX statement allows the DBA to see if an index is currently being used.

Each new database release typically provides an impressive array of new features – many are brilliant ideas that the Oracle community has enthusiastically welcomed.

Some Lessons may have to be Re-Learned

The list goes on and on. Oracle Corporation continues to add more and more database features; most will prove useful, but some will probably be discarded. As the new database versions are released, the performance specialist may discover that some of the lessons-learned in previous versions may no longer apply! Some of these lessons may have to be re-learned, or adapted to the new features.

For example, ideas that worked well for rule-based optimization may prove useless when the cost-based optimizer is used. Specifically, the old rule-of-thumb about determining which table is the driving table by looking at the order of tables in the FROM clause no longer applies. Additionally, performance experts now need to be aware of different join methods; the analyst who forgets about the hash join option will certainly be ignoring a major method of reducing I/O during table joins.

Stability in the Midst of Change

The quantity of database and optimizer changes seems to imply that earlier techniques for performance tuning might be completely obsolete, and that all those earlier lessons will have to be discarded. Fortunately for the Oracle performance expert, that is not the case; although many of the details have changed, the basic principles of SQL tuning have remained nearly the same.

> **Many of the principles of SQL performance tuning are generally applicable to most Oracle versions.**

Clearly, the options available to the performance specialist have increased greatly, but the essential tuning problem has not changed much. Many SQL problems still boil down to getting the right join order in table joins, or creating indexes with the right columns, and so on. DBAs still forget to add indexes, and developers still add functions in the WHERE clause, precluding use of most indexes. To solve problems such as these, the Oracle Pathologist will follow the same general process – but with a few more options, depending on the latest tools in the toolkit.

New Tools for the Toolkit

Most of the new tuning options serve to increase the size of the expert's toolkit. The optimizer changes don't generally do away with a tuning method; rather, they give the analyst a few more choices.

For example, when dealing with lumpy data, the analyst now has the option of creating a histogram on certain columns.

A histogram records the distribution of data for a certain column, so that the optimizer knows which values are rare, and which are plentiful.

For data warehouse applications, the new Star Transformation join technique is available. For table joins, the hash join is available. (We devote the next chapter to analyzing SQL joins, where we explain the variety of joins possible, and how to best select the join method.) In all these cases, the tuning expert should certainly be aware of these new options; nevertheless, he or she should still employ the same basic process.

We should also remember that all these new features, whether optimizer changes, or clever new application tools, aren't always perfect. This is a further complication for the performance analyst, since he must now consider the possibility that a new feature may not work as advertised:

> **Do not assume that a new database feature works exactly as it should.**

Where Do I Start?

Well, if the principles of SQL performance tuning haven't changed much, what exactly are those principles? Where do I start? What steps should I follow?

In the previous phase in our tuning process the Oracle Detective will probably have gathered enough intelligence information for us already to have a good idea of where the problem lies. For instance, at this stage in the tuning process, the relevant SQL statements will have already been identified. Also utilities, such as TKPROF, may already have been used to identify problem areas.

Before diving into detailed performance analysis, let's pause and consider one simple step that can prevent a lot of grief later – check the basics first. Regardless of the type of SQL code, there are certain steps and principles that can be applied. Before getting into the details of execution plans, it is a good idea to check some very simple things first; the time required will be short, and the payoff can be sizeable.

Check Statistics

When faced with a SQL problem, it is always a good idea to check for valid statistics first. Now that a wide variety of database applications can use the cost-based optimizer, it is critical that recent statistics be generated for all database tables.

Incorrect or missing statistics are the frequent cause of SQL performance problems. The link between outdated statistics and poor SQL performance should come as no surprise; if the optimizer doesn't have the correct numbers, how can it decide how to run the SQL statement efficiently? Many, many SQL problems are resolved once the statistics are updated:

> **Ensuring use of current table statistics averts many SQL problems.**

One simple way to check for statistics is to query the Dba_Tables view. This view contains several columns that reveal when the last statistics were gathered, and what kind of sample size was used.

For instance, the following query will list the pertinent information for all tables in the CHRIS schema:

```
SQL> SELECT Table_Name, Last_Analyzed, Sample_Size, Num_Rows
  2  FROM Dba_Tables
  3  WHERE Owner = 'CHRIS';

TABLE_NAME      LAST_ANALYZED     SAMPLE_SIZE    NUM_ROWS
------------    ---------------   -------------  -----------

STUDENT         01-JAN-2002            10000     13044456
REGISTRATION    01-JAN-2002            10000        23061
DEPT
PERS_INFO       01-JAN-2002            10000     13045656
```

In the above query, we see that the DEPT table has not been analyzed. So, when the application queries the DEPT table, the optimizer may not accurately develop the best execution plan. Clearly, the DBA should correct this oversight as soon as possible.

Generating New Statistics

New statistics can be generated using the Analyze Table command. There are two choices when gathering statistics; Compute Statistics, or Estimate Statistics. Normally, the estimate option is good enough; it is not really necessary to review every row in a table for the optimizer to develop good information; in fact, a relatively small percentage of rows can actually lead to a very good estimate. Of course, if the table is small, gathering statistics for every row will not really take much longer; in addition, you will have the benefit of exact statistics, rather than just good estimates.

So, for example, we could issue the following command:

```
SQL> Analyze Table DEPT Estimate Statistics;
```

With this syntax, the statistical sample size defaults to 1024 rows, regardless of the table size. For small tables, even this modest sample size will usually prove sufficient.

Optimizer statistics can be related to election polling activity. In the United States, election polls are taken prior to every major election. Each time a poll is taken, the statistician will note how accurate the poll should be considered, and how many people were interviewed for the pool. Typically, the number of samples in these polls is quite small, but the polling information is usually declared to be accurate within a few percent. That is, statisticians have determined that only a relatively small sampling can yield very good results.

It is very much the same in the Oracle arena. The default sample size of 1024 rows is usually acceptable for small- or medium-sized tables. Just like the polling data, the optimizer will achieve reasonably accurate results with this small sampling.

For large tables (above 1 million rows), the default sample size probably not be adequate; hence, it is common practice to explicitly specify a sample size, such as 10%. For extremely large tables (such as in a data warehouse), the sample size may be even lower, so as to avoid involving large numbers.

For our DEPT table, we could use the following syntax:

```
SQL> Analyze Table DEPT Estimate Statistics Sample 10
  2  percent;
```

An alternative method of gathering statistics is becoming more popular since the introduction of Oracle 9I; this method uses a PL/SQL supplied package called DBMS_STATS. One of the key advantages of the DBMS_STATS method is that the database will use parallel processes so as to gather the statistics as rapidly as possible. Additionally, Oracle provides the option of having the database itself decide on a good sample size.

To gather table statistics, the procedure GATHER_TABLE_STATS is used. Here are the parameters used when calling that procedure:

```
DBMS_STATS.GATHER_TABLE_STATS (
   ownname           VARCHAR2,
   tabname           VARCHAR2,
   partname          VARCHAR2 DEFAULT NULL,
   estimate_percent  NUMBER   DEFAULT NULL,
   block_sample      BOOLEAN  DEFAULT FALSE,
   method_opt        VARCHAR2 DEFAULT 'FOR ALL COLUMNS SIZE 1',
   degree            NUMBER   DEFAULT NULL,
   granularity       VARCHAR2 DEFAULT 'DEFAULT',
   cascade           BOOLEAN  DEFAULT FALSE,
   stattab           VARCHAR2 DEFAULT NULL,
   statid            VARCHAR2 DEFAULT NULL,
   statown           VARCHAR2 DEFAULT NULL);
```

Here is what the parameters mean:

Parameter	Meaning
Ownname	Schema of table to be analyzed.
Tabname	Name of table.
Partname	Name of partition (if any).
Estimate_Percent	Percent of rows to use for sampling. Null means use compute, not estimate. Insert DBMS_STATS.AUTO_SAMPLE_SIZE to have Oracle determine a good sample size.
Block_Sample	Should blocks be randomly sampled, instead of rows.
Method_Opt	Options for using histograms. Specifies which columns should receive histograms.

Parameter	Meaning
Degree	Degree of parallelism to use when building statistics.
Granularity	Options for partitioned tables.
Cascade	Options for gathering statistics on the table indexes.

Here is an example of how to use this procedure, as invoked from SQL*Plus. The command below gathers statistics on the table called DEPT, which is in the schema called PROD. We want to estimate statistics using a sample size of 10%:

```
SQL> EXEC Sys.Dbms_Stats.Gather_Table_Stats ('PROD', -
  2  'DEPT', ESTIMATE_PERCENT=>10);
```

Note a few special symbols in the above command; the operator => is used to explicitly assign values to a particular parameter. Also note that we have used the dash – character to continue the command on the next line.

Further details on the use of the DBMS_STATS package may be found in the Oracle 9i documentation, specifically, *Supplied PL/SQL Packages and Types Reference*.

Confirm that the SQL Being Run is Intended

There is yet another simple check to perform; confirm that the SQL being executed is doing what was intended. This step might seem a bit silly, but many DBAs have spent hours troubleshooting a SQL statement that no one ever intended to run!

How can this happen? Why would anyone run SQL statements that consume huge amounts of resources for no reason?

The answer is that, occasionally, applications run SQL statements that are inadvertently triggered by a user error, or a flaw in the application design. For instance, with some applications it might be easy for the user to make a mistake, and to run a query accidentally that he did not intend to run.

It is especially common for applications to allow a null search to execute; this is a query that has no limiting conditions whatsoever! For example, instead of retrieving records for certain customers using a limiting condition provided by the user, the query returns records for *all* customers. The correction for these types of application problems is usually an application change to disallow queries for which no restricting criteria have been entered.

Check the Size of the Result Set

It is very common, especially in reporting applications, for users to report database problems that are really just delays due to displaying a huge result set. These types of problems are especially common on data warehouse applications.

For instance, suppose a report user desires to see all customers for the past week or month. Depending on the application, it may be easy to mistakenly request a Detail Report that lists all customers over a one-year period. The result set for this accidental query could easily be hundreds of thousands of rows. Of course, the transfer of this data would mean a substantial network delay – usually far beyond the time for the database to actually extract the rows.

The database may contribute a small delay (perhaps half a minute), but the real delay will come when the database transfers the data to the application server, which then must format and display the report. Typically, the network and application delays will be many times greater than the database delay. The reason for this is simple; extracting data is relatively easy, but formatting and displaying the information is usually much more time consuming:

> **Be alert for performance delays due to large result sets.**

If the users do not know the size of the final result set, that information can be obtained from the SQL that is being run. (Recall that the actual SQL text can be retrieved from the database by querying the V$SQL view or, if necessary, by activating SQL_TRACE, and reviewing the trace dump file.)

With the SQL code known, one can simply re-run the SQL, with a few modifications to avoid the actual displaying of data. That is, we set up a test to determine what the size of the result set would be if we were to display all the rows, although we won't actually do so. Note also that the AUTOTRACE feature in SQL*Plus has a convenient way of accomplishing this same thing. By using the command SET AUTOTRACE ON TRACEONLY we can run the query, but not actually display the results.

For instance, an easy way to quantify the total result set is to insert the rows into a temporary table instead of displaying them on the screen. Alternatively, the SQL can be modified to return the row count, instead of the actual rows.

Summarize the Starting Position of the Problem

When tuning SQL, it is helpful to note what the starting position is. Like a scientist, it is useful to keep a sort of laboratory notebook of how the problem looked at the beginning of analysis, and what steps were taken to resolve it.

Notebook entries could contain pertinent facts such as:

- ❑ Exact SQL code of query or transaction
- ❑ Frequency of code execution
- ❑ Simplified SQL code (without formatting, and so on)
- ❑ Diagram of table joins (if applicable)
- ❑ Original execution plan
- ❑ Original run time statistics, including elapsed time, disk I/O, logical reads
- ❑ Number of rows returned
- ❑ Size of result set in bytes

Besides being helpful in the actual tuning process, these entries will prove valuable later, when a final report is made to the customer. It will be important to report the before and after statistics to management.

Now that we have presented some preliminary ideas for getting started with SQL analysis, let's examine how the Oracle optimizer actually handles a query. The manner in which an Oracle database processes a query is called the **execution plan**; this is one of the most important aspects of Oracle performance tuning.

Oracle Execution Plans

When trying to find a root cause, the Oracle Pathologist should ask the question, "What is the optimizer doing with the SQL?" In the Oracle world, this means taking a look at the steps that the database engine performs when running the SQL statement, listed in the execution plan. Before the database server can execute a SQL statement, the Oracle engine must first parse the statement and develop a road map of data access methods and other steps that must be fulfilled before the SQL statement can be fully satisfied.

For example, consider how the Oracle optimizer would deal with a simple SELECT query. Suppose that this query is against a table called Employee; this query searches for all employees that have an employee id between 1000 and 1010:

```
SQL> SELECT Emp_Name
   2  FROM Employee
   3  WHERE Employee_Id BETWEEN 1000 AND 1010;
```

How will the optimizer deal with this SQL statement? Assuming that there is an index on the column Employee_Id, the optimizer will clearly benefit by using it to narrow down the result set. Thus, whatever the format of the Oracle execution plan, we would expect that the execution plan for this query would first show an index lookup, and then a table access using the information that was supplied by the index.

There have been numerous articles written on how to use execution plans, and for good reason. This facility is central to the SQL tuning process; it is essential that you become proficient in obtaining and interpreting the execution plan for any SQL statement:

> **Practice reviewing execution plans for a wide variety of SQL statements.**

With the execution plan in hand, the Oracle specialist can often pinpoint a SQL problem. For instance, the execution plan will divulge:

❑ Which indexes are being used.

❑ Which tables are being scanned.

❑ How tables are joined – for example, nested loop, or hash join, or sort-merge (see the following chapter for more on these).

❑ The order of table joins.

❏ Whether parallelism is being used, and if so, which tables or indexes. (Parallelism refers to a way that Oracle can expedite processing by dividing a complex task into separate parts, and then launching *multiple* server processes to tackle the pieces simultaneously.)

The information supplied by execution plans is so great that the value of understanding them should be apparent. Without the execution plan, the analyst simply doesn't know how the optimizer is running a particular SQL statement; in that case, guesswork is the only resort.

Obtaining the Execution Plan

A very common way to find the execution plan for any SQL statement is to use the EXPLAIN PLAN statement. This feature allows us to submit a SQL statement to Oracle and have the database prepare the execution plan for the statement without actually executing it.

When EXPLAIN PLAN is run, the execution plan is not displayed; instead, it is stored in a special table called the **plan table**. When running this command, unless an alternative name is specified, the name of this special table is simply Plan_Table. Oracle provides a script to create this table if it doesn't already exist in your schema.; the script is called utlxplan.sql. This script can be found in $ORACLE_HOME/rdbms/admin. (Note that the term $ORACLE_HOME refers to the directory that contains the Oracle executables.)

The columns that make up the plan table are shown below:

Name	Type
STATEMENT_ID	VARCHAR2(30)
TIMESTAMP	DATE
REMARKS	VARCHAR2(80)
OPERATION	VARCHAR2(30)
OPTIONS	VARCHAR2(30)
OBJECT_NODE	VARCHAR2(128)
OBJECT_OWNER	VARCHAR2(30)
OBJECT_NAME	VARCHAR2(30)
OBJECT_INSTANCE	NUMBER(38)
OBJECT_TYPE	VARCHAR2(30)
OPTIMIZER	VARCHAR2(255)
SEARCH_COLUMNS	NUMBER
ID	NUMBER(38)

Name	Type
PARENT_ID	NUMBER(38)
POSITION	NUMBER(38)
COST	NUMBER(38)
CARDINALITY	NUMBER(38)
BYTES	NUMBER(38)
OTHER_TAG	VARCHAR2(255)
PARTITION_START	VARCHAR2(255)
PARTITION_STOP	VARCHAR2(255)
PARTITION_ID	NUMBER(38)
OTHER	LONG
DISTRIBUTION	VARCHAR2(30)

Once the execution plan is stored in the plan table, you can query the rows in it using ordinary SELECT statements executed from a SQL*Plus session. In fact, Oracle provides a script that you can use. (The script provides clear formatting; it is called utxpls.sql.) A useful feature of the plan table is that it can contain many different execution plans. Each plan is given an identifier called Statement_id; each row in the plan table is then identified with this identifier, in order to keep the plans separate.

Alternatively, the analyst may choose only to store a single plan in the table. In this case, simply truncate the plan table before obtaining a new execution plan. Another method is to roll back an EXPLAIN PLAN statement in order to remove the execution plan from the plan table. This rollback is achieved simply by issuing the command ROLLBACK while in SQL*Plus.

The EXPLAIN PLAN statement runs very quickly, even if the statement being analyzed is a query that would actually run for hours. This is because the statement is simply parsed and its execution plan saved into the plan table. The actual SQL statement is never executed by the EXPLAIN PLAN process.

Preparing to Use the EXPLAIN PLAN Feature

You don't need any special system privileges in order to use the EXPLAIN PLAN statement. However, you do need to have INSERT privileges on the plan table, and you must have sufficient privileges to execute the statement you are trying to explain. Also, in order to explain a statement that involves views, you must have privileges on all the tables that make up the view. If you don't, you'll get an ORA-01039: insufficient privileges on underlying objects of the view error.

The plan table, although traditionally called Plan_Table, can actually be given any name we like; note, however, that the definition of the table must be strictly followed – the exact names and data types of the columns are required.

The plan table is created using the script called utlxplan.sql. This script is found in the directory $ORACLE_HOME/rdbms/admin.

Recall that $ORACLE_HOME refers to the location where the Oracle executables have been installed. On a Microsoft platform, an example of this would be C:\Oracle. On UNIX platforms, a typical location would be /u01/app/oracle/product/8.7.2.

If a different table name from the default one is required, simply modify the script to use the desired name. The utlxplan script already has the correct column definitions, so it should always be used as the basis for creating the plan table.

Running the EXPLAIN PLAN Statement

Once you have used the utlxplan script to create a plan table, you are ready to run the EXPLAIN PLAN statement. The syntax is as follows:

```
EXPLAIN PLAN SET STATEMENT_ID = [Id]
INTO [table name]
FOR [SQL Statement];
```

The INTO clause is optional; if you do not specify this clause, then Oracle will assume that the name of the plan table is the default name.

The SET clause is also optional. You use it to assign a name to the execution plan, which is useful if you want to be able to have multiple execution plans stored in the plan table at the same time. Giving each execution plan a distinct name enables you to determine which rows in the plan table belong to which execution plan. If the SET clause is not used, then it will be necessary to truncate the table prior to the next EXPLAIN PLAN; otherwise, there will be no way to distinguish between the execution steps that are listed in the plan table.

When we run the EXPLAIN PLAN statement in SQL*Plus, we get back the feedback message Explained. For instance, the following commands in SQL*Plus could be used to find the execution plan for a very simple query. We will use the simple name ONE so we can later identify this execution plan in the plan table:

```
SQL> EXPLAIN PLAN SET Statement_Id = 'ONE'
  2   FOR SELECT COUNT (*) FROM Employee;

Explained
```

At this point the execution plan for the explained SQL statement has been inserted into the plan table, and we can now query the plan table to examine the execution plan.

Contents of the Execution Plan

An execution plan is a hierarchical arrangement of simple data access and processing operations. It simply shows how the Oracle engine intends to get the data, and what other processing steps will need to be implemented. In order to display the plan, we will use a simple SQL query that can be run from SQL*Plus. Just as there are many different ways to retrieve data from regular database tables, there are many different ways to format the data retrieved from the plan table. This means that there is no one way to query the plan table; individual DBAs will find different columns in the plan table more useful than others, depending on the situation.

For example, many DBAs use a script that shows indentation for the different parts of the execution plan. Some DBAs want to see more fields; others are happy with just a display of the most critical fields. Each analyst will customize his or her own script:

> **Develop and save your own favorite script for retrieving execution plans.**

Using the sample script presented below, the execution plan can be retrieved and printed in a helpful indented format. There are just a few tricks in this script that make the display a little more readable:

```
SET VERIFY OFF
SET PAGESIZE 100

ACCEPT stmt_id CHAR PROMPT "Enter statement_id: "

COL id          FORMAT 999
COL parent_id   FORMAT 999 HEADING "PARENT"
COL operation   FORMAT a35 TRUNCATE
COL object_name FORMAT a30

SELECT id, parent_id, LPAD (' ', LEVEL - 1) || operation ||
' ' || options operation, object_name
FROM plan_table
WHERE statement_id = '&stmt_id'
START WITH id = 0
AND statement_id = '&stmt_id'
CONNECT BY PRIOR id = parent_id
AND statement_id = '&stmt_id';
```

First, the script asks the user to provide the Statement_Id. Of course, this is the identifier that was used when the EXPLAIN PLAN statement was executed. Because execution plans are shown in a *hierarchy*, the script will use a CONNECT BY clause. (The CONNECT BY and START WITH clauses make use of a convenient Oracle feature that causes a traversal of the hierarchy from parent to child, or vice versa.) Another feature is the LPAD function; this causes the output to be formatted with indentations to indicate the different levels in the hierarchy The script also includes the qualification on Statement_Id; otherwise, the response would return rows for other execution plans as well!

Let's now turn to some examples to see how the process works.

Example: Creating and Retrieving an Execution Plan

To demonstrate the process for creating then retrieving an execution plan, let's consider a simple query, shown below:

```
SQL> SELECT a.customer_name, a.customer_number,
  2  b.invoice_number, b.invoice_type, b.invoice_date,
  3  b.total_amount, c.line_number, c.part_number,
  4  c.quantity, c.unit_cost
  5  FROM customers a, invoices b, invoice_items c
  6  WHERE c.invoice_id = :b1
  7  AND c.line_number = :b2
  8  AND b.invoice_id = c.invoice_id
  9  AND a.customer_id = b.customer_id;
```

This invoice item query simply retrieves customer and invoice information from three tables: Customers, Invoices, and Invoice_Items. In addition, it limits the results to only a particular invoice and line item.

The execution plan for this SQL statement, as retrieved and formatted using our sample script, is shown here:

```
ID  PARENT OPERATION                          OBJECT_NAME
---- ------- -------------------------------- -------------
 0          SELECT STATEMENT
 1      0   NESTED LOOPS
 2      1    NESTED LOOPS
 3      2     TABLE ACCESS BY INDEX ROWID     INVOICE_ITEMS
 4      3      INDEX UNIQUE SCAN              INVOICE_ITEMS_PK
 5      2     TABLE ACCESS BY INDEX ROWID     INVOICES
 6      5      INDEX UNIQUE SCAN              INVOICES_PK
 7      1    TABLE ACCESS BY INDEX ROWID      CUSTOMERS
 8      7     INDEX UNIQUE SCAN               CUSTOMERS_PK
```

The execution plan shows that Oracle is using nested loop joins to join three tables (two tables joined at a time), and that accesses from all three tables are by unique index lookup – note the phrase INDEX UNIQUE SCAN in three places. For each index lookup, the exact index name is shown.

The first table in the join is invoice_items. This table is not accessed directly; rather, the index INVOICE_ITEMS_PK is first used to find rows matching the criteria listed in the SQL query.

After the rows from invoice_items are found, this intermediate result set is used to find matching row(s) in the invoices table. The result set from this second join is then used to find matching rows in the customers table.

Other Scripts Provided by Oracle

Besides the sample script shown previously in this chapter, there are other scripts that can be used to retrieve the execution plan. For instance, for Oracle 8i and later, there are two plan query scripts in the directory, $ORACLE_HOME/rdbms/admin. utlxpls.sql is intended for displaying execution plans of statements that do not involve parallel processing, while utlxplp.sql shows additional information pertaining to parallel processing. Note that the names of the two scripts only differ by only one letter: s for single (non-parallel) processing and p for parallel processing. The output of the latter script is more complex, so it is best to use it only when parallel queries are used.

The output from utlxpls.sql for our sample invoice item query is shown in the next code snippet. Note the similarity of the output to the format shown in the output from our first example in this chapter. This new figure has a little more information; however, most analysts will probably prefer the simpler output, without the row and byte counts. There are a few confusing notations, such as pstart and pstop. These two terms refer to the partitioning option, in which data in a table is divided (for example, by date) into convenient sets, for faster query access. Pstart means the *start* partition of a range of queried partitions, while pstop refers to the *stop* partition of a range of accessed partitions:

```
Plan Table
-----------------------------------------------------------------------
|Operation                    |Name      |Rows|Bytes|Cost|Pstart|Pstop
-----------------------------------------------------------------------
|SELECT STATEMENT             |          |  1 |  39 |  4 |      |
| NESTED LOOPS                |          |  1 |  39 |  4 |      |
|  NESTED LOOPS               |          |  1 |  27 |  3 |      |
|   TABLE ACCESS BY INDEX R   |INVOICE_I |  1 |  15 |  2 |      |
|    INDEX UNIQUE SCAN        |INVOICE_I |  2 |     |  1 |      |
|   TABLE ACCESS BY INDEX R   |INVOICES  |  2 |  24 |  1 |      |
|    INDEX UNIQUE SCAN        |INVOICES_ |  2 |     |    |      |
|   TABLE ACCESS BY INDEX RO  |CUSTOMERS |100 |  1K |  1 |      |
|    INDEX UNIQUE SCAN        |CUSTOMERS |100 |     |    |      |
```

When you have completed your analysis of the execution plan for a particular SQL statement, you can delete it from the plan table. As mentioned earlier, you can do this by rolling back the EXPLAIN PLAN statement, truncating the plan table, or simply deleting rows from the plan table.

If you have multiple execution plans in the plan table, then you should delete selectively by Statement_id:

> **Be careful to use unique identifiers when using EXPLAIN PLAN.**

Besides explicitly asking Oracle to generate an execution plan (and then having to query the plan table,) there is another way to get this same information. This alternate method makes use of the standard utility, SQL*Plus. Some DBAs find the SQL*Plus method more convenient; it really comes down to a matter of personal preference.

Obtaining Execution Plans using SQL*Plus AUTOTRACE

Although it is pretty easy to generate an execution plan using EXPLAIN PLAN, it is not the only way to determine how the Oracle optimizer will process certain SQL code. Tools, such as Oracle's OEM, can also display the execution plan for the SQL that a given session is running. Recall also that TKPROF reports can include the execution plan.

Although these methods are not very difficult, there is an even easier method – SQL*Plus AUTOTRACE. With this feature, the Oracle engine automatically displays the execution plan after each statement is executed. In addition to the execution plan, the AUTOTRACE feature will show the resources, for example disk reads and logical reads, that were consumed during the SQL execution.

AUTOTRACE is controlled by using the following SQL*Plus syntax:

```
SQL> SET AUTOTRACE OFF|ON|TRACEONLY [EXPLAIN] [STATISTICS]
```

When we turn on AUTOTRACE in SQL*Plus, the default behavior is for SQL*Plus to execute each statement, display the results as usual, then display the execution plan and resource statistics. Thus, returning to our sample Invoice item query, the output from AUTOTRACE is shown here:

```
Execution Plan
----------------------------------------------------------
0      SELECT STATEMENT Optimizer=CHOOSE (Cost=4 Card=1 Bytes=39)
1    0   NESTED LOOPS (Cost=4 Card=1 Bytes=39)
2    1    NESTED LOOPS (Cost=3 Card=1 Bytes=27)
3    2     TABLE ACCESS (BY INDEX ROWID) OF 'INVOICE_ITEMS'
            (Cost =2 Card=1 Bytes=15)
4    3      INDEX (UNIQUE SCAN) OF 'INVOICE_ITEMS_PK' (UNIQUE)
            (Cost=1 Card=2)
5    2     TABLE ACCESS (BY INDEX ROWID) OF 'INVOICES'
            (Cost=1 Card=2 Bytes=24)
6    5      INDEX (UNIQUE SCAN) OF 'INVOICES_PK' (UNIQUE)
7    1    TABLE ACCESS (BY INDEX ROWID) OF 'CUSTOMERS'
            (Cost=1 Card=100 Bytes=1200)

8    7      INDEX (UNIQUE SCAN) OF 'CUSTOMERS_PK' (UNIQUE)


Statistics
----------------------------------------------------------
        0   recursive calls
        0   db block gets
        8   consistent gets
        0   physical reads
        0   redo size
      517   bytes sent via SQL*Net to client
      424   bytes received via SQL*Net from client
        2   SQL*Net roundtrips to/from client
        0   sorts (memory)
        0   sorts (disk)
        1   rows processed
```

As shown in the figure, the AUTOTRACE version of the execution plan provides the same basic information as the EXPLAIN PLAN version. Note, however, the additional details about resource usage – shown at the bottom of the figure. For our sample query, there were only eight logical reads (shown as consistent_gets). In addition, there were 517 bytes sent to the user, and 424 bytes sent from the user to the server.

There are a few words shown in the figure that need some explanation; the term Card is short for cardinality. It is a term borrowed from database theory. In this context, it is simply the number of rows in the table. This value is obtained by the optimizer when the statistics are gathered. Note that, in practice, the term cardinality is often used in a different way; typically, DBAs use it to describe the proportion of distinct values in a particular column compared to the total number of rows in the table. Technically, the correct phrase for this is *degree of cardinality*.

The term Cost represents units of work or resource used. The CBO uses disk I/O, CPU usage, and memory usage as units of work. So, the cost used by the CBO represents an estimate of the number of disk I/Os and the amount of CPU and memory used in performing an operation. The operation can be scanning a table, accessing rows from a table by using an index, joining two tables together, or sorting a row set. The cost of a query plan is the number of work units that are expected to be incurred when the query is executed and its result produced.

For further information, you can consult *Oracle9i Database Performance Guide and Reference*.

AUTOTRACE Options

There are a few different ways to use AUTOTRACE. By specifying the TRACEONLY keyword, we can have SQL*Plus suppress the query results (but still run the query). This would be very useful if the final output contained a huge result set, so that the actual display of the results is not practical. Other useful options are the EXPLAIN or STATISTICS keywords; with these, we can have SQL*Plus display just the execution plan (without the statistics), or just the statistics (without the execution plan).

In order to have SQL*Plus display execution plans, you must have privileges on the table Plan_Table. Additionally, in order to have SQL*Plus display the resource statistics, you must have SELECT privileges on V$SESSTAT, V$STATNAME, and V$SESSION. (Of course, if the analyst has DBA privileges, this is not an issue.) There is a script in $ORACLE_HOME/sqlplus/admin called plustrce.sql that creates a role with these three privileges in it; note, however, that this script is not run automatically by the Oracle installer.

The AUTOTRACE feature of SQL*Plus makes it extremely easy to generate and view execution plans, with resource statistics as an added bonus. One key drawback, however, is that the statement being explained must actually be executed by the database engine before SQL*Plus will display the execution plan. This makes the tool impractical in a situation where you would like to predict how long an operation might take to complete:

> Use SQL*Plus AUTOTRACE in cases where it is feasible to actually execute the SQL statement.

Interpreting Execution Plans

An execution plan is a hierarchical structure that resembles an inverted tree. The actual SQL statement can be thought of as the root of the tree; this will be the first line on an execution plan listing – the line that is least indented.

The SQL result can be thought of as the conclusion of one or more lower-level operations. Each of these subordinate steps can typically be broken down even further. This decomposition process continues repeatedly until, eventually, even the most complex SQL statement is broken down into a set of basic operations.

Example: A Simple Query's Execution Plan

Consider this simple query:

```
SQL> SELECT customer_id, customer_number, customer_name
  2  FROM customers
  3  WHERE UPPER (customer_name) LIKE 'ACME%'
  4  ORDER BY customer_name;
```

and its execution plan:

```
  ID   PARENT OPERATION                        OBJECT_NAME
  ---- -------- ------------------------------ ------------
   0           SELECT STATEMENT
   1        0  SORT ORDER BY
   2        1    TABLE ACCESS FULL CUSTOMERS
```

As shown, the top-most operation (that which is being explained) is a SELECT statement. The output of the statement will be the results of a sort operation (due to the ORDER BY clause in the original SQL statement). The input to the sort will be the results of a full table scan of the Customers table.

The Oracle engine will execute this query by checking every row in the Customers table to find which rows match the search criteria, and then sorting the results. In this example, the developer might have expected Oracle to use an index on the customer_name column to avoid a full table scan, but the use of the UPPER function nullified the possibility of using an existing index. A function-based index could have been created in order to make index use possible.

Example: An Execution Plan for a Nested Loop Query

Consider the query shown here:

```
SQL> SELECT a.customer_name, b.invoice_number, b.invoice_date
  2  FROM customers a, invoices b
  3  WHERE b.invoice_date > TRUNC (SYSDATE - 1)
  4  AND a.customer_id = b.customer_id;
```

and its execution plan:

```
  ID PARENT  OPERATION                             OBJECT_NAME
 ---- ------- ------------------------------------  ---------------
   0           SELECT STATEMENT
   1        0  NESTED LOOPS
   2        1   TABLE ACCESS BY INDEX ROWID         INVOICES
   3        2    INDEX RANGE SCAN                    INVOICES_DATE
   4        1   TABLE ACCESS BY INDEX ROWID         CUSTOMERS
   5        4    INDEX UNIQUE SCAN                   CUSTOMERS_PK
```

Once again, the root operation (shown at the top of the execution plan) is a SELECT statement. In this case, the SELECT statement gets its input from the results of a nested loops join operation. The nested loops operation takes, as input, the results of the invoices and customers table accesses.

Note the indenting, which indicates that the two tables feed directly into the nested loops operation. It also indicates that the invoices table is accessed by a range scan of the INVOICES_DATE index, while the customers table is accessed by a unique scan of the CUSTOMERS_PK index.

It will be helpful to explain, step by step, the exact processes that Oracle will perform to execute the query shown in the previous code snippet:

1. Oracle will perform a range scan on the INVOICES_DATE index to find the ROWIDs of all rows in the invoices table that have an invoice date matching the query criteria.

2. For each ROWID found, Oracle will fetch the corresponding row from the invoices table.

3. Using the customer_id retrieved from the invoices table, Oracle will read the CUSTOMERS_PK index to find a ROWID for the customers table.

4. This ROWID is used to fetch the correct customer record. (This, in effect, joins the rows fetched from the invoices table with their corresponding matches in the customers table.)

5. The results of the nested loops join operation are returned as the query results.

Let's now look at another example of interpreting an execution plan.

Example: An Execution Plan for a Two-Join Query

Consider the query and execution plan shown below:

```
SQL> SELECT a.customer_name, COUNT (DISTINCT b.invoice_id)
  2  "Open Invoices", COUNT (c.invoice_id)
  3  "Open Invoice Items"
  4  FROM customers a, invoices b, invoice_items c
  5  WHERE b.invoice_status = 'OPEN'
  6  AND a.customer_id = b.customer_id
  7  AND c.invoice_id (+) = b.invoice_id
  8  GROUP BY a.customer_name;
```

```
ID PARENT OPERATION                                  OBJECT_NAME
-- ------ ------------------------------------------ ---------------
 0            SELECT STATEMENT
 1        0   SORT GROUP BY
 2        1    NESTED LOOPS OUTER
 3        2     HASH JOIN
 4        3      TABLE ACCESS BY INDEX ROWID         INVOICES
 5        4       INDEX RANGE SCAN                   INVOICES_STATUS
 6        3      TABLE ACCESS FULL                   CUSTOMERS
 7        2     INDEX RANGE SCAN                     INVOICE_ITEMS_PK
```

This execution plan is more complex than the previous three, as it contains two different types of table joins. At this point, it is not necessary to know all the details of the different types of joins but, rather, to observe the method of interpreting the execution plan. The various types of joins are discussed in detail in the next chapter. This example is also illustrative of the way in which Oracle breaks down complex operations into simpler subordinate operations.

According to the execution plan, the Oracle engine will perform the following when commanded to execute this query:

1. Oracle will first perform a range scan on the Invoices_Status index to get the ROWIDs of all rows in the Invoices table with the specified status.

2. For each ROWID found, the respective row from the invoices table will be fetched.

This set of invoice records will be set-aside for a moment while the processing turns to the customers table. The next steps are:

3. Oracle will fetch all customers records with a full table scan.

4. To perform a hash join between the invoices and customers tables, Oracle will build a hash table from the invoice records.

   A hash table is simply the outcome of applying a hashing function to all the records. In this context, a hashing function means a method of placing a group of values, based on a set formula. For example, "Put the data in the bin number that matches the first number found in the string; if there is no number, put the data in bin 0".

5. Oracle will then cause the customer records to probe the invoices hash table

6. Next, a nested loops join will be performed between the results of the hash join and the INVOICE_ITEMS_PK index. For each row resulting from the hash join, Oracle will perform a unique scan of the INVOICE_ITMES_PK index to find index entries for matching invoice items.

Note that Oracle gets everything it needs from the index and doesn't even need to access the invoice_items table at all. Also note that the nested loops operation is an outer join. A sort operation for the purposes of grouping is performed on the results of the nested loops operation in order to complete the SELECT statement.

As well as this, the Oracle optimizer chose to use a hash join and a full table scan on the `customers` table instead of the more traditional nested loops join; the reason for this has to do with the data content. In this database, there are many invoices and a relatively small number of customers, making a full table scan of the `customers` table less expensive than repeated index lookups on the `CUSTOMERS_PK` index.

Consider how the optimizer would work in a slightly different scenario. Suppose the `customers` table was enormous and the relative number of invoices was quite small. In this scenario, a nested loops join might be better than a hash join. We will discuss the strengths and weaknesses of each join type in detail in Chapter 9.

Examining the execution plan allows you to see which join method Oracle is using. Later in this chapter, we will see how to use optimizer hints to persuade the optimizer to use an alternative way of performing a table join.

Example: A More Complicated Query

Now let's look at a slightly more complicated query. The purpose of query shown is to list the big customers – those who have over 100 invoice records. This execution plan is more complex because the query includes a view plus a subquery that is processed separately:

```
SQL> SELECT customer_name
  2  FROM customers a
  3  WHERE EXISTS
  4  (
  5  SELECT 1 FROM invoices_view b
  6  WHERE b.customer_id = a.customer_id
  7  AND number_of_lines > 100
  8  )
  9  ORDER BY customer_name;
```

ID	PARENT	OPERATION	OBJECT_NAME
0		SELECT STATEMENT	
1	0	NESTED LOOPS	
2	1	NESTED LOOPS	
3	2	TABLE ACCESS BY INDEX ROWID	INVOICE_ITEMS
4	3	INDEX UNIQUE SCAN	INVOICE_ITEMS_PK
5	2	TABLE ACCESS BY INDEX ROWID	INVOICES
6	5	INDEX UNIQUE SCAN	INVOICES_PK
7	1	TABLE ACCESS BY INDEX ROWID	CUSTOMERS
8	7	INDEX UNIQUE SCAN	CUSTOMERS_PK

Note that the SQL statement appears to be very compact and simple. The presence of the view, `invoices_view`, complicates things somewhat. To understand this execution plan, we should know the definition of the object called `invoices_view`.

We can easily find this by using the data dictionary view Dba_Views, which reveals the definition as:

```
SELECT a.invoice_id, a.customer_id, a.invoice_date,
       a.invoice_status, a.invoice_number, a.invoice_type,
       a.total_amount,
COUNT(*) number_of_lines
FROM invoices a, invoice_items b
WHERE b.invoice_id = a.invoice_id
GROUP BY a.invoice_id, a.customer_id, a.invoice_date,
         a.invoice_status, a.invoice_number, a.invoice_type,
         a.total_amount;
```

Referring now to the execution plan given in this example, we see that Oracle will perform the following when the SQL statement is executed:

1. First, read all rows from the customers table using a full table scan.

2. For each customer row, use the invoices_view to determine whether the customer should be part of the result set or not.

3. Assemble the view by performing an index range scan on the INVOICES_CUSTOMER_ID index and fetch the rows from the ivoices table containing one specific customer_id.

4. For each invoice record found, the INVOICE_ITEMS_PK index will be range-scanned to get a nested loops join of invoices to their invoice_items records.

5. Sort the results of the join.

6. Filter-out groups with 100 or fewer invoice_items records.

What is left at the step with ID 4 is a list of invoices for one specific customer who has more than 100 invoice_items records associated. If at least one such invoice exists, then the customer passes the filter at the step with ID 2.

Finally, all customer records passing this filter are sorted for correct ordering and the results are complete.

Let's now look a little further into how the optimizer handles views and filtering, for example, reducing the result set based on some specified criteria. These two operations are sometimes listed in the execution plan for a given SQL statement; thus, it will be helpful to understand a little more about these operations.

Views and Filtering

Recall that a view is a database object that does not really have any rows – it is just a definition of how to get the rows. In the execution plan for a SQL statement containing a view, the plan will typically not show a step corresponding to the view. This omission is not a mistake; rather, the Oracle optimizer tries to merge a view definition into the query. In this way, the table accesses required for the view just become part of the regular execution plan. In the SQL of our previous example, shown above, the GROUP BY clause in the view foiled Oracle's attempt to merge the view into the query. Thus, we see a separate view operation became part of the execution plan.

Also, the `filter` operation can take on several different forms. Generally, a `filter` operation occurs when the database engine reviews a set of candidate rows and discards some based on certain criteria. These criteria could involve a simple restriction, such as number of lines, or it could be a more elaborate subquery.

In our last execution plan, the filter at step ID 5 takes only one input. Here, Oracle evaluates each row from the input one at a time, and either adds the row to the output or discards it as appropriate. Meanwhile, the filter at step ID 2 takes two inputs. When a filter takes two inputs, Oracle reads the rows from the first input one at a time and executes the second input once for each row. Based on the results of the second input, the row from the first input is either added to the output or discarded.

Note that a `filter` operation will not always be shown in the execution plan. This is not really an omission; rather, Oracle is able to perform simple filtering operations while performing a full table scan. Thus, a separate filter operation will not be shown if Oracle performs a full table scan while discarding rows not meeting a condition listed in the WHERE clause.

Subqueries

The Oracle optimizer performs some tricky processing when it encounters subqueries. For SQL statements that involve subqueries, the optimizer will try to merge the subquery into the main statement by using a join.

If it is not possible to merge the subquery (and the subquery does not have any dependencies or references to the main query) then the optimizer will treat the subquery as a completely separate statement – almost as if two separate SQL statements were sent to the database server. These situations might be confusing, because the execution plans for these SQL statements may not include the operations for the subquery. In these cases, simply generate an execution plan for the subquery separately.

For example, consider the following SQL statement. This SQL retrieves a list of managers who belong to departments > 20. It also includes a subquery in which we find the managers who have a particular security access:

```
SQL> SELECT Manager_Name, Dept_Id
  2  FROM Department
  3  WHERE Dept_Number > 20
  4  AND Manager_Name IN
  5  (SELECT Manager_Name FROM Managers
  6   WHERE Security_Access = 1);
```

If the subquery does not appear in the execution plan, it can be produced separately with the command:

```
SQL> EXPLAIN PLAN SET Statement_Id = 'M1' FOR
  2  SELECT Manager_Name
  3  FROM Managers
  4  WHERE Security_Access = 1;
```

Note that we have used the reference M1 for the execution plan, so that we can easily identify the information corresponding to the SQL in question.

Other Tips on SQL Tuning

Now that we have discussed in detail the methods used to generate and interpret execution plans, it will be helpful to present some ideas on how best to exploit the valuable information provided.

Review Object Utilization

In reviewing execution plans, one of the most basic steps is to confirm that the objects listed in the plan table are the same objects that you expect to be part of the execution plan. Of course, there should normally not be any surprises, since the tables listed in the SQL statement will normally be the same objects shown in the execution plan; but this is not always the case.

Consider a few special cases. For instance, the last example we looked at began with a very simple SQL statement – but it actually included a reference to a view, which made the execution plan far more complicated than one would have expected. With views, the execution plan can become more complicated, because a view can comprise a SQL statement of nearly unlimited complexity. As a result, when views are involved, what at first looks like a very simple query could actually require the optimizer to perform many complicated steps.

A similar situation occurs when the SQL statement references a synonym, rather than an actual table.

> A synonym is a database object that acts like an alias for some other view or table; you can use the synonym as a shortcut to the other object. This is especially convenient if a table has a cumbersome or very long name.

The synonym could actually be an alias for a table of a completely different name, or even a table in another database (through a database link). In all these cases, a quick perusal of the execution plan will confirm the list of expected tables involved.

Review Index Utilization

A major part of SQL tuning is checking to see which indexes are being used (and why). Some important questions that should be asked include:

❑ Are any indexes being suppressed because of a function?

❑ Is the execution plan using an index when a full table scan would be better?

❑ Which columns of the index are being used?

❑ Is the index used the best choice?

❑ Would a bit-map index be a better choice?

Note that bit-map indexes are appropriate for cases where the query combines different search criteria – none of which are very selective. The Oracle optimizer, normally reluctant to combine separate indexes, is extremely efficient at combining bitmap indexes. Bitmap indexes are often used in data warehouse applications, and are discussed in the following chapter.

Quite often, the optimizer will have a choice of several indexes that could each provide the same information. This occurs when the database has a variety of indexes, each with the same leading column. Generally speaking, the optimizer will select the index that contains the fewest columns that provide all the necessary information – that is, the index that best matches the exact columns needed. The optimizer is not perfect, however, and will occasionally pick an index that is not actually the best alternative.

Remember that indexes are not always the best choices; in fact, some of the worst possible execution plans use indexes! This fact is something that many junior analysts often fail to appreciate. Many times, frustrated developers have approached the DBA and exclaimed, "I don't know what's wrong – the query is using an index!" Although indexes generally assist the Oracle engine, they are not helpful in all cases.

In situations where a full table scan is appropriate, the alternative of index scan (followed by table access) can often produce amazingly bad performance. Indexes are often a good choice, but sometimes are a poor option compared to a full table scan. In cases where most of the table needs to be accessed anyway, indexes are usually an inappropriate alternative:

> **Index usage alone does not indicate proper SQL tuning.**

Note Full Table Scans

Many analysts are focused on eliminating full table scans, but sometimes they may be appropriate. Especially with the improvements made in disk access time, disk caching, and multi-block reads, a full table scan is often an excellent alternative:

> **Full table scans need not be avoided in all cases.**

The objective of the performance expert is not to eliminate full table scans, but to minimize the runtime of the query, as well as the related resource consumption. The reason that indexes are generally a good idea is because response time is generally better, and resource consumption is generally less when indexes are used.

Thus, for queries that impose a severe selective condition, for example, Employee_Id = '12345', an index is almost certainly the best option. There is no question that queries such as this should be using an index; these types of queries are very common, and the Oracle Pathologist should not hesitate to suggest an index for these situations.

As the restrictive condition loosens, however, the choice between index and full table scan will become less obvious. At some point, the cost of the full table scan will be less than numerous index and table lookups. The resource consumption and run time for each of the alternatives can easily be checked in SQL*Plus. (SQL*Plus AUTOTRACE is an excellent way to get a quick measurement of resource consumption.) Just remember that a full table scan does not mean that the optimizer is making an error; it could be the correct choice for a particular SQL statement.

Don't Ignore Logical Reads

Since physical I/O is more expensive than logical I/O, the Oracle analyst might be tempted to ignore logical I/O. This would be a big mistake, for several reasons.

Firstly, the cost of physical I/O is much closer to the cost of logical I/O than is generally believed. The widely publicized speed of modern memory circuits might lead the analyst to believe that logical I/O is tens of thousands of times faster than physical I/O; for Oracle database systems, that is simply incorrect.

Software engineers might be tempted to think of the bare bones access time when thinking of logical access speed; that is, they equate an Oracle logical I/O to the extremely fast memory access in an integrated circuit. Of course, the two are not at all the same. For one thing, the database engine must spend a great deal of time trying to determine if blocks are already in the database buffer cache, or if they need to be read from disk. This process is not trivial, and means that logical I/O for the Oracle system will not be anywhere close to the access time quoted for microprocessors at a much lower level. Furthermore, with the improvements of disk caching and multi-block reads, physical I/O has become much faster:

> **Physical I/O is roughly 10 times more costly than logical I/O.**

All of these things taken together mean that the gap between physical and logical I/O for the Oracle system as a whole is much closer than most analysts realize. This means that Oracle performance analysts need to readjust their thinking, and focus on minimizing logical I/O, as well as physical I/O.

Another good reason to focus on reducing logical reads, is that by solving logical reads, the physical reads will be solved as a necessary side effect. If logical reads are substantially reduced, the physical reads will normally be reduced in a similar proportion. (After all, how can you have physical reads without logical reads also?)

The reverse is not true however. Changing the execution plan to reduce physical reads does not necessarily reduce logical reads – in fact, if the execution plan is drastically changed so that physical reads are eliminated, logical reads may be much higher, and lead to a much worse response time!

For instance, index blocks are often read from the cache, but blocks from tables are much less likely to be in the cache already. So, a query that requires many index reads will lead to a large number of logical reads, but few physical reads. This may or may not be a good idea, but it will make the number of physical reads look good:

> **Reducing logical I/O is usually a good way to reduce physical I/O as well.**

A further reason to focus on logical reads is that logical reads can often lead to massive CPU consumption. For instance, consider two tables that are joined in a nested loop. Normally, a nested loop is a good choice when the result set from the driving table (that is, the first table) is fairly small. The Oracle engine loops through the first table, then uses the small result set to check an index in the second table for the corresponding entries that satisfy the join condition. With a small result set from the first table, the subsequent work is small – perhaps just a few index look-ups.

But what if the result set is not small? What if the first result set is huge, or even comprises the entire table? In that case, the engine must loop through every row of the large result set, processing each row one by one. The response time could easily be an order of magnitude worse – even though very little physical I/O is occurring!

Be a Mentor to the Developers

When analyzing SQL code, the Oracle Pathologist is faced with nailing down the exact issue causing the problem. After spending all the time and effort to accomplish this, why not pass on the analysis details to the development team? That is, instead of hiding all the details, let the developers also benefit from your analysis – perhaps it will avoid a similar problem in the future.

This means that it is not good enough just to say, "The SQL was poorly written". That comment is of no value to the programmer. At the end of the SQL analysis, the analyst needs to be able to state with great confidence precisely what was wrong with the SQL code as written. Don't make the developers guess where they went wrong; rather, show them!

For example, here is a simple summary of the analysis and recommendations that could be provided to both management and the development team.

SQL statement:

```
SQL> SELECT Acct_number, Acct_Name
  2  FROM Accts_Payable
  3  WHERE UPPER (Acct_Name) LIKE 'JONES%';
```

SQL problem:
Execution plan is not using index on table `Accts_Payable`.

Analysis:
This index could not be used because the `UPPER` function makes the index unusable.

Recommendations:

1. Create function based index on `Acct_Name`.

2. Remove `UPPER` function, and redesign application to store the `Acct_Name` field in a consistent case always.

Option 2 also requires that a one-time update be performed on the existing data to convert it to the new format.

This summary succinctly states the root cause of the performance problem, and gives a few reasonable options. With this summary in hand, it is likely that the developers will not repeat the mistake mentioned:

> **Provide the developer with a summary of the solution to the SQL performance problem.**

Remember the Cache Effect

When performing sample run-time tests, remember that the second and subsequent queries will usually be faster because the majority of data fetched will probably be cached. Don't be fooled into believing that some slight change has fixed the problem, when nothing has been corrected at all. Of course, this illusion can be completely avoided if the analyst makes it a practice always to include a measurement of logical reads. If there is no reduction in logical reads, then the fix has probably done nothing.

In our next case study, the developers were fooled into believing that a particular SQL query had been corrected. Their faulty conclusion led them to release a poorly optimized report into production, where it caused unnecessary delays for the customers. The developers had fallen into the trap of believing that they had fixed a problem simply by running it a second time!

Case Study: The Cache Effect to the Rescue!

A group of report writers designed sophisticated user reports for an auto parts chain. The end users accessed the reports over the company intranet. These reports showed personnel throughout the corporation the daily revenue, parts shipped, inventory, and so forth. It was critical that these reports run quickly and efficiently, because they were run by a large number of users; any delays would be viewed very unfavorably.

The report design team was asked to correct several reports that seemed to take a very long time to run. In some cases, the reports were poorly designed; in other cases, the designers needed to add SQL hints, which were provided by the DBA.

To discover which reports needed help, several DBAs monitored them as they ran on the production system. This monitoring was especially easy because the designers had included a particularly useful feature in the application; there was a report run-time log (actually just an Oracle database table) that showed the exact run-time for each report! It even included the exact parameters that were applied to the report, and which user ran the report.

Using this run-time log, one of the DBAs discovered a particular report that ran very slowly; in fact, it ran slowly for almost any parameters that were entered. The DBA was curious as to how this report could actually have been released to production. He asked the lead report developer if he had noticed the long delay for this report during QA testing. The developer responded that he had seen the poor response time, but upon running the same report again, "it was okay".

By running the report on a development server, then querying the V$SQL view to list the SQL text, the application DBA was able to discover the SQL problem for this report. On the development system, the second and subsequent queries were indeed fast, as the physical I/O dropped off due to the caching effect. The DBA recommended a slight change to the report design, which eliminated most of the logical I/O; thus, the runtime for this report was greatly reduced for all runs, even the first run. (The initial report design had nullified index use by inadvertently including a function in the where clause.)

In this case study, the designer was led to believe that a certain SQL query was really well tuned; in reality, the subsequent reports had merely taken advantage of caching much of the data. The number of physical I/Os was substantially reduced (at least for the artificial setup in the testing environment); nevertheless, the huge number of logical I/Os was not reduced at all. Eventually, the SQL was tuned to eliminate the logical I/Os as well.

More Advanced Features of the Plan Table

Although the plan table contains 24 columns, so far we have used only a few of them in our execution plan examples. Columns such as ID, PARENT, OPERATION, and OBJECT_NAME, are indeed most important, but some of the other columns can also be helpful in specific situations:

❑ The OPTIMIZER column in the plan table shows the optimizer mode, for example, RULE or CHOOSE, used by the optimizer to generate the execution plan. One would think that the choices for optimizer mode would be RULE or COST, but not so! Cost-based optimization is only practical if table statistics have been generated. The option CHOOSE thus means that the optimizer uses cost-based optimization, if the statistics are available.

❑ The TIMESTAMP column shows the date and time that the execution plan was generated.

- ❏ The REMARKS column is an 80-byte field where you may put your own comments about each step of the execution plan. You can populate the REMARKS column by using an ordinary UPDATE statement against the plan table.

- ❏ The OBJECT_OWNER, OBJECT_NODE, and OBJECT_INSTANCE columns can help you further distinguish the database object involved in the operation. You might look at the OBJECT_OWNER column, for example, if objects in multiple schemas have the same name and you are not sure which one is being referenced in the execution plan.

- ❏ There is a special column related to distributed queries or transactions. (The term distributed means SQL statements that require access to a different database from the current one.) In these types of SQL statements, the OBJECT_NODE column indicates the database link name that leads to the object in the remote database.

Other useful fields are:

- ❏ The OBJECT_INSTANCE column is helpful in situations such as a self-join, where multiple instances of the same object are used in one SQL statement.

- ❏ The PARTITION_START, PARTITION_STOP, and PARTITION_ID columns offer additional information when a partitioned table is involved in the execution plan.

- ❏ The DISTRIBUTION column gives information about how the multiple Oracle processes involved in a parallel query or parallel DML operation interact with each other.

  Note that DML means Data Manipulation Language; it refers to commands that actually manipulate the data in a table, as opposed to commands that only define or restructure objects in the database. This second type of commands fall into the category we call DDL, which stands for Data Definition Language.

- ❏ The COST, CARDINALITY, and BYTES columns show estimates made by the cost-based optimizer as to how expensive an operation will be.

Remember that the execution plan is inserted into the plan table without actually executing the SQL statement; therefore, these columns reflect Oracle's best guess, and not the actual resources used. While these estimates are generally helpful, the estimates are just that – estimates; therefore, they should not be assumed to be 100% correct. If the exact values for a particular execution plan are required, these values may be gathered by activating SQL_TRACE, and then running TKPROF in order to format the results.

- ❏ The OTHER column in the plan table is a general-purpose field where the optimizer can store any sort of textual information about each step of an execution plan. For instance, in a distributed query, the other column will show the exact SQL statement sent to a remote database for the REMOTE step of the execution plan. The DBA can then take this statement to the remote database and tune it there.

- ❏ The OTHER_TAG column gives an indication of what has been placed in the OTHER column. For example, this column will contain valuable information during parallel queries and distributed operations.

Let's now take a look at a slightly more exotic SQL query, which involves accessing objects in a different database – that is, a distributed query. This example also shows some of the information that is retrieved from the other columns in the plan table:

Example: Using AUTOTRACE with a Distributed Query

Consider the following distributed query that was run with SQL*Plus AUTOTRACE turned on:

```
SQL> SELECT  /*+ RULE */
  2  a.customer_number, a.customer_name, b.contact_id,
  3  b.contact_name
  4  FROM customers a, contacts@sales.acme.com b
  5  WHERE UPPER (b.contact_name) = UPPER (a.customer_name)
  6  ORDER BY a.customer_number, b.contact_id;
```

AUTOTRACE shows the following execution plan:

```
Execution Plan
-----------------------------------------------------------
   0     SELECT STATEMENT Optimizer=HINT: RULE
   1   0   SORT (ORDER BY)
   2   1    MERGE JOIN
   3   2     SORT (JOIN)
   4   3      REMOTE*  SALES.ACME.COM
   5   2     SORT (JOIN)
   6   5      TABLE ACCESS (FULL) OF 'CUSTOMERS'


   4     SERIAL_FROM_REMOTE  SELECT "CONTACT_ID","CONTACT_NAME"
         FROM "CONTACTS" "B"
```

In the execution plan hierarchy, the step with ID 4 is displayed as a REMOTE operation, which is sent over the database link called sales.acme.com. At the very bottom of the execution plan you can see the actual SQL statement that will be sent for execution to the remote database. Note that the information displayed here originated in the OTHER and OTHER_TAG columns of the plan table.

Let's review what is happening in this execution plan:

1. Oracle first recognizes that a hint is being used, and switches to the RULE optimizer.

2. A remote query is sent to the database via sales.acme.com to fetch the contact_ids and names from a remote table.

3. These fetched rows will be sorted for joining purposes and temporarily set aside.

4. Oracle will next fetch all records from the customers table with a full table scan

5. The rows are sorted for joining purposes.

6. Next, the set of `contacts` and the set of `customers` will be joined using the `merge join` method.

7. The results of the merge join will be sorted for proper ordering.

8. Finally, the complete results of the query are returned.

Summary

In this chapter, we have provided an overview of effective ways to analyze SQL bottlenecks. The key to successful resolution of SQL problems is understanding how the SQL code is being processed. This is a reasonable objective, because SQL is the fundamental language by which we communicate with the database. It is, thus, imperative that the Oracle performance analyst be adept at understanding how Oracle handles SQL queries and transactions.

For the performance analyst who has a good understanding of Oracle database operation, SQL optimization is often easy; many SQL-related problems are solved by relatively simple changes, such as correcting an index, showing the developer how to use functions properly, or generating statistics that had been omitted.

In this chapter, we learned that there are three primary ways provided by Oracle to generate an execution plan: TKPROF, EXPLAIN PLAN, and SQL*Plus AUTOTRACE. Any of these three is perfectly valid; the same information will be displayed (in a slightly different format) for each method. The SQL*Plus AUTOTRACE method has the advantage that it displays the actual statistics for resource consumption. The EXPLAIN PLAN method will only generate an estimate of runtime resource consumption. In addition to these three methods of finding the execution plan, many software tools and utilities provide an easy way to view the execution plan.

In the next chapter, we continue our discussion of SQL tuning. Building on the ideas presented in this chapter, we move to an area that is often the source of SQL problems – that is, table joins.

- What are Joins?

- Optimization of Joins

- A Graphical Method of Analyzing Joins

- init.ora Parameters that Influence Joins

- Other Join Topics

9

Analyzing SQL Joins

This chapter continues our discussion of SQL tuning; moving from SQL tuning in general to focus on the specific area of joins. The aspiring performance tuning expert should pay close attention here; expertise in Oracle tuning requires a thorough understanding of join methods and optimization tactics. This subject is also a somewhat complicated area; many performance tuning problems stem from confusion as to how the Oracle optimizer handles SQL statements that join two or more tables. To do justice to this subject, we have reserved this entire chapter for its discussion.

We begin the chapter with an explanation of terms. What do we mean by join? What kinds of joins are there? We also clarify some terms that are commonly used, such as inner and outer join.

Our discussion on the various technical terms for joins leads directly into an overview of the specific Oracle techniques for joining tables. We explain the various ways that Oracle performs joins, and illustrate the strengths and weaknesses of each method. We demonstrate that no one join method is best; instead, any given SQL command can take advantage of the join method that best matches the needs of the particular SQL query.

Once we have the preliminary definitions and explanations in hand, we consider ways to optimize join processing. Optimizing joins is a lot more than determining the right join method. We present some key principles, foremost of which is reducing the result set as early as possible in the join processing.

Specifically, in this chapter, we discuss the following topics:

- ❏ Nested loops
- ❏ Sort-merge joins
- ❏ Hash joins

- ❑ Cluster joins
- ❑ Optimization of joins
- ❑ A graphical method of analyzing joins

We also explore the various `init.ora` parameters that cause the optimizer to modify its processing of join statements. These parameters can alter the model that the optimizer uses when making decisions about the best join approach. Some of these parameters are very simple to set; others are tricky and require some patience to understand.

Finally, we wrap up our discussion with a detailed discussion about special join methods used in data warehouse applications. In particular, we focus on the star join and star transformation methods – both of which are crucial in optimizing joins for star schemas.

What are Joins?

Recall that a join is a SQL query that gathers information from two tables rather than just one. The tables are related via at least one column that they have in common. The SQL that relates these corresponding columns is called the **join condition**.

For example, suppose that a certain application for a phone company displays information on a particular customer. The program uses a form that shows the customer name, address, phone number, and the long-distance plan that the customer has selected. As with most applications, the required information is not in a single table, but is spread over two tables. Thus, the query must identify both these tables, and also specify how the two tables relate to one another.

In the following diagram, we depict two tables and show which column they have in common. (We will see later that this manner of illustrating the join will in helpful in optimizing join processing):

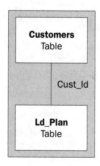

The two tables are joined on the column `Cust_Id` – that is, the `Cust_Id` column is common to both tables.

In the following SQL, we perform a join of the two tables to retrieve information pertaining to the customer `Bob Johnson`. Note that we retrieve most of the information from the `Customers` table, and just one field from the `LD_Plan` table:

```
SQL> SELECT C.Cust_Id, C.Address, C.Phone, P.Plan
  2  FROM Customers C, LD_Plan P
  3  WHERE C.Cust_Id = P.Cust_Id
  4  AND Customer_Name = 'BOB JOHNSON';


CUST_ID        ADDRESS      PHONE                 PLAN
----------  ----------  ----------  --------------------
  1001        1212 ELM    555-1212    MCI LONG DISTANCE
```

Observe that we have included the join condition, WHERE C.Cust_Id = P.Cust_Id. Without this, there would be no way to relate the information in one table to the other.

Equi-Join Versus Theta-Join

In many joins, the two columns are related using an equality. The SQL below is an equi-join, because of the clause WHERE C.Cust_Id = P.Cust_Id:

```
SQL> SELECT C.Cust_Id,
  2  FROM Customers C, Store S
  3  WHERE C.Cust_Id = S.Cust_Id
  4  AND C.Customer_Name = 'BOB JOHNSON';
```

In scientific terms, we can say that a join is an equi-join if, and only if, the left-hand side of the comparison is equal to the right-hand side.

In contrast, the following SQL is a theta-join because the > symbol has replaced the = symbol:

```
SQL> SELECT Cust_Id,
  2  FROM Customers C, Store S
  3  WHERE C.Cust_Id > S.Cust_Id
  4  AND Customer_Name = 'BOB JOHNSON';
```

In the query, we only want to retrieve rows where the Cust_Id in the Customers table is greater than the Cust_Id in the Store table. (Perhaps the analyst was doing a quality check, and believed that there was some problem with the Cust_Id values.) Of course, if the < relational operator were used instead, the SQL would still be a theta-join. The = symbol implies equi-join; any other relational operator implies theta-join.

The distinction between equi-join and theta-join is more than just an academic curiosity; certain join methods only work with equi-joins, while other join methods can work with any type of join. We will explore these distinctions in the next few sections.

Inner Join

In the last SQL sample, information was retrieved from two tables, based on the common value of Cust_Id. But what if there were a row in the Customers table that had *no* corresponding row in the Store table? In this situation, the row would *not* be returned because the information was missing in one of the tables.

For example, suppose each of the two tables contains entries for 100 customers, with Cust_Id values between 1 and 100. When we perform an equi-join (= symbol in join condition), we will retrieve all 100 rows. Now assume that the Store table is missing an entry – it only has 99 rows. When we perform the join query, we will only get 99 rows.

This manner of operation is the default way that Oracle joins tables; it is called an inner join. With this type of join, only rows that have a match in both tables are returned.

Outer Join

Although the requested information may be available in both tables specified in the join, it is also still possible to return a result even if only one of the tables had an entry. In this type of query, called an outer join, a row is still returned even if the information is missing in one of the tables.

In the previous SQL, we illustrated how to retrieve customer information for Bob Johnson. However, what if Bob Johnson has never specified a long distance carrier? That is, there is no entry for him in the Ld_Plan table. With an inner join, this means that no rows would be returned. With an outer join, however, the available information will be returned – even if some of it is missing.

For an outer join, the SQL syntax is modified to tell the Oracle engine which table might be lacking in information. The method is simply to put the + indicator next to this table. Thus, our previous inner join is easily converted to an outer join with just one change:

```
SQL> SELECT C.Cust_Id, C.Address, C.Phone, P.Plan
   2  FROM Customers C, Ld_Plan P
   3  WHERE C.Cust_Id = P.Cust_Id (+)
   4  AND C.Customer_Name = 'BOB JOHNSON';

CUST_ID       ADDRESS        PHONE            PLAN
----------    ----------    --------------    ------------------------
1001          1212 ELM       555-1212
```

We see that the PLAN field is blank (actually NULL), since this information did not exist in the Ld_Plan table. Nevertheless, because of the outer join syntax (+), the row (with information just from the Customers table) is returned anyway. Note that we could have applied the + operator to the Customers table if necessary, but only one table in a join can receive the + symbol.

Beginning with Oracle 9i, there is a new way to accomplish outer joins without using the + operator. This new method makes Oracle compliant with the ANSI SQL 99 standard. With this method, instead of the + operator, we will use the phrase Left Outer Join, or Right Outer Join.

An example will illustrate how to use this new option. Consider the case where we need to display information on our customers – especially any of those in the Late table (which means that they are reticent in their payment). We wish to display the customer id, their company, as well as their overdue date (if any). This calls for an outer join, which we would normally write like this:

```
SQL> SELECT C.CustomerId, C.Company, L.Late_Date
  2  FROM Customers C, Late L
  3  WHERE C.CustomerID = L.CustomerID (+);
```

We put the + operator on the Late table, because we want to see all customers, even if they have no entry in the Late table.

Here is the same query using the new ANSI SQL method:

```
SQL> SELECT C.CustomerId, C.Company, L.Late_Date
  2  FROM Customers C LEFT OUTER JOIN Late L
  3  ON (C.CustomerID = L.CustomerID);
```

This query will return rows for all customers, even if they don't appear in the Late table. In the same way, we could have specified RIGHT OUTER JOIN if we thought the Customers table was the table lacking the information.

A very useful feature of the next syntax is that it is now possible to perform a full outer join; this is like putting the + operator on both tables. Up to now, this has always been an illegal operation. Here is an example of a FULL OUTER JOIN.

```
SQL> SELECT C.CustomerId, C.Company, L.Late_Date
  2  FROM Customers C FULL OUTER JOIN Late L
  3  ON (C.CustomerID = L.CustomerID);
```

In the query above, all of the customers are returned no matter which table is lacking the information for a given customer.

Join Techniques

There are three main joining implementations that Oracle normally employs: nested loop, sort-merge, and hash join. These three joins account for the vast majority of all joins encountered. (In addition, there are some special purpose joins, called cluster join, star join, and star transformation, which we will also look at later on in the chapter.) Let's take a look and see what Oracle does for these three techniques.

Nested Loop

This is one of the most common join methods. The concept of a nested loop join is simple; we first retrieve rows from one table, and then find the matching rows in the second table. This method works especially well for queries that are very selective, and only return a small result set.

Let's look again at our telephone company query, and see exactly how this works:

```
SQL> SELECT Cust_Id, Address, Phone, Plan
  2  FROM Customers C, Ld_Plan P
  3  WHERE C.Cust_Id = P.Cust_Id
  4  AND Customer_Name = 'BOB JOHNSON';
```

1. Oracle starts with one table, called the driving table, and finds all rows that match the criteria in the WHERE clause. (In our SQL, Oracle would find all customers in the Customers table with the name BOB JOHNSON.)

2. Using this result set from the driving table, Oracle uses an index on the second table, the driven table, to find entries that match the value of the join field. (Find all rows in the Ld_Plan table that have Cust_Id = 1001.)

3. Using the row identifiers in the index on the driven table, Oracle retrieves the matching rows from that table (In our example the rows are retrieved from the Ld_Plan table.)

4. Oracle returns the information from both tables for all matching rows.

We can see from these steps why this method is called nested loop. We are actually using two loops – one nested in the other. For each row in the driving table (loop 1) we find all the rows in the driven table (loop 2)

For a nested loop join, the second table (the driven table) should have an index on the join column. In our example, this means that the Ld_Plan table must be indexed on the Cust_Id column.

Performance of Nested Loop Joins

Nested loop joins can run very quickly, but there are two important index requirements. When we access the driving table, it is important that there be an index to identify the desired rows. Secondly, when we retrieve the rows from the driven table, there must be an index on the join column in that driven table. In this way, the optimizer is able to use indexes to find the result set as quickly as possible, without having to scan through the table directly.

Note how well the nested loop method will work in our phone company example. Assuming that the Customers table has an index on Cust_Name:

❑ Step 1 will execute very rapidly. That is, the rows that have BOB JOHNSON as the customer name will be located nearly instantaneously by the index.

❑ Step 2 will execute just as quickly, because the index on the Cust_Id column will quickly identify which rows match the condition Cust_Id = 1001 (The customer id for BOB JOHNSON).

❑ Step 3, making use of the row identifiers found in Step 2, will be nearly instantaneous.

❑ Step 4, the culmination of the previous steps, will likewise be very rapid. The desired information – which was stringently restricted to just a single customer – is displayed.

This example illustrates a critical point, which is fundamental to understanding the strength of this form of join:

> **Nested loop joins are very efficient only for queries with highly restrictive conditions.**

There are a few other interesting aspects of nested loop joins. One benefit is that nested loop joins return the first rows faster than the other join methods. This happens because with the nested loop there is no need to wait until the loops have completed. The nested loop join provides the final result a little at a time, in contrast to both the hash join and sort-merge methods. These latter two methods must complete the entire operation before any results are available.

A second advantage of nested loop joins is that they do not require sorting; the result set from the driving table is simply used as input for the second table. (As we will see, the sorting operation is a key factor in the sort-merge join, and can make it a poor option.)

A third benefit of the nested loop join is that this join method can be used whether or not the join criterion is an equi-join. In contrast, both the sort-merge and hash join methods are only applicable for equi-joins.

Example: A Nested Loop Join

The following SQL is used by a video rental store to list the DVDs that are rented to a particular customer (in our example, the customer is Peter R. Johnson). Perhaps this customer is in doubt as to which DVDs he has checked out.

In addition to using the Customer table to retrieve the pertinent customer information, the SQL requires a join to the Rented table to locate the actual DVD title. The two tables have the column Cust_id in common, so that will be the join condition:

```
SQL> SELECT C.Cust_Name, C.Phone, R.DVD_Name
  2  FROM Customer C, Rented R
  3  WHERE C.Cust_Id = R.Cust_Id
  4  AND C.Cust_Name = 'Peter R. Johnson';

CUST_NAME              PHONE      DVD_NAME
-----------------      ---------- -------------------------
Peter R. Johnson       555-1212   Around the World in 80 days
Peter R. Johnson       555-1212   Star Wars Episode 1
```

We see that the query has successfully found the two DVD titles checked out to Mr. Johnson. Assuming that the optimizer has chosen a nested loop for this join, the execution plan for this query will look like this:

```
SELECT STATEMENT
NESTED LOOPS
   TABLE ACCESS BY INDEX ROWID CUSTOMER
      INDEX RANGE SCAN IDX_CUST_NAME
   TABLE ACCESS BY INDEX ROWID RENTED
      INDEX RANGE SCAN IDX_CUST_ID
```

We see that the `Customer` table is listed immediately below the phrase NESTED LOOPS. Thus, the optimizer is starting with the `Customer` table; this means that it will be the driving table. Why did Oracle choose this as the driving table? Well, the optimizer is smart enough to start with the table that has the restrictive condition (in this case the name of the customer). We will see later in this chapter the importance of reducing the result set as quickly as possible.

The `Customer` table is not accessed directly; looking at the execution plan above, we see that the index IDX_CUST_NAME will be scanned to find the entries meeting the condition on customer name. In our particular example (where there is only one customer named `Peter R. Johnson`), the index will have one relevant entry – the entry for `Peter R. Johnson`.

The second table listed under the phrase NESTED LOOPS is for the `Rented` table. After the row meeting the name criteria is found in the `Customer` table, the database engine looks for a matching `Cust_Id` in this second table. Once again, the engine uses an index; we can see from the execution plan (last line) that the index is called IDX_CUST_ID.

Oracle finds two entries (the two DVDs rented to Mr. Johnson) with the matching `Cust_id` in this second table. From this second table, Oracle retrieves the required information (the DVD name). Combined with the information from the first table (`Cust_Name` and `Phone`) the complete set of information is then returned as the final result set.

Limitations of Nested Loop Joins

The example above works well using the nested loop methodology; however, this was a special case. In this example, there was just one row returned from the driving table; thus, there was only one index lookup to perform in the second table. The final result was achieved very rapidly. But what if the selection criteria were much broader? What if many customers were fetched?

Let's take a look and see what happens. In the following SQL, the query has been modified to find the same information, but for those customers whose first name is `John`:

```
SQL> SELECT C.Cust_Name, C.Phone, R.DVD_Name
  2  FROM Customer C, Rented R
  3  WHERE C.Cust_Id = R.Cust_Id
  4  AND Cust_Name LIKE 'John%';
```

This query will return a fairly large result set from the first table. For a medium- or large-size business, many customers will probably have the last name that begins with the letters `John`. (There will probably be many for the last name `Johnson` alone.) This means that if a nested loop join were used, the optimizer would have to make many index lookups for the second table; this would be followed by thousands of table lookups to get the `DVD_Name` column. Not only is a nested loop join a bad idea in this new case – it is probably the worst possible choice for queries such as this.

Let's now turn to ways that are better suited to handle queries that have large result sets, such as the previous example. One such technique is the sort-merge join.

Sort-Merge

A sort-merge join reads through the rows in each of the two tables. The set of rows from each table is first sorted, and then merged with the set from the other table. Clearly, this method is radically different from the nested loop.

> *Recall that the nested loop join technique finds rows in the first table, then looks for matches in the second.*

The name sort-merge is really an accurate description of this technique. An odd thing about this join method is that the idea of a driving table does not apply. In the sort-merge join, there is no such thing as a driving table; both tables are considered equally.

Let's look at an execution plan for a sort-merge join to help us understand this better. Consider our query that lists all the customers having the name John. Using a sort-merge join, here is how the optimizer would process this query:

```
SELECT STATEMENT
   MERGE JOIN
   SORT JOIN
      TABLE ACCESS (FULL)      CUSTOMER
   SORT JOIN
      TABLE ACCESS (FULL)      RENTED
```

In this execution plan, note the use of words such as FULL, SORT, and MERGE. The optimizer will conduct a full table scan of each table, sort the rows by the join criteria (Cust_Id), and then merge the rows together. With all the rows combined, Oracle will then find the rows where the customer name begins with John, and return the information meeting the criteria.

Performance of Sort-Merge Joins

Notice that this execution plan, in contrast to the nested loop, uses full table scans. Although full table scans can be very efficient, this step could nevertheless be very time consuming for a huge table. (Of course, if the result set is going to be a large proportion of the table, a full table scan is often the only reasonable choice):

> **Sort-merge joins are a reasonable choice when the result set is large.**

Depending on the size of the sort area that is set in the database (via the init.ora parameter SORT_AREA_SIZE discussed later in this chapter), the sorting process may not fit into memory. In that case, it will be necessary for the database engine to perform numerous transfers back and forth from disk in order to accomplish the sort. This means that the sorting step is often a key factor in determining the performance of a sort-merge join.

This sorting delay may make the sort-merge join less attractive than other joins. There are some cases, however, where the optimizer can make use of a sort that has already been performed, for other reasons – such as an ORDER BY or GROUP BY clause in the SQL statement. In this case, the sort-merge join is not penalized for the sort step, since a major part of the work is already done.

In this following SQL, we retrieve a summary of sales for those items having a code beginning with 101. Assuming that there are many products with this type of item code, a sort-merge join is a reasonable choice:

```
SQL> SELECT I.Item_Code, SUM (Sales)
  2  FROM Items I, Product_Line P
  3  WHERE I.Item_code = P.Item_Code
  4  AND I.Item_Code like '101%'
  5  GROUP BY I.Item_Code;
```

The interesting part about this SQL is that a single sort can satisfy two steps of the SQL processing; in addition to the sort required by the sort-merge join, the GROUP BY clause would normally require an additional sort. In this example, however, the column to be sorted (Item_Code) is the same in each case; thus, the database engine can economize, and get two for the price of one.

The execution plan for the SQL is:

```
SELECT STATEMENT
  SORT GROUP BY NOSORT
    MERGE JOIN
      TABLE ACCESS BY INDEX ROWID ITEMS
        INDEX RANGE SCAN IDX_ITEMS
      SORT JOIN
        TABLE ACCESS BY INDEX ROWID PRODUCT
          INDEX RANGE SCAN IDX_PRODUCT
```

Thus, in spite of the sort step requirement for this type of join, the sort-merge join is sometimes still a reasonable choice. The key in this example was avoiding an extra sort.

Hash Join

As we have seen, the sorting operation in the sort-merge join can add a significant delay to the join process. This leads us to a fairly recent join method, which avoids the sort altogether; the hash join method. The hash join is yet another way in which the Oracle optimizer can join two tables. Although a relatively recent addition to Oracle (version 7.3), the mathematics for this technique was explored several decades ago.

Hash join processing beginswith the **Build Phase**. Oracle begins the process with the smaller table as the driving table. It divides the smaller table up into a set of partitions, or buckets, that will fit in memory. (Note that these partitions are not related to the Oracle object called partitioned table.) A hashing function is then applied to the join column for each entry in this table. The outputs from the hashing function yield a hash table.

After the hashing for the first table is complete, we proceed to the second phase, which is called the **Probe Phase**. Here, the second table is processed just like the first; it is divided into partitions and the same hashing function is applied. The larger table then probes the hash table from the first table, looking for a match.

Performance of the Hash Join

Like the sort-merge, the hash join is a good choice in queries where a large proportion of the table will need to be joined. As with the sort-merge join, this join method requires a full table scan of each table. (Recall that the nested loop is usually the better choice when only a small proportion of the table is retrieved.)

If the smaller (driving) table can fit entirely into the hash area (an area of memory set aside for the hash join operations), the hash join will usually be very fast, and outperform the sort-merge join. In fact, in recent Oracle versions, hash joins often replace the older sort-merge method. This success of the hash join method has even led some academics to claim that the hash join has made the sort-merge join obsolete. (Their claim has proved to be premature; the sort-merge join is still used.)

Hash joins work best when the smaller table fits into the hash area. When this driving table cannot fit into memory, it must be broken up into pieces that *will* fit. This extra step will degrade the performance of the hash join, because the parts must be swapped back and forth from disk. It is possible to minimize this delay by changing the amount of memory set aside for the hash. This allocation is controllable via the HASH_AREA_SIZE parameter. (The various init.ora parameters are discussed later in this chapter.)

Note, this method is possible only for equi-joins.

Example: A Hash Join

Consider a query that joins two tables: The Student table and the Unregistered table. The Student table is very large, and contains a list of all students for the college. The Unregistered table, on the other hand, just contains a few students, who have missed registration for some reason.

Suppose we wish to obtain a list of all unregistered students, along with their phone number and course major. The list of unregistered students is in the Unregistered table, but we will need to join to the Students table to get the Phone and Major columns. This simple query looks like this:

```
SQL> SELECT R.Student_Name, S.Phone, S.Major
  2  FROM Unregistered U, Students S
  3  WHERE U.Student_Name = S.Student_Name;
```

If the Oracle optimizer employs a hash join, the first step is to hash the smaller table – in this case the Unregistered table. Since the join column is Student_Name, Oracle applies a hashing function on this column. In this example, we will assume that the hash function is very simple – the optimizer hashes all the rows based on the first letter of the student's name. (Of course, Oracle will normally apply a more sophisticated hashing algorithm, but the concept is the same.)

The result of the first table hashing is shown in the following figure. Note that we have four buckets that represent the hash table from the Unregistered table. Remember that this first table is the driving table in this example:

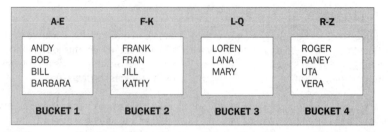

Now that the first table has been processed, Oracle proceeds to hash the second table, using the same hashing function (in our case, the first letter of the student name). The figure below illustrates the processing for this second table. The first row has a value for Student_Name of Herbert. Using the hashing function based on the first letter means that Oracle should look in bucket 2 to see if there are any Herbert's in that bucket. There are not, so Oracle will disregard this first row, and process the next row in the Students table.

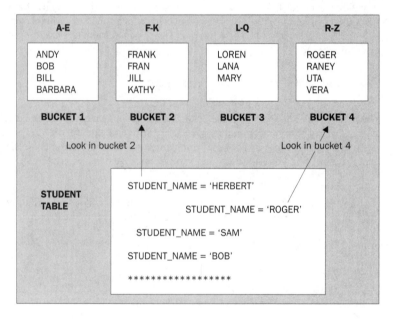

In this example, the names were nicely distributed into four buckets. Of course, Oracle will typically use more than four buckets, because the more buckets there are, the fewer entries in each bucket. The fewer entries in each bucket, the easier it will be to find a match. Ideally, there will only be one entry in each bucket.

Suppose, however, that the data is not so nicely distributed; what happens if the data is skewed? As shown in the next figure, skewed data presents a real problem for the hash join. In this scenario, all the data is hashed into the same hash bucket! In other words, the hashing function has accomplished absolutely nothing; every entry from the second table maps to the same place – bucket number one:

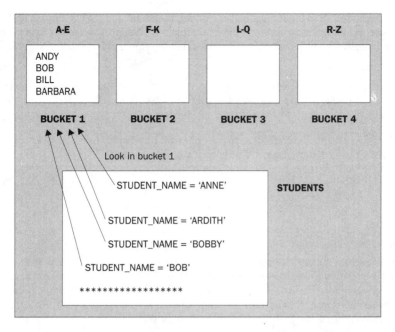

This observation reveals a serious shortcoming of the hash join method when data is not reasonably distributed:

> **Hash joins typically perform badly if data is skewed.**

Of course, this skewing of data is not usually a problem with names, since people's names cover the whole alphabet. Consider, however, a join based on department names or department numbers. If most entries in a table were assigned to a single department, the same problem with hash joins would probably be experienced.

Cluster Join

The cluster join is a rare event that few DBAs will actually encounter. The reason is simple: relatively few databases actually employ clusters! The idea of a cluster is to store the data chunks most likely to be needed at the same time in the same data block. For a join, this means storing the relevant data from both tables in the same area, which makes the data access easy, and the subsequent join extremely fast.

The cluster join will look very similar to a regular nested loop join. For each row in the driving table, Oracle uses the cluster index to find the matching rows in the driven table. As noted, these rows will probably be in the same data block.

The cluster join method can be used to join tables if the WHERE clause in the SQL statement includes a join condition that corresponds to the clustering key. Specifically, there must be a clause that equates each column in the cluster key in the first table to the respective column in the second table.

For example, in the following SQL query, let us assume that the `Customer` and `Region` tables are clustered on the `area` column. Thus, in order to perform a cluster join, the `WHERE` clause must link the two tables on the `area` column:

```
SQL> SELECT *
  2  FROM Customer, Region
  3  WHERE Customer.area = Region.area
  4  AND Customer.Lastname = 'Johanson';
```

This query meets the condition, so the optimizer can employ a cluster join. The `EXPLAIN PLAN` output for this statement would look like this:

```
SELECT STATEMENT
  NESTED LOOPS
    TABLE ACCESS    BY ROWID       CUSTOMER
      INDEX         UNIQUE SCAN    PK_CUST
    TABLE ACCESS    CLUSTER        REGION
```

We see from the execution plan that the database engine starts with the index `PK_CUST` on the `Customer` table in order to find the rows matching the criterion of `Lastname = 'Johanson'`. After each row is retrieved from the `Customer` table, the cluster index is used to find the matching rows in the `Region` table. The complete set of all columns is then returned as the final result set.

Cluster joins are rarely used in practice. Although there really is a performance benefit to storing joined data in the same blocks, the idea has not really caught on with most DBAs. One reason could be that a cluster join, as opposed to the other join methods, requires the DBA to perform extra planning up-front; the database objects that will be part of a cluster have to be built that way ahead of time.

Optimization of Joins

In analyzing a SQL statement that includes joins, there are some basic steps that should be performed. The analyst should consider the following:

❑ Selecting a join technique

❑ Reducing the result set as early as possible

❑ SQL hints that influence joins

Let's examine each one of these ideas, and see how optimization of table joins works in practice.

Choosing the Right Join

The exact method of performing a table join can make a huge difference in run-time. The most common issue is the choice between a nested loop and either the sort-merge or hash join. Generally speaking, the nested loop is excellent for cases where the filtering of the driving table produces a small result set. For instance, a join that includes the condition, `Employee_Id = 10453` looks like a good candidate for a nested loop. Assuming that duplicate employee numbers are not allowed, the result set will certainly be extremely small – most likely just one row.

The other two joins will generally outperform the nested loop in the absence of a highly restrictive condition on the driving table. Let's slightly modify the restrictive condition (`Employee_Id=10453`) above to be less restrictive: `Employee_Id > 100`. Now, the nested loop will probably be a poor choice, because the result set will be very large. Trying to use a nested loop with such a wide-open condition will most likely result in terrible performance.

This leaves either the sort-merge or hash join. It is true that both the sort-merge and hash join methods use full table scans, but consider the alternative. Even worse than a full table scan would be a fetch of many rows in a table via individual index reads, followed by table reads. This method would impose a much larger burden on the CPU, because Oracle would have to jump back and forth from index to table. Even worse, there would be no possibility of using the multi-block read feature that makes a full table scan look much more favorable.

Reduce the Result Set Early

Another important way to accelerate joins is by reducing the result set as early in the join process as possible; this means applying restrictive conditions just as soon as you can. The goal is to achieve the largest feasible percentage reduction. Note that this is not the same as beginning with the smallest table.

Let's consider an analogy to show why it is so critical to reduce the result set early in the process. Suppose a citizen of a small town goes to the county Office of Vital Statistics. He asks the clerk for all birth certificates for the year 1989.

The clerk shuffles from one filing cabinet to another, and finally carts up all birth certificates for the specified year. The citizen looks them over then says, "Now which ones are for people whose last name starts with Z?"

The clerk loads up all the boxes again, leaving the citizen with just one small folder. The enquirer finds the birth certificate of interest, jots down the desired information, and then walks out, leaving the fuming clerk behind.

Performing tuning with the Oracle engine works in much the same way. It is always best to reduce the request as much as possible, as soon as possible:

> **Reduce the result set as much as possible, as early as possible.**

SQL Hints

It is sometimes necessary to prompt the optimizer to use a different join order; this is accomplished through SQL hints, which are embedded in a comment clause at the beginning of the SQL statement. For tuning joins, here are the most common uses of SQL hints.

Specifying a Join Method

Each of the following hints prompts the optimizer to use the specified join method:

❑   USE_NL

- ❑ USE_MERGE
- ❑ USE_HASH

The syntax for each hint is very simple (and similar). To suggest that the optimizer use a certain join method, the appropriate clause is inserted into a SQL comment, with the table names listed afterwards. For a nested loop, the following syntax would be used.

```
SELECT /*+USE_NL (TABLE_1 TABLE_2 TABLE_3 ...) */
```

Similarly, the syntax for the other joins is:

```
SELECT /*+USE_MERGE (TABLE_1 TABLE_2 TABLE_3 ...) */
```

```
SELECT /*+USE_HASH (TABLE_1 TABLE_2 TABLE_3 ...) */
```

If more than one table is included in the hint, simply list the table names or aliases one after the other. In the following SQL, we want to use the sort-merge join method on the Customer and Overdue tables; note that the table alias must be used in the hint – not the actual table name (discussed in the section on *Hints Pitfalls* later in this chapter):

```
SQL> SELECT /*+Use_Merge (C O) */
  2   Cust_Name, Phone, DVD_Name
  3   FROM Customer C, Overdue O
  4   WHERE C.Cust_Id = O.Cust_Id
  5   AND Due_Date = '05-Jan-2002';
```

Ordering the Tables in a Join

Another very useful hint is the ORDERED hint. It is often used in conjunction with another hint that suggests a join method. The ORDERED hint simply requests that the optimizer join the tables in the specific order listed in the FROM clause.

> Note that this is the opposite of the convention used in the old Rule Based Optimizer approach, in which the tables tended to join in the opposite listed order.

The syntax for this hint is very simple; no table names or other argument are specified at all:

```
SELECT /*+ORDERED */
```

For instance, the following SQL suggests that the optimizer use a nested loop join to join the Customer and Overdue tables. The hint clause also includes the Ordered hint. Because of the order of the tables listed in the FROM clause, this has the effect of recommending that the Customer table be the first (driving) table:

```
SQL> SELECT /*+Ordered Use_NL (C O) */
  2  Cust_Name, Phone, DVD_Name
  3  FROM Customer C, Overdue O
  4  WHERE C.Cust_Id = O.Cust_Id
  5  AND Due_Date = '05-Jan-2002'
  6  AND C.Cust_Name LIKE 'A%';
```

When typing hints, note that the case for the hints may be either upper or lower case; the optimizer doesn't care.

Hints Pitfalls

Be sure to specify the alias name in the hint if the table listed in the FROM clause makes use of an alias. Observe the hint syntax for the following SQL:

```
SQL> SELECT /*+Use_NL (C D) */ Cust_Name
  2  FROM Customer C, Department D
  3  WHERE C.Cust_Id = D.Cust_Id
  4  AND Dept_Name = 'Engineering';
```

The SQL above correctly uses the two table aliases – C and D.

Be aware that using incorrect syntax in a hint will not always be easy to discover. Many analysts and DBAs have spent hours wondering why the optimizer is not obeying the hint, only to discover some typo in the hint syntax. In the case of wrong syntax or typos, the optimizer will simply ignore the hint – but you will not know!

Consider the following SQL, slightly modified from above. It contains a *serious error* that will prevent the hint from being accepted:

```
SQL> SELECT DISTINCT /*+Use_NL (C D) */ Cust_Name
  2  FROM Customer C, Department D
  3  WHERE C.Cust_Id = D.Cust_Id
  4  AND Dept_Name = 'Engineering';
```

Did you spot it? Of course, it is the word DISTINCT that has been (incorrectly) positioned. The optimizer does not balk at running the SQL; it simply ignores the hint!

Here is the right way to include the DISTINCT keyword:

```
SQL> SELECT /*+Use_NL (C D) */ DISTINCT Cust_Name
  2  FROM Customer C, Department D
  3  WHERE C.Cust_Id = D.Cust_Id
  4  AND Dept_Name = 'Engineering';
```

The moral of the story is simply to follow the syntax shown; don't put some other words in between the word SELECT and the SQL hint:

> **Watch the syntax in SQL hints; the optimizer will not tell you if you have made a mistake!**

243

A Graphical Method of Analyzing Joins

When there are only a couple of tables referenced in a SQL statement, it is not too cumbersome to decide which table should be driving, and which should be driven. After all, there are only two choices! Many SQL queries, however, have far more tables in the join. It is not unusual to have a dozen tables all joined in one SQL statement.

Clearly, some sort of convenient algorithm must be used to deal with these more complicated queries. The best approach I have seen is the graphical method of tuning joins. This method works equally well regardless of the number of tables in the join.

Show the Tables and Join Conditions

The first step in the graphical method is very easy; simply draw a node for each table in the SQL statement. Consider the following SQL for a DVD rental company, which is used to list the credit card expiration information.

This query lists those customers with credit cards that are within 1 day of expiration. (Note the use of the function Sysdate to mean now. For simplicity in this example, let's assume that a credit card expires on an exact day and time):

```
SQL> SELECT Customer_Name, Address, Credit_Card_Name,
  2    Expire_Date
  3    FROM Customers C, Credit_Card CC
  4    WHERE C.Customer_id = CC.Customer_id
  5    AND CC.Expire_Date < (Sysdate + 1);
```

The diagram for this SQL statement is shown in the following figure. Note the line between the two tables; this represents the join condition, which in this case is the clause C.Customer_id = CC.Customer_id:

There will often be a great difference in the sizes (row counts) of the tables in the join. It is best to show the largest tables at the top of the diagram, so we can remember where the real show stoppers are. In our sample SQL, the two tables are roughly the same size, so we have shown them side-by-side.

We have also listed the approximate number of rows in each table; roughly 3 million rows in each. It is not necessary to determine precisely the row count since a rough approximation is fine. This row count will prove useful in subsequent steps.

List the Filtering Statistics

The next step in the graphical procedure is to use the filtering conditions in the query to determine the proportion of rows that will actually be retrieved from each table. In other words, we need to know what effect the WHERE clause has on each table. Certain conditions will hardly reduce the result set at all, while other conditions will eliminate almost every single row.

The idea is to determine roughly what percentage of rows will remain after all the conditions for that table have been applied. This percentage should then be listed on the diagram. In the next figure, we have added the value 0.1% under the Credit_Card table. This indicates that we expect a very small percentage (1 out of 1000) of rows to meet the criteria for that table – credit card expiring on the next day.

Once again, this estimate need not be scientifically precise; a rough estimate is fine. In this example, we might have known that the credit card system sets the cards to expire every three years, or roughly 1000 days.

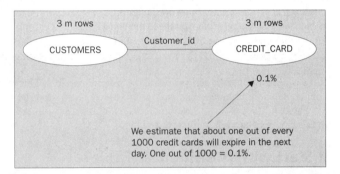

One might wonder why there is no number under the Customers table. The reason for that is simple –there is no condition listed in the SQL statement that causes any sort of restriction to be applied to that table. The only condition in the SQL that will reduce the result set is the condition on credit card expiration date. And that condition really applies to the Credit_Card table, not the Customers table.

Starting the Join

Now that we have shown the important statistics on the figure, it is possible to select a good join order. The first rule is:

> **Start the join with the table with the most restrictive percentage.**

Looking at the previous diagram again, we note that there is only one table that has any restriction condition. The Credit_Card table has a condition that only returns 0.1% of the table. This condition will greatly reduce the result set and, as a result, our choice is simple; we must begin with the Credit_Card table.

Let's take a look at the execution plan for this join. First here's a reminder of the query:

```
SQL> SELECT Customer_Name, Address, Credit_Card_Name,
  2    Expire_Date
  3    FROM Customers C, Credit_Card CC
  4    WHERE C.Customer_id = CC.Customer_id
  5    AND CC.Expire_Date < (Sysdate + 1);
```

and here's its execution plan:

ID	PARENT	OPERATION	OBJECT_NAME
0		SELECT STATEMENT	
1	0	NESTED LOOPS	
2	1	TABLE ACCESS BY INDEX ROWID	CREDIT_CARD
3	2	INDEX RANGE SCAN	EXP_DATE
4	1	TABLE ACCESS BY INDEX ROWID	CUSTOMERS
5	4	INDEX UNIQUE SCAN	CUSTOMERS_PK

The Oracle optimizer has correctly chosen the Credit_Card table as the first, or driving, table. Oracle will use an index on the credit card expiration date to find the entries in the Credit_Card table that meet the condition of expiration in one day first. Then, it will join to the Customers table, and use the CUSTOMERS_PK index on the Customer_id column to find the rows that have matching customer ids.

Note that the optimizer has correctly selected the nested loop join. This join method is an excellent choice here, because the result set is severely restricted right from the beginning. The condition of only retrieving rows matching a certain expiration date has made this a perfect candidate for a nested loop.

Why not Start with the Smallest Table?

Some analysts mistakenly believe that the first table in the join (the driving table) should always be the smallest table. At first, this idea seems to make sense – after all, isn't the small table always going to return the smallest result set?

This is an incorrect generalization, although it may happen to be correct in some cases. The correct principle is not to find the smallest result set in terms of row count, but the result set with the smallest proportion of rows returned. The two ideas are not at all the same.

Consider a join of two tables, as shown in this diagram:

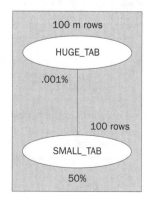

The table at the top, HUGE_TAB has 100 million rows. The SMALL_TAB table has only 100 rows. We assume that the SQL has restrictive conditions for each table. For table HUGE_TAB, only .001% of rows will be returned. For table SMALL_TAB, 50% of the rows will be returned.

Let's see what happens if we execute the join by starting with the small table; will this prove to be a good choice? Let's find out:

1. Find rows in SMALL_TAB meeting the query restriction. This returns 50 rows.

2. Join these 50 rows to HUGE_TAB. These 50 rows will find a match in about 50 million rows! Retrieve and temporarily hold these 50 million rows. This is because the rows returned from the first table will match the same proportion of the rows in the second table.

3. Determine which rows from the 50 million rows meet the query criteria. As shown in the figure, the restriction on HUGE_TAB eliminates 99.999% of all rows; thus, we will end up with about 500 rows.

We observe that this incorrect join order, based on using the smallest table first, has caused the Oracle engine to needlessly process 50 million rows – only to throw almost all of them out in the very next step! What is important is not so much that the driving table is small in terms of row count, but that the driving table is chosen so that the result set is proportionately small.

In our example, the small table provided a 50% reduction. This sounds good until we apply the 50% to 100 million rows! The 50% factor ends up applying to both tables! On the other hand, if we start with the huge table, its 99.99% reduction ends up applying to the smaller table as well:

> **Look for the proportionate reduction in the result set, not the number of rows.**

Intrinsic Table Filters

Of course, in some cases, this inherited selectivity will not correspond to the actual data distribution. It is possible that the entries in one table will not apply proportionately to the other tables in the query. In other words, merely using a certain table is like applying a filter, without the filtering condition being explicitly stated. This scenario is identical to having an extra condition in the WHERE clause that restricts the result set associated with this special table.

A simple way to deal with this situation is to estimate the selectivity of this intrinsic filter, list it on the diagram, and then look for the best join order, based on the usual selectivity criteria.

Consider the following diagram representing the SQL shown after it:

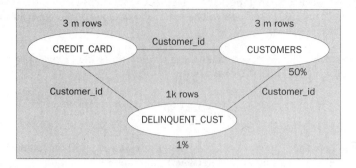

```
SQL> SELECT C.Customer_Name, C.Customer_Address
   2 FROM Customers C, Delinquent_Cust DC, Credit_Card CC
   3 WHERE C.Customer_id = CC.Customer_id
   4 AND C.Customer_id = DC.Customer_id
   5 AND CC.Customer_id = DC.Customer_id
   6 AND Customer_Name BETWEEN 'A%' AND 'K%';
```

In this query, one table is special. Although the Oracle optimizer does not know it, the Delinquent_Cust table has an intrinsic restricting condition that should be considered when selecting the join order.

The Delinquent_Cust table does not map proportionately to the other tables. That is, a selection of 100% of the rows in the Delinquent_Cust table does not map to 100% of the Customers table. Instead, it maps to only a small proportion of the Customers table – perhaps only 1%.

When the Delinquent_Cust table is used in a join, this intrinsic filtering phenomenon is like having an explicit restriction in the SQL that filters out 99% of the rows. Thus, we show a value of 1% for the filtering statistic for that table.

Since the best filtering criterion is associated with the Delinquent_Cust table, it is best to use that table as the driving table. The driven table should be Customers, since there is a 50% filtering criterion on it. Finally, we join in the Credit_Card table.

The order of joins can be shown like this:

Join 1 driving table: Delinquent_Cust
Join 1 driven table: Customers

Join 2 driven table: Credit_Card

So, even though the Delinquent_Cust table has no explicit condition in the SQL query, it is the best choice for the driving table. It implicitly eliminates 99% of the result set. Because of this, when it is joined to the Customers table, the expected result set will only be 1% x 3 million rows = 30 thousand rows.

Continuing the Join

Once the first table in the join is determined, the next step follows using the same logic. If it is best to begin the join with the most restrictive condition, it is likewise best to continue the join using the best filtering conditions that remain:

> **Continue joining to tables with the next-best restrictive conditions.**

In practice, the choice is not as simple as in some of our examples, which used only two tables.

Let's consider a slightly more complicated query, in which there are three tables. We once again return to our DVD rental company. In this query, the video store manager wants to find customers with expiring credit cards; but now, he only want to list those customers whose name beings with A-K. In addition, he only wants to list those customers who have a terrible credit rating.

Our new query adds these extra conditions:

```
SQL> SELECT Customer_Name, Address, Credit_Card_Name,
  2  Expire_Date
  3  FROM Customers C, Credit_Card CC, Credit_Rating CR
  4  WHERE C.Customer_id = CC.Customer_id
  5  AND C.Customer_id = CR.Customer_id
  6  AND CR.Credit_Rating = 0
  7  AND CC.Expire_Date < (Sysdate + 1)
  8  AND Customer_Name BETWEEN 'A%' AND 'K%';
```

To represent this SQL in a diagram, we need to make two new estimates, corresponding to the two new filtering conditions:

❑ Percentage of customers with terrible credit.

❑ Percentage of customers with names starting with A-K.

From past (and sad) experience, the store manager estimates that 10% of his customers have bad credit. For the restriction on customer names, we will assume that 50% of the customers meet the A-K restriction. The new diagram that reflects these new statistics is shown here:

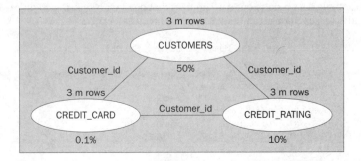

Let's decide on the best join order. Using the axiom of always starting with the most selective condition, we once again choose the Credit_Card table to be the driving table. Next, we will join to the Credit_Rating table, because it is expected to return 10% of the rows only. Finally, we join to the Customers table, because it restricts only 50% of the rows. (In this figure, note that the tables all happen to be large, so it isn't really necessary to try to put one higher than the others.)

By using this order, we have successfully reduced the result set as early as possible. The Oracle engine will have a very easy time processing this query.

The total result set from this query will be the product of the total number of rows (without restriction) times the three restrictive values:

3 million rows x .001 x .1 x .5 = 150 rows.

The execution plan for this new query is shown here:

```
ID PARENT OPERATION                              OBJECT_NAME
--- ----- ------------------------------------  -----------
 0         SELECT STATEMENT
 1     0    NESTED LOOPS
 2     1      NESTED LOOPS
 3     2        TABLE ACCESS BY INDEX ROWID      CREDIT_CARD
 4     3          INDEX RANGE SCAN               EXP_DATE
 5     2        TABLE ACCESS BY INDEX ROWID      CREDIT_RATING
 6     5          INDEX UNIQUE SCAN              CREDIT_RATING_PK
 7     1      TABLE ACCESS BY INDEX ROWID        CUSTOMERS
 8     7        INDEX UNIQUE SCAN                CUSTOMERS_PK
```

Once again, we see that the Oracle optimizer has chosen the nested loop, because the optimizer knows about all these restrictions. Note that the optimizer starts with the Credit_Card table, then joins to the Credit_Rating table; finally, the intermediate result set is joined to the Customers table.

Multiple Conditions

In the examples so far, there has been only a single restriction on each table. How should *multiple* restrictions on a table be dealt with? This is an easy problem to handle. When estimating what percentage of rows will be returned for a table, simply form an estimate that considers all the restrictions on the table. In some cases, this will simply be a matter of multiplying the percentages together. In other cases, some knowledge of the data distribution will be needed to make a good estimate.

For example, let's modify our earlier query that dealt with expiring credit cards slightly. Let's include an additional filter in the WHERE clause:

```
SQL> SELECT Customer_Name, Address, Credit_Card_Name,
  2    Expire_Date
  3    FROM Customers C, Credit_Card CC, Credit_Rating CR
  4    WHERE C.Customer_id = CC.Customer_id
  5    AND C.Customer_id = CR.Customer_id
  6    AND CR.Credit_Rating = 0
  7    AND CC.Expire_Date < (Sysdate + 1)
  8    AND CC.Credit_Card_Type = 'VISA';
```

Now, there will be even *fewer* rows returned from the `Credit_Card` table. The new restriction that the credit card must be a `VISA` card further reduces the chances that a row will meet the query conditions.

Previously, we estimated that only 0.1% of rows met the expiry condition. Knowing the types of credit cards in circulation, we estimate that only half the credit cards are VISA cards; thus, our new estimate of rows returned for the `Credit_Card` table is 0.05%. In this case, the optimum join order is the same, because we were already starting with the `Credit_Card` table.

Handling Joins to Large Tables

In some cases, it will be a close call which table should be processed next. This is where it is helpful to draw a diagram that shows the relative sizes of each table. In particular, it is helpful to show the largest tables at the top of the diagram. These huge tables will then represent steps that could conceivably slow down the join process if they are included too early. That is, if only a small proportion of rows have been eliminated, a join to a huge table will probably return a massive result set. Inevitably, this means a much worse response time.

All other things being equal, it is best to put off joining to huge tables until as many filtering conditions have been applied as possible. Of course, this may not always be possible, but a complete diagram will at least help the analyst make the best possible decision, given the SQL in hand:

> **Try to include the best filtering combinations before joining to a huge table.**

In some cases, it will be possible to include a variety of filtering conditions, so that by the time we have to join to a huge table, there has already been a large, proportionate reduction in the result set. This benefit will then also accrue as we join to the large table, giving us the smallest possible result set, and thus making the job of the database engine much easier.

init.ora Parameters that Influence Joins

There are several parameters that influence the optimizer's selection of joins. Most of these parameters cause the optimizer to change the weighting that it uses when determining the best join method. Other parameters cause the optimizer to alter its model of data access methods slightly. In addition, there are a few very special parameters added for Oracle 9i that alter the way that memory is allocated for certain work areas.

The most important parameters that influence join processing are:

- ❑ HASH_JOIN_ENABLED
- ❑ HASH_AREA_SIZE [default: 2 * SORT_AREA_SIZE]

- ❏ HASH_MULTIBLOCK_IO_COUNT
- ❏ SORT_AREA_SIZE
- ❏ DB_FILE_MULTIBLOCK_READ_COUNT
- ❏ OPTIMIZER_INDEX_COST_ADJ
- ❏ OPTIMIZER_INDEX_CACHING
- ❏ OPTIMIZER_MAX_PERMUTATIONS
- ❏ PGA_AGGREGATE_TARGET
- ❏ WORKAREA_SIZE_POLICY

Let's take a look at all these in more detail...

HASH_JOIN_ENABLED

Normally, the default value of True should be accepted for this parameter; setting it to False will make it impossible for the optimizer to select a hash join. Since hash joins frequently outperform the other join methods, there should be few cases where it is appropriate to turn this feature off.

HASH_AREA_SIZE

This parameter specifies the maximum amount of memory, in bytes, to be used for hash joins. It has a huge impact on hash join performance, because hash joins are very fast when all the partitions of the smaller (driving) table can fit into the hash area entirely:

> **Consider increasing HASH_AREA_SIZE to allow hashing of the first table completely in memory.**

HASH_AREA_SIZE is one of the existing parameters that has been provided for backward compatibility. Oracle now suggest that the DBA should allow the database to adjust a few of these parameters itself. This requires setting PGA_AGGREGATE_TARGET, discussed a little later.

HASH_MULTIBLOCK_IO_COUNT

This parameter defaults to the same as DB_FILE_MULTIBLOCK_READ_COUNT. It specifies the maximum number of blocks for a hash join that Oracle should read and write concurrently. A higher value for this parameter means that fewer partitions will be needed, since more blocks can be read at one time from each partition. Thus, increasing the value for this parameter makes a hash join appear more attractive, and increases the likelihood that the optimizer will choose the hash join method.

SORT_AREA_SIZE

A large value for SORT_AREA_SIZE makes it more likely that sorts can be handled completely in memory (or at least more of the sort can be performed without disk I/O). This makes the sort-merge join appear more attractive, since sorting is a major component of that join method. It defaults to 65536 .

This parameter impacts database performance in many ways; for instance, it is especially important for index creation. Setting a large value (say 10 MB) for this parameter usually speeds up index creation. Certain applications that need to create large indexes can exploit this benefit; in particular, data warehouse applications often dynamically change this value just prior to creating indexes on the large fact tables.

The fact table is the largest table in a data warehouse schema; it contains the entire set of business transactions.

> **Consider setting a large SORT_AREA_SIZE for data warehouse applications that need to rebuild large indexes.**

DB_FILE_MULTIBLOCK_READ_COUNT

The proper value to set for this parameter is system-dependent. It is usually set to the largest number of Oracle blocks that can be read from disk in one I/O operation. Traditionally, the largest multi-block read for most UNIX systems has been 64 KB. Thus, this parameter has customarily been set to 64Kb divided by the [Oracle block size]. It's default is 8.

In recent years, however, many servers can now perform a much larger read. For instance, some Sun Solaris systems are capable of a 1 MB read. Naturally, this means that the DB_FILE_MULTIBLOCK_READ_COUNT should be set higher accordingly:

> **Set the value of DB_FILE_MULTIBLOCK_READ_COUNT to take best advantage of the server capability.**

Proper care when setting this parameter can minimize disk I/O during full table scans and fast full index scans. With a relatively high value for DB_FILE_MULTIBLOCK_READ_COUNT, the optimizer will consider a full table scan less expensive than otherwise. As a result, it will choose full table scans instead of index lookups a little more often. This in turn means that hash joins and sort-merge joins may be selected slightly more often, because their overall estimated cost will be slightly less. (The cost of the nested loop operation is not affected, since it relies on index scans.)

OPTIMIZER_INDEX_COST_ADJ

This parameter controls how the Oracle optimizer should assess the cost of accessing index blocks. The default value of 100 tells the optimizer to use the normal costing model for estimating index access time. A higher value means that the optimizer should consider index access more expensive than the default. A lower value means that the optimizer should treat index access as proportionately less expensive. For instance, setting this parameter to 20 tells the optimizer that the cost of an index access path is one-fifth of the normal costing model.

OPTIMIZER_INDEX_COST_ADJ may be set anywhere between 1 and 10000, with a value less than 100 indicating that index access should be considered faster than full table scans. Depending on your actual system, especially the type of disk drives used, the default value of 100 may be a poor choice.

For many disk systems the cost of indexed access is not really the same as full table scan access – it is usually less. Some Oracle tuning experts recommend a much lower value, say 50, for this parameter. This lower setting is a judgment that reading an index is twice as fast as reading a block associated with a table.

Since this parameter should be set depending on the particular environment for the database, it is best to develop an estimate based on the actual system in use. We can do this by querying the database statistics to suggest an optimal value.

Recall that the wait event facility contains statistics for several types of reads. In order to estimate read access time, we will simply query the V$System_Event table and fetch the statistics for db file scattered reads and db file sequential reads. This will return a pretty good estimate because scattered reads reflect full table scans, and sequential reads will mostly be index reads.

> *Recall that scattered reads is Oracle-speak for multi-block reads used in full table scans. Remember also that the values are in centiseconds.*

Here is a sample query:

```
SQL> SELECT Event, Average_Wait
  2  FROM V$SYSTEM_EVENT
  3  WHERE Event LIKE 'db file s%';

EVENT                          AVERAGE_WAIT
----------------------------   ------------
db file sequential reads              .4561
db file scattered reads            2.04121
```

We need to estimate the ratio between these two types of reads. So, we calculate the fraction .4561/2.04121 = .223, or 22.3%. This means that index reads require only 22% of the time for full table scans. Thus, a reasonable estimate for OPTIMIZER_INDEX_COST_ADJ is 22. When we set this parameter lower, it will cause the optimizer to choose index access more frequently. The optimizer now knows that the index block accesses are much faster than it originally thought:

> **Calculate the actual time for index reads, and use this value to update OPTIMIZER_INDEX_COST_ADJ.**

OPTIMIZER_INDEX_CACHING

This parameter is similar to the parameter OPTIMIZER_INDEX_COST_ADJ, in that it modifies how the optimizer treats the cost to access blocks that contain index data. This parameter, however, affects how the optimizer models the cache of index blocks.

The parameter OPTIMIZER_INDEX_CACHING may be set to any value between 0 and 100, with the default being 0. The value indicates the likelihood of finding an index block in the buffer cache. Lower values tell the optimizer to assume that fewer index blocks are likely to be cached. At the other extreme, a value of 100 (representing 100%) means that the optimizer should assume that all the index blocks are cached.

If a value of 100 were set for this parameter, this would have a significant impact on the frequency of nested loop joins; this would occur because nested loop joins are dependent on index lookups. A value of 100 means that each index lookup is to be considered only a logical read (it is assumed to be already in cache.), so the index lookups would be assessed a much lower cost, which would translate to more frequent nested loops:

> **Use caution when changing the value of** OPTIMIZER_INDEX_CACHING; **big changes in join processing can result.**

OPTIMIZER_MAX_PERMUTATIONS

If the parameter OPTIMIZER_FEATURES_ENABLE equals 9.0.0 or higher, then the default is 2000. If OPTIMIZER_FEATURES_ENABLE equals 8.1.7 or lower, then the default is 80000. This parameter is specific to SQL that contains one or more joins. Basically, it places an upper limit on the number of join permutations (in other words, possibilities) that the optimizer is allowed to consider. Normally, there is no reason to change this parameter; practically speaking, only a moderate number of tables (for example, less than ten) are usually listed in the SQL. Fewer tables listed in the SQL in turn results in only a limited number of join combinations.

In some applications, however, the number of joined tables is so large, that the time just to parse the SQL statement becomes significant. In these cases, the optimizer may have to spend many seconds just trying all the join possibilities. By setting a lower value for OPTIMIZER_MAX_PERMUTATIONS, the parse time for the query can be reduced. Of course, the tradeoff is that it is possible (though unlikely) that the optimal join order may be missed. Acceptable values for this parameter are 4 to 80000:

PGA_AGGREGATE_TARGET

Beginning with Oracle 9i, the DBA is encouraged to use Automatic Memory Management. The key parameter for this is PGA_AGGREGATE_TARGET. This parameter specifies the target total PGA memory to be used for all server processes for that particular instance. If this parameter is used, it must be large enough to account for working memory needed for sorting, merging, joining, and so on. This parameter may be set anywhere between 10 MB and 4000 GB but by default is turned off (set to 0).

Oracle examines the value for this parameter and adjusts the various work areas in memory so as not to exceed the specified value. If the parameter is increased, this allows more work to be performed in memory, tending to decrease disk I/O, and thus slightly improving total run-time.

Starting with Oracle 9i, Oracle Corporation recommends that the DBA be willing to let the database perform self-tuning. DBAs are still allowed to tweak the work area parameters, but this capability is provided for backwards compatibility only.

For instance, this is the official line regarding the SORT_AREA_SIZE parameter:

> *Oracle does not recommend using the* SORT_AREA_SIZE *parameter unless the instance is configured with the shared server option. Oracle recommends instead that you enable automatic sizing of SQL work areas by setting* PGA_AGGREGATE_TARGET. SORT_AREA_SIZE *is retained only for backward compatibility.*

A similar recommendation is given for setting the HASH_AREA_SIZE parameter.

Understandably, most senior DBAs are very reluctant to give up the finer control that is possible with the variety of init.ora parameters in favor of an unknown (and unproven) methodology. Notwithstanding the strong suggestion from the *Oracle9i Database Performance Tuning Guide and Reference*, it is not clear whether the self-tuning methodology will prove to be the best choice for all situations. In any case, it is best to be aware of the preceding parameters, and understand how they affect the join processing.

WORKAREA_SIZE_POLICY

The default for this parameter works like this: if PGA_AGGREGATE_TARGET is set, then the default is AUTO, if not then the default is MANUAL. This parameter specifies the policy for setting sizes of several memory work areas. WORKAREA_SIZE_POLICY controls how the memory for these work areas is to be allocated.

When WORKAREA_SIZE_POLICY is set to AUTO, work areas used by memory-intensive operations are sized automatically, based on the PGA memory used by the system, the PGA memory target set in PGA_AGGREGATE_TARGET, plus the memory needs of the individual process. We can specify the AUTO option only when PGA_AGGREGATE_TARGET is defined (see the previous parameter).

When WORKAREA_SIZE_POLICY is set to MANUAL, the memory allocation for the work areas is determined explicitly via the various memory parameters set in the init.ora file.

The Oracle manual suggests that using the old manual method may result in sub-optimal performance and poor PGA memory utilization. Of course, experienced DBAs will understand that there is no guarantee whatsoever that even the automatic method will choose the right values:

> **Be aware that Oracle 9i self-tuning may not be as good as optimal tuning.**

Notwithstanding the warning from the Oracle manual about sub-optimal tuning, the best course for the performance expert is to become knowledgeable about these critical parameters so that the best decision for your particular system can be selected. In some cases, this might mean choosing automatic tuning; in other cases, the performance expert will need to make some alteration to fit the specific scenario. In short, rarely do one size fits all approaches correctly address all tuning issues for every application.

Other Join Topics

There are a few other points that the Oracle analyst should keep in mind. We now examine how the Oracle optimizer handles remote tables. Also, there is one other type of join to consider – the Cartesian product.

Joining Remote Tables

With distributed queries (SQL involving tables located on different servers), the optimizer may need the remote table to be the driving table, instead of the local table. This can be helpful in minimizing the work performed over the network.

Let's look at a simple query to see why the optimizer makes this choice. The SQL below is from our video store example. In this query, let's assume that the Credit_Card table is a remote table, accessed over the database link called Remote_Database:

```
SQL> SELECT Customer_Name, Address, Credit_Card_Name,
  2   Expire_Date
  3   FROM Customers C, Credit_Card@Remote_Database CC
  4   WHERE C.Customer_id = CC.Customer_id
  5   AND CC.Expire_Date < (Sysdate + 1)
  6   AND C.Customer_City = 'Los Angeles';
```

In this query, we include two different conditions – one for each table. The condition on the Customer table is: City = 'Los Angeles'. The condition on the Credit_Card table is our familiar restriction on the credit card expiry date: Expire_Date < (Sysdate + 1).

If the optimizer uses the local table Customers as the driving table, what will happen on the remote database? (We expect this to be the wrong way.) Let's take a look to see what the database engine would have to do.

The optimizer on our local database will first find all the rows in Customers that match the criterion of Los Angeles. Then, for each of these rows, a separate query is sent to the remote database; it will look like this:

```
SELECT Credit_Card_Name
FROM Credit_Card
WHERE Customer_Id = :b0;
```

This looks efficient – and it is! The problem is that this query will be sent for separate execution on the remote database for every row in the driving table that meets the specified condition (in this case Customer.City = 'Los Angeles').

Big problems come to mind. immediately Firstly, there will certainly be a significant network delay just to transmit this query to the remote site, and then return the results. Secondly, the SQL on the remote site will have to be read and executed many times. The simple act of re-executing a SQL statement over and over will itself often cause a performance bottleneck.

The problem with the remote table is very similar to the issue in previous case studies, in which we emphasized the importance of using set, or array processing rather than row-by-row processing. One execution that processes a million rows is much faster than one million executions that process a single row.

This thought experiment shows that a remote table usually functions badly as the driven (second) table; thus, the optimizer designers have reasonably decided to try to make the remote table the driving table when possible. Generally speaking, this is the right way to optimize these sorts of SQL.

Of course, making the remote table the driving table is a reasonable guess, and will probably be correct in most cases – but it will not always be the right choice. In some situations, there may be other filtering criteria listed in the SQL that make the local table an even worse driving table. Thus, it is possible that a SQL hint may be necessary to change the driving table selection.

Cartesian Product

There is a certain result (usually bad) that comes from not specifying the join condition in a SQL query. When the join condition is missing, the database engine will return all possible combinations between the two tables. This typically means a huge result set and, consequently, terrible performance.

Let's return to our video store query that looks for customers having credit cards about to expire. Here is the same SQL, but with the join condition (C.Customer_id = CC.Customer_id) removed:

```
SQL> SELECT Customer_Name, Address, Credit_Card_Name,
  2  Expire_Date
  3  FROM Customers C, Credit_Card CC
  4  WHERE CC.Expire_Date < (Sysdate + 1);
```

Recall that each of the two tables in this query has about 3 million rows. We had earlier assumed that only 0.1% of the rows in the Credit_Card table meet the date condition. As a result, we expect that the Credit_Card table will contribute about 3000 rows to the final result set. In the previously worded (with the correct join condition) SQL, these rows were then joined to their counterparts in the Customers table. The final result set in that case yielded a result set of about 3000 rows.

Without a join condition, however, the 3000 rows in the Credit_Card table will be joined to every possible row in the Customers table – all 3000000 rows. This makes the total expected result set 3000 rows x 3000,000 rows = 9000000000 rows!

This is a good example of what usually happens when the join condition is omitted. By forgetting that one little phrase, the Oracle engine will be burdened with trying to produce a result set of 9 billion rows! The database will work on the query "forever" and everyone will wonder why it is so slow!

> **Forgetting a join condition will drastically worsen performance, often leading to very, very long queries.**

Special Joins for Data Warehousing

Oracle provides numerous features that are specially aimed at data warehouse performance. There are two join methods that have been provided to handle the special setup of data warehousing schemas. To understand why these joins are needed, let's review the special schema arrangement that is present in most data warehouses.

The schema design in a data warehouse frequently uses a setup called **star schema**. With a star schema, there is a central table, called the **fact** table, which contains the main transaction of interest. Thus, for retail stores, the fact table will most likely contain the rows that identify each sale. For a university, the transaction might be a grade assigned by the professor; in that case the fact table would contain the rows that identify each course grade given to every student.

The diagram shown below displays a simple star schema for Jupiter Sporting Goods. Jupiter is a large (and imaginary) manufacturer and retailer of sporting goods, with retail stores throughout the United States. As shown in the figure, the Jupiter data warehouse employs a very simple star schema. The main fact table, listing all retail transactions, is called the `Sales` table. Naturally, this is a very large table; in our example this table has 100 million rows:

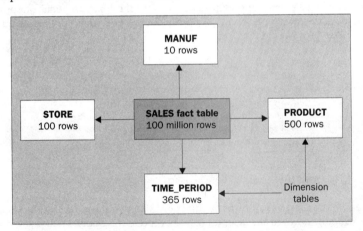

Besides the fact table, note that there are several other small tables, which are called **dimension** tables. These tables contain the attributes that describe a single transaction. So, in the previous figure, we note that Jupiter apparently uses ten manufacturers, because there are ten rows in the `Manuf` table. Similarly, there must be 100 retail stores, indicated by 100 rows in the `Store` table. Note that each transaction listed in the fact table will have a particular `Manuf`, `Store`, `Product`, and `Time_Period`. In other words, the fact table has `foreign keys` that point to the dimension tables.

For a report writer, using the star schema is very easy; if we want to find a particular set of transactions, we simply write a query that selects data based on the dimension attributes. Looking at our Jupiter diagram, we can write SQL that restricts rows based on four attributes:

Restriction	Table
Where the product was made	`Manuf`
Which store made the sale	`Store`
What product was sold	`Product`
When the sale occurred	`Time_Period`

This simplicity of the star schema is very appealing, because report writers, or others who access the database easily understand the design. Unfortunately, the very simplicity of the star schema can lead to serious difficulties for the Oracle optimizer.

Performance Issues with Star Schemas

Despite the simplicity of star schemas, they are very susceptible to performance bottlenecks. A frequent problem with queries against a star schema is that the selection criteria are spread over the dimension tables – that is, the query filtering is not very restrictive for any single dimension table. This means that even if the query as a whole only returns a few rows, the intermediate processing will probably degrade the query.

For example, let's consider a simple query against the Jupiter schema. Suppose we wish to list the sales for a certain product in the `Boston` store, for the first quarter of 2000. The query would then be:

```
SQL> SELECT Sales.Dollar from Sales, Manuf, Store, Product,
  2  Time_Period
  3  WHERE Sales.Time_Key = Time_Period.Time_Key
  4  AND Sales.Manuf_Key = Manuf.Manuf_Key
  5  AND Sales.Product_Key = Product.Product_Key
  6  AND Sales.Store_Key = Store.Store_Key
  7  AND Time_Period.Quarter = 'Q1-2000'
  8  AND Manuf.Source = 'Coleman'
  9  AND Product.Line = 'Sleeping Bag'
 10  AND Store.Store_Name   = 'Boston';
```

When we run the query, it turns out that only 250 rows meet the criteria listed. Let's now examine how the Oracle optimizer can process this query. We'll first try the methods typically used for table joins.

First, note that this is a five-way table join. How then will the optimizer deal with this query? Without resorting to some kind of trick, the optimizer has three ways to accomplish the join: hash join, nested loop, or sort-merge join. Let us consider each method, and see if good performance can be achieved.

Unfortunately, the sort-merge and hash join methods will require a full table scan of the huge `Sales` table. Considering the size of the `Sales` table, this method seems poor. What about a nested loop join? The nested loop at first might seem attractive because a full table scan is not mandatory. Upon closer examination, however, the nested loop also seems unsuitable. This is because no single search criterion is very restrictive. This fact greatly decreases the appeal of the nested loop; however, let's try a nested loop and see what happens.

Suppose that the most restrictive criterion in the SQL statement is the Store criterion, which returns a result set of 500000 rows. Using a nested loop join, the database engine will have to process many rows before it can whittle the set down to the final 250 rows.

Starting with the Store table, this is what typically happens:

1. Join SALES to STORE   returns 500000 rows

2. Join above result to MANUF   returns 50000 rows

3. Join above result to PRODUCT   returns 1000 rows

4. Join above result to QUARTER   returns 250 rows

Of course, starting with a different dimension table first will not solve the problem. The point is, no matter which table we start with, we must first wade through many rows. This is necessary because each restricting condition is considered separately, rather than jointly.

We see, then, that none of the classic join methods is satisfactory. This problem seems unsolvable – or is it? It turns out that the Oracle optimizer has a few clever solutions up its sleeve.

Star Join

With the star join, the optimizer addresses the fundamental problem with queries that join to the fact table. The solution is very clever. Instead of immediately joining to the fact table, the star join adds a pre-processing step. During this pre-processing, the database engine jointly considers the dimension constraints. It does this by building a list of all possible combinations (Cartesian product) of the dimension rows that meet the selection criteria. This set of rows is typically not very large.

Then, this set of rows is used to access the fact table, via a (**B*tree**) composite index. A B*tree index is the regular index that Oracle uses. When a DBA creates an index, it will be a B*tree index by default. This type of index is very much like an index in a book; within the index blocks, there are entries that give the row identifier for each unique value in the table. In this way, Oracle can quickly determine where to look in the table for any given value of the indexed column.

Here is how the optimizer deals with our sample query, which the normal join methods could not handle. First, it finds the Cartesian product of dimension rows meeting search criteria. In this example, we assume that the business uses 90 days in the first quarter:

Column	Restriction	Rows
Time_Period.Quarter	Q1-2000	90
Manuf.Source	Coleman	1
Product.Line	Sleeping Bag	1
Store.Store_Name	Boston	1

So, the Cartesian product equals 90 rows in total.

Second, using this set of only 90 rows, we access the `Sales` table via a single composite index on columns (`Time_Key`, `Manuf_Key`, `Product_Key`, `Store_Key`). Therefore, the result set is fetched using only 90 index lookups – certainly a very fast operation. For this query (and others of similar format), the star join has far outperformed any of the traditional join methods. In spite of this promising start, however, the star join is not a good answer for all queries.

Problems with the Star Join Method

Although the star join can provide dramatic performance improvement for some queries, there are significant drawbacks and limitations.

First, the star join method requires huge composite indexes. Note that the sample query made use of a four-column composite index. In fact, multiple huge indexes will probably be required, so that the leading columns of at least one index can meet the selection criteria. The total size of numerous composite indexes on a massive table will be huge.

For certain types of queries, the star join will simply not work well. Depending on the search criteria, the Cartesian product could be very large – even millions of rows. This would in turn require millions of index lookups against the fact table. A huge Cartesian product is especially likely if there are a large number of dimension tables.

Let's return to our Jupiter example and consider a query with selection criteria that are slightly different:

```
SQL> SELECT Sales.Dollar$
  2  FROM Sales, Manuf, Store, Product, Time_Period
  3  WHERE Sales.Time_Key = Time_Period.Time_key
  4  AND Sales.Manuf_Key = Manuf.Manuf_Key
  5  AND Sales.Product_Key = Product.Product_Key
  6  AND Sales.Store_Key = Store.Store_Key
  7  AND Time_Period.Quarter = 'Q1-2000'
  8  AND Manuf.Source LIKE 'C%'
  9  AND Product.Line LIKE 'Sleeping%'
 10  AND Store.Store_Area = 'East';
```

In this query, the restriction criterion for each dimension has changed slightly. Instead of retrieving sales just for the `Boston` store, we are looking for all stores in the area called `East`. Also, we now want to include all products starting with `Sleeping`, plus all manufacturers starting with `C`.

At first, these slight changes might seem to be insignificant. They do, in fact, reveal critical weaknesses with the star join method. To understand the core problem, remember that the star join method uses the dimension table criteria to create a list of all possible combinations first. In the original query, this amounted to only 90 rows. In the revised query, the Cartesian product turns out to be a big problem:

Column	Restriction	Rows
Time_Period.Quarter	Q1-2000	90
Manuf.Source	LIKE C%	5
Product.Line	LIKE 'Sleeping%	10
Store.Store_Area	East	20

So the Cartesian product equals 90,000 rows in total in this case.

Thus, a slight change in the selection criteria has produced a serious bottleneck. Continuing with the next step of the star join, the database engine must now perform 90,000 index lookups on the Sales table! The method that seemed so elegant before now seems no better than the traditional join methods. In order to deal with this type of problem, Oracle uses yet another solution – the **star transformation**.

Star Transformation

Oracle's newest star optimization method also employs pre-processing, but with a different (and tricky) twist. Although some documentation might imply that star transformation is similar to star join, the two methods are actually very different. Unfortunately, some parts of the Oracle documentation are particularly confusing when discussing these methods.

As we saw previously, the star join attempts to reduce the magnitude of the problem. In contrast, the star transformation accepts the size of the problem but speeds up the processing. Whereas the star join tries to avoid processing a large set of rows, the star transformation tackles the problem head-on. Instead of building a Cartesian product with (hopefully) a small set of rows to process, the star transformation method uses the inherent speed of combining bitmaps. This speed allows the database engine to perform the intermediate processing rapidly, even when large amounts of data are involved.

Bitmap indexes point to table information differently from B*tree indexes.; they have an entry for each distinct value of the indexed column. For each of these entries, there is a map of Yes/No bits that indicate whether or not a row in the table corresponds to a given value.

For instance, suppose that we are looking at a table called Engineers, which only has 10 rows. In this table, there is a column called Manager, which indicates (via YES or NO) whether a particular engineer is a manager or not. We further assume that there are only two managers, which happen to correspond to the first and last rows in the Engineers table. Here is what a bitmap index on the Manager column would look like:

```
<YES>1 0 0 0 0 0 0 0 0 1
<NO>  0 1 1 1 1 1 1 1 1 0
```

Observe that the bitmap for YES indicates that only rows 1 and 10 correspond to YES. Similarly, the separate bitmap for NO indicates that rows 2 through 9 are a match for NO.

A key to understanding the star transformation method is the referential integrity (RI) that is defined in the star schema. Recall from our last figure that entries in the fact table are children of the dimension tables. So a transaction listed in the Sales table is defined by four dimensions or attributes: Manuf, Store, Product, and Time_Period. The Sales table thus has four foreign keys, and each one points to its parent in one of the dimension tables.

This RI relationship between the fact and dimension tables identifies the key point in star transformation processing:

> **Entries in the fact table can be found using the primary keys from each of the dimension tables that meet the search criteria.**

In other words, once all the dimension keys matching the search criteria are found, these keys can be used to find the desired rows in the fact table. This point also explains why this method incorporates the word *transformation* – a query is transformed, or rewritten, to gather the keys from each dimension table first.

Let's return to the last Jupiter query that performed so badly using the star join. Using a star transformation, the optimizer will rewrite the query to fetch the primary keys from the dimension tables first. Internally, the optimizer will create a new, transformed SQL like so:

```
SELECT Sales.Dollar$
FROM Sales
WHERE Manuf_Key IN
(SELECT Manuf_Key FROM Manuf WHERE Source LIKE 'C%')
AND Prod_Key IN
(SELECT Prod_Key FROM Product WHERE Line LIKE 'Sleeping%')
AND Store_Key IN
(SELECT Store_Key FROM Store WHERE Store_Area = 'East')
AND Time_Key IN
(SELECT Time_Key FROM Time_Period WHERE Quarter = 'Q1-2000');
```

The steps that the optimizer performs for a star transformation are:

1. For each dimension table, find rows meeting the query's selection criteria. For now, fetch only the primary keys for these rows.

2. Using these PK values, fetch the corresponding bitmaps on the fact table. Merge (OR) these bitmaps. This yields a single bitmap of all fact table rows matching the query's restriction for a single dimension.

3. Merge (AND) all the summary bitmaps for the dimension tables. This yields a final bitmap of rows that meet restrictions on all the dimension tables.

4. Use this final bitmap to fetch the final result set from the fact table.

5. Fetch any other fields needed from the dimension tables (not already retrieved during the first step).

Note that this method also requires that the fact table have a bitmap index for each foreign key pointing to a dimension table.

Let's work through these steps, using the problem query that worked so badly with the star join method:

1. Scan each dimension table to fetch primary key(s) that match the search criteria. For Jupiter, there are four dimensions, so we will have four sets of primary key values:

Table	Number of PKs	Values
QUARTER	90	{1/1/2000, 1/2/2000, and so on}
MANUF	5	{Coleman, Clark, and so on}
PRODUCT	10	{Sleeping Bag, Sleepware, and so on}
STORE	20	{Boston, New York, and so on}

2. Access matching bitmap indexes on the fact table. Combine bitmaps (OR) to yield one bitmap per dimension:

   QUARTER   Merge (OR) 90 bitmaps, yielding 1 bitmap
   MANUF   Merge (OR) 5 bitmaps, yielding 1 bitmap
   PRODUCT   Merge (OR) 10 bitmaps, yielding 1 bitmap
   STORE   Merge (OR) 20 bitmaps, yielding 1 bitmap

3. Combine (AND) bitmaps from Step 2, yielding the final bitmap that encompasses all selection criteria related to the dimension tables:

   Quarter bitmap AND Manuf bitmap AND Product bitmap AND Store bitmap

4. Fetch fact table rows via ROWIDs, using this final bitmap.

The star transformation has successfully sidestepped the difficulty that made the star join unworkable. This success is primarily due to the database engine's extremely fast bitmap processing.

Summary

In this chapter, we have provided an overview of effective ways to analyze SQL joins. We have seen that the Oracle optimizer generally uses three techniques to perform a table join, namely:

❑ Nested loop

❑ Sort-merge

❑ Hash join

The first two methods have been included in database releases for many years; the hash join, on the other hand, is a relatively recent addition. The hash join has proved to be an excellent choice for many table joins, outperforming both the nested loop and the sort-merge join in many cases.

We finished the chapter by looking at the `init.ora` parameters that can affect joins, and then discussed some other important topics related to joins, namely Cartesian products, star joins and star transformations.

In future database releases, Oracle Corporation will undoubtedly offer new methods of controlling table joins, or even new types of join methods. This makes it all the more important for the Oracle Pathologist to be well versed in the basics of table join processing.

- Analyzing Slow Databases

- Address the Worst Symptoms

- Operating System Utilities

- Oracle Statspack

- Other Tips

- Summary

10

The Pathologist's Toolkit: Other Tactics

The job of the Oracle Pathologist can be very challenging. He or she must deal with a wide variety of performance issues; some are trivial (or even non-existent), while others will tax even the most experienced analyst. In this chapter, we provide an assortment of tactics that the Oracle performance analyst can use to isolate even the most puzzling performance issue. We will focus especially on the particular performance problem often described by users as "your database is working slowly".

In cases where the performance problem doesn't seem to fit into any particular pigeonhole, the Oracle analyst must be able to deal with this uncertainty, and drive the problem to a successful conclusion. Many problems are more than just a missing index; indeed, on rare occasions the solution will be very elusive and puzzling. These cases require detailed study; some require even days of analysis.

This chapter focuses on ways to handle these difficult cases professionally. We begin by exploring methods of dealing with databases that are reputed to be "just slow", which is a common complaint heard by DBAs. How should the Oracle performance analyst deal with cases like that? We provide a variety of suggestions, tactics, and proven methods that can be used to diagnose database problems.

In the second part of this chapter, we discuss the group of operating system (OS) utilities that are found on most servers, including the popular UNIX utilities top, sar, iostat and vmstat, as well as some useful tools for Windows platforms. We provide an explanation of each utility, and give an illustration of sample use. We also discuss some valuable options that are available for each of these utilities.

The next part of the chapter provides an overview of the recently released Oracle utility called `Statspack`. In recent years, Oracle has upgraded the classic utilities `bstat` and `estat`; DBAs who have appreciated the capability of these tools will especially like the much more versatile `Statspack` program. We explain how to get started with this tool, and how to run its report facility.

Finally, we provide a variety of tips that will ensure the user gets the maximum benefit from the `Statspack` utility.

Analyzing Slow Databases

When users are plagued with delays, they frequently ask the DBA to activate that special parameter – the go fast switch on the database. Well, unfortunately for us all, there isn't any go fast parameter in Oracle. Instead, the Oracle analyst must face the user's complaints head-on, by systematically dealing with each problem on a case-by-case basis.

This head-on approach requires the analyst to ask two questions, which expose the very essence of performance tuning. Let's look at them now briefly...

Is Performance Really Slow for Everyone?

The first step in dealing with slow database complaints is to recognize that databases do not run slowly just on general principle; that is, in spite of users' claims that a database is generally slow, many performance problems are only performance issues only when experienced in a specific scenario.

This doesn't mean that the users are being deliberately misleading; it just means that the scope of their experience is limited to the applications that they use every day. In most firms, application users are typically exposed to only a small subset of queries. There is really no way for any one user to know that the database is operating badly for all users.

The preceding observation means it is possible that the situation described by the users is not entirely accurate. It is possible that just a few queries executed by one or two applications are really the only programs experiencing performance problems, not the database in general:

> **Oftentimes, a slow database is really slow for only a few users.**

Could the Problem be Due to Just a Few Culprits?

Secondly, even when the database truly is slow for all users, it is still very possible that this is due to just one or two culprits. These culprits could be several poorly designed queries or batch jobs, which degrade performance for many other users – in severe cases, perhaps, even the entire user population!

This observation illustrates the beauty of performance tuning; small actions can have massive consequences – both positive and negative.

First the bad news:

> **A single design flaw can cause a massive performance problem for users.**

Now, the good news:

> **A single correction can provide massive performance improvement for users.**

Sometimes, however, the root cause of the slow database is not obvious; there doesn't seem to be any single cause of performance degradation. These mystery cases present an interesting challenge to the Oracle Pathologist, who will have to approach the problem a little differently, and use some special tactics to try to unmask the culprit.

Let's take a look at some suggestions that can be used for these go-slow databases.

Address the Worst Symptoms

When faced with a database that just seems slow, it is often helpful to pick the most egregious query (the one with the slowest performance), and then try to figure out what is happening. Very often by solving the worst performance problem on the server, the overall load goes down, the disk contention is reduced, and everyone benefits.

There are many ways to find this worst SQL. The biggest problem (or at least one of the biggest) can be found simply by interviewing users and asking them which report to function takes the most time. They should know since they are the ones stuck with the poor performance.

Another easy way to identify big bottlenecks is to list the SQL statements that are consuming the most resources (disk reads or logical reads). These statements are easily found in the V$SQL view, by retrieving entries having a high disk reads/executions ratio.

Monitor the Active Sessions

Another way to find the worst bottlenecks on a slow database is to watch the active sessions. Recall that with many applications (especially OLTP systems), very few users are actually active at any one time. It is very helpful for the analyst to get a feel for what the application is really doing. By looking at the active sessions, he will soon discover which queries are consuming the most resources, or run the most frequently.

Many popular tools, including Oracle's DBA Studio or Console), incorporate a way to show these active users, along with the SQL they are running at that moment. (Note that DBA Studio and the Console are really the latest incarnations of Oracle's OEM, Oracle Enterprise Manager, which has been available for many years.) For instance, the screenshot below shows the typical information displayed for all the connections to a database; this information was generated from the DBA Studio Report feature:

Session ID	Status	Username	OS User	OS Process ID	Machine Name	Program
1	ACTIVE		oracle	9418	alpha-db1	oracle@alpha-db1 (PMON)
2	ACTIVE		oracle	9420	alpha-db1	oracle@alpha-db1 (DBW0)
3	ACTIVE		oracle	9422	alpha-db1	oracle@alpha-db1 (LGWR)
4	ACTIVE		oracle	9424	alpha-db1	oracle@alpha-db1 (CKPT)
5	ACTIVE		oracle	9426	alpha-db1	oracle@alpha-db1 (SMON)
6	ACTIVE		oracle	9428	alpha-db1	oracle@alpha-db1 (RECO)
7	ACTIVE	SYSMAN		9430		
8	ACTIVE		oracle	9432	alpha-db1	oracle@alpha-db1 (ARCO)
9	ACTIVE	STORE	tlau	29324	DIGITALTHINK\TLAU_LT_SERVER	
10	INACTIVE	STORE	tlau	29783	DIGITALTHINK\TLAU_LT_SERVER	
14	INACTIVE	CHRIS	clawson	26986	DIGITALTHINK\CLAWSONLT-W2K	SQLPLUSW.EXE
30	ACTIVE	CHRIS	clawson	26064	DIGITALTHINK\CLAWSONLT-W2K	jrew.exe
31	INACTIVE	STORE	tlau	29594	DIGITALTHINK\TLAU_LT_SERVER	
32	INACTIVE	SYSMAN	srognes	29057	DIGITALTHINK\ORACLEDEV-W2K	Spotlight.exe

Here we see that there are only a few active users. One active user is STORE (SID = 9); another is CHRIS who has SID = 30. Looking at the far right column, we note that the CHRIS user is running a program called jrew.exe, which gives us a clue as to what he is doing. Whenever the program name can be determined by Oracle, it will be displayed. This last user is active only because he is the one running the tool that is producing this listing! The program jrew.exe is the process that runs the DBA Studio program.

Alternatively, a simple SQL script can be run to list the active users. The following script adjusts a few column widths, and then queries the V$SESSION and V$SQL views in order to find the active users. Finally, it lists the associated SQL. Note that this sample script excludes all users with a NULL username; this is intended to exclude the system background tasks:

```
Col username format a13
Col prog format a22
Col Sql_Text format a57
Col Sid format 999
Set linesize 120

SELECT Sid, username, Substr(program,1,19) PROG , Sql_Text
FROM V$SESSION, V$SQL
WHERE status = 'ACTIVE'
AND username IS NOT NULL
AND V$SESSION.sql_address = V$SQL.address
AND V$SESSION.sql_hash_value = V$SQL.hash_value;
```

Here is an example of how the results are returned:

```
  SID USERNAME   PROG           SQL_TEXT
----- ---------- -------------- --------------------------------
   29 CHRIS      SQLPLUSW.EXE   SELECT Sid, username,
                                Substr(program,1,19) PROG ,
                                Sql_Text FROM V$SESSION , V$SQL
                                WHERE status = 'ACTIVE' AND
                                username IS NOT NULL AND
                                V$SESSION.sql_address =
```

```
                                  V$SQL.address AND
                                  V$SESSION.sql_hash_value =
                                  hash_value

        30 BOB        SQLPLUSW.EXE  SELECT Emp_Name FROM Emp

        31 JOE        SQLPLUSW.EXE  SELECT Dept_Name FROM Dept
```

Note that the very first SQL_TEXT field returned is the SQL statement itself! That is, the very user that runs this script is also active.

Confirm that Sessions are not Blocked

What sometimes looks like a slow system is really nothing more than users getting blocked by other sessions. In these cases, the user's transaction is not just slow – it isn't even running! Remember, however, that a user will not be blocked for performing a query; only transactions (SELECT or UPDATE) are blocked.

There are several ways to check for blocked users. Many sites use convenient DBA tools and utilities that display which users are locking which objects, and which users are blocking other users, in a clear tree arrangement. As useful as these tools are, the same information is easily retrieved using simple SQL scripts that show the blockers.

Oracle provides such a sample script, called utllockt.sql. On most servers, this script is located in $ORACLE_HOME/rdbms/admin. Recall that $ORACLE_HOME designates the directory where the Oracle executables have been installed. On windows operating systems, the Oracle Home will be something like C:\oracle.

The only setup requirement for running utllockt.sql is that the preliminary script catblock.sql must be run first (typically as SYS), in order to create the additional views referenced in utllockt.sql.

The output from the utllockt script is an indented hierarchy of who is blocking whom. In the sample output below, the user with SID = 8 is blocking two other sessions, 14 and 16.

```
WAITING LOCK_TYPE    MODE_REQUEUE MODE_HELD LOCK_ID1 LOCK_ID2
------- -----------  ------------ --------- -------- --------
      8 None
     14 Transaction Exclusive    Exclusive  143111        90
     16 Transaction Exclusive    Exclusive  143111        90
```

The utllockt script also provides a clue as to which object is involved in the blocking. In the sample above, the field Lock_Id1 refers to the object id for the table involved. Thus, for our example, the table with id 143111 is the table being locked by session number 8.

Knowing the object number, we can then easily find the object name. The view Dba_Objects has the information that we are after; the column Object_Id contains the object number. Thus, in our case, we will look for object 143111. This query shows that the Accts_Payable table is the table being locked by the user with SID = 8:

```
SQL> SELECT Owner, Object_Name
  2  FROM Dba_Objects
  3  WHERE Object_id = 143111;

OWNER                OBJECT_NAME
----------------     ---------------
FINANCE              ACCTS_PAYABLE
```

One unusual quirk to keep in mind: the session for the user who is blocked will be shown as active, even though that user is not doing anything. This situation is a classic indicator of a blocked session. Thus, in our example, sessions 14 and 16 will be shown as active – even though they are stuck:

> **Look for blocking users who have a status of active but are not really doing anything.**

Note that the status of a session is shown in the V$SESSION view, Status column.

A simple way to see if a session is being blocked is via the view V$SESSION. In this view, the columns of interest are:

Column	Contains
LOCKWAIT	The address of the lock waiting
ROW_WAIT_OBJ#	Object number we are waiting on
ROW_WAIT_FILE#	File number corresponding to blocked row
ROW_WAIT_BLOCK#	Block number corresponding to blocked row
ROW_WAIT_ROW#	ROWID of the locked row

For example, if we wanted to see if the session with SID = 44 is being blocked by another user updating exactly the same row, we could run this SQL:

```
SQL> SELECT Username, Lockwait, Row_Wait_Obj#, Row_wait_row#
  2  FROM V$SESSION
  3  WHERE SID = 44;
```

The information from the above query is then used as the basis for querying other views; for instance, the column ROW_WAIT_OBJ# corresponds to Object_id in the view Dba_Objects. By simply querying the view Dba_Objects, we can find exactly which table is involved in the blocking. Of course, we could have joined to the view Dba_Objects in the first place. Note that the field Lockwait will be NULL if there is no locking problem.

Once the table with the blocking row is identified, it is then easy to obtain details on the row involved; we simply select from the table of interest where ROWID = Row_Wait_Row#.

In a similar way, we can query other views to get more details on the file and block number involved. To do this, we need to know how to relate columns in V$SESSION to these other views. The column Row_Wait_File# corresponds to column File_Id in the view Dba_Data_files. This can be used to retrieve the file name: likewise, the column Row_Wait_Block# matches the field Block_Id in the view Dba_Extents.

Let's now turn to some other areas that the Pathologist will need to investigate. One commonly mentioned subsystem is the network; it is often blamed (rightly or wrongly) for performance degradation.

Check Network Throughput

Some applications tend to transfer large amounts of information to and from the database server. In these cases, insufficient network bandwidth will make everything seem slow, even though the database has nothing whatsoever to do with the delays. The database will frequently be blamed for this bottleneck.

When large data transfers are suspected, a good first step is to determine how much data is really being transferred. After all, why waste time investigating the network unless a large amount of data transfer is occurring?

A simple way to check network transfer to and from Oracle is to query the view V$SESSTAT, and display the statistics for SQL*Net transfer. In the sample script below, we query the V$SESSTAT view and also the V$STATNAME view (just to get the name of the statistics.) We then return all rows that have the word NET in the statistic name.

```
Col Name Format A50

SELECT Sid, Name, Value
FROM V$SESSTAT One, V$STATNAME Two
WHERE One.Statistic# = Two.Statistic#
AND UPPER(Name) LIKE '%NET%'
AND Value > 1000
ORDER BY 1
/
```

Here is the result, when I ran the query on my database:

```
   SID NAME                                               VALUE
  ---- ------------------------------------------  -----------
     9 bytes sent via SQL*Net to client              91264636
     9 bytes received via SQL*Net from client        67900418
     9 SQL*Net roundtrips to/from client              1629676
    10 bytes sent via SQL*Net to client                  2291
    10 bytes received via SQL*Net from client            1840
    11 bytes sent via SQL*Net to client               136677
    11 bytes received via SQL*Net from client           67470
    13 bytes sent via SQL*Net to client                  5530
    13 bytes received via SQL*Net from client            7613
    14 bytes sent via SQL*Net to client                  7254
    14 bytes received via SQL*Net from client            3659
    15 bytes sent via SQL*Net to client                  3609
    15 bytes received via SQL*Net from client           13098
    17 bytes received via SQL*Net from client            1540

  14 rows selected.
```

For this particular database, there were seven sessions that had activity over SQL*Net that exceeded 1000 bytes. The SID shown for each of these active sessions is 9, 10, 11, 13, 14, 15, and 17. Of these sessions, only the session with SID = 9 had SQL*Net traffic of any significance.

If a slow network is suspected, there are many ways to get a rough idea of the network speed. A brief consultation with the Systems Administration or the Network Administrator will usually confirm the network bottleneck; it is very likely that these engineers will be well aware of the network limitations on your particular system.

Another easy way to check the network speed is to build a small file and transfer it to some other server on the network. Simply create a small file (perhaps 1 MB), and use FTP (File Transfer Protocol) to copy it to and from the database server. The SCP (Secure Copy) utility may have to be used in more secure environments; consult with the Systems Administrator to see which utility is used on your system.

Look for the Heavy Hitters

We have already mentioned the idea of looking for the big resource consumers, but the concept bears repeating. On many, many occasions the heavy hitters script shown below, has located those SQL queries that are responsible for the slow database:

```
SELECT Executions, Buffer_Gets, Disk_Reads, Sql_Text
FROM V$SQL
WHERE Disk_Reads/(.01+Executions) > 100000
ORDER BY First_Load_Time;
```

When we run this script, we are really making an assumption; we are suggesting that the database is not slow in some general sense, but in a very specific sense. This script does not tell us what is wrong in general – it tells us what is wrong specifically. In a way, we are thinking (to ourselves) that the users are really in error, the database is not just generally slow at all, it is slow in some very specific ways.

Recall one of our earlier axioms, that database problems are frequently reported inaccurately:

> **A database reported as generally slow is often specifically slow in reality.**

The following screenshot shows an actual readout from a production server that contains a data warehouse application. Using the heavy hitters script above, we sought to list all SQL statements that consumed over 100,000 disk reads per execution. As shown in the figure, there were several SQL statements that met this criterion. Of course, we would normally focus our efforts on the SQL with the most egregious consumption of resources – in this case, disk reads:

```
EXECUTIONS BUFFER_GETS DISK_READS
---------- ----------- ----------
SQL_TEXT
--------------------------------------------------------------------------------
        5     610262     514076
SELECT DISTINCT    lp.CERT_NAME             AS primary_group ,'1'                              AS secondary_group ,''
TE)            AS secondary_group_name ,slp.student_registration_key  AS drill_down_key ,AVG(slp.PCT_LPATH_COMPLE
  parent_group  ,MAX(slp.LPATH_COMPLETE_DATE_KEY)  AS pct_progress  ,sr.LAST_NAME || ',' || sr.FIRST_NAME  AS drill_down_desc ,''                          AS
path slp, student_registration sr  WHERE  slp.subdomain_key = 'STORE01'   AS certification_completion_date    FROM  learning_path lp, student_l
EARNING_PATH_KEY = lp.LEARNING_PATH_KEY    AND sr.STUDENT_REGISTRATION_KEY = slp.STUDENT_REGISTRATION_KEY    AND lp.cert_short_name = 'TECH'    AND slp.L
.cert_name, slp.student_registration_key,  sr.LAST_NAME || ',' || sr.FIRST_NAME   UNION SELECT DISTINCT   lp.CERT_NAME   Group BY  lp
         AS primary_group ,lp.learning_path_key           AS secondary_group ,lp.NAME                              AS seconda
ry_group_name ,slp.student_registration

        1     181295     181028
SELECT DISTINCT   sr.student_registration_key   As PrimaryKey  ,   sr.last_name || ',' || sr.first_name As PrimaryName,
  c.course_short_name              As SecondaryKey,   c.course_name                       As Secondaryname,   sc.ENROLLMENT_DATE_K
EY              As EnrollemntDate,    sc.LAST_ACTIVITY_DATE_KEY     As LastActivityDate,   sc.COMPLETION_DATE_KEY          As Com
pletionDate,    sc.PCT_COURSE_PROGRESS       As Progress,    sc.PCT_SCORE            As Score,  sr.JOB_CODE
         As JobCode,   sr.status                     As Status  FROM    student_course sc, registration_custom rc, cou
rse c, student_registration sr  WHERE  rc.CUSTOM_FIELD_10 = 'ccdepartment'    AND sc.REGISTRATION_CUSTOM_KEY = rc.REGIS
TRATION_CUSTOM_KEY    AND sr.student_registration_key = sc.student_registration_key    AND sc.course_key = c.course_key
       AND  sc.ENROLLMENT_DATE_KEY >= ('01-Jan-1900')   AND  sc.ENROLLMENT_DATE_KEY <= ('01-Jan-2003')   Order By  Sec
ondaryName

        1     181288     181034
SELECT DISTINCT   sr.student_registration_key   As PrimaryKey  ,   sr.last_name || ',' || sr.first_name As PrimaryName,
  c.course_short_name              As SecondaryKey,   c.course_name                       As Secondaryname,   sc.ENROLLMENT_DATE_K
EY              As EnrollemntDate,    sc.LAST_ACTIVITY_DATE_KEY     As LastActivityDate,   sc.COMPLETION_DATE_KEY          As Com
pletionDate,    (sc.PCT_COURSE_PROGRESS) * 100      As Progress,   (sc.PCT_SCORE) * 100            As Score,  sr
.JOB_CODE              As JobCode,   sr.status               As Status  FROM    student_course sc, registratio
n_custom rc, course c, student_registration sr  WHERE  rc.CUSTOM_FIELD_10 = '0034004015'    AND sc.REGISTRATION_CUSTOM_
KEY = rc.REGISTRATION_CUSTOM_KEY    AND sr.student_registration_key = sc.student_registration_key    AND sc.course_key
= c.course_key    AND  sc.ENROLLMENT_DATE_KEY >= ('01-Jan-1900')   AND  sc.ENROLLMENT_DATE_KEY <= ('01-Jan-2003')
  Order By  SecondaryName
```

Besides using a query to find big resource consumers, it is helpful to understand the overall disk I/O patterns. There are several easy ways to check disk I/O specifically caused by Oracle activity. It can be measured by the database itself, or it can be checked at the operating system level. At the database level, the view V$FILESTAT contains excellent statistics on disk I/O.

Here is a sample script to find the physical reads for every file in the database:

```
SELECT File#, Phyrds
FROM V$FILESTAT
ORDER BY 2;
```

The results are sorted by the number of physical reads:

FILE#	PHYRDS
4	96
2	589
3	1057
1	7474
6	13160
5	389458

15	1270150
17	1447316
10	1449939
12	1453450
9	1499077
14	1571555
8	1607753
13	3398210
7	3398537
11	6419747
16	278070700

Of course, the script could just have easily shown the disk writes. In that case, we would perform a SUM on phywrts instead. Note that the field File# can be translated to the actual file name using the view Dba_Data_Files.

Disk Latency

Another useful tactic is to check how fast the disk operations really are. That is, how long does it really take to read the disk? We call this figure of merit disk latency. Here is a simple script to check it:

```
SELECT Event, Total_Waits, Time_Waited,
Average_Wait*10 Wait_In_Ms
FROM V$SYSTEM_EVENT
WHERE Event LIKE 'db file seq%';
```

It gives results like the following:

```
EVENT                    TOTAL_WAITS TIME_WAITED   WAIT_IN_MS
------------------------ ----------- -----------   ------------
db file sequential read         4438        1687   3.80126183
```

Note that this script uses the wait event facility to determine the average wait for disk I/O. Recall that sequential reads is the way that Oracle refers to single block reads; thus, the script simply finds the average time for these single-block reads, and then scales the output to display milliseconds. For the database used in the example above, the latency was about 3.8 ms.

Typical values for this latency will normally range from 2 ms to 10 ms. Note that it is possible that the latency will actually be better than the latency claimed by the manufacturer! This can occur due to caching on the hardware itself. Caching has the benefit of reducing the number of actual round trips to the disk.

Review Parameters for Extreme Settings

When all queries seem to run badly, it is possible that some init.ora parameter has been set to an extreme value. This usually happens when the DBA wants to try something and forgets to reset the parameter, or document why he has used an unusual value. In some cases, it may even be necessary to reset some of the parameters to more typical values, just to remove the init.ora parameters from suspicion.

It is especially important to look closely for unusually high values for the shared pool and the other cache and pool sizes. It is sometimes helpful to see the values for the current parameters, without having to actually read the init.ora file; the values can be retrieved by querying the view V$PARAMETER.

The following is a simple SQL script that will prompt for a portion of the parameter name. It will then display the parameter and the value.

```
Col Name Format A33
Col Value Format A22

SELECT Name, Value
FROM V$Parameter
WHERE Name LIKE '%&1%';
```

In this example, we want to see the values for all parameters that have the word hash somewhere in the phrase:

```
Enter value for 1: hash

old 1: where name like '%&1%'
new 1: where name like '%hash%'

NAME                              VALUE
------------------------- ------------
hash_join_enabled                 TRUE
hash_area_size                    5242880
hash_multiblock_io_count          0
```

In the script above, the phrases old 1 and new 1 simply refer to the variable substitution activity. Oracle automatically generated the number 1 as a reference; there is no performance significance related to the number.

Let's a have a look at a case study that demonstrates how reviewing init.ora settings can solve certain performance problems:

Case Study: Too Much of a Good Thing

A plumbing material supply house ran a database to keep track of their inventory. One of the DBAs was assisting a user, and noticed that even simple queries were taking a long time. He tried several very simple queries, and discovered that the database was always slow; for instance, a query from a small table took about 10 seconds, instead of the more typical 1 second.

The DBA reviewed the init.ora settings, and discovered one very extreme setting. It turned out that the shared pool had been set to an enormous value (1GB), consuming a large portion of the memory on the server. The DBA had chosen this value in an attempt to get the best possible performance; the idea was, why not make this setting as large as possible? If big is good, then bigger must be better!

Of course, overly large values do not make the database work faster. In this case, the database engine had to search through the gigantic shared pool every time a new SQL statement was issued, which led to terrible performance for everyone. Simply resetting the Shared_Pool back to a mid range value corrected the entire problem.

Watch for Distributed Queries

Some databases use database links to retrieve data from other Oracle systems. These links slightly complicate the performance analysis, because it may not be obvious which database is causing the bottleneck.

Joins across multiple databases present a particularly tricky challenge, because different pieces of the query will be run on different databases. A new wrinkle is that a SQL statement for the driven (second) table may be executed numerous times (especially for a nested loop join). Normally, with non-distributed databases, the query on the second table in a nested loop join is not a separately executed SQL statement, it is handled internally, as part of the join. This is not the case for a distributed query.

The SQL that is run on each database may look fine at first – but note the execution count! Although each SQL statement may run fine, the remote system may be burdened with a massive number of executions (typically if the remote table has been designated as the driven table for a nested loop join). The execution count is found in the view V$SQL:

> **For distributed queries, be alert for large execution counts on the remote database.**

In our next case study, the importance of checking for the right database is illustrated:

Case Study: Right Idea, Wrong Database

The designer of a data warehouse application complained to the DBA that the database kept running out of TEMP space. This always occurred while a gigantic SQL query, called the monster query, was running. The designer had copied the error message from the application, which clearly reported the Oracle error message, and specifically mentioned the name of the temporary tablespace.

The DBA checked the TEMP space on the database in question, but there was absolutely no indication of any space problem; there were no warnings in the alert log, the file system had plenty of space, and the tablespaces were not full. The number of extents likewise was not an issue.

After spending several hours on this problem, the DBA realized that the SQL in question was actually a remote query. Although the INSERT was occurring locally, the SELECT was occurring remotely. This meant that the TEMP space was needed on the remote database, not the local database.

After checking the remote database, the problem was discovered. The TEMP space was indeed maxed-out. A simple file extension solved the problem.

Operating System Utilities

For problems that indeed seem general in nature, it is a good idea to review statistics on the server itself. The two areas that are most obvious (and easy to check) are CPU and disk. Every operating system has a variety of OS level utilities that can assist the performance analyst; some of the most popular are top, sar, and iostat. These are commonly available on most UNIX operating systems.

In the samples shown in the following sections, the commands and displays are for the Solaris operating system, but other versions of UNIX will look very similar. Use the man pages to find the exact syntax and options for your particular version, invoked by entering:

```
$ man[topic]
```

Following a discussion of the UNIX tools, we also explore valuable utilities for the Windows operating system.

top

Although slow CPUs are not generally the primary root cause of a performance problem, there are occasions where the server is indeed vastly underpowered. There are several ways to get a quick check on the overall load on the server. Perhaps the easiest (and fastest) way to check the load is to run the top command. The top command will show the processes consuming the highest level of CPU resources at that moment – hence the name, top. In addition, the overall load on the server is typically shown at the top-right portion of the display. The following example shows the top command, as run on Solaris, and its results:

```
$ top

last pid:  7550;  load averages:  0.05,  0.11,  0.17
10:54:59
93 processes:  92 sleeping, 1 on cpu
CPU states: 97.7% idle,  0.3% user,  1.6% kernel,  0.4% iowait,  0.0%
swap
Memory: 2048M real, 440M free, 1532M swap in use, 2055M swap free

   PID USERNAME THR PRI NICE  SIZE   RES STATE    TIME  CPU COMMAND
  7550 oracle     1  58    0 2584K 1656K cpu/0    0:00 0.19% top
   420 oracle    11  58    0  182M  153M sleep    6:48 0.06% oracle
 22283 oracle     1  58    0  265M  243M sleep    5:30 0.05% oracle
          . . .
   948 dt-dra     9  58    0   49M   10M sleep    6:13 0.02% java
  7515 oracle     1  48    0  181M  159M sleep    0:00 0.01% oracle
   243 root       8  58    0 2760K 2016K sleep    0:09 0.00% nscd
   500 oracle    11  59    0  267M  243M sleep  111:13 0.00% oracle
```

In this example, there was not very much activity on the server. In fact, the top command itself is the top CPU-consumer! Note that the load is provided in three distinct values; these values are the load over the last 1, 5, and 15 minutes. Thus, the first value shown is very close to the instantaneous load on the server. For this example, all three values are close to zero, confirming that the server is nearly idle. Note that load figures on a server are not necessarily comparable to other servers (which typically differ in number of CPUs, among other things). Instead, load numbers are usually compared against a baseline for the system under normal load conditions.

uptime

The uptime command is another convenient way of obtaining information on the recent load on the server. It displays the current time, how long the server has been running, and the load – which is defined as the average number of jobs waiting to be run (the run queue) over the last 1, 5, and 15 minutes.

The following example shows that the load on the local server has remained nearly constant at a little over 1:

```
$ uptime

10:21am up 7 day(s), 20 mins, 3 users, load average: 1.18,
1.26, 1.20
```

Clearly, the uptime command is a very handy way to get a feel for the recent load on the server. The load values reported are normally the same values as shown in the top command.

sar

Another powerful OS tool is the sar facility. sar stands for System Activity Report. Using it, the analyst can get a quick snapshot of the load on the server, and a bit more information about what type of activity is consuming the CPU cycles.

The sar facility can be more useful than the top command because it can also reveal historical server loads (you might need to have your Systems Administrator configure this feature for you). This is particularly helpful when you are trying to troubleshoot a performance problem that occurred at some earlier time.

Our example shows an (abbreviated) version of the sar tool. Note that the percentage load is shown sorted by the hours of the day, for 20-minute intervals:

```
$ sar

SunOS manhattan-db1 5.6 Generic_105181-31 sun4u    06/05/02

00:00:00    %usr    %sys    %wio    %idle
00:20:00      2       2       0       96
```

00:40:00	1	1	0	98
01:00:00	1	1	0	98
01:20:00	4	2	1	93
03:20:00	19	4	2	74
03:40:00	18	4	2	75
04:00:00	23	3	1	73
...				
07:40:00	13	5	1	82
09:40:00	1	1	0	97
10:00:00	1	1	0	97
Average	13	4	2	81

The fields displayed are simple abbreviations, and easily interpreted:

- %usr: Percentage of time running in *user* mode,
- %sys: Percentage of time running in *system* mode,
- %wio: Percentage of time waiting for block I/O
- %idle: Percentage of time spent idle.

In this example, the server was mostly idle, until about 03:20, at which time some user process began to consume about 20% of the CPU capacity.

sar Options

There is a large number of options that can be used with sar; the list will vary by operating system. Two commonly used options are the -e (end time) and -s (start time) selections. These options restrict the report to the specified times.

Here is a list of typical sar options that should prove useful. The list is probably similar on your system:

- -a: Report use of file access system routines iget/s, namei/s, dirblk/s
- -A: Report all data. Equivalent to specifying all options
- -c: Report system calls
- -d: Report activity for each block device (for example, disk or tape drive)
- -e time: Select data up to time. Default is 18:00
- -f filename: Give a file to use as the source of the sar display
- -g: Report paging activities such as page-out requests per second
- -m: Report message and semaphore activities
- -o filename: Save output in file
- -p: Report paging activities
- -s time: Select data later than time specified
- -u: (default option) Report CPU utilization
- -w: Report system swapping and switching activity

To get the complete list of options for your system, it is easiest to use the man pages. The man pages are help files that are invoked by entering:

```
$ man sar.
```

Using sar to Find Historical Information

When running sar in the normal way (without the -f option), the regular activity file is used, which (on Solaris systems) is typically stored in /var/adm/sa/sadd. There is another way to use sar, however. Note that one of the options shown is the -f option; this is used to have sar report on server activity using some other activity file – from some earlier time. Using the -f option, sar will report on previous load information for the local server.

When using the -f option, the filename is typically entered in the following format:

```
/var/adm/sa/sadd
```

where dd is the day of the month.

A sample use of sar to extract historical system load information is shown below. In this example, we retrieve the activity for the fourth day of the month. On this particular system, we have information on the server activity for every 20 minutes. The system was mostly idle until about 1:40 in the morning:

```
$ sar -f /var/adm/sa/sa04

SunOS manhattan-db1 5.6 Generic_105181-31 sun4u      06/04/02

00:00:00    %usr    %sys    %wio    %idle
00:20:00      2       1       0       97
00:40:00      1       1       0       98
01:00:00      1       1       0       98
01:20:00      4       2       1       93
01:40:00     14       2       3       81
04:40:00     21       4       2       73
              ...
14:40:00      2       1       0       97
15:00:00      1       1       0       97
23:40:00      1       1       0       98

Average       7       3       1       89
```

As shown in this figure, the display format is the same as the sar display that is produced without specifying the -f option. The only difference is that the day has been changed.

iostat

At the server level, it is possible to get a listing of disk activity using iostat. There are typically two arguments that are provided when using it. The first is the interval (in seconds) between scans; the second is the count – the number of times to execute. Thus, a command of:

```
$ iostat 5 10
```

means that we want to see ten executions of the `iostat` command, with a delay of five seconds between each output.

The exact syntax and options will vary slightly depending on the operating system, but the basic principles are the same for each UNIX server.

iostat Field Descriptions

Depending on your UNIX version and platform, the column titles may be slightly different. Here is a list of column definitions for my system:

- ❏ `tin`: Characters read from terminals
- ❏ `tout`: Characters written to terminals
- ❏ `kps`: Kb transferred per second
- ❏ `tps`: Transfers per second
- ❏ `serv`: Average service time (ms)
- ❏ `us`: User mode (% of CPU time)
- ❏ `sy`: System mode (% of CPU time)
- ❏ `wt`: Waiting for I/O (% of CPU time)
- ❏ `id`: Idle percent (% of CPU time)

Although each platform will usually show the information slightly differently, the columns will generally be very similar to those indicated above. Note that the `tin` and `tout` columns refer to terminal (tty) I/O, as opposed to disk I/O.

iostat Options

There are several options that may be used to format the `iostat` output in different ways. For example, on Solaris operating systems, the following options may be of interest:

- ❏ `-d`: Show transfers per second and the average service time (ms)
- ❏ `-D`: Show the reads/second, writes/second, and percentage disk utilization
- ❏ `-M`: Display data throughput in MB/sec instead of KB/sec
- ❏ `-n`: Display names in a more descriptive format
- ❏ `-r`: Display data using CSV (comma-separated values)
- ❏ `-z`: Don't print lines where data is zeros.

Our next case study illustrates how a problem with disk throughput can cause a real crimp in database performance. In this example, the application was rendered useless due to a very slow disk system. This case once again shows what odd things can happen when people are involved (that is, all the time!):

Case Study: Blame it on Sybase!

The designer of a data warehouse complained of extremely long run times for jobs that normally finished promptly. Her application was trying to pull data from a Sybase database into Oracle. The job, which normally took about 6 hours, was taking an entire day!

Investigation by several DBAs revealed that the bottleneck was on the extract side, not the insert side; that is, the dump from Sybase was the problem, not the load into Oracle. For a typical table of 1 million rows, the extract from Sybase was taking 1 hour, while the insert using SQL*Loader only required 5 minutes! Discussions with another Oracle DBA who had also used the same Sybase database confirmed that the Sybase database was extremely slow.

The extract from Sybase used a standard Sybase utility called BCP (Bulk Copy). This utility is very similar to the Oracle export/import tool; it generally runs well, and finishes in approximately the same time as the Oracle counterpart. In this case, the Sybase DBAs confirmed that the BCP utility should be able to extract 1 million rows in just a few minutes.

After a few days of confusion, one of the Systems Administrators revealed a little secret. There had not been any room on disk for the Sybase database; therefore, it had been temporarily mounted nfs (network file system; a way to mount a file system not local to the server). This caused a huge degradation in disk performance, leading to a 10x slowdown in overall system performance. With the root cause determined, the team simply decided to use another database server for the Sybase data extraction.

Even though the problem in the above case study was for a Sybase database, the symptoms would have applied equally had the database involved been Oracle. A ridiculously slow disk system will wreak havoc on any database.

vmstat

A database installed on a system with insufficient memory will usually be dreadfully slow. Almost all DBAs have heard of the consequences of paging and swapping, in which the server has either to remove a page of a process, or swap the entire process out of the insufficient memory allocation. Paging and swapping always produces a huge performance problem; performance could easily be an order of magnitude worse.

Fortunately, it is not very difficult to determine if insufficient memory is causing this degradation. On most systems, the standard UNIX command vmstat will divulge paging. The command for executing vmstat is very similar to that for iostat – you simply decide how many seconds between scans, and how many total executions you wish to see displayed.

As with iostat, the first line displayed contains the statistics for the entire time since the last reboot. Thus, we generally are more interested in the second and subsequent lines.

vmstat Options

If no options are specified, vmstat displays a summary of virtual memory activity since the last system re-boot. Here are the options most likely available on your system:

❑ -p: Report paging activity in detail
❑ -s: Display the total number of system events since the last reboot
❑ -S: Report on swapping rather than paging

The vmstat output is divided into six areas:

❑ procs
❑ memory
❑ page
❑ disk
❑ faults
❑ cpu

Let's take a look at what is displayed in each segment of the report.

procs

Procs simply means processes. This area lists the number of processes in the following states:

❑ r: in run queue
❑ b: blocked for resources I/O, paging
❑ w: runnable but swapped

memory

This area lists statistics on the usage of virtual and real memory:

❑ swap amount of swap space currently available (KB)
❑ free size of the free list (KB)

page

This section lists details on the frequency of page faults and paging (occurrences per second):

❑ re: page reclaims
❑ mf: minor faults
❑ pi: kilobytes paged in
❑ po: kilobytes paged out
❑ fr: kilobytes freed

❏ de: anticipated short-term memory shortfall (KB)

❏ sr: pages scanned by clock algorithm

disk

This section of the report provides the number of disk operations per second. Provision is made for displaying up to four disks, each identified by a single letter and number. The letter shows the disk type (For example, s = SCSI), and the number shows the logical unit number.

faults

In this area, we see the trap/interrupt rates (per second):

❏ in: (non clock) device interrupts

❏ sy: system calls

❏ cs: CPU context switches

cpu

Finally, the cpu section gives a breakdown of proportionate usage of CPU time. Note that on multi-processor systems, these statistics are an average for all processors.

❏ us: user time

❏ sy: system time

❏ id: idle time

Tools for Windows Operating Systems

On Microsoft operating systems, there are many different tools that can be used to monitor performance and assist the DBA in isolating the cause of performance bottlenecks. The most popular performance and development tools are packaged as part of a Microsoft Platform SDK (Software Development Kit). This package of tools is available for the following Windows platforms:

❏ Windows XP and Windows .NET Server

❏ Windows Advanced Server, Limited Edition

❏ Windows 2000 Windows NT versions 3.51 and 4.0

❏ Windows 95, Windows 98, and Windows Millennium Edition

The SDK includes the following performance tools:

Tool	Description
Performance Monitor	Performance Monitor
APIMon	API monitor
PerfMtr	Performance meter

Tool	Description
PStat	Performance statistics
WPerf	Performance monitor
WSTCat	Working set tuner
WSTDump	Working set tuner
WSTune	Working set tuner

Let's take a look at each of these tools. We start with the most popular, the Performance Monitor.

Performance Monitor

This tool is normally the first OS-specific tool to consider when beginning performance analysis on a Windows platform. You can start Performance Monitor by selecting: Start | Programs | Administrative Tools (Common) | Performance Monitor.

This tool is useful in determining the general area in which the problem occurs. It is possible to retrieve statistics on many different system parameters, such as CPU time, network activity, disk traffic, and so on. The relevant performance information is graphically displayed in a performance chart

In order to add a different metric, you simply select the desired statistic (for example, % Processing Time, or %Disk Time) from a menu of chart choices. You can also set the data sampling frequency; for instance, you can gather data every ten seconds.

Besides simply displaying the statistics, it is also possible to record, or log, statistics. Here are some other powerful features of the Performance Monitor tool. You can:

❑ Chart data from multiple servers in order to compare the performance counters on different machines.

❑ Export data from charts, logs, and so on to a spreadsheet or database for further analysis.

❑ Program alerts that list events in the Alert Log and notify the Administrator.

❑ Use triggers that can execute a user-defined program when a counter exceeds a certain threshold.

Definitions

There are a variety of cryptic-sounding statistics used in the Performance Monitor that need a little explanation:

❑ Memory-Pages/sec: This refers to the number of pages that the server must read from or write to disk (possibly due to inadequate memory). This statistic may be helpful in determining if the server has enough memory.

289

❑ **Memory-Available Bytes:** This provides overall statistics for available memory.

❑ **PhysicalDisk-% Disk Time:** This represents the percentage of time that the disk drive is servicing I/O requests. Continuing high values may indicate excessive disk activity.

❑ **Processor-Interrupts/sec:** This reveals how frequently processor interrupts are occurring.

❑ **System-Processor Queue Length:** This refers to the length of the processor queue (which is normally 0, except when you have activated the thread counter). If this value regularly exceeds two, the processors are overloaded.

❑ **Physical Disk-Current Disk Queue Length:** This indicates the number of requests not yet serviced (for example, queued-up). This statistic is useful in detecting unusually high disk loads.

❑ **Processor-% Processor Time:** This indicates the percentage of time the processor spends actually performing useful work. Continual high (>85%) values suggest an overworked processor.

Some Tips on Using the Performance Monitor

Although the Performance Monitor tool is very versatile, and offers a lot of good information, there are a few precautions to note:

❑ Remember that the statistics for any parameter need to be activated in the chart first. This is done by turning on the performance counters.

❑ When logging system activity, try to restrict the logging period to the minimum time possible. This is important because the Performance Monitor itself consumes resources and will degrade the system somewhat. (This is similar to what happens when the DBA runs SQL_TRACE on the entire database.) Also, note that the monitor logs can consume a lot of disk space if the logging is left on for extended periods.

❑ To get a feel for the typical load on any given system, it is a good idea to spot-check statistics over a week, including different times of the day.

Finally, Microsoft provides an excellent case study that illustrates how to use the Performance Monitor for isolating a performance bottleneck. In the Microsoft example, they debug a performance problem with the classic Solitaire computer game. This example is available at http://msdn.microsoft.com/library/.

Let's look at some of the other tools available for Windows, now.

APIMon

APIMon stands for Application Monitor. It is a performance monitor utility that shows the run time of functions within an application. It can also reveal page faults caused by the application under observation. This tool is most useful in determining which parts of the application are taking the most time.

APIMon provides two types of reports. One report shows the time and count for all functions called in the monitored application. A second report is like a debugging report, because it shows a trace of each call as it happens.

There is additional information on using this utility provided in the file APIMon.hlp, which is provided with the software for this tool.

PerfMtr

In contrast to APIMon, which has a very narrow focus, the PerfMtr utility provides a much broader set of information related to system performance. PerfMtr is invoked at the command-line simply by typing:

```
Perfmtr
```

The default activity for PerfMtr is to display CPU usage. The display is easily changed, by simply depressing a single key. Use the following keystrokes to change the type of performance information displayed:

Key	Displays
C	CPU usage
V	VM usage
F	File Cache usage
R	Cache Manager read and write operations
P	Pool usage
I	I/O usage
X	x86 VDM stats
S	Server stats
Q	Quit
H	Repeat Header line

PStat

This utility provides statistics for each process that is running. The syntax for running pstat is:

```
pstat [-u] [-s] [-v]
```

with the following option definitions:

- ❑ -u: Show statistics for user-mode processes.
- ❑ -s: Show statistics for activity related to system processes.
- ❑ -v: Verbose mode (for example, more detailed statistics).

291

WPerf

WPerf is similar to the Performance Monitor utility, but displays the performance statistics in a slightly different fashion. Like the Performance Monitor, WPerf categorizes the information to be displayed using counters.

Further information on each of these Windows performance-monitoring utilities is available at http://msdn.microsoft.com/library/.

Let's now turn from OS-specific tools to a utility that has become increasingly popular in recent years: Statspack.

Oracle Statspack

We now come to one of the most interesting and useful tools provided in recent years by Oracle Corporation. Beginning with Oracle 8.1.6, analysts have the new Statspack option. Statspack is a utility very similar to the classic utlbstat and utlestat programs, which have been available for many years.

These utlbstat and utlestat tools were designed to gather and compare statistics from two different points in time. The fundamental idea of Statspack is the same; we still capture statistics at various points in time, but there are considerable improvements over the older utilities. In fact, the entire report is far more useful and flexible than with the older method. Statspack also includes more statistical information, which is nicely formatted, scaled, and grouped. For instance, it adds the following information:

❑   Instance summary
❑   Normalization of overall instance statistics
❑   SQL statements that are resource hogs

Besides these extra features, it is also possible to slightly change how much information is collected; for instance, the list of resource-intensive SQL may be optionally excluded. At the other extreme, more information may be requested (at the cost of some performance degradation).

Another major difference between Statspack and the other stat tools is that it retains all the statistics as long as wanted; should the DBA desire, it is possible to store thousands of snapshots. With the older utilities, however, the information was always dropped once the report was completed.

Installing Statspack

It is fortunately very easy to set up Statspack. The new user, named PERFSTAT, will be created automatically; there are a few decisions to make, however. First, decide which tablespaces are required for this user – both for its default tablespace and the temporary tablespace.

The data that will be stored in Statspack will not be large, about 35 MB to start. Of course, as more and more data is captured, this the size will increase slightly; nevertheless it shouldn't become an issue.

To begin the installation process, log into the server, then connect to the database as SYS or INTERNAL (for pre-Oracle 9i), or connect as SYSDBA for Oracle 9i. Navigate to the directory $ORACLE_HOME/rdbms/admin. This is the directory where the various Statspack scripts are located. Here is a list of the most important files:

- ❏ spdoc.txt: The readme file
- ❏ statscre.sql: SQL script that sets up Statspack
- ❏ statsdrp.sql: SQL script that drops entire Statspack installation
- ❏ statsauto.sql: SQL script to automate snapshot execution using DBMS_JOB
- ❏ statsuexp.par: Sample export parameter file for exporting Perfstat user

It is a good idea to review the readme file spdoc.txt, which is located in the same place as all the other Statspack scripts. From this directory, start SQL*Plus and run the script spcreate.sql. This script will create several packages; here is an example of what will happen:

```
SQL> @ spcreate.sql

... Installing Required Packages

Package created.

Grant succeeded.

View created.

Package body created.

Package created.

Synonym created.

****
```

After a few minutes, you will be prompted for the name of the default tablespace to use for the PERFSTAT user, like so:

```
Using the SYSTEM tablespace to store statistical data is
NOT recommended.
TOOLS
RBS
TEMP
USR
STAGING
DIM_DATA
FACT_INDEX
DIM_INDEX
METADATA
```

```
METAINDEX
FACT_DATA_A
FACT_DATA_B
EPIOP
EPIMART
DRA_ADMIN

15 rows selected.

Specify PERFSTAT user's default tablespace
Enter value for default_tablespace:
```

You will then be prompted for the name of the temporary tablespace. Traditionally, this is called TEMP, but might be different on your particular database. After this information is provided, the script will run for just a few minutes more. The entire process completes in about 5 minutes.

Behind the scenes, this first script, spcreate, calls several other scripts and performs the following:

❑ Creates PERFSTAT user and required privileges using script spcusr

❑ Builds the tables and synonyms using script spctab

❑ Creates the statistics package using script spcpkg

When running the spcreate script, a spool file will be created for each step in the installation process; this makes it easier to troubleshoot any problems that may occur. If for some reason the spcreate script should fail, simply look for the spool file created in the same directory. The name of the spool file will correspond to the script that was running when the failure occurred.

Taking PERFSTAT Snapshots

Like the old bstat and estat utilities, Statspack requires two separate snapshots; statistics are gathered from the database at the moment each snapshot is taken. Once we have two snapshots, they can be compared, and used as the basis of the report.

We use the Statspack package, plus a procedure called Snap. Here is an example of how a snapshot is taken:

```
SQL> EXEC Statspack.Snap

PL/SQL procedure successfully completed.
```

With each snapshot, Oracle generates a key by which to identify this particular set of data, called a snapshot id. When future statistics are run, the report will ask for the beginning and ending snapshot id.

Besides the simple execution method shown above, the analyst or DBA may optionally specify that more (or less) detailed statistics should be gathered. This is called the snapshot level. There are just a few different levels:

❑ Level 0: Statspack collects a large assortment of statistics.

❑ Level 5: (default level): Same as Level 0, but also includes detailed statistics on SQL statements that are high resource-consumers.

❑ Level 6 (new for Oracle 9i): Captures usage information for SQL resource hogs.

❑ Level 10: Same as Level 5, but also includes more detailed latching information.

Note that the data gathered at Level 10 can cause performance degradation; in fact, Oracle recommends that this level only be used for special troubleshooting situations.

To specify a snapshot level that is different from the default, we supply a parameter called I_snap_level. Simply set this argument to the desired level when calling the snap procedure. For example, to take a snapshot at Level 0, the following command would be used:

```
SQL> EXEC Statspack.Snap (I_snap_level=>0)

PL/SQL procedure successfully completed.
```

Here is a list of some other parameters that can be used with the snap procedure:

❑ I_ucomment (default = Null): Include this comment with the snapshot statistics

❑ I_session_id (default = 0, all sessions): Specify a specific SID for which to take a snapshot

❑ I_modify_parameter (TRUE|FALSE; default=FALSE): Change the default behavior for future executions of snap

It is also possible to change the threshold that Statspack uses as the cut-off point for classifying high-resource usage. The following parameters control these thresholds:

❑ I_executions_th (default = 50): Number of executions

❑ I_disk_reads_th (default = 1000): Number of disk reads

❑ I_parse_calls_th (default = 1000): Number of parse calls

❑ I_buffer_gets_th (default = 10000): Number of buffer gets

If desired, it is easy to change the default snap behavior – without taking a snapshot at the same time; the procedure Modify_Statspack_Parameter is used to accomplish this. For instance, to change the default snap level to level 0, the following command could be run from SQL*Plus:

```
SQL> EXEC-
  2  Statspack.Modify_Statspack_Parameter (I_snap_level=>0)

PL/SQL procedure successfully completed.
```

295

Running Statspack Reports

When running a `Statspack` report, you will need to supply a little information. Since there are multiple snapshots stored in the `Statspack` tables, it is necessary to specify which two snapshots should be used as the basis for the report. After this information is provided, `Statspack` will query the tables owned by the `PERFSTAT` user, and find the delta between the two snapshots. Then, statistics will be provided that reflect this difference.

To run a report, simply connect to SQL*Plus as `PERFSTAT` (default password = `PERFSTAT`), and run the script `spreport.sql`. This script is located in the same directory as all the other `Statspack` scripts: `$ORACLE_HOME/rdbms/admin`.

After connecting as `PERFSTAT` and starting the script `spreport`, you will be shown a summary of the snapshots available for that database. You will then need to select a beginning and ending snapshot.

Here is a sample of this first section:

```
SQL> @ spreport

Current Instance
~~~~~~~~~~~~~~~~

          DB Id DB Name     Inst Num Instance
------------- ---------- -------- ------------
   2628433931 OPELSA            1 opelsa

Instances in this Statspack schema
~~~~~~~~~~~~~~~~~~~~~~~~~~~~~~~~~~~~

          DB Id Inst Num DB Name Instance      Host
------------- -------- ------- ------------ ------------
   2628433931        1 OPELSA  opelsa        alpha-db1

Using 2628433931 for database Id
Using        1 for instance number

Completed Snapshots

                         Snap                       Snap
Instance   DB Name        Id Snap Started           Level Comment
---------  ---------     ---- ------------------- ------ ---------
opelsa     OPELSA          1 30 May 2002 13:50         5
                           2 30 May 2002 13:51         5
                           3 30 May 2002 13:59         0
                           4 30 May 2002 13:59         0
                           5 04 Jun 2002 13:34         0
                           6 04 Jun 2002 13:35         0
                          11 05 Jun 2002 14:55         0
                          21 06 Jun 2002 11:09         0
                          22 06 Jun 2002 12:00         0
                             * * *
                         117 10 Jun 2002 11:00         0
                         118 10 Jun 2002 12:00         0
```

We see that for this database, there are over 100 snapshots available. Let's say we want to get a `Statspack` report using snapshot 99 as the start, and snapshot 100 as the endpoint. Here is what we see next:

```
Specify the Begin and End Snapshot Ids
~~~~~~~~~~~~~~~~~~~~~~~~~~~~~~~~~~~~~~~~~~
Enter value for begin_snap:

Begin Snapshot Id specified: 99

Enter value for end_snap: 100
End Snapshot Id specified: 100


Specify the Report Name
~~~~~~~~~~~~~~~~~~~~~~~~~
The default report file name is sp_1_100. To use this name,
press <return> to continue, otherwise enter an alternative.
Enter value for report_name:
```

In this example, we accepted the default name for the report. Of course, we could have entered any name.

Sample Report

The entire `Statspack` report is very long and cumbersome to read. Fortunately, it is divided into sections that group the statistics for related data. Some of the key sections are:

- Load Profile
- Instance Efficiency Percentages
- Top 5 Wait Events
- All Wait Events
- Instance Activity Statistics
- Tablespace Statistics
- File IO Statistics
- Buffer Pool Statistics
- Instance Recovery Statistics
- PGA Memory Statistics
- Rollback Segment Statistics
- Rollback Segment Storage
- Latch Activity
- SGA Memory Summary
- init.ora Parameters

Let's take a look at a sample report for each of these areas. In the following sections we provide a sample display for each section of the `Statspack` report. For those sections that are typically very lengthy, we have condensed the display to show just a few sample rows.

Preliminary Information

The first section of a `Statspack` report provides some basic information, such as the snapshots used and the database that is being reported. For the sample report shown, we have requested that `Statspack` use snap id 1 to begin, and snap id 3 to end. We note that the instance name is `nyathi`, and the server name is `HORATIO`:

```
STATSPACK report for

DB Name      DB Id  Instance  Inst Num  Release   Cluster Host
-------  ----------  ---------  --------  ---------  -------  -----
ORACLE   1350275712 nyathi            1  9.0.1.1.1  NO        HORATIO

             Snap Id      Snap Time        Sessions  Curs/Sess Comment
             -------  ------------------  ---------  ---------  -------
Begin Snap:        1 07-Dec-02 15:33:50         7      4.6
  End Snap:        2 07-Dec-02 15:35:35         7      5.6
   Elapsed:                  1.75 (mins)
```

Cache Sizes

In the next section of the report, the cache sizes (for the final snapshot) are shown; these values are the basic sizing for the instance. Note that although most of the `Statspack` report is based on differences between two snapshots, some statistics don't make any sense as differences, this section being one of those exceptions. In the report below, the values are not differences:

```
Buffer Cache:        256M  Std Block Size:    8K
Shared Pool Size:    64M   Log Buffer:        1,024K
```

These values are simply a reflection of the `init.ora` values set in the database at the time of the second snapshot. Thus, this section is really a configuration check, so that you know for a fact how your database was configured at the time of the second snapshot.

The `init.ora` parameters that determine the `Statspack` values above are:

❑ `Shared_Pool_Size`
❑ `Log_Buffer`
❑ `Db_Block_Size`
❑ `Db_Block_Buffers`

Remember that the cache size noted in the `Statspack` report is the product of the database block size and `Db_Block_Buffers`.

Load Profile

This section gives the analyst an idea of how busy the database was during the snapshot interval. The statistics here can give the analyst a good feel for what kind of activity is occurring on the database. This area is a good example to illustrate the importance of having a good baseline from a prior snapshot; this means taking regular snapshots.

For example, the number of sorts shown in this section is potentially good information, but its value really depends on seeing how the number has changed compared to a normal period. If the number of sorts seems gigantic, that in itself does not mean that there is some problem; perhaps it is entirely normal in a given application for the sorts to be large. We are really more interested in seeing how the various statistics have changed over time:

```
                      Per Second  Per Transaction
                    ---------------- ----------------
    Redo size:          2,392.30         2,392.30
    Logical reads:        153.00           153.00
    Block changes:          3.85             3.85
    Physical reads:         0.28             0.28
    Physical writes:        0.79             0.79
    User calls:             8.55             8.55
    Parses:                 1.57             1.57
    Hard parses:            0.20             0.20
    Sorts:                  4.20             4.20
    Logons:                 0.00             0.00
    Executes:               5.25             5.25
    Transactions:           1.00

    % Blocks changed per Read: 2.52 Recursive Call %: 77.18
    Rollback per transaction %: 95.05  Rows per Sort: 53.44
```

Once again, the value of these numbers lies mostly with their comparison to a baseline period – a report that has been run during a normal workload, with all applications working properly. However, there is a rough rule of thumb that can be used with respect to hard parsing. A hard parse rate over 100/sec generally is excessive; such a high value suggests that numerous forms of new SQL statements are being offered for execution.

Instance Efficiency

In this efficiency section, some critical performance ratios are provided, including the famous buffer hit ratio. This metric shows how often needed data is already cached in memory. Once again, these numbers are really most useful when there is a baseline for comparison; it is often difficult to judge whether they are good or bad without having such a baseline.

Here is a sample readout for this section of Statspack:

```
Buffer Nowait %:           100.00   Redo NoWait %:       99.91
Buffer Hit %:               99.91   In-memory Sort %:   100.00
Library Hit %:              95.77   Soft Parse %:        87.18
Execute to Parse %:         70.06   Latch Hit %:         99.99
Parse CPU to Parse Elapsd %: 96.91  Non-Parse CPU %:     95.52
```

In the above report, the term In-memory Sort refers to the proportion of sorts that are performed in memory. Optimally, most sorts will be small enough to be performed completely in-memory. Likewise, the parsing ratios ideally would show that the SQL statements in the system are only parsed once and executed many times.

The term Soft Parse means that a SQL statement has been processed recently; this means that the database optimizer can use the parse information already in the library cache. On the other hand, generating parse information from scratch is called a Hard Parse. Not surprisingly, hard parses consume significantly more resources than soft parses.

Oracle provides more details on distinguishing between hard and soft parses in the support document at http://metalink.oracle.com/metalink/plsql/showdoc?db=Not&id=32895.

Top 5 Wait Events

This section can be very valuable, as it shows what the database is waiting for, and how much time is attributed to the various events. It's a good place to begin serious analysis using the Statspack report. Using the wait events shown here, it is possible to drill down to the trouble spots.

Of course, the values displayed here are really the same sort of information as can be gleaned from the wait event facility. Statspack is in effect just querying the same tables that are available to anyone. A big advantage with Statspack, however, is that the information is retained for use in reports:

Event	Waits	Time (s)	Wt Time
control file sequential read	45	2	35.90
control file parallel write	31	2	25.23
db file parallel write	8	1	20.22
log file parallel write	9	1	15.19
log file sync	2	0	3.47

The information above is similar to that which we have discussed for the V$WAIT facility. These events (along with the events mentioned in the next few sections) were discussed further in Chapter 6.

All Wait Events: Foreground

In this section, the wait events related to the foreground server processes are shown. In the context of Oracle database administration, the term foreground refers to processes that are initiated by a user session, and exist in order to service a particular user:

Event	Waits	Timeouts	Total Wait Time (s)	Avg wait (ms)	Waits /txn
async disk IO	86	0	2	26	0.2
db file parallel write	28	28	1	40	0.1
control file parallel write	190	0	1	5	0.3
log file parallel write	57	56	1	15	0.1
direct path read	78	0	1	8	0.1
log file sync	33	0	0	15	0.1
db file sequential read	74	0	0	3	0.1
log file switch completion	1	0	0	62	0.0

Again, these events are the same as those gleaned using the Wait Facility, discussed in Chapter 6.

All Wait Events: Background

The concept of wait events was discussed in Chapter 6, where we provided several illustrations of using them to isolate performance problems. In this section, the wait events related to the background processes are shown. By background, we mean the Oracle processes that are automatically running as part of the nominal database operation, regardless of how many users are connected. An example of background processes would be smon and pmon:

Event	Waits	Timeouts	Total Wait Time (s)	Avg wait (ms)	Waits /txn
async disk IO	86	0	2	26	0.2
db file parallel write	28	28	1	40	0.1
control file parallel write	190	0	1	5	0.3
log file parallel write	57	56	1	15	0.1
direct path read	78	0	1	8	0.1
control file sequential read	63	0	0	0	0.1
log file single write	2	0	0	2	0.0
buffer busy waits	1	0	0	1	0.0
. . .					

One entry above deserves special consideration. The value of buffer busy waits indicates that there are some buffers that different processes are attempting to access at the same time – thus, the buffer is busy. By querying the view V$WAITSTAT you can see the wait statistics for each type of buffer.

Instance Statistics

This portion of the Statspack report is very long, as it includes just about any system-wide statistic available. (It gets this information by querying the V$SYSSTAT view.) Here are some of the statistics listed in this section:

```
Statistic                          Total    per Second per Trans
---------------------------------- -------- ------------- ---------
CPU used by this session            2,098         3.8        3.8
CPU used when call started          2,097         3.8        3.8
buffer is not pinned count         70,236       128.6      128.6
buffer is pinned count             88,522       162.1      162.1
bytes received via SQL*Net from c 519,220       951.0      951.0

...

table fetch continued row               0         0.0        0.0
table scan blocks gotten            7,636        14.0       14.0
table scan rows gotten            152,256       278.9      278.9
write clones created in foreground      7         0.0        0.0
```

The large variety of statistics provided by Statspack can be overwhelming. An excellent source of examples and further details on using this tool can be found in Oracle9i High-Performance Tuning with STATSPACK by Donald K. Burleson, ISBN 007222360X.

Tablespace Statistics

This area shows activity (reads, writes, buffer waits) for each tablespace. Here are a few sample rows:

	Reads	Av Reads/s	Av Rd(ms)	Av Blks/Rd	Writes	Writes/s	Av Buffer Waits	Av Buf Wt(ms)
TOOLS								
	1	0		1.0	210	0	0	0.0
UNDOTS								
	1	0	310.0	1.0	113	0	2	0.0
SYSTEM								
	1	0	300.0	1.0	53	0	0	0.0
INDX								
	22	0	80.9	1.0	1	0	0	0.0
DATA								
	9	0	123.3	1.0	1	0	0	0.0
INDX_CW								

With the information from this section of the report, the DBA can get a feel for where most of the transactions are occurring. Combined with information from the following section, the DBA can thus find where the hot spots are among the various database files on the system.

In the results above, note that the unusual name UNDOTS is simply the name for the rollback tablespace for the database that was being used as an example. UNDOTS stands for UNDO tablespace.

File I/O Statistics

This section of the report shows I/O details specifically attributed to each file. Once again, the DBA can easily glean most of this information from a database view. There is one important distinction, however; the statistics in Statspack reflect the difference in values between the two snapshot periods.

Here are a few sample entries for this section of the Statspack report:

```
Tablespace     Filename
-------------  ----------------------------------------------------------
                  Av     Av     Av              Av   Buffer Av Buf
        Reads Reads/s Rd(ms) Blks/Rd  Writes Writes/s   Waits Wt(ms)
        ----- ------- ------ ------- ------- -------- ------ ----------------
DATA       /u02/oradata/opelsa/data01.dbf
          19       2  123.3     1.0       1        0             0

DATA_CW    /u02/oradata/opelsa/data_cw01.dbf
          22       2  120.0     1.0       1        0             0

DATA_TR    /u02/oradata/opelsa/data_tr01.dbf
          52       5  170.0     1.0       1        0             0
```

Note that the above information is very similar to the report on tablespaces. These two sections provide abundant statistics on disk I/O that will help pinpoint any I/O problems to the exact tablespace and files involved.

Buffer Pool Statistics

This area shows activity for each pool in memory. Note the heading P refers to the pool type:

❑   D = default

❑   K = keep

❑   R = recycle

Some useful hit ratios are provided, segmented by pool type:

P	Number of Buffers	Cache Hit %	Buffer Gets	Physical Reads	Physical Writes	Free Buffer Waits	Write Complete Waits	Buffer Busy Waits
D	8,024	99.9	34,599	40	373	0	0	3
K	16,048	17.6	17	14	0	0	0	0
R	8,024	99.7	7,651	20	0	0	0	0

Some further explanation of the various cache pools is in order. A single buffer pool is used for most databases; however, when applications have a large number of tables being accessed, you can assign different objects to different cache pools. The database objects that are constantly being accessed should be assigned to the Keep Pool.

303

Conversely, the objects only rarely accessed (such as tables only used during a nightly batch job) are assigned to the Recycle Pool. This assignment keeps objects in one pool from consuming space in the other pool. Objects not explicitly assigned are sent to the Default pool.

In the report above, we see that more buffers (16,048) were allocated to the Keep pool, compared to the Default and Recycle pools (8,024 buffers each). The actual size of a pool is computed by multiplying the number of buffers times the database block size used for that particular database.

Instance Recovery Statistics

This section tells the DBA how long an instance recovery would require if the database were to crash (that is, unexpectedly abort). This information will be most useful in production databases that are critical to the firm's business. In these situations, the information here will assist the DBA in minimizing the time to re-open a database. The DBA can use these numbers to form an estimate of down time following a database crash.

In the report below, note that the abbreviation MTTR means Mean-Time-to-Recover. (Not to be confused with the oft-used MTTR in the field of logistics and maintainability that means Mean-time-to-Repair):

```
  Targt Estd                                Log File  Log Ckpt  Log Ckpt
  MTTR  MTTR  Recovery   Actual    Target     Size     Timeout   Interval
  (s)   (s)   Estd IOs  Redo Blks RedoBlks  RedoBlks  Redo Blks Redo Blks
  ----- ----  --------- --------- --------  --------  --------- ---------
B  40   21     32096      1418     15567     18432      15567   #########
E  40   22     32096       247     16889     18432      16889   #########
```

The fields shown for log file sizing and checkpointing (Ckpt above) are included here because they directly affect instance recovery time. A key method to reduce recovery time is to perform more frequent checkpoints (for example, updates of the .dbf data files). With more frequent updates, a recovery will be faster because the database files are always more current.

PGA Aggregate Memory Statistics

Let's look a little more at what some of these terms mean – in particular, the term PGA. The Program Global Area (PGA) is a private memory region that contains control information and work areas for one particular session. An example of a work area would be a sort area that is needed because the SQL run by that session contained the ORDER BY clause.

In the display below, the abbreviation W/A below means Work Area:

```
                                   %Optim %Non-W/A %Auto %Manual
  PGA Aggr    PGA      W/A PGA   1-Pass   W/A     PGA    W/A     W/A
  Target(M) inUse(M) inUse(M) MemReq(M) Execs  Memory PGA Mem PGA Mem
  --------- -------- -------- --------- ----- ------ ---------------
```

B	512	12.7	.0	3.3	99.94	.06	.00
E	512	13.2	.0	3.3	99.94	.06	.00

Starting with Oracle 9i, Oracle provides a new PGA self-tuning capability. With this new feature, the DBA sets an aggregate target for the work areas. Then, the database itself adjusts the memory assigned to each work area, as long as the target value is not exceeded. The init.ora parameter is called PGA_AGGREGATE_TARGET.

In the report section above, note the column that uses the term 1-Pass. Some of the terms used in this (and the next) section of the Statspack report are related to aspects of the automatic PGA tuning feature. When a particular PGA work area size can completely contain all the information needed to complete an operation, we call this the optimal size of a work area. When the size of the work area is smaller than optimal, and one extra pass must be performed, we call that size the one-pass size of the work area.

PGA Memory Statistics

This section provides a slight different look at the PGA; in particular, this Statspack section shows the maximum allocations for the different aspects of PGA. The difference between the snapshot periods is also listed:

Statistic	Begin (M)	End (M)	% Diff
global memory bound	.025	.025	.00
maximum PGA allocated	45.779	45.779	.00
maximum PGA memory for one-pass	3.277	3.277	.00
maximum PGA memory for optimal	3.277	3.277	.00
maximum PGA used for auto workareas	1.191	1.191	.00
total PGA allocated	21.900	22.097	.90
total PGA inuse	12.696	13.158	3.64
total PGA used for auto workareas	.008	.008	.00
workarea memory allocated	.000	.000	.00

As noted in the previous report section, many of the PGA metrics refer to features of the PGA automatic memory management, newly provided in Oracle 9i. If this feature has not been activated in the init.ora file, this section will probably not be very useful.

Rollback Segment Statistics

From this portion of the report, we note that there are ten rollback segments used in this database. The activity for each is shown:

RBS No	Trans Table Gets	Pct Waits	Undo Bytes Written	Wraps	Shrinks	Extends
0	39.0	0.00	0	0	0	0

1	55.0	0.00	1,698	0	0	0
2	63.0	1.59	15,662	1	1	0
3	51.0	0.00	1,710	0	0	0
4	51.0	0.00	1,602	0	0	0
5	167.0	0.00	275,768	7	0	6

In most cases, this section of Statspack will probably not be too interesting. In situations where the transaction rate is very high, however, the DBA might want to check the distribution of the load between the different rollback segments. Another possible use would be for systems where particular rollback segments are reserved for giant transactions.

There are a few odd terms listed above that need some explanation. The term Extends refers to situations where Oracle had to increase the number of extents allocated for a given rollback segment automatically. Similarly, Shrinks denotes cases where Oracle removed unneeded extent allocations. Generally speaking, it is best to have relatively stable rollback segments, so that the database engine is not using valuable CPU time for these housekeeping chores.

Rollback Segment Storage

The sizing statistics for each of the ten rollback segments are provided here:

RBS No	Segment Size	Avg Active	Optimal Size	Maximum Size
0	401,408	0		401,408
1	712,704	59,977		712,704
2	319,488	38,671		385,024
3	188,416	47,410		188,416
4	319,488	53,147		319,488
5	581,632	166,084		581,632
6	385,024	70,045		385,024
7	385,024	46,590		385,024
8	188,416	42,904		253,952
9	647,168	141,623		647,168
10	385,024	45,853		385,024

This information is similar to the previous section of the report, but provides a slightly different perspective; in this report, we see the total size of each rollback segment, along with the values used for Optimal and Maximum. Note that the term Optimal means the size that the rollback segment will tend to maintain; it will not shrink below this value. (Of course, it can still grow larger if necessary.)

These statistics, in conjunction with those from the previous section, can be useful in detecting excessive rollback maintenance activity. One example would be a rollback segment that is frequently expanding, only to contract back to its optimal size soon afterwards. This could be an indication that the optimal size is set too small.

Undo Segment Summary

This section lists overall statistics for the rollback activity, including the total number of transactions for the rollback tablespace. The information here is sorted by tablespace; in many systems, there will be just one tablespace housing this undo information.

Note that statistics for several errors are also shown – including the well-known Snapshot too old ORA-01555 error message. This infamous error message is a sort of classic in the DBA arena, and has been the subject of numerous articles, and probably thousands of queries to Oracle support. It refers to a situation where a user needs to see information in a rollback block that has already been overwritten by another transaction. In other words, the snapshot of data is no longer available. A better name for the cryptic message might have been Data Gone!:

Undo TS#	Undo Blocks	Num Trans	Max Qry Len (s)	Max Tx Concurcy	Snapshot Too Old	Out of Space	uS/uR/uU/ eS/eR/eU
1	308	762	190	3	0	0	0/0/0/0/0/0

End Time	Undo Blocks	Num Trans	Max Qry Len (s)	Max Tx Concy	Snapsh Too Old	Out of Space	uS/uR/uU/ eS/eR/eU
30-May 14:01	77	72	190	2	0	0	0/0/0/0/0/0
30-May 13:51	231	690	3	3	0	0	0/0/0/0/0/0

The information in the section above is not for general-purpose troubleshooting, but for analyzing very specific issues, once some problem with the rollback segments has surfaced. For instance, perhaps the developers have complained of a funny Snapshot too old message. In other cases, the DBA might have noticed an Unable to extend error message in the alert.log file. The information above can help confirm that the problem is indeed related to a rollback tablespace.

Latch Activity

Recall that a latch is a method Oracle uses to control access to critical internal database structures. Just as user-defined tables need to have some sort of traffic cop to co-ordinate updates between multiple users, the internal database structures need to be protected in a similar way. When a large number of processes are competing for access to some internal object, we use the phrase latch contention.

In the next two sections, we see a summary of locking information, including latch requests, misses, and wait time:

Latch	Get Requests	Pct Get Miss	Avg Slps /Miss	Wait Time (s)	NoWait Requests	Pct NoWait Miss
cache buffers chains	130,890	0.0	0.0	0	261	0.0

checkpoint queue latch	19,124	0.0	0.0	0	0
enqueues	7,721	0.0	0.0	0	0
messages	1,567	0.1	0.0	0	0
library cache	47,744	0.0	0.0	0	0
SQL memory manager latch	0			0	176	0.0
cache buffers lru chain	2,878	0.0		0	257	0.0
process allocation	2	0.0		0	2	0.0
resmgr:schema config	470	0.0		0	183	0.0
hash table column usage	11	0.0		0	461	0.0
redo copy	0			0	1,194	0.1

Latch	Get Requests	Pct Get Miss	Avg Slps /Miss	Wait Time (s)	NoWait Requests	Pct NoWait Miss
cache buffer handles	26	0.0		0	0	
archive control	149	0.0		0	0	
SQL memory manager worka	13,520	0.0		0	0	
JOX SGA heap latch	1	0.0		0	0	

As with most delays in Oracle, the Wait Facility can help confirm the existence of abnormal wait events, and help narrow down the problem.

SGA Memory Summary

Here we find a very convenient summary of the entire SGA memory allocation:

SGA regions	Size in Bytes
Database Buffers	268,435,456
Fixed Size	280,176
Redo Buffers	1,064,960
Variable Size	184,549,376
...	
sum	454,329,968

In the listing above, Database Buffers is the main database cache that holds copies of data blocks read from any of the data files (the .dbf files). This is the area DBAs are usually referring to when they use the phrase hit-ratio. The size of this area is the product of Db_Block_Buffers * database block size.

Fixed Size contains general information about the database which the background processes (pmon, smon, and so on) will need as a reference. This is not where user data is located; thus, this region is usually much smaller than the other areas listed.

Redo Buffers is the space used for the buffers in the SGA that hold the database change information. All changes to the database (with very few exceptions) are written to this area.

Variable Size is an accumulation of different pools, and is determined by the values used for these init.ora parameters – shared_pool_size, large_pool_size, and java_pool_size.

Beginning with Oracle9i, the SGA can be configured in a very surprising way; it can be dynamic – that is, changed while the database is running! The size of the dynamic SGA is affected by the following initialization parameters – DB_BLOCK_SIZE, DB_CACHE_SIZE, SHARED_POOL_SIZE, and LOG_BUFFER.

Oracle Corporation has provided additional information on dynamically reconfiguring the SGA. On the Metalink support site (http://metalink.oracle.com), see Note 1008866.6, How to determine SGA Size.

init.ora Parameters

In this final area of the Statpack report, we see a list of all the init.ora parameters that do not use the default value. This section will be somewhat lengthy. Here is a sample of the Statpack report:

```
                                               End value
Parameter Name                   Begin value  (if different)
-------------------------------- -----------  --------------
O7_DICTIONARY_ACCESSIBILITY TRUE
pga_aggregate_target             536870912
processes                              500
recovery_parallelism                     4
remote_login_passwordfile        EXCLUSIVE
resource_manager_plan            SYSTEM_PLAN
sessions                               555
shared_pool_size                 67108864
sort_area_size                   131072
tape_asynch_io                   TRUE
timed_statistics                 TRUE
undo_management                  AUTO
undo_tablespace                  UNDOTS
workarea_size_policy             AUTO
```

This portion of the Statpack report is really just for reference. This information will be helpful in noting the exact database setup at the time of the snapshot.

Removing Old Snapshot Data

After taking many snapshots, the DBA will probably want to clean up (or even entirely delete) much of the old information. Statpack provides several ways to perform this maintenance; it is possible to remove certain snapshot information, or truncate the tables entirely.

Purging Some Data

Beginning with version 8.1.7, a purge script is provided. With this script, you simply specify the beginning and ending snapshots (inclusive) that you wish to remove. This script, called sppurge.sql, is located in the same place as the other scripts ($ORACLE_HOME/rdbms/admin).

While in the admin directory, simply start SQL*Plus as the PERFSTAT user, then run script sppurge.sql. In the following example, we command a purge of snapshots 1 through 2:

```
SQL> @ sppurge

Database Instance currently connected to
=========================================

                                      Instance
        DB Id DB Name     Inst Num Name
    ----------- --------- ---------- ----------
     335177272 DRAQE              1 draqe


Snapshots for this database instance
====================================

            Snap
  Snap Id Level     Snapshot Started Host              Comment
  -------- -----  --------------------- ----------------   --------
        1  5      04 Jun 2002 13:02:20 dra-qedb1
        2  5      04 Jun 2002 13:06:17 dra-qedb1

Warning
~~~~~~~
sppurge.sql deletes all snapshots ranging between the lower and
upper bound Snapshot Id's specified, for the database instance
you are connected to.

You may wish to export this data before continuing.


Specify the Lo Snap Id and Hi Snap Id range to purge
~~~~~~~~~~~~~~~~~~~~~~~~~~~~~~~~~~~~~~~~~~~~~~~~~~~~~~~
Enter value for losnapid: 1
Using 1 for lower bound.

Enter value for hisnapid: 2
Using 2 for upper bound.

Deleting snapshots 1 - 2.

Purge of specified Snapshot range complete. If you wish to
ROLLBACK the purge, it is still possible to do so. Exiting from
SQL*Plus will automatically commit the purge.
```

At this point, the data for the two snapshots has been deleted. As suggested by the note above, you could issue a rollback if necessary – as long as that step is performed before leaving SQL*Plus.

Removing all the Data

Besides a purge of a particular range of data, it is also easy to remove all the snapshots. Statspack provides a script, sptrunc.sql, which accomplishes this via the truncate command. Here is a sample run:

```
SQL> @ sptrunc

Warning
~~~~~~~
Running sptrunc.sql removes ALL data from Statspack tables. You
may wish to export the data before continuing.


About to Truncate Statspack Tables
~~~~~~~~~~~~~~~~~~~~~~~~~~~~~~~~~~~~
If you would like to continue, press <return>


Enter value for return:
Entered - starting truncate operation

Table truncated.

   ...

Table truncated.

2 rows deleted.

2 rows deleted.

Commit complete.

Truncate operation complete.
```

At this point, all snapshot data is removed. Of course, the truncate command cannot be rolled back; therefore, in most cases, the purge option is a preferred choice.

Suggestions for Using Statspack

To get the most from this tool, there are some standard practices to follow. To get the reader started, we provide some suggestions here.

Take Regular Snapshots

Without a baseline for comparison, the value of Statspack will be much reduced. For instance, the Statspack report provides good information on the database load. This could be very illuminating, but how will you know if these statistics are bad if you have no other report against which to compare them? Without a standard of comparison, only more questions arise: Are there more users on the system? Maybe, maybe not! Without a baseline, the analyst can only make educated guesses. Perhaps the load is actually going down, instead of up!

Good planning, and just a few preparations easily avoid these drawbacks. In particular, since it is easy to take snapshots, there is really no reason not to execute regular snapshots, or even better, to automate the entire process.

The `Statspack` installation includes a sample script to automate snapshot execution using the DBMS_JOBS facility; this file is named `statsauto.sql`. Observe a few precautions before running this script. First of all, be sure to connect as PERFSTAT. Secondly, remember that when DBMS_JOBS is used for automation, it is necessary to set the parameter Job_Queue_Processes to some value greater than 0; otherwise no jobs will ever be run!

Of course, it is not mandatory to use the DBMS_JOBS facility; the same thing can be accomplished at the operating system level. In fact, on UNIX platforms, many DBAs prefer to automate all jobs using the `cron` facility. With `cron` jobs, it is a bit easier to see the entire list of automated jobs for all databases on the same server.

For Windows platforms, instead of using cron, you use the Job Scheduler to run periodic jobs. The utility is typically activated on Windows servers by selecting: Start | Control Panel | Scheduled Tasks

Then, double-clicking on **Add Scheduled Task** initiates the Scheduled Task Wizard, which will guide you though the steps of scheduling a new job.

Whatever platform or scheduling utility is used, remember that the value of `Statspack` is greatly enhanced when multiple snapshots are available. Some sites take snapshots every hour, others only during peak usage times. The workload at each company will vary, so customize this process to ensure that several snapshots are recorded during the busiest time for your particular application:

> **Schedule automatic snapshots for Statspack.**

Use Drill Down

The `Statspack` reports provide a huge amount of information, and might seem overwhelming at first. The information provided is so voluminous that an entire book could be written on how to interpret the `Statspack` reports and make effective use of it for performance tuning.

Fortunately for the Oracle analyst, it is not usually necessary to read the entire `Statspack` report. Instead, it is easier to use a two-pronged, drill down approach:

❑ First peruse some of the summary information – especially the Top 5 Wait Events.

❑ Then, proceed to the section that has more detail related to this summary data.

Beginning with the wait events section makes sense, because these are the areas where Oracle is admitting that there are frequent delays. From there, we can proceed to the next section that gives further information on the particular wait in question. The value of the `Statspack` report is that most information is neatly bundled and close at hand.

For example, let's assume that one of the top five wait events was for I/O events. The event could be listed as either sequential reads (single-block reads) or scattered reads (multi-block reads). From this point, we would probably want to drill down to the section of the report showing file I/O activity. After looking at the file I/O, we would certainly want to consult the section showing the resource-intensive SQL statements and their associated I/O:

> **When reading Statspack reports, start with the summary information, then drill down to the details.**

Other Tips

❑ Remember to set `TIMED_STATISTICS = True` in the `init.ora` file. Many of the statistics will be worthless without that setup:

> **Unless there is a solid reason not to do so, leave `TIMED_STATISTICS = True`.**

❑ When running a report, be sure to select a beginning and ending snapshot identifier that does not span a database shutdown. If there has been a shutdown between the two snapshots, the report will abort with the following error:

ERROR: Snapshots chosen span an instance shutdown: RESULTS ARE INVALID

❑ Remember that the Top 5 Wait Events will not list events included due to CPU time.

Recall that the wait event facility has one large drawback – delays due to CPU time are not included! This means that the information shown in the `Statspack` wait events report section will also have this same limitation. Of course, CPU activity can be one of the most critical factors in performance tuning; thus, do not depend solely on the wait events information.

Improvements with Oracle 9i Statspack

The version of `Statspack` provided in Oracle 9i is very similar to the 8i version; most of the differences are related to refinement of how the statistics are displayed, or the inclusion of a few more fields of information. In other words, if you know how to run `Statspack` on Oracle 8.1.7, you already know how to run the 9i version.

Here is a summary of the changes made for Oracle 9i:

Report Changes

❑ Columns with cumulative times are now displayed in seconds.

❑ In the summary section, all cache sizes are now reported in M or K.

❑ Two new columns, CPU Time and Elapsed Time, are provided for resource-intensive SQL statements.

Statistic Changes

❑ There are new statistics on the summary page for open cursors.

❑ User-provided comments entered prior to taking a snapshot are displayed.

❑ Child and parent latch sections now include total time spent waiting for the latch.

❑ New statistics are included for a clustered database.

New Data Captured for Level 1

❑ V$RESOURCE_LIMIT information

❑ Automatic undo management values

❑ Buffer Cache advisory data

❑ Automatic memory management statistics

❑ Multiple-sized block buffer pools

❑ Resizable buffer pool and shared pool

❑ Statistics for instance recovery

New Reports

❑ sprepins.sql: This new report allows display of data for information that originated from another database. When running this report, Statspack will prompt for database identification, as well as the beginning and ending snapshots.

❑ sprepsql.sql: This new report provides the complete SQL text and execution plan for a single hash_value.

Miscellaneous Changes

❑ Details on the SGA now show a percentage difference between the beginning and ending values.

❑ New Snapshot Level 6 captures SQL Plan usage information for resource hogs SQL.

❑ Statistics for the Dictionary Cache Stats and Library Cache Activity sections are only printed for values > 0.

❑ The install script will no longer accept the SYSTEM tablespace for either the DEFAULT or TEMPORARY tablespace for the PERFSTAT user.

❑ Executing a snapshot can now be performed via a PL/SQL function, which returns the snapshot id of the new snapshot.

❑ A new script, spup817.sql, upgrades a 8.1.7 Statspack schema to Oracle 9i.

Behind the Scenes: What Does Snapshot Actually *Do*?

You can obtain a trace file for a session that is performing a snapshot by activating SQL*Trace on the session, and then formatting the trace file using TKPROF. Looking through the SQL, you may recognize some of the object names from which data is extracted. For instance, the V$SESSTAT view is queried to obtain many of the statistics presented in the Statspack report.

You'll notice from this trace output that the Statspack utility really does nothing more than query the same views that are already available to any analyst. The same queries could be performed using standard SQL queries or PL/SQL procedures; the advantage is, Statspack has packaged these steps into an easy-to-use utility.

Summary

We began this chapter with a discussion of the various steps that the Oracle Pathologist can use to help diagnose a case of slow database. These included methods like reviewing parameters for extreme settings and keeping an eye open for distributed queries.

There are also many excellent OS-level utilities that the analyst should try. On UNIX, the most widely available tools include sar, iostat, vmstat, top, and uptime. These commands are available on most UNIX platforms, and allow the analyst to detect server-wide problems – including those problems not specifically attributable to the database. The SAR command is especially useful for reviewing historic load information.

Besides the UNIX tools, we also reviewed some popular tools for Windows systems. In particular, we saw that the Performance Monitor is one of the most versatile (and popular) utilities for helping to isolate bottlenecks on Windows platforms. This tool is especially helpful in logging system performance for later playback.

Finally, we explored one of the most recent tools available for analyzing database information, the Statspack utility. Based on the older bstat/estat routines, Statspack provides a bewildering set of statistics on exactly how the database is working – probably more information then you will even want to know!

- Painting a Solution

- Oracle Bugs

- New Tuning Options

- The "Impossible" Problem

The Oracle Artist

At this point in the Physician-to-Magician tuning process, we have should have isolated the root cause already. Our esteemed predecessor, the Oracle Pathologist, has struggled with all the evidence, and has finally pinned the blame on the guilty party or parties. Nevertheless, the job is not quite yet: even when the root cause has been identified, the show is not over. We have established what caused the problem, but now we have to *do* something about it. In other words, now we have to fix it!

To recap, this is where we are in the Physician-to-Magician approach:

Physician	Detective	Pathologist	Artist	Magician
Define problem	Investigate	Isolate cause	Create solution	Implement

When fixing the problem, the Oracle Artist needs to synthesize a solution that is acceptable to the client. Not only must the specialist produce a solution that is *technically* correct, he or she must also take care to provide a solution that really fits the customer's environment. An elegant solution that cannot be implemented is of no value to anyone. Remember, also, that the Oracle Detective has established some sort of performance baseline, so that a clear before and after summary can be cited accurately when the solution has been implemented.

In this chapter and the next, we provide guidelines, insights, and tips on how to devise a solution to eradicate the root cause that has been identified.

We first discuss a general approach to devising solutions for the *routine* issues; these are the common issues that crop up almost daily. In these cases, the solution is usually obvious because it flows right from the root cause.

The next category we address is not so simple. What if no solution to the problem is apparent? What if the solution is not a simple correction, such as adding a new index? What should the performance analyst do then?

Although there isn't any set formula that can magically generate creativity, there are certain time-tested performance solutions that can be used as a guide. To help "prime the pump" of creativity, we provide a set of real solutions that have worked in other cases. These include such ideas as using special indexes to eliminate table access entirely, using set processing instead of row-by-row processing, and using parallelism, amongst others.

In the *Oracle Bugs* section that follows, we tackle the tough issues that arise when the root cause of the problem is potentially a bug in the Oracle software itself. Among other topics, we discuss how to use Oracle's online support facility to identify and resolve the glitch. In addition, we discuss ways to gather more information that can help provide either a solution or a work-around.

For some tough problems, it may be appropriate to employ one of Oracle 9i's new or expanded features. Although these present a myriad of changes, we limit our discussion to three expanded features that offer promising new ways to deal with performance bottlenecks. We focus specifically on:

❑ Database Resource Manager with Consumer Resource Groups

❑ Materialized Views

❑ Query Rewrite

Finally, we turn to the toughest hurdle of all: how to begin to deal with those problems that just seem impossible to solve. These are the issues that go beyond mere index changes or bugs; these are the problems that tax the wits and patience of even the most experienced analysts. We offer an assortment of research tactics and tools that have proved useful in finding the root cause of perplexing problems.

It's time to get started! Our easel is set up, the paints are mixed, and our palette is in hand. Let's see what work of art we can devise as we enter our studio and begin...

Painting a Solution

The analysis we have performed so far will often hint at several possible solutions. In fact, in many cases, the solution will be totally obvious once the root cause has been identified. For example, it's not too tough to choose a course of action when our diagnosis reads, "missing index on `Employee` table, column `Email_Address`". Similarly, we will not be too stressed if the root cause presented is, "missing statistics on schema `Accounting`". Clearly, in each of these cases, the solution is pretty obvious and trivial.

Although many performance problems really are that simple to correct, we must also be prepared for the more challenging variety. For simplicity, let's divide the types of solutions into two categories: **routine** and **serious**.

Here are some typical routine solutions.; it is usually a simple task for the Oracle Artist to devise a remedy for these types of issues:

❑ Simple SQL modifications, such as changing join order.

❑ Small indexing changes, such as adding an index or two.

❑ Resetting an extreme `init.ora` value.

❑ Updating statistics on a table.

Of course, if all the solutions were that simple, the field would be far less interesting (and pay far less money). Clearly, there is a lot more to performance tuning than just adding an index or two.

At the other extreme are the more serious/complicated (and interesting) solutions. These are the types of problems that stretch our faculties, and cause us to spend many hours analyzing perplexing bottlenecks. In these cases, the analysis may reveal serious design flaws requiring complex changes, such as:

❑ Major application restructuring.

❑ Complex SQL restructuring.

❑ Working around Oracle bugs or other limitations.

❑ Hardware modifications.

Ideally, the Oracle Artist will "paint a solution" that is simple, elegant, and requires minimal modification to the application. Let's take a look at how this can be done for routine problems.

Common Solutions

Here the solution often is obvious, once the root cause is identified. In these cases, identifying the root cause is really 99% of the battle; what remains is only to formulate the correction and confirm the solution.

Fortunately for the performance analyst, the same techniques that were used to find the root cause can often be used to synthesize a solution:

> **The techniques used for analysis of a problem can also be used for synthesis of a solution.**

For instance, consider a SQL statement that includes a series of table joins. As we discussed earlier (Chapter 9), the join order is vitally important in these types of statements, so a sub-optimal join order must be corrected if it is causing performance problems. The same graphical technique we saw earlier can be used to suggest a better join order, and thus reduce the result set earlier in the join process. So, the analysis work serves a dual purpose—it helps find the *solution* as well as the *problem*.

Similarly, a SQL statement that results in many unnecessary full table scans will often need a new index. The initial analysis – perhaps involving SQL_TRACE or using the EXPLAIN PLAN command—can be re-used to assist with the solution. This will likely provide strong hints as to which column should be indexed.

In some cases, it might be helpful to list or chart the possible solutions to a performance issue. For example, the figure below is a "road map" of some common solutions to two of the frequent causes of performance degradation: full table scans and wrong join order. Of course, there are additional possible solutions, but these are the most common:

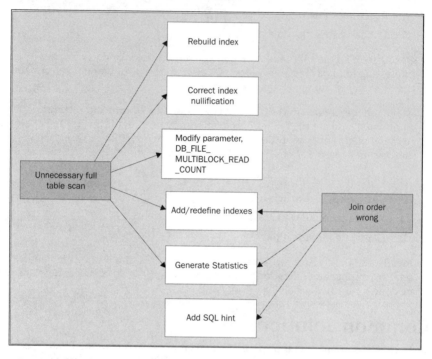

Some of the solutions shown overlap; for instance, gathering new (or more detailed) statistics for certain tables is a possible course of action for either problem. Similarly, errors with wrong or missing indexes also apply to either issue.

Of course, the previous analysis should have already included simple steps such as confirming that the statistics have been properly supplied. If not, it is simple enough to check. The view Dba_Tables can be queried to fetch the last analyzed date, along with the sample size that was used to gather statistics.

Let's now take a look at one of the most common solutions in some more detail.

Indexes

As we have already discussed, the vast majority of performance problems come down to the basic issues of database operation; in particular, index definition will play a huge role in many solutions. Despite all of the documentation available about indexes, dreadful mistakes with them are still very commonplace – even on production systems!

Do not assume that proper indexes exist – even on a production system!

Here is a checklist of issues to consider when your solution involves indexes:

- ❑ Do the leading columns of the index match the typical search criteria?
- ❑ Is the index being suppressed by a function in the query?
- ❑ Is it appropriate to use a bitmap index?
- ❑ Do indexes need rebuilding?

Let's explore each of these in turn.

Do the Leading Columns of the Index Match the Typical Search Criteria?

This relates to probably the most basic rule of all. Most developers and DBAs understand that the leading columns in an index should match the criteria listed in the SQL, but it is, nonetheless, very common to find that this isn't done. Oddly, some developers are especially reluctant to create composite indexes (indexes with more than one column), and will create a multitude of single-column indexes instead.

Our next case study illustrates what can happen when the designers have an offbeat idea about indexes.

Case Study: The More the Merrier

I was consulting for a small publishing firm in Northern California. After working there for several weeks, I noticed certain quirks about an important application where some functions seemed to run badly; I wanted to find out what was happening. No one had brought to my attention any serious issues, but I considered that perhaps the users were used to bad performance, and didn't even realize that they should be complaining.

Using the V$SQL view to find the commonly executed queries that performed a lot of I/O, I listed the actual text for these queries. Next, I obtained the execution plan using the EXPLAIN PLAN command. The queries were not really very complicated; in fact, many were simple joins involving just a few tables.

In the first few queries I examined, indexes seemed to be used properly; there was nothing obviously wrong that jumped out at me. When I checked the index definition, however, there was a big surprise. The query in question used an index that had *15* columns!

It turned out that many of the other suspicious SQL statements used the same "technique". Instead of creating a variety of indexes, with a variety of different leading columns, the designer had simply created a few, giant "one size fits all" indexes! Of course, these did *not* fit all the problems; in fact, because of this, some of the queries were not using any index at all. Further investigation revealed that there were about a dozen indexes with more than 8 columns in each. Some even had 16 columns!

It took weeks to correct this problem. The main difficulty was in determining exactly which of the leading columns were actually required, and then building the appropriate index with just those few columns. In most cases, just two or three columns were needed, but I had to work slowly—just in case! I used the V$SQL view to determine the actual SQL statements used on the system, and identify the columns that could benefit from indexing.

Is the Index Being Suppressed by a Function in the Query?

It is still common to see functions in queries that prevent index usage. It may be helpful to explain to developers that it is not helpful to put the function on the left-hand side.

Here is a typical example of a query that nullifies index usage:

```
SQL> SELECT COUNT (*) FROM Emp
  2   WHERE
  3   UPPER (Emp_Name) = 'BOB JONES' ;
```

Of course, the UPPER function on the left-hand side makes an index on the column Emp_Name useless; a full table scan of the Emp table will be required.

Fortunately, it is possible to create a function-based index as a work-around for this problem. In the example above, we would create an index on UPPER (Emp_Name).

Nevertheless, the first option in most cases should be to avoid applying a function to the column name in the WHERE clause whenever possible. The use of a function in the WHERE clause sometimes indicates that the SQL query is forced to clean up, standardize, or "fix" the data dynamically. Of course, this is really an admission that the data load process should already have performed this standardization:

> **Watch for queries that need to standardize data.**

Is it Appropriate to use a Bitmap Index?

For certain (somewhat rare) cases, it is advantageous for the database engine to *combine* several indexes in order to reduce the result set. This may be the case if there are many conditions specified for one table in the WHERE clause. For example, consider this SQL:

```
SQL> SELECT Student_Name, GPA
  2   FROM    Students
  3   WHERE   Student_Gender = 'Male'
  4   AND     Student_Year = 'Senior'
  5   AND     Student_Housing = 'On Campus';
```

Notice that no single condition for selecting the students is very restrictive. There are obviously many students who match any *one* of the search criteria used; thus, a full table scan is really the only alternative. On the other hand, if three separate bitmap indexes happened to be available (on Student_Gender, Student_Year, and Student_Housing), the situation would be different; the optimizer could easily combine the bitmaps to produce selection criteria far more restrictive than just one of the conditions alone.

Generally speaking, the optimizer will be loathe to perform this index-combining step with the regular B*tree indexes. This reluctance is reasonable, because it is usually not very efficient to search one index, get the results, search another index, then merge the results. With *bitmap* indexes, however, the optimizer is able to combine these indexes more rapidly. In fact, that is exactly what bitmap indexes are designed for!

Do Indexes Need Rebuilding?

It is good practice to perform regular index rebuilds on tables that have frequent updates or deletes; in Oracle, indexes for active tables can become filled with useless space, called *stagnant* space, if you don't. These areas in the index blocks cannot be reused by new index entries and new index blocks are added instead.

If nothing else, a rebuild makes the index much more compact, and will substantially reduce the disk space required by it. It is not unusual to have an index rebuild reduce space by 50%.

In addition, a simple rebuild will occasionally clear up the performance problem; this happens because the leaner index appears much more attractive to the optimizer. The optimizer realizes that it will get "more bang for its buck" because the database engine will need to read fewer blocks in order to retrieve the same data:

> **When the optimizer is reluctant to use an index, consider rebuilding the index.**

Index rebuilds can easily be scheduled using `cron` (on UNIX platforms) or `AT` (on Windows) to run every month or so, at off-peak hours. It is often a good idea to rebuild an index `unrecoverable` (same as `nologging`) with parallel processing; these two steps can often speed up the process several-fold. For example:

```
SQL> ALTER Index BIG_INDEX Rebuild
  2   Unrecoverable
  3   Parallel 4;
```

Not logging the index rebuild does not put us at a disadvantage usually, since an index does not have any data that can be "lost". In the case of a database failure or recovery, the index can easily be rebuilt if necessary.

Fortunately for the DBA, the stagnant space phenomenon does *not* apply to tables; with tables, the formerly used space in data blocks *can* be reused.

Let's now move on to discuss some solutions that might be appropriate in more difficult circumstances.

Solutions to More Complex Problems: Special Performance Tactics

In some cases, the performance problem will be a bit more challenging. The solution will not be so obvious as simply rebuilding an index, or adding an index with an additional column or two. In these cases, the conventional tactics either don't apply, or they don't help enough.

Let's take a look at some special tactics that have proved useful in solving tough performance issues. These ideas are not intended to be an exhaustive list of potential solutions; instead, they are really meant to "prime the pump" of creativity. The reader will certainly think of other possible solutions that are not listed.

Super Indexes

In practice, there is sometimes an even *better choice* for an index than the super efficient indexes we were discussing above. Besides looking at how well an index satisfies the WHERE clause, it's useful to see if an index can also satisfy the SELECT clause! This performance tactic requires that we build an index such that the table listed in the SQL is *never accessed*.

The key to this idea is that every single field in the SELECT clause must be fully satisfied via the index. Of course, the leading column(s) of the index must match the column(s) of the search criteria but, in addition, we add extra index columns that match the columns listed in the SELECT list.

The benefit we achieve by doing this might seem to be minor, but this trick has proved its worth time and time again. It is most beneficial when trying to extract the last little bit of performance improvement. For instance, this tactic may be useful for some table joins, when it is a close call between choosing a nested loop join or one of the other join methods. The super index can make the nested loop option achieve much better performance than otherwise. With the new super index, many table accesses can be eliminated, even though there might still be a large number of index accesses. This can sometimes make a huge difference in run-time:

> **Consider super indexes that make table reads unnecessary.**

The optimizer may detect the existence of a super index on its own; in some cases, however, it will be necessary to use the SQL hint INDEX to persuade it to do this. To use the hint INDEX, simply insert the table name (or alias, if applicable), plus the index name, like so:

```
SELECT /*+ INDEX(Table Indexname1 Indexname2. . .) */
```

Note that the second argument, Indexname, is optional. If more than one index is provided, the index with the lowest cost will be used. If no indexes are listed, the optimizer will once again choose the index that appears to provide the lowest cost.

In the next case study, the DBA was faced with trying to tune a SQL query – but without changing the application. The super index tactic was just what the doctor ordered:

Case Study: Super Index for a Super Problem

A utility company had a billing-inquiry application with a problematic query. The vendor was unwilling to correct the problem, so the DBA had to perform whatever tuning could be accomplished without any change to the application code.

The query in question was a join of several large tables. By a process of simplification (eliminating the irrelevant portions of the query), the DBA was able to isolate the essential issue.

The SQL for the "bad" part of the query looked like this:

```
SELECT  Last_name, First_Name, City
FROM    Customer
WHERE   Customer_status = '1'
AND     Billing_Code = '2';
```

It was not possible to structure an index that would be extremely selective, due to the distribution and size of data, so creating an index with both columns (`Customer_Status` and `Billing_Code`) was only partially successful. There were still substantial delays while the many rows from the table were accessed.

Further investigation showed that additional improvement was still feasible. In fact, it was possible to build a five-column super index (having three columns from the `SELECT` clause and two columns from the `WHERE` clause), such that table access was completely avoided. That is, all the fields needed to satisfy the SQL query could be contained in one index of five columns. Of course, there would still be an index lookup, but no subsequent table lookup.

The index was created, and the run -time was substantially reduced.

Although a five-column index is a little rare, in this case it reduced the query time significantly – from 10 minutes to 1 minute. Of course, that length of time still wasn't perfect, but the users were very happy with this improvement. The new index was very large, but all parties considered the trade-off of space for performance completely acceptable.

Index-Organized Tables

Since the release of Oracle 8, there has been a powerful option available for improving query performance; this feature is called the **index-organized table**. When this type of table is used, its structure really resembles an *index* more than a *table*. Whereas the rows are more-or-less randomly stored (in a heap) in a regular table, the entries in an index-oriented table are stored just like a B*tree index. Instead of being randomly placed, the entries are sorted by the primary key of the table. Although the internal table structure is entirely different, to the users, the index-organized table looks just like a normal table.

In an index-organized table, both the key columns and the non-key columns are stored in the index-like structure. This makes the access time via the key very rapid, since there is no separate database object to access. Just like the super index, all the information is in one place, which suggests that there will probably be space savings; instead of maintaining two separate database objects (table plus separate index), the database need only contain one object.

Although a very powerful option, using an index-oriented table requires a little more planning than just adding an index or two. Whereas indexes are usually very easy to add, or drop, redefining a table obviously has much larger ramifications should a mistake be made. In addition to the greater care that should be taken when using this option, there are also a few limitations, such as the data types that can be used. For a complete list of restrictions and other suggestions on using index-organized tables, see the *Oracle9i Database Performance Tuning Guide and Reference* at http://otn.oracle.com/.

Consider Using Set Operations

There are some forms of SQL queries that set off alarms when the DBA sees the code. In particular, most DBAs will become curious about SQL that contains the clause NOT IN; this attracts attention because it has proved to be especially troublesome in many programs.

Queries such as WHERE NOT IN and WHERE NOT EXISTS are not "wrong" or illogical; in fact, they are very logical and seem intuitive. Nevertheless, they are often the root cause of SQL problems. Let's take a deeper look and see why.

Typically, these clauses require the database engine to perform one table or index access for every row that needs to be checked for the NOT IN condition. So, if the preliminary result set contains 10,000 rows, Oracle will typically perform 10,000 additional steps in order to qualify the NOT IN condition:

Case Study: When MINUS Beats NOT IN

The following code was deployed for a data warehouse for an educational firm that wanted to track student progress. Its purpose is to DELETE rows from a table that is supposed to contain only the *last* module number for a course – that is, the last quiz. Therefore, it deletes all rows that are not really the last quiz:

```
DELETE FROM Last_Quiz_Course
WHERE (Course_id, Module_Number) NOT IN
(SELECT Course_Id, Max(Module_Number)
 FROM Last_Quiz_Course
 GROUP BY Course_Id);
```

We see that this original method first finds all rows, and then excludes each row that is NOT IN the list of maximum module numbers. Although this is functionally correct, it has an intrinsic performance flaw; for every row in the "first" query, it will have to check the table again to make sure it is NOT IN. So, if there are 10,000 rows in the table, the database engine will have to perform 10,000 lookups. Even if this can be accomplished via indexes, it is clearly not the best way to perform this processing.

The designer decided to rewrite the SQL to use a set operation; instead of finding which rows should not be included, she switched it around. In the next set of code, we find the entire set of all rows first, and then simply subtract the set of "bad" rows. The new method uses MINUS to produce an effect similar to set processing, instead of row-by-row processing:

```
DELETE FROM Last_Quiz_Course
WHERE (Course_id, Module_Number) IN
--
--Get all Rows
--
(SELECT Course_Id, Module_Number
 FROM Last_Quiz_Course
 MINUS
```

```
--
--Now DELETE the set of Max Rows
--
   (SELECT Course_Id, Max(Module_Number)
    FROM Last_Quiz_Course
    GROUP BY Course_Id));
```

Although the actual lines of code might look longer using this new method, the concept is simple: get the whole list with one table scan, then subtract the set of undesired rows. This change in the SQL resulted in a 90% reduction in logical reads and a commensurate performance speed-up.

As we have seen, in cases such as these it is useful to consider using set operators, such as MINUS, INTERSECT, or UNION. Although a full table scan will probably be required, eliminating the huge number of index lookups will offset this.

Here is a brief summary of these key set operations:

Operation	Action
MINUS	Returns distinct rows in the first query that are *not* in the second query.
INTERSECT	Returns the list of distinct rows returned by both queries.
UNION	Returns distinct rows returned by *either* one of the queries.
UNION ALL	Same as UNION, but also returns the duplicate rows.

The point of using these set operators is to try to process a big group at a time, rather than make the database engine execute a huge number of minor operations. Normally, the performance gain will be substantial:

> **Consider using set operations to avoid NOT IN clauses.**

Increase Sample Size for Statistics

Although using the default sample size when estimating statistics may be adequate for many tables, it may prove inadequate for very large tables. When dealing with tables having many millions of rows, using a small sample size can throw the optimizer off, and lead to costly performance delays. Remember also that tables should be re-analyzed if there has been a large (that is, more than 20%) increase in the number of rows, or a substantive change to the data distribution:

> **Be careful about using the default sample size when analyzing huge tables.**

Fortunately, the re-gathering of statistics, using a larger sample size, is very simple and fast. For example, the following command uses a sample size of 20,000 rows, which is probably adequate for most large tables:

327

```
SQL> ANALYZE TABLE Monster Estimate Statistics
  2   Sample 20000 Rows;
```

Another option is to specify the sample in percent, instead of the absolute number of rows. For example:

```
SQL> ANALYZE TABLE Monster Estimate Statistics
  2   Sample 2 Percent;
```

Of course, don't forget to automate statistics gathering; the AT facility on Windows or cron facility on UNIX is very suitable for this task:

Case Study: When an Estimate was not Good Enough

While consulting at an insurance company, I had occasion to upgrade a production database from Oracle 7 to Oracle 8. This particular application was critical to the firm and was used by many attorneys. I was allowed several hours over the weekend to make this change.

The upgrade completed without any problems whatsoever. To be sure that all the objects were still in place, I did a quick count of the number and types of objects in the main schema; everything looked fine. To wrap things up following the upgrade, I gathered statistics on the schema that owned all the application objects. I used the estimate statistics clause, and accepted the default sample size.

Unfortunately, when the lawyers and clerks began to try the system, they received an unpleasant surprise – response times for some important functions were terrible! In fact, as users wearied of the long delays, many tried to abort the application by pressing *CTL-C* on their workstation. This made matters much worse. Although their action successfully stopped the GUI on their PC, the SQL continued to run on the database unabated. This caused the load on the server to climb higher and higher.

Watching the server begin to crash, I had to abort many of these "duplicate" user sessions frantically. As I did this, I prayed that I picked the right ones.
It turned out that one of the key problems was due to my re-analyzing the schema with a small sample size. In this database, some of the tables were fairly large, up to a few million rows. For these tables, the default sample size (about 1000 rows) was insufficient. In the prior version of the database, a small sample size had been adequate, but not in the new version!

There had apparently been some changes in the optimizer design in the new database release. For my particular application set up, the optimizer began to make different (that is, *wrong*) decisions for some complex SQL statements. Unfortunately for the production DBA, database upgrades sometimes lead to unexpected (and *unwanted*) behavior—especially with the Oracle optimizer. This reminds us of the need for careful testing before executing a database upgrade on a production system.

Ultimately, re-analyzing a few tables with a larger sample size (25,000 rows) corrected most of the most serious problems.

Consider Special Join Techniques

For data warehouse applications, we have a few more options for join processing; in particular, consider the star join and star transformation methods. These methods (described in detail in Chapter 9) are applicable to joins where many small tables are joined to one huge table; they avoid processing a huge number of intermediate rows when the final result set is really quite small.

Hints in Views

Here is another tactic that is usually overlooked. Suppose we wish to use a SQL hint, but the application code cannot be changed; how can we somehow supply this hint without tampering with the code?

SQL hints are the subject of a large part of Chapter 12.

One easy way is to substitute a view for the table and then, in the view definition, supply a SQL hint. The database engine will see the hint, even though we have never changed the application!

Suppose, for example, that we have a table called Sales. We have previously concluded that for our particular application, queries to this table need to use a particular index called Sales_Index. (Perhaps the optimizer was selecting a different index, which was not ideal, or was conducting a full-table scan instead.) We will rename the table T_Sales and then create a view called Sales. In the new view, we supply the INDEX hint; the view definition will be:

```
SQL> SELECT /*+INDEX (Sales Sales_Index) */
  2  * FROM T_Sales;
```

Now, whenever the application queries Sales, it will really be accessing the view instead. The hint in the view will then guide the optimizer to use the right index.

Note that the INDEX hint usage includes the table name first, then the index name, with just a blank space in-between. Remember also that it might be necessary to add object privileges so the application user can properly access the new view.

Of course, one drawback with this whole idea is that the same SQL hint will be provided every time the special view is used. Hints that make no sense, such as giving the ORDERED hint when there is no join, will be ignored, but the possibility remains that a particular SQL hint may not be right in some cases.

Plan Stability

Recent database releases provide a way to maintain the current execution plan for a SQL statement, even when the optimizer might otherwise be prompted to change it. This feature is useful when you are happy with the performance of a critical application, and you don't want the execution plan to change—no matter what!

Oracle uses a construct called a **stored outline** in order to preserve an execution plan. When this feature is enabled (discussed below), the optimizer generates an execution plan based on the stored outline, which is really a set of SQL hints that instruct the optimizer to follow a particular execution plan. This plan will be followed even when the table statistics change, or even if the optimizer design is changed in a new database version. It is also important to know that there must be one stored outline for each different SQL statement; if there is any change whatsoever to the SQL, a new outline must be generated.

A word of caution is in order here. By using this feature you are really overriding the optimizer's decision; thus, even if the content of the database drastically changes, the optimizer will follow the execution plan provided by the outline— even if it is a terrible choice! This feature may not be a wise choice in cases where the data content or distribution is expected to change drastically.

Creating and Using Outlines

Outlines can be created for all future SQL statements by setting the init.ora parameter CREATE_STORED_OUTLINES = True; alternatively, you can create them one at a time, by using the SQL command CREATE OUTLINE.

To keep track of stored outlines, you can, optionally, group them into categories, which are specified at the time the CREATE OUTLINE command is run. Alternatively, if you choose to use the parameter CREATE_STORED_OUTLINES, you can list the category with that parameter, instead of specifying True. Each outline will then be assigned to the specified category until the parameter is changed.

For the optimizer to actually follow a stored outline, the init.ora parameter USE_STORED_OUTLINES must be set to True. If it is set to False, any stored outlines will be ignored.

There is an easy way to tell if a stored outline is being used for a given SQL statement that has been executed. In the view V$SQL, the column OUTLINE_CATEGORY will show the category of the stored outline being used (or DEFAULT, if no category was specified). If the value in OUTLINE_CATEGORY is NULL, then no stored outline is being used.

For further information on using plan stability, see the *Oracle 9i Database Performance Tuning Guide and Reference*.

Parallelism

In many cases, it will be necessary to perform full table scans of very large (> 1 million row) tables. This is common in data warehouses, where the nightly or weekly data load must scan through most of, if not all of, some large tables.

When faced with these large scans or sorts, a very effective solution is to have the database engine divide up the job, and start a separate process for each part.

The general rule of thumb is to use one to two "degrees" of parallelism for each CPU on the system. Of course, this is only a rough guideline; a few tests on your particular system can determine which value is best for your particular SQL statements. Remember, also, that the extra parallel processes will increase the load on your server; so this feature is best used only when there is spare CPU capacity:

> **Consider activating parallel processes when performing full table scans of huge tables.**

The parallelism degree is generally specified via the SQL hint PARALLEL. The syntax of the hint is simply:

```
SELECT /*+ PARALLEL (Table DEGREE) */
```

The DEGREE field is optional; if it is not specified, the parallelism degree will be the default for your particular database instance. This default is controlled by the init.ora parameter PARALLEL_THREADS_PER_CPU. On most servers, this parameter is set automatically to 2.

As an example of specifying parallel processing in an actual query, the following SQL text commands the optimizer to process the query using a parallelism degree of 5. Note that the hint for parallelism has specified the table alias and a degree of 5:

```
SQL> SELECT /*+ PARALLEL (BT 5) */
  2  Emp_Name, Emp_Id
  3  FROM Big_Table BT;
```

Let's now consider what the database engine is actually doing during the processing of such queries. While the query is running, we can find this information by querying the V$SQL and V$SESSION views to find the SQL that is being executed by each active session:

```
SQL> SELECT Sid, SQL_Text from V$SESSION, V$SQL
  2  WHERE USERNAME = 'CHRIS'
  3  AND status = 'ACTIVE'
  4  AND V$SESSION.SQL_Hash_Value = Hash_value
  5  ORDER BY SID;
```

Here is an example of the response, from processing a query with a parallelism degree of 2:

```
SID SQL_TEXT
--- ------------------------------------------------------------
 22 SELECT /*+ PIV_SSF */ SYS_OP_MSR(MAX(A1.C0)) FROM
    (SELECT /*+ NO_EXPAND ROWID(A2) */
    A2".PCT_LAST_QUIZ_SCORE"
    C0 FROM EPIMART".STUDENT_COURSE_0_B"
    PX_GRANULE(0,BLOCK_RANGE, DYNAMIC) A2) A1
 25 SELECT /*+ PIV_SSF */ SYS_OP_MSR(MAX(A1.C0)) FROM
    (SELECT /*+ NO_EXPAND ROWID(A2) */
    A2".PCT_LAST_QUIZ_SCORE"
    C0 FROM EPIMART".STUDENT_COURSE_0_B"
    PX_GRANULE(0, BLOCK_RANGE, DYNAMIC) A2) A1
 13 SELECT Sid, SQL_Text FROM V$Session, V$SQL Where
    USERNAME = 'CHRIS'
    AND status = 'ACTIVE' AND v$session.SQL_hash_value =
    hash_value ORDER BY SID
```

This shows that two parallel slaves have divided up the work, and are actively performing the scan of the specified table. These processes are in addition to the original session (known as the **query coordinator**), which is not shown here because it is not active at the moment; instead, it is waiting for the slaves to perform their work. (Note that the session with SID = 13 is not relevant to this discussion; it is actually the query that was used to obtain these results.)

The SQL actually retrieves results on a total of *3* processes, one of which is not shown, as we have noted. If we were to specify a degree of five, there would actually be *six* processes – one query coordinator and five slaves.

When the SQL query requires *sorting*, there will be twice as many slaves, as the work is divided up even further. The processes that read from disk are called **producer slaves**; they feed the information to the **consumer slaves**, which actually perform the sorting.

Besides using a SQL hint to initiate parallel queries, there is another way to achieve the same thing; the table itself can be set to a certain degree, just as we set the degree with the SQL hint above. This is a good potential method when the application code cannot easily be changed, or cannot be modified to use hints. Some data warehouse applications, for instance, are known to filter out comments that have been placed in the SQL; with these applications, it is impossible to implement hints in the usual fashion.

> Note that parallelism specified via a hint will override any value set in the table itself.

Here are some init.ora parameters that you should keep in mind when using parallel queries:

❑ PARALLEL_MAX_SERVERS: Default = Derived from the values of CPU_COUNT, PARALLEL_AUTOMATIC_TUNING, and PARALLEL_ADAPTIVE_MULTI_USER. This parameter controls the maximum number of slaves that will be used. Setting this to 0 turns off parallel query.

❑ PARALLEL_MIN_SERVERS: Default = 0. The number of slaves started at instance startup; these will remain active.

❑ PARALLEL_MIN_PERCENT: Default = 0. A throttle on parallelism. Sets a threshold of CPU resources that must be available before parallel processing is activated. For example, a value of 80 means that 80% of CPU resources must be available for parallelism to activate. Setting a value of 0 means that parallelism will not be used.

❑ PARALLEL_THREADS_PER_CPU: Default = 2. This sets the default degree of parallelism for the instance, as we have already mentioned.

A new parameter that can be considered is PARALLEL_AUTOMATIC_TUNING. (Default: False). When set to True, the database itself will decide what default values to use for parallel processing. As with all the new automatic tuning features, this option should be used with great care, and thoroughly tested before release into production. Of course, this same caution is really applicable to making *any* change to a production system—test thoroughly first!

Oracle Bugs

The Oracle Artist will discover that in some cases, the evidence begins to suggest that there is a bug in the Oracle software. These bug cases present some of the most challenging problems; they are often very hard to detect and solve because they seriously disrupt the analytic process. In fact, the "normal" methods of troubleshooting may not work at all.

The usual process of analysis and troubleshooting assumes that each system is "telling the truth". When a bug is present, however, the rules are thrown out of the window. It is as though the database, usually a most reliable system, is lying to us; we don't know what to believe!

To illustrate the difficulty implicit in an Oracle bug, consider what happens when people try to use information from untrustworthy sources. A certain party game is sometimes played in which each person is secretly assigned the name of a famous character; the goal being to guess your own character. Each person is allowed to ask the others in the group 10 "yes/no" questions in an effort to try to discover their character. This game becomes very difficult when it is played with the "lie" option. With this option, the other players are allowed to lie once; the questioner knows that all the answers will be true except one, but he doesn't know *which* answer is false.

It is the same thing when dealing with Oracle bugs. The database does something strange, but we don't know where, or when, or how; the job of the Oracle Artist becomes much more difficult.

Bugs, Bugs Everywhere?

Note that some DBAs are very quick to "discover" rare bug in the RDBMS internals. Sometimes they are right; but, more often, the real problem lies elsewhere. Experience shows that the odds of finding a new bug in a seasoned database version are relatively low compared to the odds that the application is the problem:

> **Don't be too eager to blame database versions that have stood the test of time.**

Of course, this is not to say that any database release is perfect; on the contrary, there are certainly minor bugs in every version – and the bugs may be substantial when a new database version is released. If you are working with a fairly new release, or trying something unusual, it stands to reason that the odds of finding a bug will be much higher. This next hint is the flip-side of the prior one:

> **Be cautious, even suspicious, when using new Oracle releases.**

DBAs often joke that they don't want to be the first one to implement a new Oracle version; the reason for this is that the odds are much higher that there will be a major "show stopper" in a brand new release. Instead, it is much easier (and safer for your career) to let one of your colleagues find the bugs first!

This doesn't mean that the new Oracle versions always run poorly, or should never be used; rather, it just means that DBAs, designers, and developers need to be wary. Recall the great fanfare that accompanied the first release of Oracle 8i (version 8.1.5)? It soon became clear that Oracle 8.1.5 contained flaws; in fact, the Oracle site soon suggested that DBAs should not use 8.1.5, but upgrade to Release 2 (8.1.6).

Of course, one hopes that more recent Oracle releases will not repeat the same mistakes; nevertheless, new software products, no matter where they are from, will inevitably have bugs. The number of combinations of all features for all situations is simply too large to check; it is almost certain that some bugs will be overlooked, no matter how diligently the QA group looks.

The DBA should keep these points in mind when working on performance issues. If the application is using a brand new feature, it is *just possible* that the feature is not quite working in the way it has been advertised. Even if the new feature is working correctly, the documentation may not be complete. Once in a while, the precise manner of operation of brand new features is not documented as carefully as we would like.

There are some methods of finding out about bugs though, and these are what we will go on to look at next.

Finding the Big Bugs: Alerts

Severe Oracle problems and bugs are sometimes documented with **Oracle Alerts**. These are listed on Oracle's Metalink web site (http://metalink.oracle.com/), under Documentation. If you have never used Metalink, you will first have to register, and provide your CSI (Customer Support Identifier) number - see the next section to find out if you have one.

> Note that most of the Alerts are actually warnings that Oracle will soon be "desupporting" certain product versions.

The problems listed in Alerts are so severe that Oracle Corporation feels compelled to warn the user community. For example, the Alerts section shows the following information in the section on Oracle 9i release 1:

RDBMS release 9.0.1 fix - JDBC Thin Driver (ORA-600 when pre-9i talking to 9i)
ALERT: Transportable Tablespaces can Corrupt Target Database
IMPORTANT: Set "_SYSTEM_TRIG_ENABLED=FALSE" When Upgrading / Downgrading
ALERT: "CONNECT INTERNAL" Syntax to be DeSupported
DESUPPORTED: SVRMGRL Desupported in Oracle 9i

Note, especially, the consequences of using the Transportable tablespace option; under certain conditions, database corruption can result! Pity the poor DBA who first discovered this bug! He will very probably remember our adage, "be cautious, even suspicious, when using new Oracle releases".

It is possible to supply your email address to the Metalink site, so that you can be notified of new alerts automatically. It is highly recommended that you do so!

The Sticky World of "TARs"

In most cases where a bug is suspected, it is good procedure to start a **TAR** (**Technical Assistance Request**) with Oracle Corporation. Gaining access to Oracle support requires that you have a support agreement with Oracle, called "metal" support (traditionally bronze, silver, or gold) - you will only have a Customer Support Identifier if you have one of these agreements.

It is easy to create a TAR online at the Oracle Metalink support site; once that's done, it is also easy to check its status or make additions. The TARs for your company can be sorted by several options, such as by date or by TAR Status (open or closed.)

Here are some suggestions on making the TAR process as painless as possible:

❑ Know the exact Oracle RDBMS version that you are using. If you are in doubt, you can see this version revealed when you start a new SQL*Plus session.

❑ Know the exact operating system level; for example, Sun Solaris 2.8.

❑ Have the Oracle ORA- error number, if any, handy.

❑ Have your script and trace files close by; they will be uploaded to Oracle support.

When opening a TAR, you will be asked several questions; these are designed to "triage" your problem. Oracle Corporation wants to understand accurately how critical your problem is, and whether your *production* system is down (development databases don't count in the same way).

The support organization will prioritize your request based on your answers to these questions:

❑ Can you easily recover from, bypass, or work around the problem?

❑ Does your system or application continue normally after the problem occurs?

❑ Are the standard features of the system or application still available; is the loss of service minor?

Other questions require you to supply details on your particular environment, such as:

❑ Platform and O/S version, including patchset or service pack level?

❑ What version and patchset level of the database are you running?

❑ Are you running the most recent patch set?

For minor problems, your answers will typically cause your TAR to be given a low priority, such as level 4. This level means that you do *not* have a serious production problem; your problem is more routine—certainly not a production system show stopper.

A level 1 problem, on the other hand, means that your production system is down, and that you need immediate help. (Of course, in this case, a phone call would be used, not the Metalink site.) With a level 1 issue, Oracle customer support will take immediate action on your problem, so be ready to supply all necessary information. You must be prepared to respond to their questions in the same way that you expect them to respond to yours; if you do not supply this information promptly, your priority will be reduced. This policy is actually very fair; why should they treat your problem as top priority if you don't treat it the same way?

The Metalink site also allows an easy upload of your trace files, SQL scripts, and so forth. This is done at the end of TAR creation process. After you have supplied the various details on your difficulty, the TAR program will remind you to upload them; it provides instructions and a link to accomplish this. If you fail to upload the necessary files, it is very likely that the Oracle support analyst will ask you to do it later, leading to further delays.

Other Ways to Smash Bugs

Most Oracle bugs will not be uncovered by a simple check of the Alerts section on Metalink; many of them are far more elusive. Let's take a look at some suggestions for confirming and dealing with a suspected Oracle bug.

Reduce the Problem to the Bare Essentials

When dealing with a suspected flaw in the database or application, try to strip away all the irrelevant information. That is, focus on listing the minimum set of information – SQL statements, special parameters, procedures, and so on, that are required to trigger the problem. In performing this step, you will often uncover some important clues about the source of the problem.

Determine How the Problem can be Duplicated

Without a clear definition of how to duplicate the problem, it will not be easy for anyone, including you, to confirm that a bug really exists. Oracle support will be especially reluctant to spend much time on such a "fuzzy" issue that promises to waste a great deal of time. In fact, as we've already heard, they will probably insist that you provide numerous kinds of trace files, queries, and so on, before they agree to spend valuable resources on your problem. Your request will be reset to "Waiting for Customer Action" in the meantime.

It is also important to capture the SQL statements leading up to the problem. This is easily accomplished using SQL_TRACE, or simply copying and pasting the SQL into a text file. Be as precise as possible; if you cannot clearly state how to duplicate the problem, how can you expect anyone else to try to solve it?

Search Metalink for Similar Issues

If you have uncovered a genuine bug, it is unlikely that you are the first victim; there are probably several other users who have encountered similar issues on the same database version and operating system. Even if other users have not encountered exactly the same problem, there are usually many similar cases— perhaps on slightly different OS versions.

A simple Metalink search will often uncover many relevant discussion threads in the various Oracle Forums. You can find these discussions by using the Metalink Search facility; the search option is shown on just about every page on the site. Then, once you have spotted and reviewed these discussions, you can post further questions, or even email these other users.

In the same way, you should co-operate with other DBAs who ask how *you* handled a problem.

New Tuning Options

Beginning with Oracle 8i and Oracle 9i, there are expanded tuning options for the Oracle Artist. Three expanded features are worth special consideration, because they offer significant new capability: **Database Resource Manager**, **Materialized Views**, and **Query Rewrite**.

> *The Materialized Views feature is actually an extension of the Snapshot facility that has been available for a long time; however, the functionality of this facility has been greatly expanded in Oracle 9i.*

These three expanded features stand out because they appear to offer substantial new possibilities for the performance specialist. Although not overly complicated, none of them is trivial to set up and use.

Although each of the three appears to work "as advertised", exercise caution when implementing in a production environment; as always, test!

> **Thoroughly test new database functionality; do not assume it works precisely as advertised.**

Let's take a look at each of the new facilities in turn.

Database Resource Manager

Prior to Oracle 8i, there was no easy way to assign system resources to a group of users. For instance, there was no way that the DBA could grant CPU time based on the user's business need, or assign a prioritization to users that reflected the importance of their tasks.

Of course, the profile feature has long been available, but assigning a profile to users is a crude approach that offers little flexibility. A profile allows the DBA to set some overall restrictions, such as maximum session time, CPU time, and so on, but this option is pretty limited—there's not much "intelligence" to it. In contrast, the Database Resource Manager offers much greater flexibility, plus many more options not available with a simple profile.

The term Database Resource Manager is rather confusing, because it suggests that there is some single application or tool that the DBA starts; it is actually a set of procedures and run-time controls provided by the Oracle engine. This entire set of controls is really the "Manager" that gives the DBA a good way to distribute system resources to various users.

The concept is very simple. The Database Resource Manager is a system to distribute scarce system resources efficiently; for example distributing CPU cycles, undo space, and session connections to competing groups of database users. At first, this capability might sound just like the old profile feature, but consider these possible uses of the Database Resource Manager that were not possible with profiles:

❑ Limit the degree of parallelism for a certain group of users

❑ Limit the maximum number of sessions for a group

❑ Set prioritization of long-running SQL operations

❑ Limit maximum rollback ("undo") space

Clearly, then, the Database Resource Manager has substantially more versatility than a simple profile.

Using the Database Resource Manager

Both the command line (via SQL*Plus) and the OEM utility DBA Studio may be used to build resource consumer groups and resource plans.

> Note that the OEM tools have been renamed and repackaged over the years. In Oracle 8i, the features are bundled as DBA Studio; in Oracle 9i, this functionality is now part of the DBA Console.

The command line method makes use of various calls to the package DBMS_RESOURCE_MANAGER. In Oracle 9i, this package has 18 procedures that are used to set up resource plans and consumer groups. Using the command line is certainly feasible, but finding the correct syntax will try the patience of most DBAs; simply to change the CPU allocation requires up to 20 lines! This is a compelling argument for using DBA Studio instead, where the same operation takes a *single keystroke*. Most DBAs will find the GUI tool to be good for performing the various tasks involved in setting up the Database Resource Manager.

Prior to actually setting up a resource plan (see later in this section for a detailed discussion these), the DBA should first assign proper privileges. The database user that will be administering the Database Resource Manager must be granted administrative privileges via the Grant_System_Privilege stored procedure. For example, if user CHRIS were the resource administrator, the following command would allow that account to manage the resource manager (but not allow it to grant it to others):

```
SQL> EXEC Dbms_Resource_Manager.Grant_System_Privilege -
  2  (GRANTEE_NAME => 'CHRIS', -
  3  PRIVILEGE_NAME => 'ADMINISTER_RESOURCE_MANAGER', -
  4  ADMIN_OPTION => FALSE);
```

To revoke administration privileges, the Revoke_System_Privilege procedure is called. Note that the usual method of assigning privileges using grants will not work; the above PL/SQL procedures must be used.

After permissions are assigned, the DBA should group the users into broad categories, or *levels,* and decide how resources should be prioritized. A tree can be drawn as an example. When creating a resource plan, it is easiest to use DBA Studio's Resource Plan Wizard to help you; the wizard will prepare the numerous calls to the Dbms_Resource_Manager.

Resource Consumer Groups

To properly allocate resources among users, the Database Resource Manager uses a feature called **resource consumer groups**. Each consumer group is set up by the DBA to identify users with similar usage patterns or priority. For instance, all the critical OLTP users could be assigned to a group called CRITICAL, while the remaining users could be assigned to a group called LOW_PRIORITY. There can be a large number of these groups, but practically speaking, a handful will probably prove adequate.

The advantage of assigning users to consumer groups is that it becomes possible to guarantee important users a minimum level of resources. For instance, in our example above, the users in the CRITICAL group could be guaranteed 90% of CPU resources.

Besides this, we can also ensure that lower priority groups are restricted in their consumption of resources to a maximum level. For instance, we could restrict the users in LOW_PRIORITY to just 10% of CPU time. Of course, caution should be exercised when establishing these priorities; unreasonably low (or high) settings could easily result in an angry group of users!

While the DBA can create new consumer groups, there are some "pre-built" groups:

❑ Default_Consumer_Group: users that have not been explicitly assigned to a consumer group are automatically assigned to this one.

❑ Other_Groups: contains users who are part of a group that is not defined in the current resource plan.

❑ Sys_Group: assigned to Sys and System users.

❑ Low_Group: provided by Oracle, but has no users pre-assigned.

Resource Plans

It is not enough to build just the resource consumer groups; in addition, the DBA must decide how to allocate resources among them. This feature is called a **resource plan**. As its name suggests, the resource plan is the administrator's instructions on how resources will be distributed.

In a resource plan, the DBA assigns the various consumer groups to different levels. The concept of level is very simple:

❑ Level 1 gets first priority

❑ Level 2 only gets CPU resources if there is a surplus at level 1

❑ Level 3, in turn, only gets resources if there is a surplus at level 2

❑ This continues up to eight levels.

When planning resource allocation, it is helpful to draw a tree to visualize it. For example, the following figure illustrates a resource plan called Plan One. In this plan, as in *all* plans, the CPU time is first allocated to Level 1:

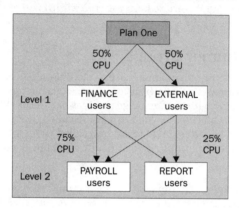

We see that Level 1 has two important consumer groups, FINANCE and EXTERNAL, that need to have first call on CPU cycles. At this level, the CPU time is evenly divided between them. If these two groups do not consume all CPU cycles, then 75% of the spare CPU time goes to PAYROLL group, and 25% goes to the REPORT consumer group, because they are at Level 2.

Several resource plans can be created, but only one is active at any time. The active plan is identified with an init.ora parameter:

```
RESOURCE_MANAGER_PLAN = [Resource Plan]
```

It is also possible to change the current resource plan dynamically:

```
SQL> ALTER SYSTEM SET Resource_Manager_Plan = PLAN_A;
System Altered.
```

Although only one resource plan can be active at a time, there are advantages to defining several at once. Different resource plans can be activated at different times using the resource plan schedule; for example, one resource plan could be scheduled for the day, and another, giving higher priority to batch jobs, could be scheduled for night-time.

Switching Consumer Groups

As a DBA monitors a database, some adjustments to consumer groups may be necessary; for instance, it might become necessary to switch an active session to another consumer group. This might be required if a particular user is consuming excessive resources, or interfering with critical database transactions. Conversely, a critical user may need to be switched and given a *higher* priority on resources.

To switch a user to another consumer group, first find the session identifier (SID) and SERIAL#. These are easily fetched from the V$SESSION view (see Chapter 6 for more information on doing this). Then, call the procedure Switch_Consumer_Group_For_Sess, supplying the SID, Serial Number, and new consumer group.

> *The field Serial# might at first seem redundant, since the SID value already identifies a user session. There is an internal complication, however, that is resolved via this field; Oracle uses Serial# to distinguish between objects for sessions that have just ended and newly started sessions that happen to be assigned the same SIDs.*

For example, suppose the user with SID = 100 and SERIAL# = 5000 needs to be switched to a consumer group called NEW_GROUP; the DBA simply executes the following:

```
SQL> EXEC -
  2  Dbms_Resource_Manager.Switch_Consumer_Group_For_Sess -
  3  ('100', '5000', 'NEW_GROUP');
```

Besides switching just a single session, it is also possible to switch all sessions using the same username. For instance, suppose the database has been made available to a set of outside users. They each log in using the username ACCT1 and, after monitoring database activity, the DBA decides to switch all these users to the consumer group GROUP_Z. The protocol is very similar to switching a single user; however, instead of calling the procedure Switch_Consumer_Group_For_Sess, we call Switch_Consumer_Group_For_User instead:

```
SQL> EXEC -
  2  Dbms_Resource_Manager.Switch_Consumer_Group_For_User -
  3  ('ACCT1', 'GROUP_Z');
```

Automatic Switching of a Consumer Group

One of the most powerful features of the Database Resource Manager is **automatic consumer group switching**. Besides manual switching (described above), it is possible to enable dynamic switching to another resource consumer group, based on the user's activity.

For instance, if a certain group of users is getting starved of CPU time, and never finishing their queries, the resource manager can automatically shift them to another, higher priority group. Alternatively, users can also be switched to a *lower* priority group if their queries consume system resources beyond a certain limit. Once again, great care should be exercised in deciding exactly how you want this to work; this is a very powerful feature, and must be wisely used.

To activate automatic switching, the procedure Update_Plan_Directive is used to change the resource plan. This has three special parameters that must be specified:

❑ Switch_Group: to which group should the user be switched?

❑ Switch_Time: how many seconds of processing before switching?

❑ Switch_Estimate: use the database estimate of run-time?

Note the significance of the last parameter, Switch_Estimate. If set to True, the Oracle engine will first calculate an estimate of total run-time for the SQL statement that is about to be executed. If the projected run-time exceeds the Switch_Time, Oracle will automatically switch that user to the specified group *before* the statement is even executed!

Let's consider an example of how this could work:

Example: Setting up a Resource Group to Switch Automatically

Suppose our Oracle 9i database is currently using a resource plan called PLAN_A. Now we want to update this plan, so that users in the consumer group Outside_Users will be switched automatically to the group called Limit_CPU if the projected run-time exceeds 5 minutes. Therefore, we will use the following special parameters:

```
New_Switch_Group = LIMIT_CPU
New_Switch_Time = 300
New_Switch_Estimate = True
```

We now call the procedure Update_Plan_Directive, using these parameters:

```
SQL> EXEC Dbms_Resource_Manager.Update_Plan_Directive -
  2  (PLAN => 'PLAN_A', -
  3  GROUP_OR_SUBPLAN => 'OUTSIDE_USERS', -
  4  NEW_SWITCH_GROUP => 'LIMIT_CPU', -
  5  NEW_SWITCH_TIME => 300, -
  6  NEW_SWITCH_ESTIMATE => TRUE);
```

Note that the automatic switching feature cannot be activated using the GUI; instead, the package Dbms_Resource_Manager must be called manually.

Performance Tuning with the Database Resource Manager

Now that the basics of the resource manager have been covered, let's look at some performance tuning examples. The first of these is from a large American power company, and illustrates how to prioritize competing demands for parallel processes. Here we can see how a DBA can use the Database Resource Manager to reconcile competing demands for CPU time from different user groups:

Example: Batch Jobs During the Day

Traditionally, long-running batch jobs have been restricted to night runs. This is usually necessary because it is too risky to allow a batch job to degrade important OLTP queries that service important customers. This also means, however, that spare resources available during slack time during the day (perhaps at lunchtime) will be wasted. With the Database Resource Manager, however, batch jobs can be scheduled to run, on a *non-interference basis,* during the day as well. We can also enable plan switching, so that after hours, the batch users are given a much higher priority.

In this example, we assume there are two resource consumer groups – one for the batch users who perform long-running batch jobs, and another for OLTP users who run critical, short queries. (In this company, the two groups are entirely separate; of course, this will not always be the case.) After providing appropriate permissions using the Grant_System_Privilege procedure, we use DBA Studio (in Oracle 8i; use Console in Oracle 9i) to perform the following:

1. Create two resource groups: BATCH and OLTP.

2. Assign the users to their respective resource groups.

3. Create a resource plan called DAY, in which the OLTP users are given all the CPU time (that they can use), and the BATCH group is given the "leftover".

4. Prepare another resource plan called NIGHT. In this plan, the BATCH group is guaranteed 75% of CPU time, with the remainder going to the OLTP group.

5. Specify that the resource plan should switch from DAY to NIGHT at 6 PM. This will ensure that the BATCH group receives the necessary resources (just in case their OLTP colleagues try to get sneaky, and begin working late hours).

6. Finally, set the init.ora parameter RESOURCE_MANAGER_PLAN = DAY to indicate that the DAY plan should be active by default.

Let's consider another example of how we can use the Resource Manager to control the systems resources; here we have some "runaway" queries that need to be reined-in. In this example, instead of assuming use of the GUI tool, we illustrate how to use the package Dbms_Resource_Manager:

Example: Controlling "Runaway" Queries

As with our previous example, let's assume that we have an OLTP group working during the day; in addition, however, there are certain reports that are expected to run during the day too. Normally, this is not a problem, because these reports only take 10 minutes to run. However, due to an application flaw, certain reports can take up to 1 hour! We have confirmed with management that these long-running reports can be deferred to off-hours.

We will first assign the report users to a consumer group called REPORTS. We will also setup a new consumer group called BAD_REPORT, which will receive the runaway SQL queries. At startup, no users will actually be in the BAD_REPORT group; rather, it will contain the users running those "one-hour reports" as they are detected.

Our resource plan, shown in the following figure, will split the CPU cycles at level 1 between the regular OLTP users and the REPORT users. Any users in BAD_REPORT will be allocated only the surplus CPU cycles from level 1. In this way, the bad reports will not degrade system performance for the other users.

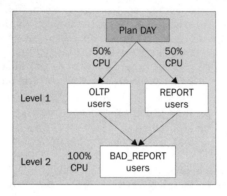

We will enable consumer group switching to handle these runaway reports; since the good reports finish in 10 minutes, we will set the switch threshold at 15 minutes (900 seconds). Also, we will specify that the Oracle optimizer should estimate the run-time (and switch, if necessary) *before* the SQL is ever executed. In this way, we move the problem reports to the lower priority group as soon as they are detected.

Using these figures, we define the special parameters for switching:

```
New_Switch_Group = BAD_REPORT
NEW_Switch_Time = 900
NEW_Switch_Estimate = True
```

Assuming the resource plan is called DAY, we now update it using the procedure Update_Plan_Directive:

```
SQL> EXEC Dbms_Resource_Manager.Update_Plan_Directive -
  2  (PLAN => 'DAY', -
  3  GROUP_OR_SUBPLAN => 'REPORTS', -
  4  NEW_SWITCH_GROUP => 'BAD_REPORT', -
  5  NEW_SWITCH_TIME => 900, -
  6  NEW_SWITCH_ESTIMATE => TRUE);
```

Now, whenever a long-running report is sent for execution, it will be automatically switched to the BAD_REPORT group; in that group, it will not take away any CPU time from the more critical users.

Let's move on to the next example:

In a large financial services company, several critical users are running reports for end-of-quarter accounting. They all connect to the database with the usernames beginning with ACCTG. As part of a previous setup, these users are part of the resource consumer group REPORTS, which is only guaranteed 30% of CPU time.

The DBA receives a frantic call from the accounting manager, complaining that these critical reports are not finishing in time. He decides to switch all these users manually into the resource consumer group CRITICAL, which is guaranteed at least 70% of CPU time.

Since all users with a certain username will be switched, there is no need to find SID and SERIAL#. Instead, the procedure Switch_Consumer_Group_For_User will be invoked to transfer all the ACCTG users into the other resource consumer group:

```
SQL> EXEC -
  2 Dbms_Resource_Manager.Switch_Consumer_Group_For_User -
  3 ('ACCTG', 'CRITICAL');
```

At this point, all the ACCTG users will participate in the 70% allocation that is specified for the CRITICAL resource consumer group. Of course, it would be possible to create additional resource consumer groups with different CPU cycle allocations. Remember to use great care in changing CPU allocations, however; as always, thoroughly test your setup before implementing in production.

Other Tuning Suggestions

Although allocation of CPU time is probably the most important use of the Database Resource Manager, there are other system resources that can be restricted. For example, the maximum number of sessions for a group of users can be limited via an **active session pool**. This pool sets a maximum threshold, beyond which users are not connected, but are placed in a queue instead, awaiting their turn to connect when someone else logs out. Optionally, waiting sessions may be aborted after a designated time.

This feature uses two special parameters:

- ❏ NEW_ACTIVE_SESS_POOL_P1: the maximum number of active sessions for a specified consumer group.

- ❏ NEW_QUEUEING_P1: the time, in seconds, to remain in queue before aborting.

The resources allocated to rollback space can also be restricted, using an **undo pool**. This sets a limit on the total size of undo generated by all members of a resource consumer group. On reaching this threshold, all attempts by members of this group to use more undo space are prevented until spare space becomes available. The parameter for this feature is:

NEW_UNDO_POOL: the maximum size, in KB, of undo for a specific consumer group.

A session may be restricted to a maximum estimated run-time using the parameter NEW_MAX_EST_EXEC_TIME, which is the maximum run-time in seconds for a user in a specific consumer group.

Similarly, the degree of parallelism may be restricted using the parameter NEW_PARALLEL_DEGREE_LIMIT_P1, which is the maximum parallelism for a specific consumer group.

Let's consider another example using these non-CPU restrictions:

Example: Setting Non-CPU Restrictions

Suppose you decide to limit a group of users in the EXTERNAL resource consumer group to only 50 sessions, and allow each session to wait 5 minutes before termination.

There is no need to create a new resource plan from scratch; instead, a simple update to the DAY resource plan is made, placing restrictions on the EXTERNAL resource consumer group:

```
SQL> EXEC Dbms_Resource_Manager.Update_Plan_Directive -
  2  (PLAN => 'DAY', -
  3  GROUP_OR_SUBPLAN => 'EXTERNAL', -
  4  NEW_ACTIVE_SESS_POOL_P1 => 50, -
  5  NEW_QUEUEING_P1 => 300);
```

At this point, the EXTERNAL resource consumer group will be appropriately restricted.

Let's now turn to a real-life example of how these features can be used. In our next case, the Database Resource Manager was used at a large power company to control the degree of parallelism:

Case Study: Limits on Parallel Queries

At one of the largest electric utilities in the United States, there are several huge (2 Terabyte) databases that are used to generate reports on revenue, electricity consumption, meter readings, and so on. The whole system is very similar to a large data warehouse, except that there is no star schema. In the reporting database, there are hundreds of tables; many of these tables have millions of rows.

Naturally, run-time of the reports is a big concern. To speed up the reports, the database designers rely extensively on the parallel query option, in which several processes are automatically activated each time a report is requested. This is a suitable method of operation for this system, due to the many CPUs available; there are 16 available CPUs, and more CPU boards can be dynamically activated when needed! This setup makes it likely that there will be spare CPU cycles that can be used to service parallel processes.

The production DBA found it helpful to divide the users into several consumer groups. Members of each group have an upper limit on the degree of parallelism that can be activated for their queries (set using

NEW_PARALLEL_DEGREE_LIMIT_P1). Here is the breakdown:

Consumer Resource Group	Degree of Parallelism
System_Activity	Unlimited
Administration	20
Infrastructure	8
Reporting_Priority	4
Reporting_Normal	4

With this arrangement, the critical (but few) administrative jobs can effectively capture more CPU cycles when necessary; the report users, on the other hand, cannot overwhelm the server, since they are limited to a parallel degree of just 4. The production DBA reports that this arrangement has worked well, and has avoided any server meltdowns.

Checking on Resources

To confirm proper resource allocation, it is possible to see the cumulative CPU time that has been consumed for each consumer group. This is easily accomplished by querying view V$RSRC_CONSUMER_GROUP:

```
SQL> SELECT Name, CONSUMED_CPU_TIME CPU
  2  FROM V$RSRC_CONSUMER_GROUP;

NAME                      CPU
--------------------     -----
BATCH                    15000
OLTP                      5000
OTHER_GROUPS             12000
```

A list of all resource plans defined in the database can be seen in the view DBA_RSRC_PLANS. Note that column COMMENTS displays the notation that is given by the DBA when the plan is first created; for example:

```
SQL> SELECT PLAN, COMMENTS
  2  FROM DBA_RSRC_PLANS;

PLAN            COMMENTS
-------------   ------------------------------------
DAY             Regular resource allocation
NIGHT           Special plan for nighttime batch reports
PLAN_A          Test plan
```

The view V$SESSION shows the allocation of resource consumer groups to particular sessions; this can be useful in confirming that all users have been assigned to the correct group. For example, the query below shows that one of the accounting users has apparently been assigned to the wrong resource consumer group:

```
SQL> SELECT SID, USERNAME, RESOURCE_CONSUMER_GROUP
  2  FROM V$SESSION;

   SID USERNAME      RESOURCE_CONSUMER_GROUP
------ -----------   ---------------------------
    25 ACCTG_101     BATCH
    26 ACCTG_102     BATCH
    32 ACCTG_103     BATCH
    49 ACCTG_104     OLTP
```

Let's now turn to another option that the performance specialist can use, **materialized views** with **query rewrite**. The query rewrite feature is an exceptionally powerful feature of Oracle 8i and Oracle 9i. It is also one of the more unusual features, because the Oracle optimizer actually *changes* the original SQL query to speed up processing. To understand this feature, we need to discuss briefly the concept of materialized views first.

Materialized Views

Materialized views are objects equivalent to what were formerly called **snapshots**. Many of the concepts and procedures used with snapshots are equally applicable to materialized views; in fact, in some database platforms and versions, several Oracle messages and warnings may still use the term snapshot.

> *After creating a materialized view, some versions of the database will respond Snapshot created. Also, in Oracle 8i, the package Dbms_Mview is really nothing more than a synonym for the old package DBMS_Snapshot!*

As its name suggests, a materialized view really contains the rows that are defined by the SQL provided during its definition. This means that storage space is consumed, similar to the space consumed by a table or index. When a materialized view is created, a tablespace name and storage parameters are specified in the same manner as for a table.

A materialized view is, thus, very different from a "normal" (non-materialized) view; which is actually only an equation residing in the data dictionary. A normal view consumes no storage space because the rows are dynamically fetched when the view is queried (a view is like a "window" into the underlying tables). In contrast, a materialized view consumes space because the rows are *materialized*.

> *For more information see the Oracle documentation online at http://otn.oracle.com/.*

Why use Materialized Views?

Although a materialized view can be used in conjunction with any application, the feature is most useful in data warehouse applications. To understand why this is so, we will briefly describe some features of a large data warehouse and explore some typical performance problems.

In a large data warehouse application, the volume of data often makes it unwise repeatedly to perform complex SQL queries that must process millions of rows (and typically based on a certain time restriction). For instance, a common report for a large corporation might tabulate the yearly sales, sorted by region, for all product lines; this type of report might take 30 minutes to run *each time it is requested.*

These long wait times are often considered unacceptable when associated with reports. As a way to reduce them, the database architect has traditionally built tables that hold *aggregate*, or pre-joined data. These pre-built tables are typically called summary tables. With these new summary tables, the reports can run much faster. Instead of performing the time-consuming joins and fetches, the report will simply query the summary tables instead.

> Note that this traditional method--the summary table--is not a *special Oracle object; rather, it is just a regular database table that is populated according to some custom-built script. The manner of refreshing the summary table is thus left completely to the programmer — there is nothing automatic about it. So, while the traditional summary table method is an acceptable option, it does have some disadvantages.*

Materialized views, in contrast to summary tables, provide some unique advantages, especially for the refreshing of data. With summary tables, the table must be truncated or rebuilt every time the database is updated; alternatively, a complex script must be designed to keep track of changes. Materialized views, on the other hand, have several refresh options that simplify and expedite the repopulation of the summary data. In addition, they allow the use of query rewrite, an important performance improvement measure that we discuss next.

Query Rewrite

Using query rewrite, the optimizer considers querying from the materialized view instead of the tables listed in the query, even though the view is not even mentioned in the query. In other words, the optimizer *changes the SQL* so that it can process the search more quickly.

To use query rewrite, you must first create a materialized view beforehand. This view is constructed so that it stores information that will fulfill the resource-intensive queries. Then, when the SQL is executed, the Oracle optimizer automatically rewrites the query to select from the materialized view instead; which means that a query that might have run for many minutes can be completed in seconds.

For example, suppose a company has an Oracle database that stores all retail transactions in a large table called Sales. In this company, there are many long-running reports that are delayed because of repeated queries against this table. This scenario, thus, seems to be a good candidate for query rewrite.

When using query rewrite, there is one critical database initialization parameter: QUERY_REWRITE_ENABLED. Be sure to set this parameter to True. There is also one important thing to note when creating the materialized view – it must be created using the option ENABLE QUERY REWRITE:

Example: Creating a Materialized View for Query Rewrite

Returning to our Sales example, we decide to use a materialized view with query rewrite enabled. We will create it, and include the clause, ENABLE QUERY REWRITE:

```
SQL> CREATE Materialized View Emp_Sales_Summary
   2  Tablespace Finance
   3  Storage (Initial 1m next 5m pctincrease 0)
   4  Build Immediate
   5  Refresh Complete
   6  ENABLE QUERY REWRITE
   7  AS
   8  SELECT Employee_Name,
   9  SUM (Sales_Amt) Sales_Total
  10  FROM Sales
  11  GROUP BY Employee_Name;
```

In the code above, the clause Build Immediate means that we want to populate the materialized view right away. The phrase Refresh Complete means that each time we update the view, we want to repopulate the entire view from scratch, rather than only keeping track of the changes.

In this example, notice that we have not accepted the default tablespace and storage, but have explicitly defined these parameters – just like a regular table. Of course, it is not *required* that we specify these parameters; the default values may be used.

One special condition for query rewrite should be mentioned; all the underlying tables must be analyzed. In our example above, this means that we should analyze the Sales table. In cases where there are many tables in the FROM clause, all of the tables should be analyzed. For completeness, be sure to analyze the materialized view itself, just so the optimizer has all the necessary information.

Which Queries are Eligible for Query Rewrite?

Obviously, not every SQL statement executed will use query rewrite. As shown below, there are some restrictions on the type of SQL that is compatible with it:

❑ The query cannot reference CONNECT BY clauses.

❑ Only local tables may be used in the query.

❑ Objects in the query cannot be owned by Sys.

❏ The query cannot refer to Raw or Long Raw datatypes.

❏ The SQL used in the materialized view cannot refer to non-repeatable expressions, such as ROWNUM or SYSDATE.

❏ The SQL used in the materialized view cannot use set operations, such as MINUS or UNION.

Fortunately, these restrictions do not affect most SQL queries. For instance, it is very unlikely that queries will SELECT from objects owned by Sys. (Sys is the owner of the internal data dictionary; user objects should never be placed in this area.)

Besides these restrictions, the main qualification for query rewrite is that a materialized view exists that definitely contains all the data needed to perform the query in question. This could occur, for instance, if the SQL under consideration closely resembles the SQL in the materialized view definition.

Tips on Using Materialized Views and Query Rewrite

Here are some other suggestions that will help you get started with materialized views and query rewrite:

❏ Don't forget to create indexes on large materialized views. These indexes are created in exactly the same way as for tables.

❏ For very large materialized views, consider partitioning; this is done in the same way as for tables.

❏ When initially trying the query rewrite feature, consider testing using a query with the *identical* SQL used to define the materialized view. This ensures that query rewrite will not be rejected because of some difference in the SQL code.

❏ Consider using the initialization parameter QUERY_REWRITE_INTEGRITY. If this is set to STALE_TOLERATED, query rewrite is allowed without consideration of the "freshness" of the data in the materialized view. Alternatively, setting the parameter to ENFORCED (the default) prevents query rewrite if the materialized view has stale (that is, out of date) data.

Although materialized views and query rewrite are most often used in large data warehouse applications, these features can really be used in any application. Materialized views are a good alternative to summary tables, where regular refreshing of the data is required. Query rewrite is a good choice where long-running SQL statements can make use of data pre-stored in a materialized view.

Let's now turn to discuss some other ideas for solving really tough problems. What can we do when faced with a problem that simply looks "impossible"?

The "Impossible" Problem

Sooner or later, we all encounter a problem that stumps us. It might be a case where we have successfully isolated the root cause, but just can't figure out what to *do* about it, or it might be that we can't even figure out what is going on. The whole thing looks "muddy".

Not to fear – we have not exhausted our toolkit. We still have a large assortment of hints and suggestions to try. Let's take a look at some ideas for solving those really baffling puzzles.

Network with Other Oracle Professionals

On more than one occasion, I have mentioned a (supposedly) difficult problem to a colleague, only to have the problem solved instantly; instead of hearing sympathy about how difficult my problem is, I get a *solution*! The point is that often, what looks terribly difficult to one person appears *trivial* to another.

Given the huge variety of database issues, it is not reasonable to hope that any one DBA can possibly know it all. Each Oracle analyst possesses a special set of expertise, along with a background different from anyone else. For instance, some DBAs enjoy researching the more unusual database features, such as advanced replication, while others prefer to concentrate on performance tuning of SQL problems. Each could very well be a true expert in that particular field, but may be relatively weak in another.

This wide variety of experience means that a skillful analyst, by nurturing a growing list of contacts, can theoretically "consult" with many experts on almost any conceivable database issue. It really doesn't make any difference who actually knows the answer, or who gets credit for it; the important thing is to locate efficiently the information needed to solve your customer's performance problem.

Besides your immediate place of business, these contacts can be made through the local Oracle user groups. which frequently feature speakers of national reputation and expertise. These groups should not be ignored!

> All serious performance analysts should participate in their local Oracle user group.

Another possibility for Oracle networking is the various Internet forums, such as the one on the IOUG-A web site (International Oracle Users Group, Americas – http://www.ioug.org/). Other discussion forums can be found at the web sites of the larger software and hardware vendors; these often include white papers, lessons learned, and other research articles of interest. You will probably also find it useful to participate in discussion forums provided by Oracle as well. (Later in this chapter, we provide some good web sites that have popular discussion forums.)

By cultivating a list of contacts, you will soon find that you have generated a mini network of valuable consultants with whom you can share information. Besides the benefit of technical exchanges, there is another big plus; this sort of networking arrangement is a smart career move, and could easily lead to your next challenging assignment. Also, don't be surprised if one of your network consultants has an immediate solution to your next really tough problem.

System Administrator Consultation

This suggestion is similar to the previous tip; every DBA should view the Systems Administrator as their "best friend". A good Systems Administrator can make the analyst's job much easier, and can help uncover server-specific performance problems.

Do not neglect to take advantage of the special skills of whatever Systems Administrator is available. They can offer guidance on setting up disks, checking memory, CPU statistics, and so on. Often the Sys Admin knows of special utilities that can help confirm "hot spots" on the system, or help you with checking network speed, and so on:

> **Practice teamwork with your Systems Administrator.**

It might be hard for some DBAs to admit but, *generally speaking*, the Systems Administrator is more qualified in detecting and solving problems like network throughput, disk I/O, and CPU load. Like DBAs, most Systems Administrators love a challenge – especially if it is some problem on *their* system!

When two qualified professionals – a good DBA and a good Systems Administrator – team-up together, excellent system performance is the rule, not the exception.

Metalink

As we heard in relation to Alerts, the Metalink resource has become extremely valuable in the last few years; in fact, almost all analysts use Metalink at one time or another. In recent years, Oracle Corporation has added many new features to this facility, and has greatly improved its value. This makes it imperative that every Oracle analyst be very experienced at using it to investigate the solutions to performance problems. Metalink also has the official Oracle documentation for all Oracle products:

> **Become an expert at finding information using Metalink.**

Oracle Forums

Metalink also makes it possible to participate in Oracle forums where any user can search for discussion threads on just about any type of database issue; they can also start a brand new discussion. Oracle Corporation provides analysts who watch these forums, and provide answers if no one else chimes in.

> *A similar forum is also available on Oracle's* OTN *web site,*
> *http://technet.oracle.com. (OTN stands for Oracle Technology*
> *Network.)*

It is also possible to email Oracle forum participants directly; simply move the cursor over the person's name, and their email address will be revealed. When first contacting other users in this way, remember that some time has probably gone by since they encountered the difficulty documented. I have found it helpful to remind them of the details of the problem, and then ask them for their perspective. How did *they* deal with the problem? Was a bug confirmed? Did Oracle supply a patch?

Note that the forums are really a place for informal questions and answers. If you have an urgent production problem, the forums are *not* the right place to log the issue; instead, log a TAR – either online or via phone.

White Papers

There is a huge number of free research articles available on the Internet; some written by novices, but a great many by experienced experts. Many of these papers represent the state-of-the-art in Oracle database knowledge; in fact, they are sometimes far more valuable than the official Oracle documentation!

Often, papers published by the IOUG-A are especially valuable. These papers are not marketing papers, but in-depth analysis by some of the top experts in the field. Many will make you re-think some of your assumptions; others will reinforce your understanding.

> As with Metalink, there is a cost associated: you must join the IOUG-A group to have access to most information. The fee is about $75 per year, and is an excellent investment in your career. With your membership you also receive the technical journal, Select.

Useful Web Sites

Here is a list of some of my own favorite web sites. All of them offer free information, such as white papers, presentations, tips, scripts, and so forth. Many also provide discussion forums monitored by the best DBAs in the field; a great deal of the information found on these sites is truly state-of-the-art.

http://www.dbspecialists.com/. This site is sponsored by Roger Schrag, who is one of the "master" instructors for the IOUG. It includes a large number of technical papers, tips, and presentations by noted experts. Many of these are on advanced performance tuning topics, as well as on more general DBA issues, such as proper installation techniques.

http://www.ixora.com.au/. This site is sponsored by Steve Adams, and includes many valuable articles and tips on advanced performance tuning. It is especially good for those really meaty Oracle internals questions that nobody can answer. If you have a tough Oracle internals question, submit it here! Steve also publishes a free newsletter, emailed to subscribers.

http://www.dba-oracle.com/. This site is sponsored by Don Burleson, who has written more Oracle books than anyone. Don provides an impressive assortment of Oracle tips and articles. The articles available for viewing span all the way back to 1994!

http://www.hotsos.com/. This site is sponsored by Cary Millsap, whose writings have greatly influenced the art of performance tuning. It provides many outstanding research articles of interest to performance tuning experts. He also includes short reviews of his top book recommendations.

http://www.nocoug.org/: This is the official web site for the Northern California Oracle Users Group - NOCOUG). It lists meeting dates and other information for Oracle users in Northern California. You can also download recent presentations.

http://www.jlcomp.demon.co.uk/. This site is sponsored by Jonathan Lewis, a well-known performance tuning expert and regular speaker at many Oracle conferences. It includes a nice topical index, making it easier to find information on various subjects: for instance, the *Internals* section alone comprises 19 articles.

You can also visit the author's web site at: http://www.oraclemagician.com/. On it, you can download technical papers on subjects such as data warehousing, performance tuning, high-availability, and so on. Plus, don't forget to check out the latest issue of the online magazine, *The Oracle Magician*, at the same site.

Finally, be sure to check out the web site of your own local Oracle users group. Many of these groups offer outstanding content, with valuable information for the Oracle practitioners in the local area. You can find out about the next user group meeting, or download useful tips and technical articles. Although most of these organizations are staffed by volunteers, many of the web sites are of professional quality.

Summary

In this chapter, we introduced ways for the Oracle Artist to devise solutions to various types of performance problems. For routine issues, such as indexing problems, the solution is usually derived directly from our prior analysis into the root cause; that is, the previous investigation conducted to determine a root cause often suggests the solution as well. We saw that the solution to these routine cases is often trivial, and usually involves simple actions, such as creating a new index, generating statistics, or making a minor change to the SQL code.

For the more complicated cases in which no solution to the problem is readily apparent, we reviewed various solutions that have been proved to work in past cases. One of the most important tactics is parallel processing; which is often a good idea where full table scans are the best choice.

In the following chapter, we continue our discussion of ways for the Oracle Artist to devise solutions, and we provide further ideas on synthesizing solutions that are acceptable to your customer.

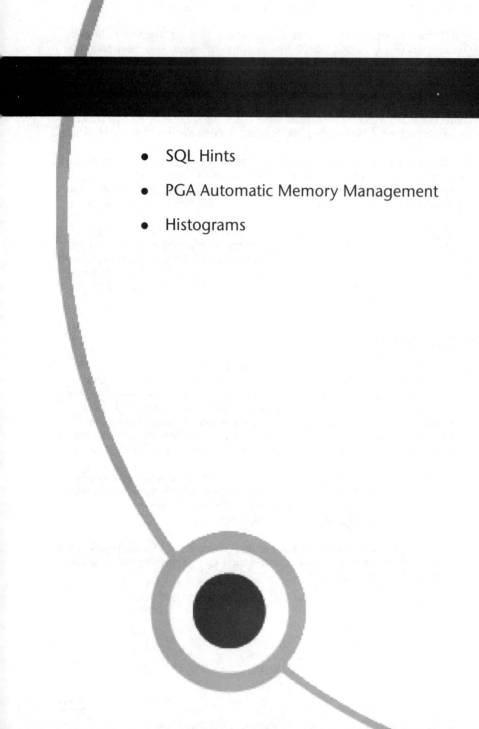

- SQL Hints

- PGA Automatic Memory Management

- Histograms

12

The Artist's Palette: More on Devising Solutions

In this chapter, we continue our discussion of ways to synthesize a solution. Recall that we are at the following position in our five-phase approach to tuning:

Physician	Detective	Pathologist	Artist	Magician
Define problem	Investigate	Isolate cause	Create solution	Implement

We provide here a detailed overview of three facilities that will probably prove useful for the Oracle Artist. Two of these areas involve techniques and features that are time-tested, and one facility is brand new for Oracle 9i.

First of all, we discuss the important facility of SQL hints. SQL hints are often misunderstood and frequently misused; nevertheless, they are an important resource for any serious Oracle analyst. The Oracle performance expert who is not comfortable using SQL hints will be severely handicapped; he or she will miss many opportunities to correct severe performance problems easily and create happy clients. This means it is imperative that the serious performance analyst fully understands what SQL hints are available, and how to use them effectively.

In our discussion on SQL hints, we explain how to persuade the optimizer to do things our way. We discuss how to modify the optimizer operation in many different ways, such as when to use a table scan, what indexes to use, or ways to change the method of performing joins. For each of these hints we provide the exact syntax that should be used.

After discussing SQL hints, we move to our second topic – a technique that is brand new in Oracle 9i. This new feature is called PGA automatic memory management (discussed briefly in Chapter 10). This feature provides a very clever way to better allocate the use of server memory to various work areas.

To fully understand the use of the new PGA feature, we provide detailed examples that illustrate how to activate automatic PGA memory management, how to retrieve the PGA statistics, and how to revise the PGA target value, if necessary.

Finally, in the last part of this chapter, we look at histograms. This feature is not brand new, but many DBAs are unaware of how best to use this technique. The histogram offers the performance expert a special option that can often dramatically improve performance in certain situations. In particular, histograms offer a powerful way to deal with non-uniform data. In this section, we provide several examples that identify situations where histograms should be considered, and how to go about creating a histogram.

SQL Hints

SQL hints are one of the greatest resources that the Oracle Artist has available; at the same time, they are also one of the most misunderstood of all Oracle features. Once the performance analyst understands how to employ them, SQL hints provide the opportunity to drastically enhance the way in which the Oracle engine processes queries. A correct hint, sometimes just a word or two, can often improve the runtime of a SQL statement dramatically. (Conversely, a wrong hint can likewise drastically worsen performance!)

For example, perhaps the optimizer believes that a full table scan is best. With one SQL hint (the INDEX hint), it is easy to convince the optimizer to use an index instead. The optimizer will not normally balk at such a switch, as long as the requested optimizer action is really possible; of course, suggesting the opposite (switch from index use to full table scan) is as easily accomplished.

Hints about index scan versus table scan, or an alternate way to join tables, will generally be accepted without difficulty. Nevertheless, there is a limit to the understanding of the optimizer. Hints that appear to make no sense will be ignored – with no warning to the analyst!

When to Use a SQL Hint

Remember that using a SQL hint is really the same thing as saying, "I know better than the optimizer". A hint is in effect asking the optimizer to disregard its own calculations, and listen to the DBA or developer. This means that the performance analyst is actually assuming responsibility for the future performance of that particular SQL statement.

A SQL hint means that the optimizer will continue to rely on your guidance – even when the size or composition of the tables changes drastically. Potentially, this means that if the wrong hint is used, future performance can be worse than expected. As a result, be a little cautious before writing a SQL hint into the application; while a SQL hint is not really the last resort, it should not be the first either:

> **Your first tuning option should *not* be a SQL hint.**

The optimizer in recent Oracle releases is accurate most of the time; this means that a SQL hint should not be the first course of action. If you find that almost every SQL statement is running poorly, it is very unlikely that SQL hints are the best treatment. Instead, it is more likely that something very serious has been overlooked; perhaps statistics have not been generated, or critical indexes are missing.

Remember that a hint embedded in the application will prevent the optimizer from adjusting the execution plan when the data size or the distribution changes. This can have a disastrous result if not carefully planned.

Suppose, for instance, during preliminary testing with a small database, that a designer inserts a SQL hint since it seems to make everything work so well (at least for that moment). Later, when the application is in use at a large customer's site, this hint may no longer be appropriate, because the table sizes are much larger. Nevertheless, the optimizer dutifully follows the hint, leading to more work for the database engine, and very likely an irritated customer.

This suggests an important point:

> **An incorrect SQL hint is worse than no hint at all.**

In other words, the Oracle Artist should remember that SQL hints have the power to do a whole lot of good, but also a whole lot of harm. As with any program modification, thoroughly check the operation of the modified SQL code before implementing it in production.

How to Use Hints

Although hints are mostly used after a `SELECT` statement, they can be provided after `INSERT`, `UPDATE`, and `DELETE` operations too. A hint is included with the comment syntax; that is, you embed the SQL hint in the code as though it were just a comment. (And if the syntax for the hint is incorrect, that is all it will be – just a comment!)

There are two different ways to provide comments, and consequently two different ways to specify a SQL hint. One way is to use the special pair of symbols, `/*` to begin the hint, and `*/` to end the hint. Here is the syntax for a hint that is used with a `SELECT` statement:

```
SELECT /*+ HINT1 HINT2 HINTN */
Emp_Name FROM Emp;
```

Note the addition sign that begins the hint; note also that several hints can follow one another in the same SQL statement. Multiple hints are most commonly used for join operations where both the join order and join method need changing.

359

Alternatively, the same hint can be specified using two dashes, like this:

```
SELECT --+ HINT1 HINT2 .. HINTN
Emp_Name FROM Emp;
```

The syntax is critical when providing a hint; for instance, if commas or some other symbol are incorrectly added, the hint will be ignored, even though the main SQL portion will still be executed.

Although the syntax is critical, Oracle is more forgiving with the case; it is not important to use a certain case when entering SQL hints.

Optimizer Mode Hints

There are dozens of SQL hints but, in practice, only a handful is used very frequently. Also, as the optimizer changes with each new release, it is possible that some of the more dated hints will become obsolete. In particular, the hints that change the optimizer mode are used less frequently in recent Oracle versions.

In older database releases, it was common to use a few particular hints whose sole purpose was to cause a switch from rule-based optimization to cost-based optimization. Of course, these hints should be very rare now, as more databases are purely cost-based.

In the older rule-based technique, the optimizer followed set guidelines when deciding how to execute a SQL statement. One very simple example of an optimizer rule would be, "When accessing a table, use an index if it exists." The more sophisticated cost-based techniques, however, take into account the resource consumption, or,cost, of performing each step. Simply put, the cost-based optimizer is much smarter than the rule-based version.

Let's discuss each of the main hints related to changing the optimizer mode.

FIRST_ROWS

Specified like so:

```
/*+ FIRST_ROWS */
```

With this hint, the optimizer endeavors to return the first row in the result set as fast as possible. This hint could be useful in a Forms application in which it is desirable to return a few rows quickly; by doing this, the user doesn't see a blank screen while waiting for the entire result set. Of course, this means that the overall time may actually be longer. For instance, the optimizer may change the order or method of joins to extract the very first row almost immediately, even though the process to get all the rows may actually be more lengthy.

This hint will often be ignored if the SQL contains group processing or ordering functions; the reason for this is that these functions require a complete result set before they can perform. This limitation includes the clauses GROUP BY and ORDER BY.

*This hint is only provided by Oracle for backward-compatibility;
consequently, it should not be used in new applications. Instead, a hint
for a particular join method can be specified (discussed later in this
chapter).*

ALL_ROWS

This is really the opposite of the previous hint and is specified like this:

```
/*+ ALL_ROWS */
```

It instructs the optimizer to choose the execution plan that has the lowest total cost –
that is, the cost for the complete result set. This may mean that the first row returned
may take longer that normal.

CHOOSE

Here the optimizer is given the option of using either rule- or cost-based optimization,
depending on whether statistics have been gathered:

```
/*+ CHOOSE */
```

As a general rule, if at least one table referenced in the SQL has statistics, the cost-
based optimization method is used; otherwise, rule-based optimization is used.

RULE

When this hint is supplied, rule-based optimization is used:

```
/*+ RULE*/
```

*This hint should not be used in new applications, as rule-based
optimization is scheduled for de-support after Oracle 9i.*

While the Oracle Artist needs to be aware of the various optimizer-mode hints, in
practice they are really becoming less and less relevant. Almost all new applications
are written with the cost-based optimizer in mind; this means that the hints
mentioned in this section will become even less common.

So, we will now turn to an entirely new group of SQL hints. We will consider those
that specify how the database engine should access various database objects. These
hints are methods that the Oracle Artist can use to improve the speed of retrieving
information from critical database tables and indexes.

Table and Index Hints

Another group of hints instructs the optimizer to fetch data in a particular way, such
as by using an index or, alternatively, by not using an index. Oracle provides various
hints that allow the developer to control these data access methods.

361

Note that there is one aspect of using hints for tables that bears repeating; if an alias is used for a table, then it is mandatory that the alias, not the real table name, be used in the hint. If the alias is not used, the hint will be ignored!

> **Remember always to use the table alias (if any) in a SQL hint.**

Let's take a look at the most commonly used hints for tables and indexes.

INDEX

This hint is specified like this:

```
/*+ INDEX (Table Index1 Index2 IndexN) */
```

This hint requests that the optimizer use an index scan for accessing the table referenced. Optionally, one or more index names can be provided. If more than one index is provided, the optimizer will select the index that achieves the lowest estimated access cost. If no index is listed, the optimizer will evaluate each index for that table and use the one with the lowest estimated cost. Note that the syntax for this hint, as for SQL hints in general, requires that the individual objects be separated by a space, not by a comma.

INDEX_FFS

This requests that the optimizer conduct a fast full scan of the table, using the listed index(es):

```
/*+ INDEX_FFS (Table Index1 Index2 IndexN) */
```

Using a fast full scan for an index is appropriate if the analyst knows that many separate lookups would be required for a particular index. In these cases, it is much better to have the database engine scan through the entire index just one time, and get it over with.

The idea behind fast full index scans is the same as the reasoning for full table scans. A fast full index scan is able to use the multi-block read technique, just like the read method used for full table scans.

AND_EQUAL

The parameters in the following hint are listed in the same way as shown for the INDEX hint listed above:

```
/*+ AND_EQUAL (Table Index1 Index2 IndexN) */
```

This hint instructs the optimizer to combine the results of several indexes. You must list at least two indexes, but no more than five.

This method is unusual (and probably questionable in many cases), because the effort of reading, then combining multiple indexes is rarely the best execution path. The Oracle optimizer is very reluctant (and correctly so) to make multiple passes through different indexes, and then combine their results. Practically speaking, this method of figuring out which rows to fetch just doesn't achieve great performance. The one exception to this is for bitmap indexes, which have been specifically designed to be combined in this way.

FULL

This hint suggests that no indexes be used; instead, a full table scan will be performed, using the multi-block read method:

```
/*+ FULL(TABLE) */
```

It would be appropriate if, for instance, the selectivity of the search criteria will always be poor, and the use of an index would only degrade the response time.

Finally, be careful when hard-coding this hint into an application. A better option might be to create a histogram (discussed later in this chapter) so that the optimizer can account for any unusual data distributions that impact the cost of using an index. Remember that the FULL hint will usually stop the optimizer from using any index – even if the index could drastically speed up the query.

Join Hints

The Oracle Artist has yet another set of SQL hints at his or her disposal; these are the join hints (Recall the discussion on join hints in Chapter 9 – we will expand on that section here.) Some type of join hint is often used when there is a large number of tables specified in a SQL statement. As the complexity of the query increases, the number of different ways that the optimizer can process the query goes up dramatically. Thus, it becomes a little more likely that the optimizer will be fooled into making a poor choice. This means that it also becomes more likely that a SQL hint will be required.

Let's take a look at the most useful join hints in turn.

USE_NL

This is a very commonly used hint, and suggests to the optimizer that a nested loop join be used for the listed tables:

```
/*+ USE_NL (TABLE1 TABLE2 TABLE3 . . .) */
```

It is usual to use this hint in conjunction with the ORDERED hint, so that the exact join method and join order are explicitly controlled. It is most often needed when the analyst knows that the result set from the join is quite small. In that case, a nested loop is usually the best choice, as nested loop joins generally outperform any other join method for small result sets.

USE_MERGE

The next hint asks the optimizer to use the sort-merge join method for the tables listed. Following advances in join processing in recent Oracle versions, it will probably now be used less often:

```
/*+ USE_MERGE (TABLE1 TABLE2 TABLE3 . . . ) */
```

The sort-merge join has classically been a good option for large result sets, in which full table scans are often used for the tables in the join. In recent database releases, however, the sort-merge join has proved to be an inferior choice compared to the hash join method.

USE_HASH

As its name suggests, this hint requests that the optimizer use the hash join method for the tables listed:

```
/*+ USE_HASH (TABLE_NAME1 TABLE2 TABLE3 . . . ) */
```

It is somewhat rare; not because a hash join is a poor choice, but because the optimizer so often correctly makes this choice!

LEADING

The next hint was introduced for Oracle 8i:

```
/*+ LEADING (TABLE) */
```

It suggests to the optimizer that the specified table should be the first table to begin the join. It can be especially convenient when trying to push a certain table (and its related search criteria) up to the front of the join. Only one table should be listed in this hint. We could use it, for instance, when the search criteria for a particular table listed in the SQL are far more restrictive than any other condition. Sometimes, the optimizer will be able to make this call correctly by itself, but not always.

ORDERED

Another very useful hint, which can be used in conjunction with another SQL hint that suggests a join method. The syntax for it is very simple; no table names or other argument are specified at all:

```
/*+ ORDERED */
```

This hint simply requests that the optimizer join the tables in the specific order listed in the FROM clause. (Note that this is the opposite of the convention used in the old rule-based optimizer approach, in which the tables tended to be joined in the opposite order to that listed.)

The ORDERED *hint will override the* LEADING *hint.*

It is not unusual to need multiple hints on one line; thus, in order to specify both a nested loop and a particular join order, we would use the following syntax:

```
/*+ ORDERED USE_NL (A B) */
```

The hint above assumes that the table names (or aliases) are A and B; this combination of ORDERED plus USE_NL is fairly common. This is fairly self-explanatory since if the DBA wants the optimizer to use a nested loop, it is also likely he or she will want to control the join order.

Special SQL Hints

Here are some SQL hints that are used only in special circumstances. They are not used as frequently as those discussed in the prior sections, but they should definitely be considered in certain cases. These hints are not more "dangerous" than the other hints; rather, they just don't fit as many circumstances.

PARALLEL

This hint is used to activate the Parallel Query Option, or PQO. The DEGREE field is optional; if it is not specified, the parallelism degree will be the default for your particular database instance:

```
/*+ PARALLEL (TABLE DEGREE) */
```

The default for a database is controlled by the init.ora parameter PARALLEL_THREADS_PER_CPU.

For example, the following SQL text commands the optimizer to run the query using a parallelism degree of 3. Note that the hint for parallelism has specified the table alias and a degree of 3:

```
SQL> SELECT /*+ PARALLEL (X 3) */
  2  Ex_Emp_Name, Ex_Emp_Id
  3  FROM Ex-Employees X;
```

See Chapter 11 for a complete discussion of parallel processing.

APPEND

The hint is very valuable, but is often overlooked. It is used in INSERT statements, and can provide substantial (even two-fold) performance improvements:

```
/*+ APPEND*/
```

It causes row inserts to complete much faster usually. This occurs because the rows are inserted in Oracle's direct-path mode. In this mode, much of the database overhead is skipped in order to get the information stored as rapidly as possible. It is important to note, however, that this also means that the INSERT transactions are not written to the REDO log.

Transactions that are not written to the REDO log will not be recovered in the case of a database failure and subsequent recovery; instead, these transactions will have to be repeated. Of course, if it is important for your particular database that these row inserts are written to the redo logs, this SQL hint is probably not a good choice.

Note that rows inserted with the APPEND hint are put after the "high-water mark" – at the end of the table. This can potentially use more space than otherwise because none of the gaps in the table will ever be filled with rows added via APPEND. An export followed by import would be required to regain the lost space.

STAR

The STAR hint encourages the optimizer to use star join processing. As discussed in Chapter 9, this step is normally only used in a data warehouse application, where there is a huge fact table surrounded by smaller dimension tables:

```
/*+ STAR */
```

In a star join, the Oracle engine adds a pre-processing step in which the database engine jointly considers the dimension constraints. It does this by building a list of all possible combinations (Cartesian product) of the dimension rows that meet the selection criteria. Then, this set of rows is used to access the fact table, via a (B*tree) composite index.

The star join method may not be quite as good as star transformation, discussed next.

STAR_TRANSFORMATION

Specified like this:

```
/*+ STAR_TRANSFORMATION */
```

this hint is also used for data warehouse applications, in which there is a large fact table of many million rows. It activates the star transformation join method, which is a reasonably recent innovation, first available beginning with Oracle 8i.

The star transformation method uses the inherent speed of combining bitmaps to determine which rows in the fact table should be retrieved. It is very successful even when large amounts of data are involved.

See Chapter 9 for detailed examples and analysis covering both the star and star join processing.

Troubleshooting SQL Hint Problems

Although SQL hints are amazingly effective, simply adding a hint to the SQL statement does not guarantee that the optimizer will obey it. In most cases, it is not a bug in Oracle that is preventing the hint from working; instead, the problem is most likely due to:

❑Wrong hint syntax, such as comma instead of space.

❏ Referring to non-existent object (for example, incorrect table or index name).

❏ Using the table name rather than the table alias.

Observe the hint syntax for the following SQL, which correctly specifies the hint USE_NL to use a nested loop:

```
SQL> SELECT /*+ USE_NL (C D) */
  2   Cust_Name
  3   FROM Customer C, Department D
  4   WHERE C.Cust_Id = D.Cust_Id
  5   AND Dept_Name = 'Engineering';
```

This SQL correctly uses the two table aliases – C and D. Observe also the allowable mix of case. Even with a mix of upper and lower case in the hint, the optimizer will accept the statement.

Syntax Caveats

Unfortunately, incorrect syntax in a hint will not always be easy to discover. Many analysts and DBAs have spent hours wondering why the optimizer is not obeying the hint, only to discover some typo in the hint syntax later. In the case of wrong syntax or typos, the optimizer will simply ignore the hint – but you will never be told!

> **You will not be notified of an error in your SQL hint.**

Remember that a SQL hint is placed in the area reserved for comments; that's what the delimiters /* and */ really indicate. This makes it a little more understandable that Oracle doesn't display an error indication when the syntax for a hint is incorrect. How is Oracle supposed to know when a real hint is intended, or when the words are just supposed to be a comment?

To re-iterate from Chapter 9, be sure to put the SQL hint immediately after the SELECT (or DELETE, and so on) key word. Placing other words after SELECT will invalidate the hint.

SQL hints are one of the most important options available to the performance specialist. The art of selecting the right SQL hint is definitely a skill worth honing. For some reason, many developers and DBAs never fully understand how to use SQL hints; of course this puts them at a huge disadvantage in the craft of performance tuning. There is simply no reason to shy away from SQL hints – they really aren't all that difficult to master!

It should now be clear that, when crafting a solution to a tough performance problem, the Oracle Artist has a large number of options at his or her disposal. A major theme in the art of performance tuning is deciding which options are appropriate for a given problem, and which options should be left unused.

Let's take a look at another performance feature, one that is brand new for Oracle 9I; it is called **Automatic Memory Management**.

PGA Automatic Memory Management

The term **PGA** stands for Program Global Area. This is the area in memory set aside for a particular server process. When a user connects to the database, a PGA will be created and assigned to that session. The PGA is then available to facilitate whatever processing is required, by holding results of intermediate processing, such as sorts.

Depending on the exact SQL executed, the PGA may actually be comprised of many work areas that need memory to complete their processing. The most common type of work area is that used for sorting. When a SQL statement contains a phrase, such as ORDER BY or GROUP BY, a sorting work area is generally used. (If the sort can be fully accomplished via an index, a sorting work area may not be needed.)

Another work area is also used for hash joins. When the hashing function is being applied, a hash work area is also needed in the PGA. Of course, it is very important that these work areas be adequate to hold all the data needed for this intermediate processing. For instance, sorts that cannot be completed in memory must be swapped back and forth from the Temp tablespace. Similarly, hash joins that cannot be completed entirely within the hash work area will also suffer substantial performance degradation. Thus, providing an adequate size for these work areas is very important for performance optimization.

Setting a PGA Target

With Oracle 9i, it is possible for the database itself to increase or decrease sizes for the various work areas automatically as more memory is requested by a particular session. With this option, the DBA just specifies an overall target value that limits the total size. Thus, the key decision for the DBA when using this option is to choose a sufficiently large value for the overall target parameter – not for the individual work areas.

To accomplish automatic PGA sizing, the database engine examines the value of the PGA target parameter and adjusts the various work areas in memory so as not to exceed the specified value. If the DBA sets a PGA target sufficiently large, more work will be completed using the respective work area in memory. This in turns tends to decrease disk I/O, thus improving total run time for the queries that need the large work area.

Advantages of the PGA Target

Recall from Chapter 9 that the DBA specifies the overall target value with the parameter called PGA_AGGREGATE_TARGET. At first, this feature might not seem so important; after all, since there is only a handful of different work area types, one might wonder why anyone would bother to use this feature. Simply eliminating a few init.ora parameters hardly seems worth the trouble.

Actually, the PGA tuning feature is deceptively versatile; the important point to notice is that the PGA target is an aggregate in two entirely different ways. Firstly, the PGA target is an aggregate limit over the different types of work areas (hash, sort, and so on). More importantly, however, the PGA target limit is an aggregate over the PGA areas for all sessions:

> **Use the PGA aggregate target to cover work areas for all sessions.**

Thus, if an individual session requires a huge work area for sorting or hashing, the memory will probably be available, as long as many other sessions don't simultaneously request similar gigantic areas.

If multiple users do request large work areas, one or more requested sizes will have to be reduced in order to keep the PGA within the target value. These deprived sessions will simply have to run with a smaller work area, and presumably run slower than otherwise. The judgment required to select a good value for the PGA target once again illustrates the art of performance tuning; it's not just a matter of simply solving an equation. There is always room for creative solutions to those impossible problems.

In contrast to the PGA target method, the traditional method of setting work areas requires that the DBA explicitly set a huge size for each work area type. This would then mean potentially many sessions could grab this amount of memory, with no limit enforced on the total PGA memory acquired.

Using the New PGA Parameters

There are two `init.ora` parameters to set when using PGA automatic memory tuning, the first of which we have looked at briefly:

PGA_AGGREGATE_TARGET

The default for this parameter is 0 (automatic memory management off). Remember that this parameter specifies the target total PGA memory to be used for all server processes for that particular instance. It must be large enough to account for working memory needed for sorting, merging, joining, and so on.

The PGA target may be set anywhere between 10 MB and 4000 GB. When entering values, you can optionally use the abbreviations K, M, or G; thus, any one of the following `init.ora` entries could be used to specify a PGA target of 1 Gigabyte:

```
PGA_AGGREGATE_TARGET = 1G
PGA_AGGREGATE_TARGET = 1000000K
PGA_AGGREGATE_TARGET = 1000M
```

Using the K method for a large number seems a bit awkward, but that usage is acceptable.

WORKAREA_SIZE_POLICY

This parameter specifies the policy for setting sizes of several memory work areas, if `WORKAREA_SIZE_POLICY` is set to AUTO, work area sizing is automatic. When this parameter is set to MANUAL, the memory allocation for the work areas is determined explicitly – via the several memory parameters in the `init.ora` file.

By default, the WORKAREA_SIZE_POLICY parameter simply follows the lead of the PGA_AGGREGATE_TARGET parameter. If PGA_AGGREGATE_TARGET is set to some legal value, then the WORKAREA_SIZE_POLICY defaults to AUTO; if there is no value set for PGA_AGGREGATE_TARGET, then WORKAREA_SIZE_POLICY defaults to MANUAL.

Of course, despite the setting of PGA_AGGREGATE_TARGET, the DBA can always turn automatic memory tuning off simply by setting WORKAREA_SIZE_POLICY to MANUAL.

You can only specify the AUTO option when there is some value set for PGA_AGGREGATE_TARGET. This is logical, since it would make no sense to use automatic memory management without providing some target value.

Estimating PGA Requirements

Since it is so critical, the DBA should spend a little time estimating a good starting value for the PGA target. Fortunately, it is not necessary initially to be extremely precise, as the value can be changed at any time without harming any structures in the database.

The PGA target value should be set based on the type of application that is being run. For databases that support OLTP applications, Oracle suggests setting aside 20% of the total memory for database usage in the PGA. For databases that require more intensive sorting, such as data warehouses, a much larger proportion of the database memory allocation can be used for the PGA. For cases where very large sorting or hashing is required, even 70% of the total database allocation could be allocated for the PGA.

For example, let's assume that 1 GB has been set aside for Oracle. On an OLTP system, a reasonable starting point would be 20% of 1 GB, or 200 MB. Thus, we would set the init.ora parameter as follows:

```
PGA_AGGREGATE_TARGET = 200M
```

Obviously, this initial setting is simply a rough order of magnitude estimate; you should not assume that it would be very precise; it is simply a place to start:

> **Use the initial PGA target as a very rough estimate only.**

Special PGA Views

After the database has been subjected to at lease one complete cycle of heavy load, it is advisable to check on the memory management, and then make adjustments to the target value if necessary. Oracle provides some simple ways to check the automatic memory management, and reveal whether the target value has been set high enough. To accomplish this, the following views are provided:

View	Description
V$PGASTAT	Shows instance-level statistics on work areas.
V$PROCESS	Shows PGA usage by each connected session.
V$SQL_WORKAREA_HISTOGRAM	Histogram showing how well all the past SQL executions fit into the allotted PGA work areas. (Not related to histograms built on certain columns in a table.)
V$SQL_WORKAREA	Shows active work areas, by session, over 64 KB.
V$PGA_TARGET_ADVICE	Shows expected work area hit ratio for various values of the PGA target.
V$PGA_TARGET_ADVICE_HISTOGRAM	Histogram showing how well all the SQL executions would fit for a higher PGA target.

In the next sections, we will be discussing how these views are used. Note that the histogram PGA views are only available for releases beginning with Oracle 9i release 2. In addition, the PGA views are not available unless the automatic PGA tuning feature is actually activated.

Special PGA Terms

When querying from the new PGA views, there are some special terms that might seem confusing at first. The names are rather odd, but their meaning is really simple.

Consider a simple SQL statement that, when executed, requires a work area. It will run in one of three different modes, depending on its specific memory requirements and the available work area:

Mode	Description
Optimal	Everything fits in the work area allotted.
One-pass	The data cannot fit entirely in the work area; one extra pass through the data is required.
Multi-pass	Similar to the one-pass mode, the data cannot fit entirely in the work area; however, two or more separate data passes are required.

Generally speaking, the performance will be excellent for queries running in optimal mode, very good for one-pass mode, and bad for multi-pass mode operations. This happens because more effort, and time, is required to perform the extra passes through the data.

Note that the work area size needed for one-pass is typically far less than the optimal mode requirement. That is, it takes a lot of memory to accommodate everything, but if the optimizer is given the luxury of just one extra pass, the memory requirement drops substantially. This means that SQL queries requiring large sorts, such as for data warehouses, can often run in one-pass mode. Thus, a reasonable goal for data warehouse is to fit most queries into the one-pass mode.

Monitoring PGA Memory Tuning

Since it is critical to avoid numerous multi-pass operations, it follows that we need a way to see how the various work area operations are being handled with automatic PGA tuning. That is, we need a way to get some statistics on the proportion of operations that have been optimal, one-pass, or multi-pass.

The view V$SQL_WORKAREA_HISTOGRAM, available in Release 2 of Oracle 9i, provides just that information. With PGA tuning enabled, Oracle will record statistics on every operation that has used one of the work areas. So, the cumulative statistics will be available by querying this view.

Using this view is easy; simply run a query to show how many operations fell into each of the mode buckets. If the query shows that many operations are in the optimal bucket, we know that the PGA target is sufficient (or even too large!). On the other hand, many operations that are categorized as multi-pass indicate that our target for PGA memory is probably too small.

Let's build a sample query. We will select the columns that list the number of operations for each of the three different run modes (optimal, one-pass, multi-pass). Here are the column names:

❑ Est_Optimal_Executions

❑ Est_Onepass_Executions

❑ Estd_Multipass_Executions

It is also helpful to group the output according to the memory used by each operation; we also scale the memory usage by dividing by 1K. Here is the entire query:

```
SQL> SELECT Low_Optimal_Size/1024 Lowkb,
  2  (High_Optimal_Size +1)/1024 Highkb,
  3  Optimal_Executions Optimal,
  4  Onepass_Executions Onepass_Md,
  5  Multipasses_Executions Multipass
  6  FROM V$SQL_WORKAREA_HISTOGRAM
  7  WHERE Total_Executions <> 0
  8  ORDER BY 1;
```

LOWKB	HIGHKB	OPTIMAL	ONEPASS_MD	MULTIPASS
8	16	90451	0	0
16	32	344	0	0
32	64	192	0	0

64	128	43	1	0
128	256	22	5	1
	. . .			
262144	524288	0	0	0

In our particular example, we see that there have been 90,451 cases of operations that needed between 8 and 16 KB of memory. Naturally, all of them ran in the optimal mode. For higher levels of memory usage, there was only one operation that ran in multi-pass mode. Finally, only a handful of operations ran in one-pass mode.

From these results, we can conclude that the DBA for this system has done a good job of selecting the PGA target. These results are what can be expected for an OLTP system that only runs very small sorts or hash joins. Since OLTP systems typically run quick lookups, it would be unusual (and probably wrong) to see massive sorting operations occurring. It would not be unusual to see 95% of all OLTP work area operations fall into the optimal category.

A DSS (Decision Support System) application, on the other hand, will probably have many large sorts. By their very nature, DSS programs often need to summarize large amounts of information, which in turn requires reading, sorting, and joining extremely large tables. For DSS applications, it might only be possible for 50% of the work area operations to fall into the optimal category.

Note that the V$SQL_WORKAREA_HISTOGRAM view has a side benefit; besides showing the work area modes, it also exposes the presence of odd SQL statements. For example, suppose the above query listed many operations that required a huge work area; if this were an OLTP system, that result would be strange, and would indicate some sort of SQL problem. The DBA would certainly want to investigate why an OLTP program was running SQL that required large work areas in memory:

> **On OLTP systems, there should be very few multi-pass operations.**

Calculating a New PGA Memory Target

Once the database has been subjected to at least one cycle of peak-load processing, it is appropriate to consider resizing the PGA target. Two special views are provided to help guide the DBA to a good decision:

❑ V$PGA_TARGET_ADVICE

❑ V$PGA_TARGET_ADVICE_HISTOGRAM

The purpose of these views is to show you what would happen if you were to change the target size for PGA memory; in other words, how would the PGA memory hit ratio change? Naturally, we would expect more operations to fit completely in memory as the PGA target is increased; with these views we can obtain a good estimate of how much improvement would be achieved.

To use any of the PGA histogram views, the init.ora parameter STATISTICS_LEVEL should be activated (for example set to TYPICAL, which is the default). Naturally, the main parameter, PGA_AGGREGATE_TARGET, must already have been set, or else these views won't even exist!

Remember that these histogram PGA views are available beginning with Oracle 9i release 2. Similarly, the new init.ora parameter STATISTICS_LEVEL is not available before Oracle 9i release 2.

V$PGA_TARGET_ADVICE

The entries in V$PGA_TARGET_ADVICE show the cache hit percentage for possible target values; the entries are shown as potential sizes (in MB) for the PGA target, both above and below the current target. The values retrieved from the view reflect all operations since the last instance startup.

Let's try a sample query and see how this works; in particular, let's see how our PGA hit ratio would change for a variety of target values. The query is very straightforward; there are really just three columns of interest:

```
SQL> SELECT ROUND (pga_target_for_estimate/(1024*1024))
  2    TARGET, Estd_pga_cache_hit_percentage HIT_RATIO,
  3    Estd_Overalloc_Count WARN
  4    FROM V$PGA_TARGET_ADVICE;

TARGET   HIT_RATIO WARN
------   --------- ----
   100          45   10
   225          47    8
   350          65    0
   475          70    0
   600          77    0
   725          78    0
   850          78    0
```

In this query, we divide the TARGET values by 1024*1024 so that the values displayed will be in MB (rounded to nearest MB). The results show the expected hit ratio for different PGA targets. As expected, the hit ratio is higher as the PGA target increases. Note, however, that we have diminishing returns as the target value continues to increase. When the target is increased past 600 MB, we fail to achieve any significant cache improvement. This means that a reasonable value for the PGA target would be roughly 600 MB.

It may be helpful to draw a simple graph that shows how the PGA cache hit ratio improves with larger target values. The following figure shows the graph for our current example:

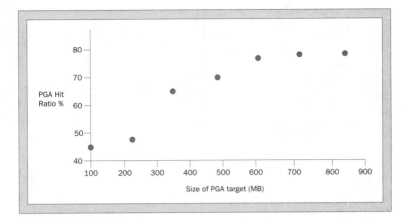

One column in the query above needs a little explanation. This column is called Estd_Overalloc_Count. In our query, we have renamed this field WARN. The information in this column is really a warning about some unusual Oracle behavior for very small values of PGA targets. Oracle calls this the **overallocation zone**.

With Oracle 9i, if you set the PGA target too low, Oracle may overallocate the PGA memory beyond the target that has been set in the init.ora file. That is, the database violates the very principle of automatic PGA tuning!

When there are non-zero values for this overallocate column, it means that the respective PGA target is excessively low. In our example, a PGA target value of less than 350 MB is in the dangerous overallocation zone; thus, we should not even consider setting a target less than 350 MB.

> **Avoid setting a PGA target in the overallocation zone.**

V$PGA_TARGET_ADVICE_HISTOGRAM

Another useful view is the V$PGA_TARGET_ADVICE_HISTOGRAM. It is the counterpart of the view V$SQL_WORKAREA_HISTOGRAM, and shows the projected impact for various values of the PGA target. In fact, these two views are nearly identical, differing only in that V$PGA_TARGET_ADVICE_HISTOGRAM has two extra columns (PGA_TARGET_FOR_ESTIMATE and PGA_TARGET_FACTOR).

To use this view, you insert a multiplier for the column PGA_TARGET_FACTOR. The multiplier reflects how much larger the PGA target should be. For instance, if you want to see a histogram that assumes the PGA target is three times the current setting, simply add the criterion WHERE PGA_TARGET_FACTOR = 3.

For example, here is a query that provides a histogram for a multiplier of 3:

```
SQL> SELECT Low_Optimal_Size/1024 LOWKB,
  2   (High_Optimal_Size +1)/1024 HIGHKB,
  3   Est_Optimal_Executions OPT,
```

375

```
4   Est_Onepass_Executions ONEPASS,
5   Estd_Multipasses_Executions MULTI
6   FROM V$PGA_TARGET_ADVICE_HISTOGRAM
7   WHERE Pga_Target_Factor = 3
8   AND Estd_Total_Executions <> 0
9   ORDER BY 1;
```

LOWKB	HIGHKB	OPTIMAL	ONEPASS_MD	MULTIPASS
8	16	90451	0	0
16	32	344	0	0
32	64	192	0	0
		. . .		
64	128	44	0	0
128	256	28	0	0

We see that increasing the PGA target pushes every single operation into the optimal bucket. The query results show that the PGA target will be adequate for 100% of the work area requirements. Of course, this is really a hint that the DBA may be *over-sizing* the PGA.

Let's move on now to look at histograms in more detail.

Histograms

We now turn to our third major option – the use of **histograms**. Histograms are an excellent way to keep the optimizer informed as to an unusual distribution of data for a table. This statistical information is then used when a query is presented for execution. With a histogram, the optimizer can determine the selectivity of search criteria, so that the best choice for data access can be made; without one, the optimizer has far less information on which to base its decision.

When statistics are gathered in the usual way, the optimizer does have some information on the data content (but no histogram). For instance, the regular statistics tell the optimizer the high and low values for a column, as well as the approximate number of distinct values for that column. Usually, that information is good enough, and allows the optimizer to make a correct decision as to index-lookup versus full table scan.

In some cases, however, the optimizer may be fooled into picking the wrong form of join, or making the wrong choice about index usage; this error usually happens when the data is badly skewed. In these cases, the optimizer is tricked into making a bad decision because its assumptions about the data distribution are wrong. With regular statistics, the optimizer assumes that the values in the table follow a uniform data distribution.

The Need for Histograms

Let's look at a situation that would benefit from a histogram. Consider a table called `Orders`. This table contains 10,000 rows – one row for each order. Each row shows the order details, including the name of the customer who placed the order. This column is called `Customer_Name`.

Let's assume that the firm has 1000 different customers; thus, there will be 1000 distinct values for the `Customer_Name` column. Of these 1000 different customer names, the high value is `ZZZZ` (for `ZZZZ Answering Service`) and the low value is `AAAA` (for `AAAA Choo-choo Trains`). Assuming that the table has been analyzed in the traditional fashion (no histogram), the optimizer will assume that all 10,000 values are evenly distributed from `AAAA` to `ZZZZ`.

The reason for a histogram is that for this firm, the uniform data distribution assumption is completely wrong! In reality, the data in this table is not at all evenly distributed; in fact, it is very lumpy. Here is the actual data distribution for the `Orders` table:

```
CUSTOMER NAME                     ROWS
-------------------------------   -------------------
'AAAA Choo-choo Trains'           5 rows
'Bob the Handyman'                7 rows


            . . .


'George Smith Golf Lessons'       8,110 rows


            . . .


'ZZZZ Answering Service'          11 rows
```

We see that the data is not anywhere close to evenly distributed. It turns out that one particular company, George Smith Golf Lessons, is responsible for about 80% of the entries! We call this type of data distribution lumpy. In our case, there is a big lump of data around the G rows.

Let's see what the ramifications of this lumpy data are. Consider how the optimizer would handle the following query:

```
SQL> SELECT SUM (Sales)
  2  FROM Orders
  3  WHERE Customer_Name LIKE 'George Smith%';
```

To process this query, the optimizer will (incorrectly) use an index. It will mistakenly believe that each customer name will be listed in about 10 rows (10,000 rows divided by 1,000 unique customer names). Of course, this particular customer actually has over 8,000 rows – but there was no way for the optimizer to realize that!

Using an index scan for this query will cause a big performance delay. The database engine will use an index on Customer_Name. From there it will have to perform a table lookup 8,110 times (once for each George Smith row). Performance will probably be ten times worse than a simple full table scan using a multi-block read.

This type of data distribution is not as unlikely as it may seem at first. There are many companies that have a few big customers that account for a disproportionate share of orders.

What Does a Histogram Look Like?

A histogram is a statistical convenience; it is simply a way to arrange data points so that the data distribution is easier to see. To accomplish this, the data is first sorted, and then grouped into buckets. Each bucket contains all the data points that are very close in value. These buckets make it easy to see what percentage of values reside at any given point.

Let's make a histogram for something with which we are all familiar. Consider the distribution of school grades for a college class. We first order all the grades for a class from highest to lowest; then, we'll make buckets that hold similar scores. In this example, we would have five buckets that stand for the grades A through F; each bucket might be 10 percentile points wide. That is, the A bucket houses the scores from 91 to 100; the B bucket holds the scores from 81 to 90 and so on.

Oracle-Style Histograms

When Oracle creates a histogram, the style is different from what many people expect. Oracle does in fact use buckets, just like our grades example; however, the buckets do not have equal width. Instead, Oracle creates a histogram with equal heights. This means that the width of a bucket changes so that nearly the same number of data points are in each bucket.

To illustrate this principle, consider a table called Students that is used in a database for a university. The Student table has 10,000 rows, which represent the enrollment at this school. We have decided to create a histogram, and use 10 buckets to represent the values in the column Major_Code. This column has numbers that range from 1 to 100, which represent the student's choice of academic major.

In the Student table, there is at lease one row for each of the 100 major choices; however, let's say that there is a big lump of data at major codes 33, 34, and 35. These codes all stand for an undeclared major.

If you didn't know about the special way that Oracle makes histograms, you might think that the histogram would look something like the next figure – but you would be wrong:

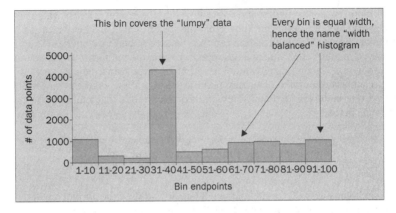

Note that each bin in this figure has the same width. In our example, there are 100 possible major codes, so each bin holds the data points that correspond to any of 10 different major codes. The height of each bin reflects the actual number of data points in that range.

In contrast, the following figure shows the way that Oracle would actually build this histogram. Note that the bins in the area of major codes 33-35 are very narrow:

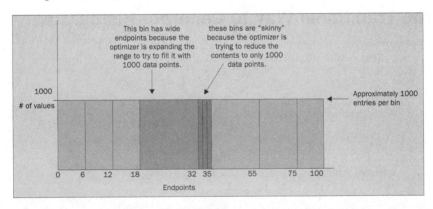

At first, this illustration might seem incorrect, since the major codes 33-35 have lots of values. Remember, though, that Oracle will make the bins very skinny (a narrow range) because it is trying to make the count of values in that bin smaller. The optimizer would ideally like to put exactly 1000 data points in each bin; this means that bins with a narrow range will be used in areas of high population, and very wide bins in areas of very sparse population.

Oracle's way of building histograms seems odd, but there is an excellent reason for this approach. Oracle's height-balanced histogram makes it possible to pinpoint the data distribution for the lumpy data points accurately. In contrast, the regular way of building a histogram simply can't give us the information we need.

Look again at the last figure, and notice how thin the bucket is for the value of 34. Using that fact, the optimizer knows that the specific value of 34 will return a large number of rows. This information can then be used to optimize queries. Thus, if a query were to use the value of 34 as search criteria, the optimizer would certainly not use an index. The optimizer would know that an index scan for the value 34 would return a massive number of entries, requiring the database engine to retrieve these rows from the table individually. It would correctly judge that a full table scan would be much better:

> **Use histograms to tell the optimizer about lumpy data.**

Now let's consider what would happen if Oracle had used the normal method of histograms – the width-balanced type. Given the same query (`major = 34`), Oracle would look at the histogram in the first figure to see how selective the value of 34 is. Unfortunately for the optimizer, the histogram is not nearly as helpful; the value of 34 is in a tall bucket that holds values from 31 to 40. The optimizer knows that there are lots of major values in the range 31-40, but no further information is available. The optimizer knows that the value of 34 might return a lot of rows, but then again, maybe it won't!

The Traditional Way to Generate Histograms

Histograms have traditionally been generated by using the ANALYZE command, with just a slight modification to indicate which columns should receive a histogram. The syntax is:

```
ANALYZE TABLE Table_Name Compute Statistics
FOR COLUMNS Col_Name SIZE Buckets;
```

or:

```
ANALYZE TABLE Table_Name Compute Statistics
FOR ALL COLUMNS SIZE Buckets;
```

or:

```
ANALYZE TABLE Table_Name Compute Statistics
FOR ALL INDEXED COLUMNS SIZE Buckets;
```

The user-supplied value for Buckets represents how many bins in which to distribute the data. This should immediately follow the keyword SIZE. The default is 75, which is adequate in most cases. Remember that the purpose of a histogram is to detect where the lumps are: this can usually be accomplished with the default number of buckets, or perhaps just a few hundred. Of course, more buckets can be used if there are many close values in the lumpy region.

Note that you can also use the Estimate Statistics clause (as opposed to Compute Statistics). This method is acceptable, except in those cases where it is critical to get an extremely accurate count of every single value for a column.

Let's return to our example of the Orders table. Recall that there was one customer, George Smith Golf Lessons, who accounted for a disproportionate number of rows in the table. We would use the following command to create a histogram on the Customer_Name column:

```
SQL> ANALYZE TABLE Orders Compute Statistics
  2   FOR COLUMNS Customer_Name;
```

With this histogram in place, the optimizer would now recognize the odd distribution of data, and would not use an index when looking for the value George Smith%.

The New Way to Generate Histograms

With later versions of Oracle (8i, 9i), the supplied package DBMS_STATS can be used instead of the ANALYZE command. In fact, Oracle recommends that DBAs use the DBMS_STATS package instead of the traditional ANALYZE method, which will not be developed any further.

Within the DBMS_STATS package, the procedure Gather_Table_Stats should be called. The key parameters for this procedure are:

Parameter	Meaning
Ownname	Schema owner
Tabname	Table name
Estimate_Percent	Sample size to use for the estimate (optional).
Method_Opt	Options to be used while gathering statistics

In its simplest form, you simply supply the schema name, table name, and number of buckets to be used for the histogram. Thus, to generate a histogram on our Student table, the following command would be used:

```
SQL> Exec Dbms_Stats.Gather_Table_Stats -
  2   ('chris','student',method_opt => -
  3   'FOR COLUMNS major SIZE 10')

PL/SQL procedure successfully completed.
```

In the code above, note the use of the hyphen symbol - to continue the long command over to the next line.

In this example, we supplied the schema name, Chris, as well as the number of buckets (10) to use for the histogram. Note that instead of specifying the individual column, we could have used the clause FOR ALL INDEXED COLUMNS. In most cases, however, creating histograms on a large number of columns is not necessary.

Checking Histograms

It is possible to check on the histograms using the view Dba_Tab_Histograms (or User_Tab_Histograms to see only histograms in your own schema). Use this view to retrieve the values for the list of bucket endpoints for the column that has the histogram.

To illustrate how this works, let's start with an ideal case in which the data is evenly distributed. Going back to our Student table, let's assume that the students had selected their major evenly; that is, there were an equal number of values for each Major_Code. Let's choose 10 buckets and generate the histogram:

```
SQL> ANALYZE TABLE Student Estimate Statistics
  2   FOR COLUMNS Major SIZE 10;

Table Analyzed.
```

With 10 buckets used for this histogram, let's see how they are represented inside the database. To accomplish this, we simply select from the User_Tab_Histograms view and include the search criteria so as to retrieve data for the column Major:

```
SQL> SELECT Endpoint_Number, Endpoint_Value
  2   FROM User_Tab_Histograms
  3   WHERE Column_Name = 'MAJOR'
  4   ORDER BY 1;

Endpoint_Number Endpoint_Value
--------------- --------------
              0              1
              1             10
              2             20
              3             30
              4             40
              5             50
              6             60
              7             70
              8             80
              9             90
             10            100
```

The endpoints shown are a reflection of the actual values that are in the table. (Recall that the values for the student academic major are in the range 1 through 100.) In this query, also note the shortcut way of specifying the ordering; the clause ORDER BY 1 simply means order by the first column in the SELECT clause. This is just an easy way to avoid having to type the column name.

These results are exactly what we would have thought! The view contains 11 endpoints, corresponding to 10 buckets. Each bin is nicely separated to cover the values from 1 to 100. We see that the first bin covers the major codes from 1-10, the second bin from 10-20, and so on. (A data point exactly on the bucket endpoint line will be assigned into one bin.) Of course, a histogram would not really be necessary for such a tidy data distribution, but it shows how the histogram is stored in Oracle.

Let's consider a more realistic example. Using the same Student table, consider a case where there are 3 big lumps at values for MAJOR of {33,34,35}. After producing a 10-bucket histogram, let's see how the buckets turn out:

```
SQL> SELECT Endpoint_Number, Endpoint_Value
  2  FROM User_Tab_Histograms
  3  WHERE Column_Name = 'MAJOR'
  4  ORDER BY 1;

ENDPOINT_NUMBER ENDPOINT_VALUE
--------------- --------------
              0              1
              3             33
              6             34
              9             35
             10            100
```

Observe that even though we requested 10 buckets, the optimizer deemed that only 4 were really required. We ended up with two very narrow buckets (33-34 and 34-35), and two very wide buckets (1-33 and 35-100). Remember that Oracle will make very skinny buckets for values that have a lot of entries, because it is trying to keep the height about the same for every bucket.

Note that the views Dba_Tab_Histograms and User_Tab_Histograms each have two columns that provide endpoint values. The column titled ENDPOINT_ACTUAL_VALUE provides the actual string value that is in the table analyzed. The column ENDPOINT_VALUE provides a value that is normalized – that is, adjusted statistically to facilitate sorting the values into bins.

Now that we have established the theory of histograms, let's see how they might work in practice. Our next case involves a strange city (with strange employees):

Case Study: The City of Miscellaneous Employees

A certain West Coast city employed 10,000 workers. They used an Oracle database to keep track of their staff. In the table called City_Workers, each of the workers was assigned an Employee_Id along with a Job_Description. Due to a clerical oversight, almost all the job descriptions were the same: Miscellaneous.

Beginning in the last year, however, new employees had received a more meaningful job description. For instance, the city recently hired several new clerks; the new clerks were correctly given the job description Clerk.

Since this correction had been applied relatively recently, almost all the employees had the older job description. Here is a breakdown:

```
EMPLOYEE_ID JOB_DESCRIPTION
------------------- --------------------------------
001 -  9,984  "Miscellaneous"
9,985 - 10,000  "Street Sweeper", "Clerk", "Typist",
                "Section Manager"
```

This lumpy data made it very difficult for the database to execute certain queries. Proper statistics were generated, but there were simply too few distinct values for the column Job_Description. Whenever that column was specified in a condition, the optimizer used a full table scan, even though there is an index on that column. Of course, this behavior was frequently wrong; for instance, if the query was looking for a Street Sweeper, a full table scan was a poor choice, since there are only a few rows that represent the job description Street Sweeper.

Here is a specific example of a query that ran badly. For the following SQL, the optimizer performed a full table scan of the City_Workers table, even though the search criteria was extremely selective:

```
SQL> SELECT Employee_Name, Employee_Id
  2  FROM City_Workers
  3  WHERE Job_Description = 'Clerk';
EMPLOYEE_NAME EMPLOYEE_ID
------------- -----------
HERBERT JONES        9992
VERONICA HILL        9998
```

Having recently read a book on Oracle performance tuning, the DBA was well acquainted with histograms and tried to improve the performance of the query above. Noting that there were only a few values for the Job_Description column, she decided to generate a histogram with 4 buckets on the City_Workers table, in the schema CITY. She used the new method of generating the histogram via the DBMS_STATS package:

```
SQL> Exec Dbms_Stats.Gather_Table_Stats -
  2  ('CITY', 'CITY_WORKERS', -
method_opt => 'FOR COLUMNS Job_Description size 4')

PL/SQL procedure successfully completed.
```

Satisfied that the optimizer was now aware of the funny data distribution, the DBA ran the query again. As expected, the optimizer now knew that there were extremely few rows that had the job description Clerk. Exactly the same query was now using an index, reducing the run-time substantially.

As a result of this clever step, the DBA received several cheerful phone calls from users; they all want to know, "What did you do?"

Note that any query that uses the lumpy portion of the data as search criteria will still require a full table scan. In our case study, this means any query that relies upon Job_Description = 'Miscellaneous' as the search criterion. Using an index to look up such a large percentage of the table would cause a disastrous performance drop.

Histogram Limitations

In spite of their great value, histograms cannot be used in all cases. There is one big limitation to their use; they will not work when the SQL statement uses a bind variable. This limitation makes sense, because a bind variable temporarily obscures the actual value. Without knowing the literal value, the optimizer cannot possibly judge how the specified value fits into the histogram.

In Oracle 9i, the concept of bind variable peeking was introduced. With this feature, the optimizer is able to decode the bind variable, and develop an execution plan accordingly. Note, however, that the optimizer then assumes this same execution plan for all subsequent executions of the same SQL statement.

Of course, in a case where a histogram is the right answer to a performance problem, the designer and the DBA might decide to forego bind variables for a few parts of the application.

Summary

In this chapter, we have examined three more resources for the Oracle Artist: SQL hints, Automatic PGA memory management, and histograms. These facilities provide a wealth of options when trying to solve aggravating performance problems.

SQL hints are one of the most important facilities for the performance analyst to master. They have the power to improve performance dramatically, but they also can wreck it: thus, they should be used with caution, and should not be the first option used. Instead, the analyst should make sure that the basics are covered. In many cases, there are fundamental problems that should be addressed first, such as forgetting to gather statistics on the tables involved.

We also reviewed the promising new feature provided with Oracle 9I, PGA Automatic Memory Management. We saw that this method has the potential to provide memory for the needs of a particular session more accurately. The sessions that need more memory can get it, as long as the overall total is not surpassed. This facility has the potential to improve the performance of queries that occasionally need a very large work area in memory.

Finally, we saw that histograms are useful for cases in which the data distribution is skewed. Oracle uses a special histogram technique, called height balancing, in which the width of the histogram buckets varies according to the data distribution. This method of generating histograms makes it very easy for the optimizer to determine whether particular search criteria should use an index or not.

This chapter concludes our discussion of the Oracle Artist, and the various ways that we can paint a solution to deal with those vexing performance problems. It's time to put the final touches to our performance painting, and temporarily drop a tarp over the canvas.

The curtain is now ready to open on our final act. In the next chapter, we introduce our final performer, the Oracle Magician.

- Set The Stage

- Wave The Wand

- If You Make A Mistake

- Tie Up Loose Ends

- Your Next Performance

13

The Oracle Magician

We have now arrived at the last step in the performance tuning process. The problem has been defined, investigated, and thoroughly analyzed; furthermore, the root cause has been isolated, and a solution has already been prepared. It's time for the performance analyst to don his final hat – this time, the hat of a magician. It's time to implement the solution:

Physician	Detective	Pathologist	Artist	Magician
Define problem	Investigate	Isolate cause	Create solution	Implement solution

This last step is really the easiest in the tuning process, but also the most exciting. With the solution in hand, the Oracle Magician will "make the magic happen". This step represents the culmination of all the labor that has gone before.

This should also be a fun time for the *audience*. Everyone loves a good magic trick, and competent performance tuning often does seem like magic to the customer. It is very common for a function that has performed miserably to run much faster instantly, immediately after the analyst has run a few commands.

Performance tuning magic often evokes comments very similar to those heard at a magic show; after seeing dramatically improved performance, database users will often say, "How did you do that?" Other DBAs or database analysts will often ask, "Please will you show me how to do that?"

In this chapter, we discuss ways to make the magic happen, and to bring our performance to a successful conclusion. Exciting as it usually is, this step will normally be very simple to execute; after all, the Oracle Physician, Detective, Pathologist, and Artist have studied the performance problem for long hours behind the scenes. You now have a solution that truly addresses the root cause of the performance bottleneck.

This chapter is divided into the following main sections:

❑ *Set the Stage*: here we will look at the necessary steps of a successful magic act. We examine the elements of a successful performance tuning engagement, and consider some ways in which to make *our* "performance" go smoothly. In particular, we will suggest ways that the Oracle analyst *prepares* for implementing the solution, including precautions such as taking a database backup, and testing the solution in a development environment.

❑ *Wave the Wand*: we discuss the actual implementation of the performance fix. The magic here is quite simple to execute; what is more complicated is watching the system *after* the solution is implemented.

❑ *Tie Up Loose Ends*: we investigate ways to ensure that the customer is happy with our work. One good idea is to document the solution. This is simply smart business; since you have gone to all the trouble of solving a perplexing performance problem, why not share your results with your customer?

❑ *Your Next Performance*: we close the chapter with some suggestions on further steps for the Oracle Magician. Now that the curtain has fallen and the theatre is empty, what can the Oracle Magician do next? Isn't there some way to make use of all this good work?

Quick! It's now time for our entrance. The audience is seated, and the lights have dimmed. Let's grab our hat and wand—it's curtain time!

Set the Stage

The first step in any performance of magic is to *set the stage*. Before a major show, the stage magician will ensure that the apparatus is all working: the trap doors are oiled, the secret handcuffs are tested, and the smoke bombs are ready to go. The stagehands ensure that the mirrors are in place, and that the magician's assistants are waiting in the wings.

In the same way, all the apparatus needed for a valid performance solution must be put in place and be ready to go: the optimizer "smoke and mirrors" must be checked, the SQL hint "trap doors" must be ready, and the magic histogram handcuffs must be checked for smooth operation.

Clearly, a dazzling performance – either by the stage performer or the Oracle tuning expert – doesn't happen by accident; in both professions, thorough preparation is mandatory. For the Oracle performance tuner, preparation takes a slightly different form.

There are three facets to our stage preparation:

❑ Testing the solution on a development system
❑ Considering the impact on the production users
❑ Preserving the existing system

By following these simple steps, the implementation of your solution will likely run very smoothly. Let's consider each of these precautions in turn.

Test the Solution

Often , the required modifications will be so significant that some trials will be necessary on a development or test instance. Almost all firms have a development environment, so this is not usually a big problem.

The whole idea of checking the solution is to avoid nasty surprises; remember that we are trying to surprise the customer, not ourself:

> **Test the solution before implementing; leave nothing to chance.**

Whatever system is used to test the modification, be sure that your setup closely matches the actual production environment. To achieve this, it may be necessary to create various indexes, analyze some database tables, import data, and so on. Again, most sites already have databases that are close copies, or even "clones" of production; if not, this is a good time to recommend that practice.

Our next case study illustrates the consequences of "trying things" on a production system:

Case Study: When in Doubt, Try on Production!

While consulting for an electric service utility, one of the more inquisitive DBAs in the group decided to implement some performance enhancements. Specifically, he wanted to re-analyze many of the tables, so that the optimizer would have the latest statistics.

The young DBA prepared a script that would run the ANALYZE TABLE command on various schemas and tables in a specified database. Unfortunately, he tried his script for the first time on one of the production systems. The syntax for the ANALYZE command was fine; the problem was that the script also operated on the data dictionary – that is, the Sys tables.

The results were catastrophic. After running the "performance enhancement" script, the production database crashed, some of the data dictionary objects became unusable, and the entire application was down for almost an entire day! The database had to be completely rebuilt, with special assistance from Oracle Support Services.

The DBA in this case should not be faulted for trying to improve performance; gathering proper table statistics is certainly good practice. The real error was not the flaw in the script, but rather the oversight of not testing the scripts in a "safe" place first.

Analysis of the data dictionary (that is, the Sys tables) has traditionally been a terrible mistake. The Metalink support site is filled with dire warnings against taking this step. For one thing, the internal data dictionary relies on *rule-based* optimization and therefore does not need (or want) DBA-activated statistics. Fortunately, with Oracle 9i there are, apparently, no serious consequences to this action. Nevertheless, there is no reason to take the risk; do not try to analyze the data dictionary without specific instructions from Oracle:

> **Never try out a script on a production system.**

Consider the Impact on the Production System

Closely related to testing a fix is the idea of considering the impact of that fix on the production system. Just as the wise stage performer never attempts a new trick without certain precautions, the Oracle analyst also needs to consider the consequences of his actions.

Just a few moments consideration can prevent some major production issues. This step is critical because many production disasters occur due to human error – not some mechanical or electrical problem. These errors are typically some careless action by a well-meaning engineer who just "didn't know".

In the Oracle area, the situation is exactly the same; many database crashes are entirely preventable, and are due to a simple mistake by a DBA or Systems Administrator:

> **Remember that many system crashes are due to human error.**

For example, here are some possible consequences of prematurely deploying a fix in production:

❑ Degraded performance during the implementation.
❑ Missed permissions or public synonyms causing application failure.
❑ Temporarily blocked users due to index or table changes.

Of course, many of these problems will be discovered in time – if the solution is first tested in a development environment. A missed object synonym would usually be detected, for example, because the part of the application that needs the synonym won't work! (Recall that a synonym is a database object that is a short-cut way of referring to a table or another object.)

Degraded performance is a harder consequence to predict; there are, however, some wise precautions that can reduce the likelihood of a blunder that leads to degraded performance. One good practice, followed by most experienced DBAs, is to include the SQL in a pre-built script always. When it is time to implement the fix on production, the script is run, rather than asking the DBA to "type in" the commands one by one. Typing in commands on a production system opens the door to all kinds of potential errors (and is just plain slow):

> **All production changes should be incorporated in scripts.**

In the next case study, the author was a little hasty in implementing some tuning fixes. Like the DBA in the previous case, the author did not spend enough time considering its potential impact. The result was some nasty consequences for an important production system:

Case Study: "Nice Job!"

While consulting for a large utility, I had occasion to analyze and try to improve performance on the main OLTP system, used by the customer service agents. This system was extremely important to the firm; a problem with this database could result in many angry customers. In fact, after an unplanned database outage, several of the DBAs would usually have an opportunity to meet the senior management in the company.

Performance for this customer service application was patchy; some functions worked very well, but others were quite slow. Several weeks of investigation showed that revising the provision of indexes could make many performance gains. In many places, important indexes were simply missing!

For instance, there were indexes that allowed a quick lookup of a customer by his or her last name; however, other commonly used search criteria, such as phone number, were not indexed. This meant that many large full table scans were performed unnecessarily.

While checking the sizes of the various indexes used by the application, I uncovered several large ones that had *never* been rebuilt. Their huge size suggested to me that a rebuild was in order; if nothing else, the rebuilding would certainly result in them being much smaller. I also suspected that a little performance improvement could be achieved by this simple step.

I identified one very large index that needed to be rebuilt. Without trying this first in development, and without checking with the other DBAs, I executed the script to rebuild the index on the production system. This was a big mistake. I had forgotten that any database user who tried to update an entry in the underlying table would be *blocked* by the index rebuild.

Of course, a little planning and forethought would have quickly revealed that issue, but this planning hadn't happened. Instead, I started the rebuild, and then went to lunch. Since the underlying table was large, I estimated the rebuild would take about a half hour. When I returned, the main production DBA calmly informed me that he had killed my job because the rebuild process was blocking numerous users on the production system!

Naturally, the other DBA was quite right to kill my job; my script had blocked all updates to a database table on the most critical database in the company! This had meant that the customer service agents could not perform simple (but important) functions, such as updating a customer's phone number.

In this case, I had erred by failing to consider the ramifications of my decision. I had failed to follow this simple idea:

> **Consider the impact on the production users.**

As a result of this index rebuilding, the application "hung" for a large number of users. While the customer service representatives were frantically trying to make the application work, the culprit (me) was blissfully ignorant – I was out to lunch! I was very fortunate that the other DBA had quickly spotted my blunder.

Preserve the Existing System

The Oracle Magician needs to set in place certain safeguards – just in case! The most basic point to remember is this; backup the production system before making changes. This is a standard precaution, and ridiculously obvious, but it is often disregarded. As amazing as it seems, it is quite common for software engineers to make a change to a production application without confirming that backups have been taken.

To avoid any possibility of mishap, confirm that some type of sure backup has been taken. In fact, many DBAs believe in having *two* forms of backups; physical and logical (exports). This is sound practice and only takes a little time; why take a chance? If backups have not yet been performed, do not proceed with making changes until this step has been completed.

One easy way to perform a backup is to run either a complete export, or an export of just the database tables that will be affected. An export is easy to carry out, and reasonably fast for most databases. For extremely large databases, such as those used in data warehouse applications, it may not be feasible to perform a complete database export; in those cases, either a selective export of certain tables, or a physical backup will be required.

If a database export has purportedly already been taken, it is easy enough to verify. The validity of an export can checked by looking at the export log. This log will show exactly which tables have been exported, and the number of rows in each table. Be sure to check the log for any error messages, especially at the end of the log file.

For physical backups, besides checking the logs to make sure that the backup completed without errors, it is helpful to look at the time stamp on each backup file. Does the time stamp on each .dbf file match the backup time?

For cold backups, verify that the database was indeed shut down properly. (Recall that a cold backup is a backup of all database files after the database is completely shut down.) A cold backup of a database that is "not quite shut down" is useless; thus, check the alert log, and compare the time of the backup with the time of the database shutdown. It is *imperative* that the database was completely shutdown prior to the cold backup.

When in doubt, take a new backup, using a method with which you feel comfortable. Whatever method you choose (perhaps both), just be sure that a backup has completed with zero errors:

> **Never modify production systems without taking a backup.**

Readers might think that the advice in this section is so basic that no one could possibly fail to observe it. Think again! The recommendation is indeed very basic, but DBAs omit this step all the time. Don't be one of them.

Our next case, based on an actual incident, shows the consequences of forgetting this simple step:

Case Study: I Don't have Time for Backups!

A large New York advertising agency was preparing to implement a pilot data warehouse application. Several consultants had designed the initial application, and worked with the DBA to prepare a prototype database. So far, the first release of the application was working well, and it was time to hand over the database to the client.

Shortly after assuming responsibility for it, the DBA decided to perform some modifications and upgrades on the production database. Not having read this book, he did not consider protecting the database by taking a complete database backup; instead, he proceeded to run some scripts immediately against the production system!

What happened next is a bit fuzzy (and no one wants to further embarrass the people involved). Somehow, the DBA modified (and ruined) the Sys objects in the SYSTEM tablespace. Of course, as all DBAs know, an Oracle database is worthless with a damaged SYSTEM tablespace.

The consultants had to be called back in to reconstruct the database as best they could, given that no backup was in place.

The mistake in this case was three-fold. Firstly, the scripts were not tested on a development system; secondly, the production system was not adequately protected; finally, the DBA should have asked for a review by a more experienced DBA. The reviewer could have cautioned him about possible consequences of his action, and the need for a good backup. All the embarrassment could have been avoided by a simple 1-hour export.

Although the advice in this section has been directed mostly at protecting the database, the same reasoning applies to all application code. In fact, *anything* related to the production system should be preserved before any changes are made. This includes the database, application, utilities, setup scripts, and so forth.

Wave the Wand

With all the groundwork completed, we're ready to work our magic! Without further delay, we now proceed to wave our wand, say "Abracadabra", and watch the results!

Abracadabra! Making Angry Users Disappear

Throughout this book, we have used the term *magic* to describe competent performance tuning. To those who have witnessed a skilled Oracle practitioner, the term will seem fitting; one minute the database is running terribly, with frustrated users, the next, all the users are happy. In the client's eyes, this performance really does look like magic; all the mad users have vanished!

Often, the magic comes down to running a simple script, or implementing a slight change to a few SQL statements. It is ironic that many performance solutions boil down to just a few lines of code, or a few commands. Nevertheless, these few lines of code carry with them enormous consequences.

Angry users especially want to know what the DBA section or other support service is doing about their problem. Some may even drop hints about wasting money on so-called performance tuning experts, or scorn your efforts.

Actually, in one way, this scenario is perfect for the skilled Oracle tuning expert; in fact, the madder the users, the better! With a backdrop of furious users, the performance change will be even more dramatic.

Our next case illustrates a situation where the customer really didn't think any DBA could do much about the sluggish performance. The problem was so severe that the users did not even consider the possibility that fast performance was possible:

Case Study: The DBA Broke the Program!

At a large insurance company, one group of inside users needed to run nightly reports that tracked customer claims. These reports had first been activated months ago. The programs were working functionally, but running dreadfully slowly. Another DBA was assigned to support this particular group, so I had never worked with this team before.

As time went on, these nightly reports began to consume almost all available night-time hours. The degradation worsened to the point that they finally had to ask for help (I don't know why they delayed so long).

One report in particular required eight hours to complete. This report was so important that every morning the project manager would personally check the run logs to make sure that it was nearing the end of its run.

Due to the temporary absence of one of the DBAs, I had an opportunity to look at these performance problems. The problem definition was very clear in my mind; it could have been written like this, "report R1 takes eight hours to complete".

My first step was to gather some more information on report R1, and look at the SQL statements generated by it. At the start, my investigation advanced little, because the SQL statements had always aged-out of the shared pool by the time I checked the database in the morning. Obviously, *something* was causing the delay but, so far, I couldn't see what!

To capture the relevant SQL, I activated a simple cron job to trap all offensive statements from midnight to 5 am. They were automatically stored in a temporary table, with all the relevant statistics – executions, buffer_gets, and disk_reads.

The following morning, I checked my "traps", and found the culprits. In three separate places, the report ran a correlated subquery that required thousands of full table scans. It was not surprising that this report required eight hours to complete; in fact, it was more surprising that it had ever completed at all!

A massive reduction in processing could easily be accomplished by a slight change in the SQL formulation. After proving to the designers that the new SQL was functionally identical to the old, they agreed to make this change.

The next day, the manager checked the run logs in the morning to make sure that the reports were running OK, and were nearing their finish. He was not happy with what he saw. The report was not even running! Very irritated, he immediately called the Systems Administrator to complain, "You guys broke our report. It's not running!"

The Systems Administrator calmed the manager down and asked him to check the run log, "Are you sure that the program is broken? How do you know?" With great reluctance, the manager checked the logs (just to satisfy the pesky Sys Admin). Amazed, the manager saw the truth. The reason the report was not running was very simple; it had finished 7 ½ hours earlier!

In this example, the run-time had changed so drastically that the manager had simply assumed that the DBA had broken the report. In his mind, it was quite inconceivable that the report could finish so fast. It was magic!

Following this incident, I found it much easier to persuade this particular group to implement various performance suggestions.

Confirm the Performance Change

After the magic fix has been performed, one should not assume that everything has gone perfectly; instead, the Oracle Magician should take the time to measure the improvement.

On a busy OLTP system, most transactions are run many times throughout the day; thus, the function that has been responsible for the sluggish performance previously will probably be run very soon. This makes it easy to confirm quickly that the solution has indeed fixed the problem.

If the application is rarely used, one can simply contact a sample user on the production system, and ask them to try it. When the user tries the "bad" function, the response is: "Wow! What happened?" Hearing this exclamation is a good sign.

Checking Statistics

Following implementation of a correction, it is also useful to watch the statistics provided in the V$SQL view. For instance, we can use a script to see the number of executions of a particular SQL statement, and the cumulative disk and logical reads.

In the script below, we retrieve the statistics for the SQL statement that selects from the table ACCTS_PAYABLE:

```
SELECT Executions, Buffer_gets, Disk_reads, Sql_Text
FROM V$SQL
WHERE Upper(Sql_Text) like 'SELECT%ACCTS_PAYABLE';
```

If the SQL statement has indeed been corrected, the number of executions will increase, but the disk reads and logical reads will now advance much more slowly.

On non-OLTP systems, where the impacted functionality is not run throughout the day, it may be more difficult to confirm the improvement. If possible, however, it is better to get some indication that the problem has been corrected.

Instead of waiting for the next run of the batch job or report, it is usually possible to confirm the fix by simulating what the report *would* do on the production system. In fact, the SQL script to accomplish this was probably already written during an earlier phase – for example, when the proposed solution was being tested. It is usually possible to run the relevant SQL statements in a SQL*Plus session, and measure the run-time. In some cases, the designers may be able to run part of a batch job early, just to see how fast it runs.

Watch for Unintended Consequences

When the correction has been applied, it is important to monitor the production system for *unintended consequences*. Even when the performance bottleneck has been fixed, the Oracle analyst must be careful to watch for degradation in other areas of the application. This might seem like a bizarre occurrence, but it happens occasionally.

This response is most likely when a new index has been added, and the optimizer incorrectly uses the new index for some other SQL statement. This can occur, for example, if the new index appears to be an excellent choice for some query, and the optimizer is "lured" into making a wrong decision. Also, in applications with a large amount of INSERT activity, the new index can potentially slow down the processing.

Remember that each time a SQL statement is presented for execution, the optimizer decides upon the best execution plan; this means the one with the lowest overall cost. When a new index is created, the optimizer has more options – including the option to use the new index instead of the one it was using previously. This can sometimes be the wrong choice.

Of course, it is actually more likely that some other SQL statement will run faster with the new index. The reverse case does happen occasionally, however:

> **When a new index is added, watch for other SQL statements that suddenly run poorly.**

Should a new SQL bottleneck appear, the analyst has two options. Firstly, if the new bottleneck is serious, you can temporarily reverse the change (such as removing a new index) until a correction for the other SQL is prepared. Before taking this step, however, you should capture the sluggish SQL and the execution plan for the new bottleneck. This will give you a head start on correcting this new problem.

Alternatively, if the new bottleneck is not severe, the change can be left in place while a solution is prepared for the newly discovered problem. Remember, however, to watch for any other functions that also begin to run poorly.

To ease the impact of unforeseen responses (and avert a panic), it is a good idea to consider various ways to reverse an implementation. Of course, a backup of the production system will allow you to revert back to the original configuration, but there might be simpler ways of doing this without having to restore the original database. Perhaps you could have a "back-out" script ready, or a list of steps to follow to reverse the changes? Of course, these tools should also be verified *before* you need them.

If You Make a Mistake

Despite your best precautions, you might still find yourself in a situation where you have simply erred. Instead of an immediate fix to the bottleneck, your recommendation has not solved the problem. For some reason, yet to be determined, the production system has behaved differently from the system on which you tested the fix.

The safest way to deal with these cases is to recognize a certain principle right from the start; in spite of diligent preparation, you will occasionally make mistakes. When this occurs, accept the criticism. Almost everyone will forgive a mistake or two by someone who owns up to it, and takes steps to correct the error. (See Chapter 4 for further ideas on establishing a trusting relationship with your customer):

> **If you err, accept responsibility.**

The real issue is not who to blame, but understanding why the fix didn't work. When a problem is "fixed" on the development system, but the correction doesn't work on another system, there are only two possibilities:

❑ You have not used exactly the same fix.

❑ The two systems are different in some important area.

Let's now take a look at what we might be able to do to rectify the situation in both cases.

Exactly the Same Fix?

It should be very simple to confirm that the correction applied to the production system is the same as the one applied in the development environment. This is another good reason to use scripts always, rather than typing in the command afresh. If you determine that there is a discrepancy, then you obviously need to ensure, by using the same script, that exactly the same correction is applied after all.

If, on the other hand, there have been no typos or other alterations to the performance-correction script, we must conclude that there is something different about the production system. The question is, "What is different about the production system?"

How are the Systems Different?

Here are a few possibilities that can be checked easily:

❑ Different statistics exist on production

❑ Different indexes have been created

❑ There are different init.ora parameters

❑ There is a big difference in data content

❑ The database version is different

❑ The database patch level is different

❑ The application is different

Technically speaking, even the disk layout or CPU speed could impact the performance; normally, however, the disk layout on production will not be worse than on the development system. Also, it is unlikely that disk layout or CPU speed alone can account for a drastically different run-time for just one form of SQL statement; if the CPUs or disks are that bad, then the entire application will probably run badly.

In practice, the most common reason for inconsistent performance between servers is not due to some arcane difference in disk layout, faster CPU speed, or even patch level. Instead, the reason is usually much *bigger* and much more *basic*. Probably the most common cause of performance discrepancies between two systems is a missing index. Fortunately, it is very easy to compare the objects in two separate databases.

Compare Database Objects

One easy and fast way to check for missing indexes or other objects is to get a count of objects in both databases for the particular schema of interest. For instance, here is a useful script that lists the count for each of the individual object types in the FINANCE schema:

```
SELECT Object_type, count (*) FROM Dba_Objects
WHERE Owner = 'FINANCE'
GROUP BY Object_type;
```

Of course, agreement with the mere object *count* doesn't prove that the objects are the same in both databases, but it's still a very simple way to rule out the most likely cause of varying performance. Should an inconsistency in index count be detected, for example, the view Dba_Indexes can be queried to isolate the missing indexes further. This view lists the indexes by table name, so it is easy to get a list of indexes for each table.

A more complete way to check on object differences requires that you create a database link from the test database to production. Then, you simply run a query that lists the variations in object names between the two databases. In the SQL below, we assume that the database link is called PROD:

```
SELECT object_name FROM user_Objects
MINUS
SELECT object_name FROM user_objects@PROD;
```

Another common cause of differing performance is a difference in application versions; this typically means that the SQL statements that can be executed are not the same on the two systems. Tracing the session activity using SQL_TRACE is once again a good idea in this case.

Review init.ora Settings

A common reason for performance discrepancies between production and test databases is a different setting in the init.ora file; for example, production servers often have more memory, CPUs, and so on. The parameters defined in the init.ora file may, thus, be set differently to exploit the divergent resources available. Typically, inconsistencies can be found in the settings for DB_BLOCK_BUFFERS and SHARED_POOL. Discrepancies in these settings can lead to (seemingly) odd performance differences.

It is wise to review the set of init.ora parameters, and compare the production values to the system where you performed your testing. Look for any drastically different setting; for instance, different values for SORT_AREA parameter. Or the production system (alone) may be configured to use some new database feature, such as PGA Automatic Memory Management.

Besides directly examining the init.ora file visually, an easy way to check the database parameters is by running a script to query the view V$PARAMETER.

Since DBAs and designers almost always have a SQL*Plus session open, this is usually a little faster; it saves the time of logging into the server, finding the right directory, then reading the correct init.ora file. Also, it can be especially confusing tracking down the right init.ora file if there are various "versions" on different directories. By looking at the V$PARAMETER view, you can determine positively what the current setting for any parameter is.

When running the script below, it is not necessary to remember the exact parameter name; a portion of the name can be entered (in upper case):

```
Col Name format a35
Col Value format a40

SELECT Name, Value FROM V$PARAMETER
WHERE Upper (Name) LIKE Upper ('%&PARNAME%');
```

As an example of this in action, here's what happened when I ran the script to look for the value of all parameters that contain the phrase SHARED on my instance:

```
Enter value for parname: SHARED

NAME                           VALUE
------------------------------ ---------
shared_pool_size               41943040
shared_pool_reserved_size      2097152
shared_memory_address          0
hi_shared_memory_address       0
```

This script is useful when trying to find parameters for which you don't know the exact name. In our example, we simply wanted to know the settings for all parameters related to SHARED.

An even easier way to list parameters is available in SQL*PLUS; simply type the command:

```
SQL> SHOW PARAMETER [PARAMETER-NAME]
```

For example, suppose we want to see the value of all parameters that have the phrase *shared pool* anywhere in their name; in SQL*PLUS, we simply type:

```
SQL> show parameter shared_pool
```

to get this result:

```
NAME                                    TYPE      VALUE
------------------------------------- -------- ---------
shared_pool_reserved_size               string    10485760
shared_pool_size                        string    209715200
```

Oracle 9i

We should note at this point that there is a significant new feature available to DBAs beginning with Oracle 9i; instead of maintaining the usual init.ora file, you have the option of using a *binary parameter* file. The main advantage of this is that parameter updates made while the database is running will *persist* even when the database is shut down then restarted. Traditionally, of course, the DBA has had to change the init.ora file manually to make parameter changes permanent; now, that extra step can be eliminated.

When this feature is used, the binary parameter file should never be edited directly; instead, there are special database commands that you should use. It is also possible to export the parameter file for backup purposes, or for documenting the state of the parameters for future reference or diagnostic purposes.

For further information on using the binary parameter file feature, see the *Oracle 9i Database Administrator's Guide*.

Capture the Relevant SQL

When faced with application performance that doesn't make any sense, it is a good idea to review the SQL that is actually being run. This can be achieved by activating SQL_TRACE for the session of interest (or the database as a whole, if necessary). Remember also, that the view V$SQL will contain the recently run SQL statements.

In the V$SQL view, the column First_Load_Time can be especially useful in confirming exactly when a statement was first executed, by using that field as a search criterion. For instance, the script below retrieves all SQL for statements that were first run at 9:00 am:

```
SELECT Executions, Buffer_gets, Disk_reads, Sql_Text
FROM V$SQL
WHERE First_Load_Time like '%09:00%' ;
```

Tie Up Loose Ends

Assuming that the fix has been applied, and unforeseen results have not occured, it is important to follow-up and resolve any loose ends. In particular, the Oracle Magician should perform these two final steps:

- ❑ Document the solution.
- ❑ Close the loop with the customer.

Document the Solution

Once the fix is confirmed, it is appropriate to document the solution and inform the customer of the results. This simple step is important because the manager overseeing the case is often anxious to cross the item off his to-do list. Notification of the final solution helps everyone to understand that the problem has indeed been resolved.

401

In addition, the manager is probably getting some "heat" from upper management about solving this problem as soon as possible. Thus, documenting the solution is really helping your customer out in several ways.

When documenting a performance fix, I have found it helpful to list before and after statistics that clearly indicate the performance change. In other words, use *metrics*. Be sure to quantify the results in simple terms; make the performance summary understandable, and avoid mumbo-jumbo that only DBAs can interpret.

Without some clear metrics, it will be difficult, if not impossible, to quantify exactly how well you have done. How do you know *for sure* if the performance has improved? How will you know when you have met your tuning goals, and your work is finished? To answer questions such as these, it is important to document each step along the way, along with the new metric. This means that you should list the performance statistics before and after each change, along with the new execution plan. If you have made index changes, be sure to list these. In general, anything that has an impact on performance should be carefully documented, along with the new performance metric.

> **Document and quantify the performance improvement.**

The customer will appreciate a simple, concise explanation with accompanying evidence, because they are probably under pressure to report some type of results to upper management. With a nice, simple document, the customer can just copy and paste from your report into their *own* .

In the performance summary, it is not necessary to list some arcane statistic that only the DBAs will understand; for instance, most people will not appreciate jargon like *Buffer Gets* or *Cache Hit Ratio*. On the other hand, almost everyone can identify with the simple terms like *disk reads* or *run-time*.

Imagine, for instance, that you have been working on solving a (seemingly) tough problem for an accounting report. The accounting manager has been hovering around your desk, eagerly awaiting the solution. After examining the execution plans, you trace the problem to an index that everyone *assumed* was correctly defined, but which in fact was defined with the wrong columns.

After proper preparation, you drop the index, rebuild with the correct columns, and then confirm the solution. Everyone is satisfied that the problem has been solved. However, you wisely decide to go the final mile and provide the manager with a simple summary of the fix.

Although the problem has really been trivial from the DBA's standpoint, the customer did not think it was trivial; he or she deserves an explanation! Here is a sample performance summary that could be submitted:

Problem:	Audit Report runs too slow.
Before:	Report requires **1 hour** and requires **1 million** disk reads.
After:	Report finishes in **3 minutes** and requires **50** disk reads.
Solution:	Created index with proper columns for the `Accounts` table.

Note that this report is very simple and written in "layman's language." It did *not* use some technical buzzwords that only a DBA would understand:

> **When reporting, avoid technical terms that only a few technicians really understand.**

Performance Improvement Log

In addition to a simple report showing how the immediate problem was solved, it is also helpful to add other documentation that summarizes all the performance improvement steps. A table showing new run-times for various functions is probably the most helpful way of presenting it.

Once again, this step is beneficial to both the customer and the analyst. Naturally, the customer wants to see regular improvement (and to check whether they are getting their money's worth). This track record of performance improvement obviously benefits the Oracle analyst as well; by letting everyone see the results, he or she will begin to earn a reputation for competent performance analysis. Who can argue with success?

> **Post a chart showing the overall performance gains.**

The performance improvement log can be a simple table, listing run-time or other metrics, as shown in the following figure. The report could be posted on a nearby bulletin board, or even included on the firm's intranet:

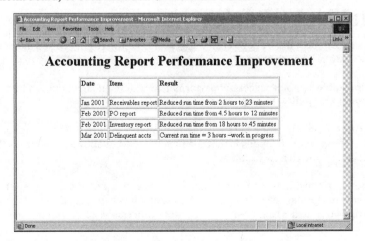

Accounting Report Performance Improvement

Date	Item	Result
Jan 2001	Receivables report	Reduced run time from 2 hours to 23 minutes
Feb 2001	PO report	Reduced run time from 4.5 hours to 12 minutes
Feb 2001	Inventory report	Reduced run time from 18 hours to 45 minutes
Mar 2001	Delinquent accts	Current run time = 3 hours —work in progress

Everyone likes to see progress, and here you are really only spreading the good news. In addition, a performance improvement log can be the start of a performance "portfolio" that provides objective proof of the analyst's performance tuning abilities – we'll return to this topic a little later.

Close the Loop with the Customer

After the magic has been performed, and the fix has been implemented, it is important to confirm that the customer is satisfied. That is, we intend to close the loop with the responsible manager, as well as the users of the application. We want to make sure that the problem that was solved is the one that they wanted solved.

At many companies, there is a formal problem-tracking system that should be updated. With these systems, you can document the steps taken to solve the problem, along with any special notes related to them. This is an excellent way to document the solution for future DBAs or developers.

We have now come full circle in our tuning process. Recall that we began with the step of careful listening to our "patient". The Oracle Physician asked the patient, "What seems to be trouble?" In that earlier stage, the Oracle analyst wanted to define the problem as accurately as possible; the goal was to delineate the real problem, as seen from the customer's perspective.

To be consistent then, we need to finish the tuning process in the same way, by focusing on what the customer thinks. In this final step of the Physician-to-Magician process, our new question is, "Was the problem solved?"

> **Confirm that the customer is happy with the solution.**

It's really just as simple as that. The ultimate goal of the Physician-to-Magician tuning approach is to hear the customer say: "Yes. The problem is solved."

Your Next Performance

At last! All the hard work has come together, and the result is a satisfied client. The customer has confirmed that the problem has been completely resolved.

This completion of a successful performance-tuning engagement is a huge boost for your credibility, but why stop there?

By careful planning, one big success will probably lead to further assignments. In fact, what usually happens is that the firm will be so happy with your results, they will assign you to new problems.

Whether a consultant or a permanent employee, the performance analyst thrives on new performance challenges. Let's look at a few key steps that will facilitate getting your next assignment to solve that "impossible" performance problem.

Publish your Lessons-Learned

Your Oracle colleagues will probably be very interested to hear about an intricate performance case. That tough performance puzzle that took many days to solve will probably prove to be an fascinating read for others in the field. Why not take the time to write it up?

Once again, this is a good win-win situation; both the writer and the readers will benefit.

First of all, by writing up your case, you will consolidate your understanding of the principles used; you will gain an even better knowledge of the methods you used (or how to do even better next time). Readers may point out possible solutions that you have overlooked, or different ways to use the technology. All of these responses can only help you to become an even better Oracle tuning expert and, of course, the publicity from a published article might also come in handy.

Besides the benefit to the writer of a tuning article, the readers will gain insight into sound tuning tactics. Almost all DBAs and designers are interested in learning about new tricks or clever methods to improve performance. Performance tuning is always a hot topic; of special interest are any suggestions about how to use new database features. Many software engineers would like to know if the new database feature really works as advertised.

Even if you decide not to submit your article for formal publication, it is always a good idea to consider writing a white paper. If nothing else, the document will serve as a valuable technical reference for future projects.

Create a Performance Portfolio

Every professional artist has a portfolio to illustrate his or her best work: why not do the same thing? A proficient Oracle tuning expert can build an impressive performance portfolio. This document need not be large; it can be as simple as a single binder that documents the substantial performance gains achieved for various applications and customers.

Such a portfolio's value is twofold. Firstly, it provides objective facts that attest to the analyst's skills by showing that they are not just theoretically capable, but have actually demonstrated performance tuning skills. The cases are listed in black and white; who can argue with the facts? A past record of substantial achievement is far more important to the customer than training, degrees, or certification that may have been earned. Those types of accomplishments are fine, but they suggest only possible competence; they don't really prove that the analyst is capable of solving a tough performance problem:

> **Demonstrated performance tuning is far more impressive than training or certificates.**

Secondly, in addition to providing evidence of performance tuning prowess, the performance portfolio also indicates the quantitative measures of improvement. Showing metrics of improvement is a wise decision, because that is exactly what most managers want to see – they want to know how much faster their particular application can run.

Most managers are interested in time statistics, such as the elapsed time to run certain functions of their application. For billing programs, the units of this time metric are typically hours; for OLTP systems, such as customer care applications, this means seconds.

A sample page from a performance portfolio is shown below. Here, we simply explain, in layman's terms, what performance improvements have been accomplished. It is not necessary to delve into a lot of detail; rather, emphasize the before and after numbers:

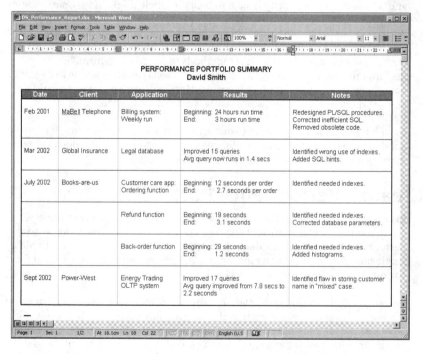

The DBA or designer who has a detailed performance portfolio will gain instant credibility. The citations in the portfolio show that the analyst indeed knows how to use SQL hints, or how to build a histogram, or how to trace a session. In short, the performance portfolio shows the reader that you really know what you are doing – you must be an Oracle Magician!

Summary

We have now reached the end of our performance. The curtain has fallen, the lights have come on, and the happy audience is streaming out of the exits. While the audience is chatting about the evening's feats, let's review what we learned in this chapter.

First of all, we saw how to set the stage. The solution should be tested adequately, the database backed up, and consideration given to possible consequences for the production user. These steps ensure that there are no unpleasant surprises.

After this, the actual magic of implementing the solution should be an easy feat. Everything should have been incorporated into a script, so there really shouldn't be much else to do except run it. Of course, the Oracle Magician will not be surprised by how smoothly everything goes; the act will have been thoroughly rehearsed beforehand, so a positive outcome is almost a certainty.

With the solution in place, the Oracle Magician closes the loop with the audience. It is critical to wrap up the performance by touching base with the customer. Just as the Oracle Physician earlier asked the customer to describe the problem, the Oracle Magician now asks the customer whether they are *satisfied* with the solution.

We have seen that it is helpful for both the customer and himself that the Oracle analyst summarizes how the performance problem was corrected. The client is usually curious as to why the problem existed, and how they can prevent a reoccurrence. This summary also validates the work that the Oracle analyst has performed. It tells the customer they've won, and that this was time and money well spent.

For his next performance, the Oracle analyst follows up a successful tuning engagement by documenting the lessons learned from an interesting performance problem. This documentation can easily be turned into a white paper for publication in a technical journal, presented at an Oracle conference or local user group, or simply kept for future reference.

Of course, the other big winner is the performance analyst himself. Whether DBA, designer, or developer, a competent performance tuning analyst earns the gratitude and respect of his or her customers. After implementing a fix for a tough performance problem, there is nothing quite like hearing the user say, "Wow! How did you do that?"

There are very few fields in any profession today that offer such positive and meaningful words of appreciation: for the Oracle Magician, that's the *real* magic.

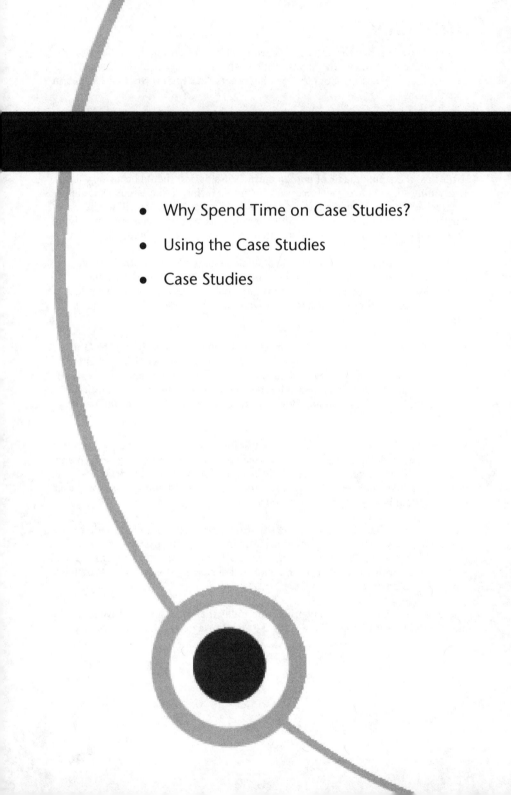

- Why Spend Time on Case Studies?
- Using the Case Studies
- Case Studies

14

Case Studies

In this final chapter, we present real-life database performance problems, each providing a unique challenges. These cases represent some of the most instructive scenarios that the author has encountered. After reading a book on Oracle performance tuning, the reader will, hopefully, find it useful to test his or her analytical skills on some real problems.

Most of these cases occurred on critical production systems, where it was important that the analyst reach a sound resolution fairly promptly. All the cases were eventually solved – some quickly, others over several days. For the most critical production cases, the problem was typically resolved in just a few hours. Some of the cases, however, showed up on low-priority development systems, where the DBA or designer had the luxury of pondering the problem for several days.

Depending on your personal experience, some of the puzzles presented here may seem trivial or commonplace; other cases will certainly seem bizarre. Note that most of the cases have a simple explanation and a simple resolution. I hope that the reader finds these puzzles as much fun and as challenging as did the author.

Why Spend Time on Case Studies?

As we have seen in this book, the Oracle performance analyst is part scientist and part artist. Many problems they are faced with demand solutions requiring creativity and perspective. Much of this creativity and breadth of understanding is experience gained from solving difficult, or even crazy cases; this suggests that the analyst with the broadest experience will be the best Oracle Magician.

This observation also explains why the best tuning experts are always on the lookout for ways to stretch and learn new ways to handle difficult problems. In fact, the very best performance analysts look forward to difficult performance challenges. These new challenges help the analyst test and hone his skills. New puzzles also give the analyst a more diverse set of tools to use in solving database problems.

Case studies are an important way to share experiences and ideas. Each analyst has a unique set of experiences and biases; what one DBA thinks is obvious, another will not. What one designer thinks is a great design, another might regard as terrible. Clearly, when we analyze a problem, we each draw upon a different background and different skills. By sharing these skills and ideas, everyone wins.

All these cases are based on true events. I hope that each of these database mysteries presents an enjoyable challenge for the reader.

Using the Case Studies

Please note that the solution provided is really just one possible answer; it happens to be the answer that the author chose, but it may not be the best one. In fact, it is very likely that the reader will uncover a different, and even better solution. Keep in mind, also, that as database versions change, the possibilities will vary slightly.

To get the most from these case studies, I recommend that the reader first review each case thoroughly, and spend some time pondering the problem before turning to the solution.

Let's now take a look at our first case study:

Case Study 1: The Disobedient Hint

A few designers at a dot-com firm were trying to solve a perplexing problem for a data warehouse application. Each night, several programs were run to load the previous day's data into the warehouse. The application made extensive use of Perl scripts. When the program needed to access the database, the Perl script read-in a separate SQL file, prepared the transaction or query, then called a Perl library function to execute the SQL.

Here was the problem: a developer had made a slight change (added a simple SQL hint) to a SQL file. The new hint simply requested that the optimizer use parallel degree 5 for the query. Now, every time the data load was run, the program bombed out at this routine.

The error message indicated that the newly added SQL comment was not correctly terminated; however, the format used for the hint was the same format as previously used!

Here is the SQL that was being run:

```
SQL> INSERT /*+ APPEND */
  2  INTO Lesson_Page_Progress (
  3  Student_Id,
  4  Course_Id,
  5  Lesson_Pages)
  6  SELECT /*+ PARALLEL (Sh 5) */
```

```
 7  Sh.Student_Id, Sh.Course_Id,
 8  COUNT (DISTINCT Sh.Page_Id) Lesson_Pages
 9  FROM Student_History Sh
10 GROUP BY Sh.Student_Id, Sh.Course_Id;
```

Both the developer and the DBA reviewed the script several times; both confirmed that the syntax was exactly correct. To check it even further, the DBA copied the entire SQL from the file, and ran the command directly in SQL*Plus. Everything worked fine!

Since the SQL was actually read-in and interpreted from a Perl script, there was only one thing left to do; call the SQL script from Perl. Therefore, the DBA decided to build a very short Perl script wrapper that just did one thing, run the problem SQL script.

While building the script, however, the DBA noticed something peculiar about the Perl code that was used in production. Here is the relevant portion of the Perl script:

```
while (<SQL>) {
    next if (/^(#|--)/);        # skip whole line comments
    next if (/^$/);             # skip blank lines
    s/[;\/]\s+\Z//;             # delete trailing ';' or '/'
    $sql_command .= $_;
}
close SQL;
```

What was causing Oracle to reject the SQL hint?

Solution

The Perl script used in production removes certain portions of the SQL before submitting to the database engine for processing. In particular, it removes comments, blank lines, and the / symbol (run command) that is included at the end of a SQL script.

Notice, in the Perl presented above, that the script is designed to remove the slash symbol, / when it is the last character on a line. This was a seemingly reasonable idea of the script designer, because the / symbol is not really a SQL statement, but just the command to run the script.

Note, however, that the / symbol is often used to terminate a comment. So, the line that reads:

```
SELECT /*+ PARALLEL (sh 5) */
```

will be changed by the Perl script to read:

```
SELECT /*+ PARALLEL (sh 5) *
```

Of course, the syntax in the line above is incorrect, since the trailing / symbol is missing. The Oracle parser reads the altered line, and correctly flags the comment as being incomplete.

Once the cause of the incorrect syntax was identified, the solution was simple. The line that ended with the / character was modified so that the SQL on the next line was brought back one line. The new line looked like this:

```
SELECT /*+ PARALLEL (sh 5) */ sh.student_id,
```

The functionality is identical, and now the Perl script does not see a trailing / symbol. This completely corrected the problem. From that point on, the SQL hint was accepted.

Case Study 2: Running Ahead of Schedule

A medium-sized educational services firm provided online training classes for various corporations. As part of this service, the training administrator for the customer could request a training status report. There were about six standard reports that could be run. For instance, a typical report might show the number of students who were enrolled in a class, and how many students achieved a passing score on the quizzes.

These reports were dynamically generated using the Actuate report utility. (Actuate is a third-party application used to build user reports for web access.) Each time a report was requested, the Actuate report server formulated the report request, and then submitted a query to the data warehouse database.

The training company wanted to deliver this type of status reports very rapidly – no more than five seconds. This goal was achievable for most customers; for a few large customers, however, the quantity of information was so large that a few minutes was required to extract the data and format for viewing over the Internet.

Normally, data warehouse reports queries can be expedited by preparing summary tables, which contain pre-built aggregate information. In this way, the information is only prepared once, and all reports can make use of the summary tables to expedite the process greatly. In this case, however, the design team quickly realized that database aggregates could never eliminate this delay. Database-specific changes would miss the real root cause of the problem.; for these particular reports, the amount of information requested was very large – it was more than just a brief summary.

The bottleneck was not due to database delays but, rather, due to the time for the report server to process such a huge amount of data. The database was able to extract the data fairly quickly, but then the report server choked on the huge amount of information. Clearly, a more radical solution would be needed.

What step could be taken to vastly speed-up these reports?

Solution

The lead designer on the project, Steve, understood the concept of pre-built summaries. Realizing that a summary at the database level would not solve the problem, he took the concept of pre-built aggregates one step further.

Steve suggested that the entire report for the largest customers be pre-run, and stored on the report server. That is, instead of just pre-building a data aggregate, we would pre-build the entire report. Then, each time the report was requested, the pre-built version would automatically be used.

This innovative solution almost seemed like cheating. The idea was even better than the summary table method. With Steve's approach, the database would not even be accessed for the large reports!

This solution was immediately accepted. The design group created a cron job to pre-build all customer reports with a size over a certain threshold. Each report would be built well before the busy morning hours. The exact run-time of the report building process was not particularly important, since it would be performed off-hours.

This alternative was a huge success. The load on the database was greatly reduced, and the large customers all got their reports nearly instantaneously.

Case Study 3: Sleazy SQL

A large publishing/shipping firm was using an MRP system very similar to Oracle Manufacturing (part of the Oracle Applications suite of software designed by Oracle Corporation). For this application, the database stores a variety of detailed inventory information, such as stock on hand, part number, vendors, and so on.

Although the application was working as advertised, the users reported that certain common operations were very slow. They asked the DBA supporting the application to see what he could do to speed things up a little.

The DBA decided that he needed more information. Thus, he used the following script to list the top resource consumers on the database:

```
SQL> SELECT Sql_Text, Disk_Reads, Buffer_Gets
  2  FROM V$SQL
  3  WHERE Disk_Reads/Executions > 1000;
```

This SQL simply listed the statistics for those statements that consumed over 1000 disk reads per execution. It yielded just one troublesome SQL statement, with these stats:

```
Disk_Reads Per Execution    = 5,000
Buffer_Gets Per Execution   = 5,100
```

With these facts in hand, it was then necessary to look at the SQL in question to see what was going on. It was not difficult to discover why the statement was running so badly; the SQL had been accidentally written to ensure the worst possible performance by making index usage totally impossible.

Here is the form of the troublesome SQL statement:

```
SQL> SELECT *
   2  FROM Inventory
   3  WHERE NVL (Col_W) = NVL (:1)
   4  AND NVL (Col_X) = NVL (:2)
   5  AND NVL (Col_Y) = NVL (:3)
   6  AND NVL (Col_Z) = NVL (:4);
```

The Inventory table had about 25,000 rows; due to the NVL function, Oracle would have to perform a full table scan every time the SQL was executed. In most cases, this would in turn translate as a large number of disk reads.

After spotting the incorrect SQL formulation, the DBA requested that the developers alter the SQL statement to eliminate the Nvl functions. In response, the DBA was advised that no changes were authorized for this program, as "No resources were available to make the changes".

If the application can't be changed, what can be done to improve performance of this SQL statement?

Solution

The DBA decided to cache the table! In other words, he decided to keep the table in memory at all times. The command to do this is simple:

```
ALTER Table Inventory Cache;
```

Normally, blocks from full-table scans are designated for rapid age-out; otherwise, the churning of these blocks would wipe out the database cache with huge rates of block turnover. When the table is cached, however, the database engine treats these blocks as normal blocks, so that they don't immediately leave the cache. (Note that implementing the Keep Buffer Pool would have achieved the same thing.)

Of course, this step was not intended to reduce logical reads; as expected, the logical reads remained constant, but the disk reads per execution were reduced to near zero.

Since the database cache was partly used up by this step, the DBA slightly increased the init.ora parameter DB_BLOCK_BUFFERS. This increase to the buffer cache compensated for the cached Inventory table that now permanently consumed a few megabytes of database cache.

Case Study 4: The Reluctant Index

The lead DBA for a distribution company was asked to analyze and tune a manufacturing database. This assignment was a little unusual because the users and database were in Australia. A quick analysis (using the usual V$SQL view) revealed one particularly bothersome SQL statement. Investigation showed that this single query was responsible for most of the performance degradation.

The SQL was very simple, and looked like this:

```
SQL> SELECT Inventory_Level, Inventory_Name
  2  FROM Products
  3  WHERE Inventory_Code = '123456';
```

In this query, the search criterion in the WHERE clause was nearly ideal; due to the data distribution, a query based on an Inventory_Code of 123456 would return very few rows. Clearly, an index would be a great option for the optimizer to use for this query.

The DBA quickly created a new index on the Inventory_Code column. Additionally, the Products table was freshly analyzed (just in case).

To the surprise of the DBA, the database consistently refused to use this index, and insisted on always making the wrong decision – full table scans. The DBA thought of using a SQL hint to encourage index usage, but the third-party application could not be changed.

How can the optimizer be persuaded to use an index for this query?

Solution

Further research showed that the values for this particular field (Inventory_Code) were very skewed. In addition, the table contained only a few different values for this column. Thus, even though this particular query was a good candidate for using an index, the optimizer did not know that. In general, a full table scan would indeed be the best choice if the only search criteria were Inventory_Code.

Recall that the Oracle optimizer, not having any special information, can only assume a uniform data distribution. In this case, that assumption was completely wrong.

The DBA also suspected that the data distribution for several other columns was similarly skewed. Thus, the DBA decided to build a histogram on all the indexed columns – just in case the optimizer was making a wrong decision for other SQL statements as well.

The command used to build these histograms was:

```
SQL> ANALYZE TABLE Products COMPUTE STATISTICS
  2   FOR ALL INDEXED COLUMNS;
```

This command built several histograms, each of which used the default value of 75 buckets. With this extra information, the optimizer realized the unique distribution of values for this column; thus, it made the correct decision to use an index. No change to the application was needed.

Case Study 5: The Hanging Database

I was part of a DBA support team for a large phone company. I divided my time between performance tuning and more routine maintenance activities, such as working on backups. There were about 8 DBAs on the team altogether.

To everyone's consternation, there was one very large (and unsolved) problem on the Oracle database: At random intervals, the database would simply hang. When this occurred, all database usage simply stopped. There were no trace files, and nothing unusual in the alert log.

The initial symptoms of this problem were very embarrassing for the DBAs. Suddenly, without any warning, there would be no response to any new connection request; additionally, over 1,000 existing database connections would simply hang. The only known correction was to abort all existing connections and restart the instance.

As a result of our failure to solve this issue speedily, the DBAs on the support team got to know some of the senior IT management on a first name basis. Management was very interested in "helping" the DBAs to correct this problem.

When the problem first occurred, the lead DBA notified Oracle Support, and asked that this issue be assigned priority number one. Oracle Corporation was very co-operative, and enlisted experts from across the world to investigate this serious issue. Unfortunately, the Oracle experts were (temporarily) puzzled by this as well.

Finally, early one morning, one DBA happened to be using a popular utility called OEM (Oracle Enterprise Manager) Lock Manager. The DBA noticed that a batch job was suddenly blocking about 25 other users on the production database. As the DBA was monitoring this, and trying to get additional details, the lead DBA announced that the infamous hang had occurred.

With this information, Oracle Australia recommended checking for correct indexes. This insightful suggestion led to the solution.

How did index problems hang the database?

Solution

Oracle Australia was correct in suggesting we look for missing indexes. To understand why, it is necessary to explain indexing practice when RI (referential integrity) is used.

Generally speaking, it is always advisable to build an index on a foreign key. The purpose of the index is to avoid locking the entire table during an update. Depending on the exact version of the database, an update on a table with RI can block the other table.

For instance, in some versions of Oracle, updates of the referenced column in the parent table completely block updates on child. Note that even in the very recent Oracle releases, where there have been substantial improvements in the locking mechanism, Oracle still recommends that foreign keys be indexed.

In the database of interest, there were hundreds of foreign keys in the database; each of these should have been indexed. Almost all of these columns had indexes, but a few did not, which was a violation of good design practice.

When a certain batch program was run (the same session that was observed blocking the other users), locking increased rapidly, and dozens of users were prevented from completing their transactions. The number of locks quickly grew so large that; the database engine became completely overwhelmed by the huge number of locks, and was unable to function. This meant that all users were eventually frozen, not just the ones who were blocked due to the missing index.

Once the proper indexes were created on all the foreign keys, the problem completely disappeared.

Case Study 6: The Odd Package

At a firm that specializes in supply-chain management, a new manufacturing application was installed on a medium-sized Sun server. A small database was then created for testing purposes.

At first, the application ran well, and there were no problems. Then, when the users began to try a few of the new features, they would sometimes receive an odd error message about insufficient memory for a PL/SQL package. Whenever the users saw this error message, the application failed, and they had to restart their work.

The odd thing about this problem was that the new functions sometimes worked without any problem; the errors seemed almost random. The one constant thread was that the problem always related to a PL/SQL package and memory.

The DBA investigated, and retrieved a sample trace file that had been produced at the time of one of the errors. The trace file indicated that a PL/SQL package was not able to fit in memory. It further suggested that an increase in the shared pool would be appropriate. The DBA complied, but even with a fairly sizeable shared pool (100 MB), the problem still happened occasionally.

The DBA was reluctant to increase the shared pool further without understanding why the problem was occurring. Besides, a shared pool of 100 MB should have been large enough for such a simple application.

What can be done to allow the PL/SQL package to fit in memory?

Solution

A more detailed analysis revealed that the application was much more complicated than earlier thought; for instance, the application used about 20 massive PL/SQL packages. Some of these packages were five times the Standard PL/SQL package that is supplied with the database.

Research showed that depending on the exact application usage, a new PL/SQL package might not fit into memory when requested. For instance, at any one time there might be a large number of small PL/SQL packages already in memory; these smaller objects were apparently fragmenting the memory allocation, not leaving a big enough chunk for the big package.

The solution was to keep the largest packages in memory, so that there would never be a question about them fitting. The small PL/SQL procedures would probably fit every time, due to their much reduced memory requirement.

The DBA built a simple script to pin the memory-intensive packages in the shared pool after RDBMS startup. For the database version in use, the command used to pin an object in memory is:

```
SQL> EXECUTE Sys.Dbms_Shared_Pool.Keep ('OBJECT_NAME');
```

But first, the DBA had to find the PL/SQL objects that needed pinning. After the application had been running for several hours, he decided to list those objects that required more than 100 KB of memory. Here is the script that was used to list these big packages:

```
SQL> SELECT Owner, Name, Sharable_Mem
  2    FROM V$DB_OBJECT_CACHE
  3   WHERE Sharable_Mem > 100000;
```

Finally, the DBA decided to create a SQL script that would build another SQL script. This first "SQL to make SQL" script would be run with the output spooled as pin.sql. The second script, pin.sql, would then be run after each database restart to perform the actual pinning. (Note that with Oracle 8i and Oracle 9i, a special trigger, AFTER STARTUP, can be used to run a procedure right after database restart.)

Here is what the first script looked like:

```
SELECT 'Execute
sys.dbms_shared_pool.keep
('||''''||owner||'.'||name|'''' ||');'
FROM V$Db_Object_Cache
WHERE Sharable_Mem > 100000
AND TYPE NOT IN ('VIEW', 'SYNONYM', 'TABLE')
AND NAME NOT LIKE '%SHARED_POOL%';
```

This script finds the large packages (over 100,000 KB in size), and prepares the commands to pin each package. (The extra single quote marks were necessary to produce single quote marks in the output spool file.) The output of this script was then run each time the database was re-started. In this way, the huge PL/SQL packages were immediately inserted into memory. This eliminated any more error messages, and the users were able to use the application without any further interruptions.

Case Study 7: The Slow Physician

At the largest HMO (Health Maintenance Organization) in the world, a DBA was analyzing a performance problem on a new electronic medical record application. The users had complained about some functions that ran slowly, and they called in the DBA to resolve the problem.

Queries from the V$SQL view revealed one particularly slow SQL statement, which was related to a database view for Co-signed medical treatment. This was a common function in the application, so a delay in this feature would have a substantial impact on the overall system performance.

The SQL statement in question was very simple in form, but was causing about 3000 disk reads for each execution. Here is how it looked:

```
SELECT *
FROM COSIGN_VIEW
WHERE Doctor_Id = 'DR. MCKENZIE';
```

The only complication in this SQL was the object COSIGN_VIEW that was actually a join of 2 tables (DOCS and COSIGN), joined on the column Patient_id. By substituting the view definition, the DBA was able to see what work the database engine really had to do. In essence, then, the query was really this:

```
SQL> SELECT *
  2    FROM DOCS D, COSIGN C
  3    WHERE D.Patient_Id = C.Patient_Id
  4    AND D.Doctor_id = 'DR.MCKENZIE';
```

Obviously, there was only one filtering criterion – that the Doctor_Id must match DR.MCKENZIE. In the table Docs, the column Doctor_Id was already indexed, and the data for that column was very well distributed. Thus, any query of the table Docs should have used the index on the Doctor_Id column (and not a full table scan).

The perplexing thing was that whenever the view was referenced, the optimizer refused to use the index on the Doctor_Id column. If the two tables were explicitly listed (instead of the view), the index was used!

The DBA confirmed that the index was valid; he also confirmed that statistics had been properly generated.

Why did the view cause the optimizer to make the wrong choice?

419

Solution

Everything seemed to point to a problem with the view, because everything worked normally as long as the view was excluded. The view was definitely valid, but the DBA decided to check the exact view definition.

Using the Oracle OEM utility, Schema Manager, to list the view definition, the DBA made a startling discovery; the columns in the view definition did not match the corresponding columns in the underlying tables!

The script to create the view switched column names, so that column Doctor_Id in the view did not match column Doctor_Id in the table! This meant that the index on the Doctor_Id column in the Docs table was completely irrelevant, since the search criterion was actually for a different column!

To clarify, let's look at the query again:

```
SELECT *
FROM COSIGN_VIEW
WHERE Doctor_Id = 'DR. MCKENZIE';
```

Substituting the underlying tables, the DBA (wrongly) assumed that this was equivalent to the following, where he assumed a match with Doctor_Id in table Docs:

```
SELECT *
FROM DOCS D, COSIGN C
WHERE D.Patient_Id = C.Patient_id
AND D.Doctor_Id = 'DR. MCKENZIE';
```

But, in reality, Doctor_Id in Cosign_View matches Emp_Id, so the actual equivalent SQL is different:

```
SELECT *
FROM DOCS D, COSIGN C
WHERE D.Patient_id = C.Patient_id
AND D.Emp_id = 'DR. MCKENZIE';
```

Thus, an index is in fact needed on the column Emp_Id. Once this index was added, the query was greatly expedited.

Of course, the real problem in this case was not really the index, but the terribly deceptive step of creating a column name in the view that did not actually correspond to the same name in the underlying table. This poor design led to many hours of bewilderment on the part of the DBA.

Case Study 8: The Failing Failover

While assisting a customer service center, I occasionally helped with a database for a very critical customer support application. This particular database was definitely a HA (High Availability) system, in which 24 x 7 operation was crucial. Each month, there were millions of customer interactions that made use of the database.

HA was achieved using IBM's HACMP high-availability clustering software. With this system, any hardware glitch causes immediate failover to a backup node; a shared file system then shifts automatically from one node to another. When this occurs, there is just a brief (say, one minute) interruption in service.

For this particular setup, the original DBAs had used raw devices, rather than a cooked file system. This was done because the designers wanted to be prepared for OPS (Oracle Parallel Server), which requires raw devices. The system had not been changed to OPS (and that idea had been shelved); thus, the raw devices were really an unnecessary leftover.

In this database, each .dbf file that was known to the database was really just a symbolic link to the actual data on the raw device. For instance, Oracle used a temp file on the local disk system, called temp01.dbf; in reality, however, temp01.dbf was not really a file, but just a link.

This same idea was applied to all the .dbf files. For example, here is how four sample files would be arranged:

```
Local filename              raw device (on shared file system)
/u04/oradata/data01.dbf  >  /dev/r001
/u04/oradata/data02.dbf  >  /dev/r002
/u04/oradata/data03.dbf  >  /dev/r003
/u04/oradata/data04.dbf  >  /dev/r004
```

The raw devices were located on the disk system that was shared between the two nodes in the failover cluster. Upon failover, the raw devices would then automatically move over to the other node.

This arrangement necessitated that each node have a symbolic link for every local filename to point to the raw device. Thus, whenever a new file was added to the database, a new link had to be added from the local file name to the raw device. Of course, this link would have to be added to both nodes, so that upon failover, Oracle could find all the files.

One morning, disaster struck; there had been a failure on the primary node, and the secondary node failed to start the database! A critical application was down!

Upon startup, Oracle complained of a missing data file; however, investigation showed that all file systems were mounted!

Why is the backup node complaining of a missing file?

Solution

All file systems were indeed mounted; the HA software had done its job correctly. The DBA noticed, however, that the missing file in question was simply not there. Had someone deleted it?

Fortunately, no one had removed any files. Recall that each .dbf file is not supposed to be there – only a symbolic link is supposed to be present. Each node was supposed to have symbolic links pointing from nice-looking paths to the actual location of raw device. For example, the link for the file data01.dbf should look something like this:

```
/u04/oradata/data01.dbf  > /dev/r001
```

Normally, the database ran on the primary node, and the primary node had all the required symbolic links; the backup node, however, was missing two symbolic links due to a DBA oversight. This meant that whenever the database tried to start on the backup node, Oracle would not be able to find two database files. Unfortunately, with this overly complicated arrangement, any missing links would never be noticed until the very moment they were needed (in other words, just after a failover).

The moral of the story is that high reliability hardware is only as good as the weakest link. In this case, it was imperative that the DBAs update the symbolic links on both nodes each time a new .dbf file was added. Clearly, this arrangement was very susceptible to human error; one slight omission completely destroyed the high-availability plan.

Once the missing links were created, the database started up properly. This case illustrates the mistake of using an overly complicated solution; there was no reason to be using raw devices. That decision, along with the tricky symbolic link business, made the entire application much less reliable.

Case Study 9: The Impatient Insurance Agent

At an insurance company in San Francisco, a team of consultants was working to build a new billing application. This application was designed to review and correlate the incoming customer billing information, which was called Responses. The application would store this information in the Response table, and then associate the data with the matching policies (in the Policy table).

One particular query was not running well; this listed the details for expired insurance policies. Although the query only returned 50 rows, it was taking two minutes to finish. The DBA agreed to investigate, since the run time seemed excessive for such a small result set.

The query was just a simple join of two large tables: Response and Policy. Each of these tables has several million rows. The form of the query was like this:

```
SQL> SELECT P.Policy_Id, R.Resp_Date, P.Cust_Name,
  2  P.Cust_Phone, P.Cust_Address, P.Cust_City
  3  FROM Response R, Policy P
```

```
 4  WHERE R.Policy_Id = P.Policy_Id
 5  AND R.Col1 = 'abc'
 6  AND R.col2 = 'def'
 7  AND R.col3 = 'ghi'
 8  AND R.col4 = 'jkl'
 9  AND R.col5 = 'mno'
10  AND P.col1 = 'xyz';
```

What makes this query unusual is the criteria in the WHERE clause. Although the entire result set is very small, the result set from just one of the tables is very large; that is, the filtering criteria on the two tables only reduce the result set when combined.

Here is a summary of the result set for the search criteria:

```
Response table            Policy table
5 where-clause 'filters'  1 'filter'
Result set: 20,000 rows   Result set: 15,000 rows
```

Tuning of this SQL statement thus presented a challenge. How could the large intermediate result sets be bypassed?

Normally, a join begins with the table that has the most restrictive filtering criteria. In this case, however, neither table filters out many rows; thus, no matter which table we choose as the driving table, the initial result set will be at least 15,000 rows (and thus wreck the performance).

The above facts are consistent with a two-minute response time. Clearly, something clever would have to be done, but what?

How can the database engine avoid processing tens of thousands of rows?

Solution

In some ways, this problem is like tuning a join in a star schema; the final result set is small, but the filters from any one table are not very selective. One needs to somehow jump to the final result set without wading through all the intermediate rows.

The method in this case is to break the processing into two main steps. In the first step, we retrieve only the Policy_Id keys that meet all the search criteria. Since we only need one field, this can be done very rapidly with indexes. (We made use of a super index that included the search criteria in the leading columns and the Policy_Id in the final column.) Since this step requires no table access whatsoever, this query runs extremely fast. Remember also that this result will only be about 50 keys.

For a reminder on super indexes, see Chapter 11.

423

In the second step, we use the list of keys from step one to repeat the query, this time retrieving all the fields required to satisfy the query. That is, we repeat the query, but we only need to use the 50 keys already found in step one.

Here is a summary of the exact implementation steps:

1. Perform a join that uses all the query filters, but retrieve only the key (`Policy_Id`) that is used as the join column. Use this small result set as the starting point in another join.

2. Join to the `Policy` and `Response` tables, repeating the query just to get the rest of the columns needed.

Here is the entire query:

```
SQL> SELECT P.Policy_Id, R.Resp_Date, P.Cust_Name,
  2  P.Cust_Phone, P.Cust_Address, P.Cust_City
  3  FROM (SELECT P1.Policy_Id FROM Response R1, Policy P1
  4  WHERE R1.Policy_Id = P1.Policy_Id
  5  AND R1.Col1 = 'abc'
  6  AND R1.col2 = 'def'
  7  AND R1.col3 = 'ghi'
  8  AND R1.col4 = 'jkl'
  9  AND R1.col5 = 'mno'
 10  AND P1.col1 = 'xyz') PART1,
 11  Response R, Policy P
 12  WHERE R.Policy_Id = P.Policy_Id
 13  AND PART1.Policy_Id = R.Policy_Id;
```

Note that the pre-processing step above is called PART1. This inline view returns only the small set of policy numbers that meet the search criteria; it is the driving table in the query. Note also that we had to include a join condition from PART1 to one of the other tables.

In essence, the query is actually performed twice – the first time to get the keys for the final result set (about 50 rows), the second time to get the selected columns for just these 50 rows. By employing this pre-processing step, the entire query time was reduced by 90%.

Case Study 10: All Primary Keys Are Equal?

In application tuning, it is sometimes necessary for the analyst to lure the optimizer into using certain indexes. It is not always possible to use SQL hints, because the application may be under the control of a third party. The owner of the application code may not be responsive to tuning suggestions, or may simply not want to spend the resources to investigate the suggestions. Also, in rare cases, the optimizer may even refuse to obey the hint; the analyst knows what the best execution plan is, but the optimizer refuses to comply.

This case once again involves a large insurance company, and a large database (version 8.0.4). This particular release had provided very reliable performance; like all database versions, however, the optimizer had certain preferences and biases.

The query that needed performance help involved a join to a table called `Policy`. The join to the `Policy` table was on the column `Policy_Id`, which was also the primary key.

The key factor in this case is the observation that the Oracle optimizer likes certain indexes, because they are typically faster to use than others. The optimizer's favorite index is an index on the primary key.

In our particular query, then, the optimizer always wanted to use the primary key index to perform this join. In this instance, however, the primary key index was really not the best choice. The best performance required that Oracle use an index built on two columns – the primary key plus another column. (The second column made it possible to avoid a table access because the entire query could then be satisfied by the index alone.)

The DBA created the new composite index, but the optimizer would not co-operate. The optimizer foolishly insisted on using the primary key index; it would not budge – even when a SQL hint was added.

How can we convince the optimizer to use the concatenated index?

Solution

In this case, the DBA needed a way to lure the optimizer into not using the primary key index but, instead, use the extra column index. This was particularly difficult because the primary key index is the number one choice of the optimizer. This bias is very understandable; after all, what could be better than an index on the primary key?

The tactic in this case was to make the primary key index look less favorable, so that the other index could be used. To accomplish this, we disguised the primary key index as just a unique index.

The DBA observed that whenever a primary key was created, the primary key would make use of an existing unique index, and treat it as the primary key index. Then, when determining the execution plan, the optimizer would treat this index as if it were just a unique index, not a primary key index. In other words, the primary key index would be given a slightly lower preference than normal.

With this background, the fix for this case was simple. The DBA:

1. Dropped the primary key

2. Built a matching unique index

3. Added the primary key again

The optimizer no longer stubbornly insisted on using the primary key index, because it was no longer a true, pedigreed primary key index. It was merely a unique index.

425

Case Study 11: The Phantom Users

While consulting at a medium-sized shipping company, I was informed that there was a performance problem at one of the firm's remote sites in Sydney, Australia. I had had good success with tuning some SQL statements on the U.S. databases, so management suggested that I take a look at the international databases as well.

Following my usual practice, I queried the view V$SQL to find all resource-intensive SQL statements. This query revealed several oft-run statements that often were consuming large amounts of disk reads. These statements were run multiple times per hour, so a correction would probably have a substantial effect on the entire system.

The SQL statements were easily analyzed; this was a simple case of a few missing indexes, which were soon created. Naturally, I wanted to confirm that the queries now ran well, so I re-ran my script to check the statistics in the V$SQL view. I was expecting to see executions happening each hour, but with just a few associated disk reads. This would prove that the queries were properly using the new indexes.

I queried the V$SQL view several times, but the statistics were precisely the same. The statistics showed exactly the same number of executions as before. I continued to query the view over the next 4 hours, but the execution statistics showed no change. It was almost as though the database knew that I wanted confirmation, so it refused to provide any new execution statistics.

I pondered this enigma for several more hours, until I realized that nothing whatsoever was wrong.

What did the DBA finally realize?

Solution

Nothing was wrong because the query was not being run – the users were still asleep! The database was in Sydney, Australia, where it was still 5:00 A.M.

Summary

I hope you have enjoyed reading the case studies presented in this final chapter. Each of these cases was very puzzling for whoever was involved at the time, but they all taught me something extra about being a good DBA, and how to find creative solutions to tough problems. I have no doubt that many of you have discovered even better solutions to the problems discussed here.

By working through actual examples and challenging case studies, I believe it's possible for the DBA to really broaden his or her capabilities. Learning new features or methods is often very hard work, but the end result is worth the extra effort.

Oracle performance tuning really is an exciting and rewarding profession. I hope you are as eager as I am to learn even more. In addition to reading books and articles, a good next-step would be to join your local Oracle user group. I think you will find your involvement with these groups to be a profitable move, both professionally and personally. Why not share your ideas with others? By relating your experience, everyone benefits.

Finally, I hope you find the Physician-to-Magician approach useful in solving many of the performance problems you tackle.

- V$LOCK

- V$PROCESS

- V$SESSION

- V$SQL

- Wait Event Views

    - V$EVENT_NAME

    - V$SESSION_EVENT

    - V$SESSION_WAIT

    - V$SYSTEM_EVENT

Useful V$ View Definitions

This appendix acts as a reference for the V$ views that appear most frequently in this book, and shows the most often used columns of those views. It is certainly not comprehensive in its coverage, including only:

- ❏ V$LOCK
- ❏ V$PROCESS
- ❏ V$SESSION
- ❏ V$SQL

and these wait event views:

- ❏ V$EVENT_NAME
- ❏ V$SESSION_EVENT
- ❏ V$SESSION_WAIT
- ❏ V$SYSTEM_EVENT

For definitions of views or columns that are not included here, please see the section on *Dynamic Performance Views for Tuning* in *Oracle 9i (Release 2(9.2)) Performance Tuning Guide and Reference*, located at:
http://download-west.oracle.com/docs/cd/A97630_01/server.920/a96533/sqlviews.htm#PFGRF023

V$LOCK

This view shows the locks currently held, as well as requests for a lock or latch.

Column	Datatype	Description
ADDR	RAW(8)	Lock state object address
KADDR	RAW(8)	Lock address
SID	NUMBER	Session identifier for session holding the lock
TYPE	VARCHAR2(2)	Lock type:
		TM – DML enqueue
		TX – Transaction enqueue
		UL – User supplied
ID1	NUMBER	Lock identifier number 1
ID2	NUMBER	Lock identifier number 2
LMODE	NUMBER	Mode in which the session holds the lock:
		0 – none
		1 – null (NULL)
		2 – row -S (SS)
		3 – row -X (SX)
		4 – share (S)
		5 – S/Row -X (SSX)
		6 – exclusive (X)
REQUEST	NUMBER	Mode in which the process requests the lock
CTIME	NUMBER	Elapsed time for current lock mode
BLOCK	NUMBER	Blocking another lock

V$PROCESS

This view contains information about the currently active processes.

Column	Datatype	Description
ADDR	RAW(4)	Address of process state object
PID	NUMBER	Oracle process identifier
SPID	VARCHAR2(12)	Operating system process identifier

Column	Datatype	Description
USERNAME	VARCHAR2(15)	OS process username
SERIAL#	NUMBER	Process serial number
TERMINAL	VARCHAR2(30)	OS terminal identifier
PROGRAM	VARCHAR2(48)	Program in progress
TRACEID	VARCHAR2(255)	Trace file identifier
BACKGROUND	VARCHAR2(1)	1 for a background process; NULL otherwise
LATCHWAIT	VARCHAR2(8)	Address of latch the process is waiting for; NULL if n/a
LATCHSPIN	VARCHAR2(8)	Address of latch the process is spinning on; NULL if n/a
PGA_USED_MEM	NUMBER	PGA memory currently in use
PGA_ALLOC_MEM	NUMBER	PGA memory currently allocated
PGA_FREEABLE_MEM	NUMBER	Allocated PGA memory that can be freed
PGA_MAX_MEM	NUMBER	Maximum PGA memory ever needed

V$SESSION

This view lists sessions currently connected to an instance.

Column	Datatype	Description
SID	NUMBER	Session identifier
SERIAL#	NUMBER	Session serial number
PADDR	RAW(4)	Address of the process that owns this session
USER#	NUMBER	Oracle user
USERNAME	VARCHAR2(30)	Oracle username
COMMAND	NUMBER	Command in progress
STATUS	VARCHAR2(8)	Status of the session: ACTIVE (currently executing SQL), INACTIVE, KILLED (marked to be killed)

Table continued on following page

Column	Datatype	Description
SCHEMA#	NUMBER	Schema user identifier
SCHEMANAME	VARCHAR2(30)	Schema user name
OSUSER	VARCHAR2(30)	OS client user name
PROCESS	VARCHAR2(9)	OS PID
MACHINE	VARCHAR2(64)	OS machine
TERMINAL	VARCHAR2(30)	OS terminal
PROGRAM	VARCHAR2(48)	OS program
TYPE	VARCHAR2(10)	Session type
SQL_ADDRESS	RAW(4)	In conjunction with SQL_HASH_VALUE identifies the current SQL statement
SQL_HASH_VALUE	NUMBER	In conjunction with SQL_ADDRESS identifies the current SQL statement
LOGON_TIME	DATE	Time of logon
LAST_CALL_ET	NUMBER	The last call

V$SQL

This view contains cursor level details for SQL queries. It can be used when trying to locate the session or person responsible for parsing the cursor.

Column	Datatype	Description
SQL_TEXT	VARCHAR2(1000)	First 1000 characters of the SQL text
SHARABLE_MEM	NUMBER	Amount of shared memory (bytes)
PERSISTENT_MEM	NUMBER	Amount of memory (bytes)
RUNTIME_MEM	NUMBER	Amount of memory required during execution
SORTS	NUMBER	Number of sorts performed
USERS_OPENING	NUMBER	Number of users opening this statement

Column	Datatype	Description
EXECUTIONS	NUMBER	Number of executions of this statement
USERS_EXECUTING	NUMBER	Number of users executing this statement
LOADS	NUMBER	Number of times the object was loaded (or reloaded)
FIRST_LOAD_TIME	VARCHAR2(57)	Time stamp of cursor creation time
INVALIDATIONS	NUMBER	Number of times this cursor has been invalidated
PARSE_CALLS	NUMBER	Number of parse calls for this cursor
DISK_READS	NUMBER	Number of disk reads for this statement
BUFFER_GETS	NUMBER	Number of logical reads
ROWS_PROCESSED	NUMBER	Total number of rows this SQL statement returns
COMMAND_TYPE	NUMBER	Oracle command type definition
OPTIMIZER_MODE	VARCHAR2(10)	Mode under which the SQL statement is executed
OPTIMIZER_COST	NUMBER	Cost of this query as determined by the optimizer
PARSING_USER_ID	NUMBER	User ID that built this child cursor
PARSING_SCHEMA_ID	NUMBER	Schema ID used to build this cursor
KEPT_VERSIONS	NUMBER	Indicates whether cursor is marked to be pinned in cache
CPU_TIME	NUMBER	CPU time (microseconds) attributed to parsing/executing/fetching

Table continued on following page

Column	Datatype	Description
ELAPSED_TIME	NUMBER	Elapsed time (in microseconds) attributed to parsing/executing/fetching
SQLTYPE	NUMBER	Version of the SQL language used for this statement
OBJECT_STATUS	VARCHAR2(19)	Status of the cursor (VALID/INVALID)
OUTLINE_CATEGORY	VARCHAR2(64)	Category of the stored outline being used (or DEFAULT, if no category was specified)

Wait Event Views

V$EVENT_NAME

This view lists all wait events and definitions of the associated parameters, P1-P3.

Column	Datatype	Definition
EVENT#	NUMBER	Reference number for this event
NAME	VARCHAR2(64)	Name used by Oracle for this event
PARAMETER1	VARCHAR2(64)	Description of P1 information
PARAMETER2	VARCHAR2(64)	Description of P2 information
PARAMETER3	VARCHAR2(64)	Description of P3 information

V$SESSION_EVENT

This view lists all wait event statistics, grouped by SID.

Column	Datatype	Definition
SID	NUMBER	Session ID of the process waiting
EVENT	VARCHAR2(64)	Name of this event
TOTAL_WAITS	NUMBER	Total number of times this session has waited for this event

Column	Datatype	Definition
TOTAL_TIMEOUTS	NUMBER	Total number of times this session encountered a timeout while waiting for this event
TIME_WAITED	NUMBER	Cumulative time spent by this session waiting for this event, in centiseconds
AVERAGE_WAIT	NUMBER	Average time spent by this session waiting for this event, in centiseconds
MAX_WAIT	NUMBER	Maximum amount of time the process had to wait for this event, in centiseconds

V$SESSION_WAIT

This view provides detailed information on the current wait event for a session. (If none, statistics are for the most recent wait event.)

Column	Datatype	Definition
SID	NUMBER	Session identifier
SEQ#	NUMBER	Wait sequence counter -- increments each time the process begins a new wait
EVENT	VARCHAR2(64)	Name of wait event
P1TEXT	VARCHAR2(64)	Name of the P1 parameter for the wait event
P1	NUMBER	Value of the P1 parameter identified above
P1RAW	RAW(4)	Value of the P1 parameter in binary form
P2TEXT	VARCHAR2(64)	Name of the P2 parameter for the wait event
P2	NUMBER	Value of the P2 parameter identified above
P2RAW	RAW(4)	Value of the P2 parameter in binary form
P3TEXT	VARCHAR2(64)	Name of the P3 parameter for the wait event

Table continued on following page

Column	Datatype	Definition
P3	NUMBER	Value of the P3 parameter identified above
P3RAW	RAW(4)	Value of the P3 parameter in binary form
WAIT_TIME	NUMBER	Length of the last wait, in centiseconds
SECONDS_IN_WAIT	NUMBER	Wait time in seconds
STATE	VARCHAR2(19)	Indicates whether process is waiting or has completed a wait

V$SYSTEM_EVENT

This view lists all wait event statistics for the entire instance.

Column	Datatype	Definition
EVENT	VARCHAR2(64)	Name of the wait event
TOTAL_WAITS	NUMBER	Total number of times a process has waited for this event since instance startup
TOTAL_TIMEOUTS	NUMBER	Total number of times a process encountered a timeout while waiting for an event
TIME_WAITED	NUMBER	Cumulative time spent by processes waiting for this event, in centiseconds
AVERAGE_WAIT	NUMBER	Average time spent by processes waiting for this event, in centiseconds

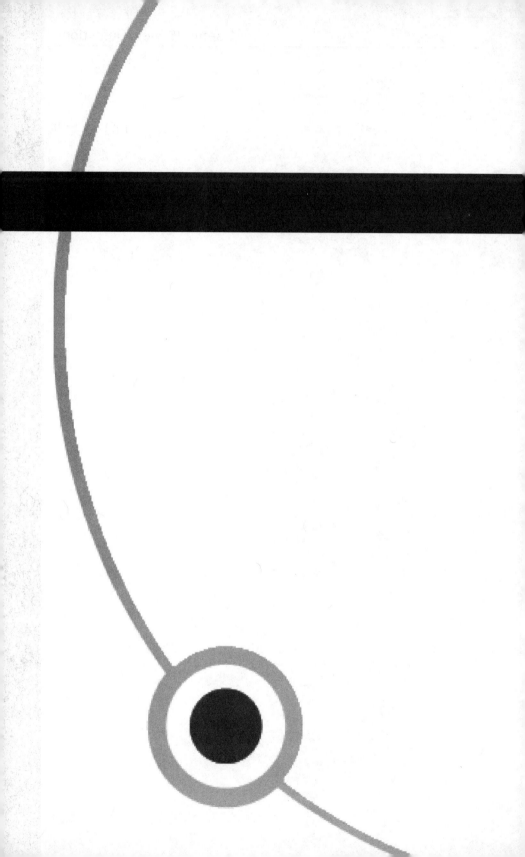

Index

A Guide to the Index

The index is arranged hierarchically, in alphabetical order, with symbols preceding the letter A. Most second-level entries and many third-level entries also occur as first-level entries. This is to ensure that users will find the information they require however they choose to search for it.

I

J

K

L

451